Crisis and Disaster Management for Tourism

ASPECTS OF TOURISM
Series Editors: Chris Cooper *(Nottingham University Business School, UK)*, C. Michael Hall *(University of Canterbury, New Zealand)* and Dallen J. Timothy *(Arizona State University, USA)*

Aspects of Tourism is an innovative, multifaceted series, which comprises authoritative reference handbooks on global tourism regions, research volumes, texts and monographs. It is designed to provide readers with the latest thinking on tourism worldwide and push back the frontiers of tourism knowledge. The volumes are authoritative, readable and user-friendly, providing accessible sources for further research. Books in the series are commissioned to probe the relationship between tourism and cognate subject areas such as strategy, development, retailing, sport and environmental studies.

Full details of all the books in this series and of all our other publications can be found on http://www.channelviewpublications.com, or by writing to Channel View Publications, St Nicholas House, 31–34 High Street, Bristol BS1 2AW, UK.

ASPECTS OF TOURISM
Series Editors: Chris Cooper *(Nottingham University Business School, UK)*, C. Michael Hall *(University of Canterbury, New Zealand)* and Dallen J. Timothy *(Arizona State University, USA)*

Crisis and Disaster Management for Tourism

Brent W. Ritchie

CHANNEL VIEW PUBLICATIONS
Bristol • Buffalo • Toronto

To Maria and my family

Library of Congress Cataloging in Publication Data
A catalog record for this book is available from the Library of Congress.
Ritchie, Brent W.
Crisis and Disaster Management for Tourism/Brent W. Ritchie.
Aspects of Tourism
Includes bibliographical references and index.
1. Tourism–Management. 2. Crisis management. 3. Travel–Safety measures. I. Title. II. Series.
G155.A1R543 2009
910.68′4–dc22 2009009364

British Library Cataloguing in Publication Data
A catalogue entry for this book is available from the British Library.

ISBN-13: 978-1-84541-106-0 (hbk)
ISBN-13: 978-1-84541-105-3 (pbk)

Channel View Publications
UK: St Nicholas House, 31-34 High Street, Bristol BS1 2AW, UK.
USA: UTP, 2250 Military Road, Tonawanda, NY 14150, USA.
Canada: UTP, 5201 Dufferin Street, North York, Ontario M3H 5T8, Canada.

Front cover: The photo illustrates the impact and recovery of Banda Aceh, Indonesia after the 2004 tsunami. The shipping container was dumped approximately 2 kilometres inland from the force of the tsunami. It now acts as a tourist attraction and has also become a focal point for a memorial located on the left hand side and a souvenir shop to the right. Further to the right is evidence of buildings that have not yet been rebuilt illustrating that recovery is still continuing.

The policy of Multilingual Matters/Channel View Publications is to use papers that are natural, renewable and recyclable products, made from wood grown in sustainable forests. In the manufacturing process of our books, and to further support our policy, preference is given to printers that have FSC and PEFC Chain of Custody certification. The FSC and/or PEFC logos will appear on those books where full certification has been granted to the printer concerned.

Typeset by Datapage International Ltd.
Printed and bound in Great Britain by Short Run Press Ltd.

Contents

Preface and Acknowledgements. ix

**Part 1: Setting the Context for Tourism Crisis and
Disaster Management**
1   Introduction to Tourism Crisis and Disaster Management. 3
    Introduction. 3
    Crisis and Disaster Definitions 4
    Understanding Tourism. 8
        Tourism definitions. 8
        The tourism industry 10
        A systems approach to tourism 11
        Tourism system attributes. 11
    Growth, Uncertainty and Vulnerability 13
    The Emerging Paradigm: Embracing Tourism Crisis/Disaster
    Management 16
    Book Aim and Content 21
    Conclusion 24

2   Classifying and Understanding Crises and Disasters. 26
    Introduction. 26
    Nature and Impacts of Tourism Crises and Disasters 26
        Natural and technical disasters. 31
        Political crises/disasters 36
        Economic crises/disasters. 39
    Differentiating Between Incidents or Natural Events and
    Crises or Disasters. 41
    Models for Understanding Crisis and Disaster Lifecycles 44
    Dealing with Complexity: Chaos, Complexity and
    Interdependence 50
    Conclusion 55

3   Strategic Crisis and Disaster Planning and Management. 57
    Introduction. 57
    Planning and Management 58
    Strategic Planning and Management 60
        The concept 60
        Elements of strategic planning and management 62

The rationale approach contested 67
Strategic Planning and Management of Crises and Disasters. . . .69
   A rationale 69
   From response and management to reduction and
   planning. 70
   A Proposed Strategic Framework for Tourism Crises/Disasters. . 74
   Conclusion 79

Part 2: Tourism Crisis and Disaster Prevention and Planning
4 Tourism Crisis Prevention and Disaster Mitigation 83
   Introduction. 83
   Organisational Crisis Prevention 84
      Scanning the environment 85
      Forecasting techniques and information gathering 88
   A Critique of Forecasting. 95
   Disaster Prevention, Reduction and Mitigation 97
      Considering risk and vulnerability .97
      Considering mitigation measures 104
         Modifying the loss. 107
         Event modification. 107
         Vulnerability modification 109
   Conclusion 111

5 Tourism Disaster and Crisis Preparedness and Planning 113
   Introduction. 113
   Disaster Preparedness: Emergency Planning 113
   Disaster Preparedness: Precursors 116
   Disaster Preparedness: Mobilisation and Warning Systems 116
   Disaster Preparedness: Contingency Plans and
   Simulation Exercises 118
   Tourism Disaster Planning Research 120
   Integrating Crisis Scanning with Planning:
   Development of Crisis Plans 127
      Crisis management systems and tools. 129
   Tourism Crisis Planning and Preparation 132
   Conclusion 141

Part 3: Tourism Crisis and Disaster Response,
Implementation and Management
6 Coordination, Control and Resource Allocation. 145
   Introduction. 145
   Coordination, Collaboration and Leadership 146
      Stakeholder coordination and control 146
      Decision-making, leadership and resource allocation 152

Government Resource Allocation. 160
Organisation and Business Resource Deployment 167
   Communication and information resource
   deployment 167
   Pull-based resource allocation. 168
   Diversification of business or target markets 169
   Cost control measures. 170
   Human resource deployment 172
Conclusion 173

7 Crisis and Disaster Communication and Recovery
   Marketing 175
   Introduction. 175
   Perceptions of Risk: Understanding Destination Choice. 175
      Image 177
   The Media Effect 179
   Organisational Crisis Communication and Control 181
   Crisis Communication in the Emergency and
   Intermediate Stage. 185
      Quick response. 187
      Consistency 188
      Access to information. 189
      Openness, honesty and sympathy. 192
   Long-term Recovery Marketing Actions 193
      Consumer advertising and partnership marketing 194
      Industry and media roles in recovery marketing 202
      Monitoring recovery marketing 203
   Conclusion 204

**Part 4: Tourism Crisis and Disaster Recovery, Resolution
and Feedback**
8 Long-term Recovery and Resolution 209
   Introduction. 209
   Understanding the Long-term Recovery and
   Resolution Phase 209
   Long-term Transformation. 213
      Organisation transformation. 213
      Destination transformation 216
      Human and community transformation 219
   The Role of Livelihood Assets and Capital in Long-term
   Recovery and Resolution. 220
   Conclusion 224

9   Knowledge Management and Organisational Learning 226
    Introduction. 226
    The Knowledge Management Imperative 227
    Organisational Learning and Feedback 230
    Managed Reflection for Organisational Learning. 235
    The Role of Knowledge Brokers, Spanners and Objects. 238
    Steps to Encourage Evaluative Enquiry and
    Managed Reflection. 245
        Asking questions 245
        Identifying and challenging values, beliefs
        and assumptions. 247
        Reflection 248
        Dialogue. 248
        Collecting, analysing and interpreting data. 250
        Action planning and implementation 251
    Conclusion 251
    Acknowledgements 252

10 Conclusion and Reflections on Tourism Crisis and
    Disaster Management 253
    Introduction 253
    Book Summary 253
        Setting the context 253
        Tourism crisis and disaster prevention and planning 255
        Tourism crisis and disaster response, implementation
        and management 256
        Tourism crisis and disaster recovery,
        resolution and feedback 258
    Future Crisis/Disaster Challenges. 259
    Future Research Issues and Topics 261
        Understanding tourism crises and disasters 266
        Planning, preparation and preparedness. 266
        Response, implementation and management 267
        Long-term recovery, resolution and feedback 268
        A post-disciplinary approach to research 268
    Conclusion 270

References 272
Index 292

Preface and Acknowledgements

It would be no surprise to many readers that tourism academics have become increasingly active in researching and publishing in the areas of tourism crisis and disaster management. However, as outlined in this book, research has tended to focus on the response and recovery phase of such incidents at the expense of the planning and prevention phase, as well as the role of organisational learning and adaptive management during such incidents. Furthermore, research has tended to follow a descriptive path rather than develop or test models and concepts from other disciplines, which could be applied. Indeed, Faulkner's (2001) tourism disaster framework model is one model which has not been tested extensively. This book is different from current books on this topic by taking a research focus.

This book provides an integrated and strategic approach to understanding tourism crisis and disaster planning and management. The book provides an integrated approach in two main ways. First, it synthesises literature from a wide range of theoretical perspectives (from natural hazards, geography, crisis public relations, communication and knowledge management theory, etc.), alongside tourism crisis and disaster literature published in the mainstream tourism field. It is important to attempt to integrate these often-disparate fields to help our understanding and the future development of knowledge in the tourism field. One of the challenges of writing such a book is that it required reading, understanding and synthesising a vast amount of literature and research. I apologise in advance for any omissions, mistakes or misinterpretations, which I take full responsibility for. Second, the book proposes an integrated view by taking a strategic planning and management approach to the topic, examining the major stages of the crisis and disaster lifecycle alongside strategic planning and management theory.

The book hopes to contribute to the debate and future research in the field of tourism crisis and disaster planning and management through its strong research base and by outlining future research issues, questions and topics in the conclusion. It is hoped that future research will use the theory, concepts and models outlined in the book to expand our collective knowledge in this important field.

This book has had a long gestation period starting with the 2001 foot and mouth outbreak, while I was living in the South East of England. A number of my honours students at the University of Brighton focused their theses on this topic, with some of their work being published in tourism journals and finding their way into this book. I would also like to thank my former research students at the University of Canberra. Dina Andari's MA research on the Indonesian government's tourism policy, subsequent to the Bali bombings, examined the important aspect of policy making and organisational learning from tourism crises. Kate Armstrong's PhD thesis on the long-term recovery of the tourism industry from the 2003 Canberra bushfires also helped my thinking, and parts of their theses have also found their way into this book. I thank them for sharing their ideas and testing mine through primary research.

Special thanks should also go to my former employers, the University of Brighton, who provided time release during the start of this book in 2003. The book was stalled in late 2003 as I travelled back from England to Australia and settled back into academic life at the University of Canberra. Study leave from July 2007 to December 2007 helped me to update the parts of the book already written. Thanks go to the University of Canberra Outside Studies Program (OSP) committee for approving my leave. The book was finally completed once I moved to the University of Queensland in Brisbane, Australia.

Special thanks go to the following people for their support, encouragement and assistance in the production of this book, which ranged from asking about progress, providing literature, writing articles with me, reviewing some of my chapters or assisting during tough times (such as that of a major hard disk crash). Thanks go to Kate Armstrong, Helen Ayres, Deborah Blackman, Peter Burns, Tracey Dickson, Paul Frost, Steven Goss-Turner, Jeremy Huyton, Nigel Jarvis, Monica Kennedy, Joanne Lester, Daniela Miller, Graham Miller, Trevor Mules, Susan Nicholls, Teone Nutt, Cathy Palmer, Christof Pforr, Bruce Prideaux, Carla Santos, Noel Scott and Sue Uzabeaga.

I should acknowledge the support of the publishing team and book series editors at Channel View for their assistance and patience throughout this process. It has been a long wait! Finally, thanks to my family and wife Maria for their love and support.

Note

Every reasonable effort has been made to locate, contact and acknowledge copyright owners. Any errors will be rectified in future editions.

Part 1
Setting the Context for Tourism Crisis and Disaster Management

Chapter 1
Introduction to Tourism Crisis and Disaster Management

> *International tourism flows are subject to disruption by a range of events that may occur in the destination itself, in competing destinations, origin markets, or they may be remote from either. The consequences may be either mild and relatively short term or have catastrophic impacts on existing industry systems. Major disruptions, also referred to as shocks, are felt in both origin and destination areas, affect both the public and private sectors and disrupt the travel plans of intending travellers.*
>
> Prideaux *et al.* (2003: 475)

Introduction

This chapter provides an introduction to crisis and disaster management for the tourism industry. First, it defines tourism and the tourism industry and acknowledges tourism from a systems perspective. It notes the main characteristics that make tourism unique but also susceptible to change as a result of shocks, crises and disasters. The chapter suggests that decision-making of consumers can be vastly impacted by crises or disasters impacting upon business and society. Second, the chapter notes a move from crisis and disaster management to prevention and planning, suggesting a growing awareness of the impact of disasters and crises on society.

It advocates that far from ignoring crises and disasters and viewing them simply as a threat, tourism managers and destinations should embrace them as a part of the tourism system and should strategically plan for such events by identifying and understanding crises and disasters, developing and implementing management plans, and evaluating the success of those plans for more effective planning and adaptive management systems. The chapter concludes with an overview of the two main fields of theory and literature: organisational crisis management, and disaster and emergency management. It also provides a brief overview of key tourism literature and concludes with an outline of the book structure.

Crisis and Disaster Definitions

A number of authors have attempted to understand crises and disasters by first defining them. According to Keown-McMullan (1997: 8), a universally accepted definition of what constitutes a crisis has not yet been developed and it is unlikely to emerge in the near future. Pauchant and Mitroff (1992: 15) believe that a crisis is a 'disruption that physically affects a system as a whole and threatens its basic assumptions, its subjective sense of self, its existential core'. Selbst (1978 in Faulkner, 2001: 136) defines a crisis as 'any action or failure to act that interferes with an organisation's ongoing functions, the acceptable attainment of its objectives, its viability or survival, or that has a detrimental personal effect as perceived by the majority of its employees, clients or constituents'. Selbst's focus on perceptions implies that if an organisation's public or stakeholders perceive a crisis, a real crisis could evolve from this misconception, illustrating that perception management is an important consideration in managing crises. Other definitions of crises are displayed in Table 1.1. Santana (2003) suggests that the definition of the term 'crisis' is problematic due to the construct itself, its application by different fields and its use jointly in the literature with terms such as disaster, catastrophe, jolt, problem and turning point. However, Laws and Prideaux (2005) make a useful point that agreement on a consistent typology for the terms describing tourism crises will help facilitate a dialogue with other researchers in the crisis management field, vital to advancing knowledge and understanding.

Common characteristics of crises tend to be that they are internal and thus the organisation has some power or influence over a crisis. Another common theme expressed in the definitions is that the scale of damage appears to be a key differentiating factor. If an incident or event can or does impact upon the survival, viability or foundation of an organisation, then it may be considered a crisis. The urgency and speed of dealing with an incident is also a key point in many of the definitions and suggests that crises may be surprises, which is why a proactive approach to crisis planning and management is important. For instance, Keown-McMullan (1997) notes that speed of a crisis developing and the speed of response is critical for managers. Nevertheless, as Santana (2003) suggests, crises are emotional situations, putting pressure on managers ensuring quality decisions are difficult to make and implement. Another theme is that a crisis is often a turning point for an organisation, which can have both positive or negative impacts and transformations for businesses and communities. This point is discussed throughout the book and especially in Part 4 of the book, which explores the transformation of organisations and destinations at the resolution stage of a crisis or disaster (Chapter 8), and the role of knowledge

Table 1.1 A comparison of crisis definitions

Author	*Definition*
Herman (1972)	Crisis is characterised by three dimensions: high threat, short decision time, and an element of surprise.
Fink (1986)	Crisis is an unstable time or state of affairs in which decisive change is impending – either one with the distinct possibility of a highly undesirable outcome or one with the distinct possibility of a highly desirable and extremely positive outcome.
Brewton (1987)	Crisis should have some or all of the following features: severe disruption of operation, increased government regulation, negative public perception of the company, financial strain, unproductive use of management time, and loss of employee moral and support.
Reilly (1987)	A crisis implies elements of magnitude, the need for taking action, and the necessity of a timely response.
Shivastava and Mitroff (1987)	Corporate crises threaten a company's most important goals of survival and profitability.
Darling (1994)	What defines a crisis in international business depends on a number of variables: the nature of the event; importance of the issue to foreign and US governments; impact on other firms and industries; how many and how quickly people inside and/or outside of a particular firm need to be helped or informed; who and how many individuals need interpretation of the events, and how accessible those people are; how much interaction with the media is necessary; what the media choose to emphasise; who and how many people need emergency care; how much the organisation needs to assert control and demonstrate that it is capable of responding; and how quickly the firm needs to respond. A crisis may also be defined by feelings of panic, fear, danger or shock.
Soñmez *et al.* (1994)	Any event which creates negative publicity and the period of time after a disaster occurrence which lasts until full recovery is achieved and pre-disaster conditions resume.
Keown-McMullan (1997)	Contrary to popular opinion, a crisis is not always bad or negative for an organisation. A crisis could, therefore, be considered as a turning point. To qualify as a crisis, the entire foundation of an organisation or business must be threatened. The idea of urgency and the speed with which decisions must be made are key components.

Table 1.1 (*Continued*)

Author	Definition
Beeton (2001)	Crises occur at all levels of tourism operations with varying degrees of severity, from much publicised environmental, economic and political disasters through to internally generated crisis such as accidents and sudden illness.
Prideaux *et al.* (2003)	Crises can be described as the possible but unexpected result of management failures that are concerned with the future course of events set in motion by human action or inaction precipitating the event.
Laws and Prideaux (2005)	1. An unexpected problem seriously disrupting the functioning of an organisation or sector or nation. 2. A general term for such problems.

management and organisational learning in improving future crisis and disaster plans and reducing the chances of an incident occurring through development of future prevention and mitigation strategies, and adaptive management (Chapter 9).

Many of the features attributed to crises are equally applicable to disasters (Faulkner, 2001), and so confusion between their distinctions can occur with common overlaps between the two, where a crisis may occur as a direct result of a disaster. Kim and Lee (1998) in their paper use the two terms together, while Hills (1998) suggests that the boundary between natural and human-induced behaviour has blurred. Faulkner (2001) considers the principal distinction between what can be termed a 'crisis' and a 'disaster' to be the extent to which the situation is attributable to the organisation itself, or can be described as originating from outside the organisation. Thus, a 'crisis' describes a situation 'where the root cause of an event is, to some extent, self-inflicted through such problems as inept management structures and practices or a failure to adapt to change', while a disaster can be defined as 'where an enterprise (or collection of enterprises in the case of a tourist destination) is confronted with sudden unpredictable catastrophic changes over which it has little control' (Faulkner, 2001: 136). Here, Faulkner (2001) suggests that crises are able, to some degree, to be controlled and within the influence of managers, whereas disasters are often external and more unpredictable. As Prideaux *et al.* (2003: 478) suggest, 'disasters can be described as unpredictable catastrophic change that can normally only be responded to after the event, either by deploying contingency plans already in place or through reactive response'. The key point is that external events and change may provide a greater degree of risk and uncertainty than internal events and change (Evans & Elphick, 2005).

Hills (1998) suggests, from an emergency planning perspective, that disasters are sudden and overwhelming events which occur for a limited duration in a distinct location. Although they may be limited by time and location, it may take a significant amount of time after a disaster to recover while some victims may never fully recover if they indeed survive. Therefore, disasters, and even crises can have a profound psychological aspect associated with them, which is discussed in Chapter 8 in the context of the recovery and final resolution of a disaster.

A disaster, as defined by the ISDR (2004: 338) is:

> a serious disruption of the functioning of a community or a society causing widespread human, material, economic or environmental losses which exceed the ability of the affected community/society to cope using its own resources. A disaster is a function of the risk process. It results from the combination of hazards, conditions of vulnerability and insufficient capacity or measures to reduce the potential negative consequences of risk.

Although disasters induced by natural conditions or ecosystems are beyond the control of humans, vulnerability is a direct result of human activity and living conditions, and a disaster is the realisation of a hazard (Smith, 1995). While natural disasters have been termed a 'humanitarian disaster with a natural trigger' (Pelling, 2003: 4), John Twigg (in ISDR, 2004: 22) elaborates by stating:

> strictly speaking, there are no such things as natural disasters, but there are natural hazards. A disaster is the result of a hazard's impact on the society. So the effects of a disaster are determined by the extent of a community's vulnerability to the hazard (or conversely, its ability, or capacity to cope with it). This vulnerability is not natural, but the result of an entire range of constantly changing physical, social, economic, cultural, political, and even psychological factors that shape people's lives and create the environments in which they live. 'Natural' disasters are nature's judgment on what humans have wrought.

This quote clearly illustrates the wide variety of ways researchers and managers are able to perceive a natural disaster. Many authors have approached the study of disaster management through the application of concepts and theory from sociology, politics, geography, economics, information technology and the physical sciences. Readers are directed to the edited work by Quarantelli (1998), which illustrates how some of these different disciplines perceive or define the term 'disaster' from their own perspectives. Hazards are 'potential threats to humans and their welfare ... risks are the probability of hazard occurrence' (Smith, 1995: 6) which lead to triggering events causing the disaster situation and possible impacts on tourism or tourist destinations.

As Cioccio and Michael (2007: 1) state, '[t]he nature of the tourism environment is often hazardous, where it is congruent with exotic scenery, unusual experiences or volatile natural settings. In such a landscape, inevitably in one locality or another, or across whole regions, there occur natural events which disrupt or destroy the physical base for tourism, and so threaten the existence of these regional enterprises', not to mention both visitor and local lives. It is likely that the tourism environment in some destinations may become even more hazardous due to global environmental change and climate change. As Becken and Hay (2007) suggest, climate-tourism hotspots such as the European Alps and small island states are susceptible to increase in global warming resulting in reduced snow cover, increased avalanche risk and increased tropical cyclones. Furthermore, as de Freitas (2006) notes, there is no clear evidence to suggest whether climate change is producing extreme weather events.

With respect to disasters, there are a range of natural hazards that may occur as a result of natural or human processes. In both instances, a disaster (or indeed a crisis) threatens the existence of a system whether it is a nation state, social community, government, organisation, natural environment, eco-system or some other established system (including tourism). The next section of this book defines tourism, the tourism industry and considers the vulnerability of the tourism system to incidents such as shocks, crises and disasters. In particular, it notes increasing concern over natural hazards and disasters as a result of climate change and concerns over global environmental change.

Understanding Tourism

Tourism definitions

The growth of tourism has been fuelled by general improvements in leisure time combined by increased discretionary income for many people. This has helped to fuel a desire to escape from work routine and engage in holidays, whether domestically or internationally. Definitions of tourism vary with respect to whether the term is applied from a supply side (industry) perspective or a demand side (consumer) perspective. As Smith (1988: 181) has noted, 'there are many different legitimate definitions of tourism that serve many different, legitimate needs'. Moreover, many of the tourism definitions vary due to organisations or individuals trying to define their own motives for tourism activities and opportunities. However, there is common ground covered by many of the definitions, although there is debate over whether tourism can be called an industry or whether it is simply a composite of organisations or industry sectors. Recent developments in quantifying tourism through satellite accounting systems show how many organisations or sub-sectors combine to form tourism.

An early definition of tourism stated that a minimum of a 24-hour stay at a site was required for an individual to be considered a 'tourist'. However, this has been modified to an overnight stay which, according to Weaver and Oppermann (2000: 28) 'is a significant improvement over the former criterion of a 24 hour stay, which proved to be both arbitrary and extremely difficult to apply'. If a person's trip does not incorporate at least one overnight stay, then the term 'excursionist' is usually applied (Weaver & Oppermann, 2000). This definition can be applied to both international and domestic travellers. For example, international stay-overs (or tourists) are those who stay in a destination outside their usual country of residence for at least one night, while international excursionists (or same-day visitors) are those who stay in an international location without residing overnight. Furthermore, a domestic stayover (or tourist) is someone who stays overnight in a destination, that is, within their own country of residence but outside of their usual home environment (usually specified by a distance of some kind). Domestic excursionists (or same-day visitors) undertake a similar trip but do not stay overnight. Tourists can also be classified based on their motivations or purpose of visit including:

- leisure travellers who may be sightseeing or visiting friends and relatives;
- business travellers; and
- other travellers such as students or people travelling for medical reasons.

Tourists can also be differentiated based on whether they are inbound, outbound or domestic tourists. Inbound tourists are those who visit a country from overseas, and combined with domestic tourism (those travelling within their own country) can be classified as internal tourists (Pender, 1999). However, inbound tourists provide much-needed foreign exchange to countries and influence the balance of payments. Domestic tourists simply circulate money within the national economy and do not add to the income of the country, although they may spread money to specific parts of the country. The majority of tourism demand is domestic in nature, with a significant proportion comprising excursions followed by overnight stays. However, for some countries, the level of outbound tourism (to other countries) for holidays is actually higher than their country's inbound tourism, generating a trade deficit. In countries such as the UK where the exchange rate is favourable and holidays abroad are cheaper, factors lead to a large outbound tourism market. In other countries, such as Japan, the outbound market is still small in comparison to the UK but is growing due to social and economic factors.

The tourism industry

Smith (1988) believes that it is difficult to determine the precise magnitude of the tourism industry due to an absence of an accepted operational definition of tourism. As Mill and Morrison (1985) note, tourism is a difficult phenomenon to describe because all tourism involves travel, yet not all travel is tourism. All tourism involves recreation, yet not all tourism is recreation. All tourism occurs during leisure time, but not all leisure time is given to touristic pursuits. Nevertheless, the tourism industry has been defined in principle as the 'aggregate of all businesses that directly provide goods or services to facilitate business, pleasure, and leisure activities away from the home environment' (Smith, 1988: 183). The primary tourist product usually consists of transport, the travel trade (tour operators and travel agents), accommodation and catering, as well as tourist attractions. Secondary and tertiary businesses can exist in sectors such as:

- the retail sector (for crafts and souvenirs);
- banks and insurance sector;
- entertainment and leisure sector;
- excursion and tour sector; and
- personal services (such as newsagents, hairdressers, etc.).

Hall (1995: 9) believes that three factors tend to emerge when examining various definitions about the tourism industry:

- the tourism industry is regarded as essentially a service industry;
- the inclusion of business, pleasure and leisure activities empha- sises 'the nature of the goods a traveller requires to make the trip more successful, easier, or enjoyable' (Smith, 1988: 183); and
- the notion of a 'home environment', refers to the arbitrary delineation of a distance threshold or period of overnight stay.

McIntosh *et al.* (1995: 10) take a more systems-based approach when defining tourism as 'the sum of phenomena and relationships arising from the interaction of tourists, business suppliers, host governments, and host communities in the process of attracting and hosting these tourists and other visitors'. This definition goes beyond viewing tourism as a business and includes the potential impacts that tourists may have upon the host community (and environment), which until recently was a neglected component of definitions.

A systems approach to tourism

The above discussion illustrates that there are many different components to defining tourism, which range from tourists themselves, the tourism industry and even the host community or destination. In essence, tourism is a system and therefore a systems-based approach to the study and research of tourism is vital. According to Hall (2000), a system is an object of study and comprises three main parts:

(1) a set of elements (sometimes also called entities);
(2) the set of relationships between the elements; and
(3) the set of relationships between those elements and the environment.

Hall (2000) notes that simple linear relationships and casual chains cannot help us understand complex situations in the physical or social sciences (including tourism), while systems thinking can help further the understanding of tourism and its complexity. A number of authors therefore view tourism as an integrated system of components (Gunn, 1988; Leiper, 1989; Mathieson & Wall, 1982; Mill & Morrison, 1985; Murphy, 1985; Pearce, 1989), although most view tourism as a closed system with tight boundaries. However, tourism can be perceived as an open system, which is impacted by external events often beyond the control of individuals or destinations. Nevertheless, this integrated set of components generally contain a number of interrelated factors:

- a *demand side* consisting of the tourist market and their characteristics (motives, perceptions, socio-demographics);
- a *supply side* consisting of the tourism industry (transport, attractions, services, information) which combine to form a tourist destination area;
- a tourism *impact side* whereby the consequences of tourism can have either direct or indirect positive and negative impacts upon a destination area and tourists themselves; and
- an *origin–destination approach* that illustrates the interdependence of generating and receiving destinations and transit destinations (on route) and their demand, supply and impacts (see Figure 1.1).

Tourism system attributes

Tourism has a number of attributes that differentiate it from other industry sectors (which are non-service based). Tourism lacks homogeneity and standardisation because it involves a large range of businesses and product fields ranging from transport, retail, hotels and restaurants, and so offers a range of different experiences or products. Activities related to travel or tourism can cross industrial sectors such as manufacturing (souvenirs), fishing and agriculture (for food) as well as

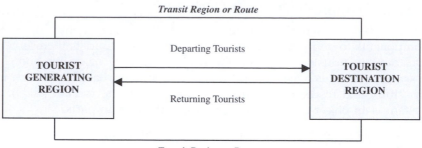

Figure 1.1 Geographical elements of a basic tourist system
Source: Modified from Hall (1998: 10) and Simmons and Leiper (1998: 91)

transportation. In comparison, the manufacturing industry has a large number of similar businesses, where products are standardised and mass produced with similar characteristics. However, the tourism industry is experience orientated and each experience can be different and evaluated quite differently amongst consumers. As Peattie and Moutinho (2000) suggest, for manufacturers there is a distinct location where the service encounter takes place, whereas for tourism it can occur at the other side of the world even at a consumer's home destination.

Tourism also has a number of other unique characteristics:

- it is *intangible* compared with other products as it cannot be tested or touched prior to purchase. Similarly, the tangible elements of a tourism or travel experience tend to be photographs or souvenirs rather than a physical product;
- it is *perishable* as inventory cannot be carried or stored away for later use. Once a date has passed and a hotel room or an airline seat has been left vacant, then revenue is lost. Unlike other industries where orders are taken in advance for products or inventory carried, the nature of the tourism industry means that managers need to try and reduce perishability (often through overbooking flights or offering discounts to stimulate purchase in the low season); and
- it is *volatile* and based on a wide range of external factors as well as the successful integration and distribution of a number of businesses spanning a number of industries providing a tourism experience.

In many senses, tourism is a system of interrelated processes that combine to create an experience for consumers. The term 'industry' has been applied to this system not only to simplify it but also to make it more identifiable, or as Seaton and Bennett (1996) note, to help unify it for political and economic reasons. The use of the term 'industry' has also proved useful in understanding the size and economic importance of tourism, and therefore a useful lobbying exercise for those businesses involved in tourism and travel.

Growth, Uncertainty and Vulnerability

According to the World Tourism Organization (WTO, 2007), tourism is predicted to increase with future tourist arrivals growing to 1.6 billion by the year 2020 at an average growth rate of 4.3%, with 2005 recording a 5.5% growth. Despite the effect of external variables and crises, tourism growth years are assured. According to the World Travel and Tourism Council (WTTC, 2007), tourism currently generates 12.2% of total world exports and employs one in every 12 workers worldwide. It is predicted that by 2017 it will support 2.8% of all employment and 10.6% of total world exports (WTTC, 2007). Despite the crises in the tourism industry in 2001, the industry bounced back in 2002 to record a 3.1% increase in world visitor arrivals to 715 million (WTO, 2003) and in 2004, an estimated 764 million international arrivals (WTO, 2005). However, predictions of large growth in world visitor arrivals may need to be reconsidered in the context of peak oil, rising fuel prices and climate change.

The growth of tourism has spread geographically with the market share of tourist arrivals reducing in Europe and increasing in the Asia-Pacific region which has the fastest growth rate of world tourist arrivals. Since 2003, the Asia-Pacific region world arrivals put the region ahead of North America and behind only Europe. There has also been a growth in tourism to developing countries with their share of tourist arrivals and expenditure increasing especially in destinations such as Eastern Europe, South America, the Middle East and Africa. Tourists are now more than ever travelling further in search for new and unusual experiences. Despite reductions in tourism to the Middle East of 4% in 2001, this region grew by 10.1% on average between 2000 and 2005, and in Africa, arrivals were ahead of the average growth rate at 5.5% (WTO, 2007).

As mentioned earlier, the characteristics of tourism create an integrated and open system which is impacted by external factors making it vulnerable to crises and disasters. According to Peattie and Moutinho (2000), although business in other sectors (such as manufacturing) have to acknowledge the external operating environment and deal with change, they are able to do so with less effort than the tourism and travel industry. This is because tourism is highly interdependent and there is no place for the industry to hide from the turbulent and unpredictable world (Gee *et al.*, 1994). The globalisation of the tourism industry has led to a rapid expansion of tourism businesses on an international scale in order to expand their market share and profitability. However, this process has also opened businesses up to a wider set of 'global risks' involved in running businesses at such a scale, as globalisation is often seen as complex and chaotic (Jessop, 1999). Greater exposure to political, economic, social and technological change in countries often removed from the bases of tourism companies requires tourism managers to effectively deal with crises and disasters (often located a substantial distance away).

The world is also becoming more interdependent and connected so that small scale crises in one part of the world can have a significant impact on other parts of the world. Political instability, or the outbreak of war in one part of the world can dramatically reduce tourist travel patterns to other parts of the world. Tourism is therefore highly susceptible to external factors and pressures in the wider operating environment. McEntire (2001) believes that a number of interrelated factors (caused by the development process and changing values, attitudes and practices) are creating increased vulnerability and risks for society and business (see Table 1.2). As Gössling and Hall (2006) note, global environmental change threatens the foundations of tourism through reductions in biodiversity, climate change, land alteration, loss of non-renewable resources and unsustainable use of renewable resources. Furthermore, as Santana (2003) observed, many tourism destinations are economically dependent on tourism and vulnerable to natural disasters due to their location, while crisis management has been identified as an important part of overall tourism destination competitiveness (Ritchie & Crouch, 2003).

For tourism organisations to successfully manage in an unpredictable and volatile world, they should be aware of the external operating environment and its potential impacts upon the destination or organisation. A series of interdependent external factors can influence tourism and travel demand and cause severe problems for tourism organisations and businesses. Common analysis of those factors that can influence tourism demand and the management of tourism organisations is called a PEST (political, economic, social and technological) analysis. However, as Peattie and Moutinho (2000: 17) note, the use of PEST is a 'broad brush' approach which may be less useful in industries, such as tourism, which are more prone to environmentally related disruption. The authors propose a SCEPTICAL analysis, which examines the influence of:

- Social factors (including demographic change, urbanisation, and health).
- Cultural factors (including cultural values and cultural changes).

Table 1.2 Factors which could augment vulnerability

Type	*Examples*
Physical vulnerability	• the proximity of people and property to triggering agents • improper construction of buildings • inadequate foresight relating to the infrastructure • degradation of the environment
Social vulnerability	• limited education (including insufficient knowledge about disasters) • inadequate routine and emergency health care • massive and unplanned migration to urban areas • marginalisation of specific groups and individuals
Cultural vulnerability	• public apathy towards disaster • defiance of safety precautions and regulations • loss of traditional coping mechanisms • dependency and an absence of personal responsibility
Political vulnerability	• minimal support for disaster programmmes among elected officials • inability to enforce or encourage steps for mitigation • over-centralisation of decision-making • isolated or weak disaster related institutions
Economic vulnerability	• growing divergence in the distribution of wealth • the pursuit of profit with little regard for the consequences • failure to purchase insurance • sparse resources for disaster prevention, planning and management
Technological vulnerability	• lack of structural mitigation devises • over-reliance upon, or ineffective warning systems • carelessness in industrial production • lack of foresight regarding computer equipment/programs

Source: Modified after McEntire (2001: 191–192).

- Economic factors (including economic shifts, exchange rates and taxes).
- Physical factors (including global climate change, deforestation and pollution).
- Technical factors (including information technology and the risks that they provide).
- International factors (including relations or stability between countries).
- Communication and infrastructure factors (including investment in infrastructure and communication links).
- Administrative and institutional factors (including the influence of organisations such as trade unions, government organisations, consumer and interest groups).
- Legal and political factors (including regulations, political instability, war and terrorism).

These influencing factors may not only provide distinct risks but also opportunities for tourism destinations and businesses depending on their impacts and how these factors are managed by organisations. In particular, with respect to crises and disasters, the economic, physical, communication/infrastructure and legal/political factors can have a distinct impact on tourism and travel. However, the above list includes factors that business managers and tourism organisations need to consider on a regular basis as part of the strategic management and planning of their organisations. Large-scale crises and disasters which are often economic, physical or political are perhaps ignored by managers due to their infrequency and reactive or pessimistic managerial mindset (Santana, 2003). Nevertheless, although economic crises or physical incidents may not be frequent, managers and destinations should expect to encounter them at some point in their lifecycle and should be prepared to do so. However, despite their probable occurrence, managers are often not prepared. Augustine (1995) discovered in a survey of Fortune 500 Chief Executive Officers, that although 85% said that a crisis in business is inevitable, only 50% had undertaken any action in planning and preparing a crisis plan. Absence of formal prevention and planning for crises and disasters, which are discussed in Chapters 4 and 5, is also evident in the tourism sector (see Drabek, 1995; Gonzalez-Herrero, 1997; Henderson, 1999a, 1999b, 2002).

The Emerging Paradigm: Embracing Tourism Crisis/ Disaster Management

The threat, time pressure, and intensity of incidents noted above differentiate normal strategic management from crisis management (a point discussed in more detail in Chapter 2). Faulkner (2001) notes an increasing number of disasters and crises that affect the tourism industry, ranging from natural to human-influenced incidents. In recent years, the global tourism industry has experienced many crises and disasters including terrorist attacks, political instability, economic recession, biosecurity threats and natural disasters.

Lee and Harrald (1999: 184) state that 'natural disasters can disrupt the supply and distribution chains for even the best prepared businesses ... service businesses are increasingly vulnerable to electrical, communication and other critical infrastructure failures'. Organisations of all shapes and sizes all have to deal with change at some point in their lifecycle, and all destinations will have to deal with a disaster at some stage (Faulkner, 2001). Kash and Darling (1998: 179) claim that it is no longer a case if an organisation will face a crisis; it is rather a question of 'when', 'what type' and 'how prepared' the organisation is to deal with it. Fink (1986: 7) believes that all businesses are on the edge of chaos. A core competency of managers is therefore to manage such change. Such skills are required due to climate change and global environmental change which will dramatically affect the tourism industry into the future (Becken & Hay, 2007; Gössling & Hall, 2006).

Faulkner (2001) argues that there is a lack of research on crisis or disaster phenomena in the tourism industry, on the impacts of such events on both the industry and specific organisations, and the responses of the tourism industry to such incidents. This lack of interest and research is somewhat surprising considering that crisis management, disaster recovery, and organisational continuity are important competencies for managers in both the public and private sector (Lee & Harrald, 1999: 184) and surprising considering the size, economic importance of tourism (Henderson, 1999b) and its reliance on positive images and perceptions (Santana, 2003). Faulkner (2001: 136) notes that the industry does not seem to make any progress in understanding the importance of crisis and disaster management planning due to 'the limited development of theoretical and conceptual frameworks required to underpin the analysis of this phenomena'. However, there has been a growing interest in this subject area and more research has been undertaken, particularly since September 11, 2001. A growing number of books have been published along with special issues of journals such as the *Journal of Travel and Tourism Marketing* which have focused on tourism crisis management and recovery marketing. Nevertheless, tourism academics are only beginning to research chaos and complexity which has been the domain of mathematicians, physicists, biologists, chemists, ecologists and economists since the 1970s (Gleick, 1987), and the body of knowledge in tourism crisis or disaster management is small but growing.

As noted earlier, tourism is now an important economic sector for many countries and destinations are dependent upon tourism for their growth and survival. This puts increasing pressure on tourism managers and planners concerned to consider the impact of crises and disasters on the industry and develop strategies to deal with the impacts to protect tourism business and society. There is a need to understand such incidents and examine strategies that can be used to stop or limit their impacts on a growing and important industry sector. Crisis and disaster management should be a core competency for tourism destination managers as well as business managers. Considering that tourist decision-making is based on perceptions (particularly of risk and safety), managers should consider strategies to deal with the impacts of economic, physical, and especially political crises. Research in this field is concentrated in two main areas: crisis management, and disaster and emergency management.

The need for crisis planning and management emerges when a crisis occurs through human or organisational action or inaction (such as accidents, financial crises, rumours or corruption). Most of the research and writing here appears to be related to organisational crisis management and the strategic planning, implementation and evaluation of business crisis management strategies. In particular, readers should note a specific journal called *Journal of Contingencies and Crisis Management*. A number of other publications deal with elements of crisis management including *Public Relations Review*, the *Leadership and Organizational Development Journal*, *Management Decision* and *Disaster Prevention and Management* which also discuss natural disasters. Crisis communications including public relations and understanding the media have been noted in the general crisis management literature as being important in managing crises (Ashcroft, 1997; Marra, 1998; Zerman, 1995). Crisis communication has also been discussed in the tourism crisis management context for both tourism destinations and organisations (see Beirman, 2002; Beritelli & Gotsch, 1999; Gonzalez-Herrero, 1999; Nielsen, 2001). Other crisis and disaster literature suggests the need for recovery marketing for destinations and organisations, and similar discussion can be found in the tourism and travel literature regarding crises (see Ritchie *et al.*, 2003; Rittichainuwat *et al.*, 2002; Soñmez, *et al.*, 1999).

Related research has focused on the causation factors for crises and disasters. Terrorism, war and political instability have also been discussed in the context of crisis management by tourism researchers. Beirman (2002) outlines the impact and management of the prolonged Arab–Israeli conflict, while Soñmez (1998) and Soñmez *et al.* (1999) provide an excellent discussion of the links between terrorism, political instability and crisis management. The impact of the Asian economic crisis on tourist attractions in Singapore is explored by Henderson

(1999a) and also the role and response of National Tourism Organisations which dealt with the crisis (Henderson, 1999b, 2002). The majority of work in the field of crisis management related to tourism and travel has focused on organisational crisis management.

Gonzalez-Herrero (1997) examined and compared the overall pre-paredness of the tourism industry for crises in Spain and the USA, while Rousaki and Alcott (2007) explored crisis readiness in hotels in the UK. Other research has focused on the crisis strategies of senior Australian tourism managers (Anderson, 2006), managers in Israel (Israeli & Reichel, 2003), and strategic decision-making following shock events (Bonn & Rundle-Thiele, 2006). Barton (1994b) explored crisis management in hotels, French (1991) noted the impact of the Gulf War on airline profitability and strategy, while Beeton (2001, 2002) explored crisis management in the context of adventure horseback tourism. Work has also been conducted on crisis management in a convention and visitor bureau context (Young & Montgomery, 1998). Other research has examined the impact of crises on the tourism economy and broader society. Leiper and Hing (1998) note the impact of crises and disasters on the tourism industry and economy of Asia, while Dwyer *et al.* (2006) examined the economic impact of world crises in Australia. Other authors noted the economic impact of the 2001 economic crisis on Turkey (Okumus & Karamustafa, 2005) and the aviation sector (Sadi & Henderson, 2000). These studies are discussed in relevant chapters throughout the book.

The need for disaster or emergency planning and management emerges when a disaster occurs through some natural phenomena or external human action (such as floods, cyclones, earthquakes, fires, terrorist attacks or biosecurity threats). According to some authors, the current state of the world is directly responsible for an increase in disasters and crises (Berke, 1998; Blaikie *et al.*, 1994; Brammer, 1990). As Richardson (1994) notes, our environment has become more crowded and as the population increases pressures such as urbanisation, the extension of human settlement, and the greater use and dependence on technology have perhaps led to an increase in disasters and crises, and in disaster reporting. A (ISDR, 2004) report on disaster reduction notes that although the number of affected populations has increased by over three times since 1970, the number of deaths has halved, through reduction and planning measures. However, the cost of disasters and hazards has been estimated at US$30 billion for 2000, which compares favourably to the US$100 billion in 1999 and US$591 billion for the 1990s alone (ISDR, 2004). Hoyios *et al.* (2007) in their annual statistical review of disasters note a US$129 billion cost for Hurricane Katrina alone in 2005, and an upward trend in cost for disasters generally. The authors also note a large increase in flood and related disasters, which in 2006 were responsible for 59% of all reported disasters with China in 2006 reporting the most number of disasters (38 in total), the most victims (more than 88 million) and the most economic damage (US$13.5 billion).

In the context of climate change and tourism, Becken and Hay (2007) explain that in alpine Europe, there has been an increase in surface temperatures, retreat of glaciers, increased precipitation in winter, increased wind speeds and reduction in the length of the snow season. The outcome of this, according to the authors, will be increased avalanches, changes in river flows and reduced demand for snow sports activity in Europe's alpine region. While the IPCC (2001) have noted that mountain tourism will be severely affected by global climatic change, increasing travel and trade has also increased the risk of biosecurity and disease threats to destinations through human mobility (Hall, 2006).

It is clear why most of the literature has focused on disaster preparation and the implementation of integrated safety and emergency actions. There has been a distinct move away from disaster management to disaster reduction (in the hope of reducing damage to economies and lives). Because of the growth of disasters and natural hazards, a growing emphasis has been given to disaster management and reduction in the last decade through the United Nations declaring 1989–1999 the International Decade for Natural Disaster Reduction (IDNDR) under resolution 235 of the General Assembly. For the tourism industry, this culminated in a joint publication by the World Tourism Organization and the World Meteorological Organization on natural disaster reduction for tourism. In particular, the publication noted that 'tourism development is frequently located in areas which are exposed to, or more likely to be exposed to, sudden-onset disasters, in particular in beach and coastal areas, river valleys and mountain regions' (WTO, 1998: 1). Considering that beach and coastal areas, and mountain regions not only host substantial number of visitors but also local communities, the potential damage of disasters is great. As the former United Nations Secretary General Kofi Annan notes in the foreword of the ISDR (2004) publication:

> communities will always face natural hazards, but todays disasters are often generated by, or at least exacerbated by, human activities. At the most dramatic level, human activities are changing the natural balance of the earth, interfering as never before with the atmosphere, the oceans, the polar ice caps, the forest cover and the natural pillars that make our world a liveable home. But we are also putting ourselves in harm's way in less visible ways. At no time in human history have so many people lived in cities clustered around seismically active areas. Destitution and demographic pressure have led more people than ever before to live in flood plains or in areas prone to landslides. Poor land-use planning; environmental

mismanagement; and a lack of regulatory mechanisms both increase the risk and exacerbate the effects of disasters.

However, tourism has been slow to respond to issues concerning climate change and global environmental change. The first world conference on climate change and tourism was hosted by the United Nations World Tourism Organization (UNWTO) in 2003, while the second international conference was held in Davos, Switzerland, in 2007 resulting in the Davos Declaration. The declaration called for a number of actions by government and international organisations, tourism industry and destinations, consumers and for the further development of research and communication networks.

In the tourism literature, research has been carried out on natural hazards and disasters generally (Mèheux & Parker, 2006), and more specifically:

- hurricanes (Chandler, 2004; Higgins, 2005; Soñmez & Backman, 1992; Young & Montgomery, 1998);
- flooding and tsunami (Carlsen, 2006; Cheung & Law, 2006; De Sausmarez, 2005; Faulkner & Vikulov, 2001; Garcia *et al.*, 2006; Henderson, 2005, 2007; Ichinosawa, 2006; Reddy, 2005; Sharpely, 2005);
- earthquakes (Huang & Min, 2002; Young & Montgomery, 1998);
- bushfires (Armstrong & Ritchie, 2007; Cioccio & Michael, 2007; Hystad & Keller, 2006, 2008);
- biosecurity and disease with an emphasis on the Foot and Mouth Disaster in the UK (see Baxter & Bowen, 2004; Coles, 2003; Irvine & Anderson, 2005; Miller & Ritchie, 2003; Ritchie *et al.*, 2003; Rodway-Dyer & Shaw, 2005; Sharpely, 2001; Williams & Ferguson, 2005, 2006); and
- biosecurity and disease with an emphasis on the impact of Severe Acute Respiratory Syndrome (SARS), particularly in the Asia-Pacific (see Au *et al.*, 2005; Chien & Law, 2003; Henderson & Ng, 2004; Huimin & Wall, 2006; Kim *et al.*, 2005; McKercher & Chon, 2004; Pine & McKercher, 2004; Tse *et al.*, 2006; Wen *et al.*, 2005; Zeng *et al.*, 2005) and wine tourism (Hall, 2005).

Book Aim and Content

The aim of this book is to examine both organisational crisis management and disaster/emergency management for tourism businesses and destinations. The synthesis of literature and theory from the crisis and disaster management areas with tourism crises and disaster literature is an important part of advancing knowledge and understanding. There is a need for a holistic systems approach to manage crises and disasters in the tourism and travel industry, for three main reasons. First, the number of crises and disasters impacting upon the tourism industry and destinations in recent years appear to be growing, in part due to changing practices and environmental change. Second, because tourism is a system of interrelated and interconnected sectors, it is therefore more vulnerable to external crises and disasters than other industries. Third, the nature of tourism suggests that business viability could be impacted because of the perishability of tourism as a result of impacts from a crisis or disaster. Although some authors believe that crises and disasters are too complex and chaotic to manage, there are others who disagree. Smallman (1997) and Santana (2003) note there is a need for managers to move from a current dominant reactive paradigm to a more proactive integrated and comprehensive approach to dealing with crises and disasters. Richardson (1994) notes a move away from 'crisis management' to 'crisis avoidance', which has also been suggested by Barton and Hardigree (1995) as a more modern approach to crisis management. Referring to natural disasters, Kofi Annan suggests in the International Strategy for Disaster Reduction publication (ISDR, 2004):

> we are far from helpless in the face of natural hazards. Early warning and risk reduction measures have been important factors in helping to reduce significantly the number of people who lose their lives to disasters. New planning and forecasting tools are helping to mitigate the devastation regularly wrought by floods. We can and must build a world of resilient communities and nations.

In particular, because of the points made above, there is a need for the tourism industry to take a holistic and strategic approach to understanding and managing disasters and crises, working alongside other industry sectors and other agencies (such as emergency groups and aid organisations). There is also a need to evaluate the body of literature on crisis and disaster management for tourism to highlight good and poor practice related to theory. This ability to learn from crisis and disaster management is a useful exercise for the tourism industry and can help move crisis and disaster management closer to crisis and disaster reduction and readiness, through understanding crises, their impacts and possible effective responses to such incidents.

Part 1 of the book helps set the context to the book and introduces elements important to the remainder of the book and the proposed framework for the book illustrated in Chapter 3. Chapter 2 of the book defines crises and disasters and notes that managers of tourism organisations and destinations need to understand what differentiates a crisis and disaster from each other, and more importantly, when an issue or incident evolves into a crisis or disaster. This chapter argues that the first step to managing crises or disasters requires increasing our understanding of such phenomena including what types of crises and disasters exist, exploring their complexity and lifecycle and considering approaches to view crises and disasters (including how they can be managed). Chapter 3 extends the context by proposing a strategic and integrated approach to planning and managing crises and disasters. However, it notes the need for flexibility in dealing with such incidents, but suggests that proactive planning can help tourism organisations and destinations more effectively deal with crises, disasters and global environmental change. In particular, strategic planning and management can help reduce the likelihood of disasters or crises occurring or, if they do occur, limit the damage they may cause to businesses or destinations. The role of knowledge and information is vital for tourism businesses and destinations to develop suitable tourism crisis and disaster plans and provide feedback into their success for future refinement and adaptive management.

Part 2 of the book consists of two chapters that examine crisis and disaster prevention, reduction and readiness including forecasting techniques that can signify the likelihood of emerging crises and disasters. However, despite the growing threat of natural disasters to tourism businesses and destinations, few tourism businesses are prepared to handle the impacts of such threats, yet crisis planning should be a core competency of tourism managers. Understanding risk and vulnerability and their broader links to sustainable development and sustainable tourism are vital and suggest the need for longer-term reduction of natural disasters. The concept of 'invulnerable development' should be considered in combination with structural and non-structural mitigation measures, and are discussed in Chapter 4.

If prevention or mitigation of crises and disasters are not possible, then contingency plans have to be developed and tested for dealing with these incidents at an organisational and destination level, and are outlined in Chapter 5. Plans should be developed which include the development of manuals and procedures, staff training and simulation exercises. All of these activities can help ensure an organisation or destination is prepared and able to respond more effectively to both emerging incidents and unpredictable shocks. To date, the evidence suggests that the tourism industry has had less formal planning than other industries, possibly because of its nature (many small enterprises and interconnected with many sectors).

Part 3 outlines the implementation of strategies to source, administer and control resources and systems for effective crisis and disaster management in Chapter 6. It emphasises the importance of coordination between stakeholders, both within the tourism industry and between the tourism industry and external stakeholders such as emergency services personnel in order to effectively and efficiently use resources.

Furthermore, leadership is required at a local, regional, national, and perhaps even international level depending on the size and scale of the tourism crisis or disaster. Chapter 7 outlines the importance of image and perceptions for the tourism industry and the effect crises and disasters can have on consumer destination choice. In particular, it suggests that the media has an important role to play in crisis communication, perceptions management and recovery marketing. The media can encourage the flow and the intensity of a crisis or disaster, or even help turn an incident or issue into a crisis due to negative media coverage. Subsequently, organisations need to work with the media to ensure that a consistent and accurate message is transmitted to the various public and stakeholders.

Finally, Part 4 focuses on the long-term recovery and resolution phase of tourism crises and disasters. The chapter begins by defining the resolution phase, which is where a routine is restored or a new and improved state established. Long-term positive and negative transformation can occur at an organisational, destination and human scale. The final chapter of Part 4 (Chapter 9) focuses on knowledge management and organisational learning from tourism crises and disasters, vital for adaptive management. This chapter begins by outlining the knowledge management imperative, defines knowledge management and argues the importance of knowledge for dealing effectively with a tourism crisis or disaster. Following on from this, the chapter focuses on organisational learning and feedback by focusing specifically on the review and reflection phase of the crisis or disaster lifecycle. The book concludes with a conclusion and reflections chapter outlining key challenges and emerging threats to tourism, highlights particular research issues, questions and topics which require future research to better understand, prepare and manage tourism crises and disasters in a complex and interdependent world. In particular, it should be noted that a lack of research exists concerned with the planning/prevention and resolution/feedback stage of tourism crises and disasters. Most research to date has focused on the response of organisations and destinations and has limited theoretical or conceptual focus. This section of the chapter calls for more interdisciplinary research to better understand these phenomena and possible future crises and disasters tourism may face.

Conclusion

This chapter provided an introduction to crisis and disaster management for the tourism industry. Firstly, it defined tourism and the tourism industry and acknowledged tourism from a systems perspective. It not only noted the main characteristics that make tourism unique but also susceptible to change as a result of shocks, crises and disasters. The chapter suggests that decision-making of consumers can be vastly impacted by crises or disasters impacting upon business and society. Secondly, the chapter noted a move from crisis and disaster management to prevention and planning, suggesting a growing awareness of the impact of disasters and crises on society, especially due to global environmental change and questions surrounding peak oil.

It advocated that far from ignoring crises and disasters and viewing them simply as a threat, tourism managers and destinations should embrace them as a part of the tourism system and should strategically plan for such events by identifying and understanding crises and disasters, developing and implementing management plans, and evaluating the success of those plans for more effective future crisis and disaster plans. The chapter concluded with an overview of the two main fields of theory and literature: organisational crisis management and, disaster and emergency management and provides a brief overview of key tourism literature and an outline of the book. The next chapter of the book continues setting the context of the book proposed in Part 1, by discussing the nature of crises and disasters to help improve our understanding of these phenomena.

Chapter 2

Classifying and Understanding Crises and Disasters

Introduction

This chapter discusses the difference between crises and disasters, the interrelationship between the two and how the 'ripple effect' can turn a crisis into a disaster or vice versa. It then outlines the type of crises and disasters that exist and can impact upon the tourism industry. Incidents can range from small-scale organisational issues ranging from staff illness, staff challenges and breakdowns, malevolence, organisational misdeeds to external factors such as natural disasters (earthquakes, floods, fires), global environmental change and terrorist incidents. An anatomy of a crisis or disaster is presented and the lifecycle of such incidents are identified and discussed.

Understanding when an 'issue' becomes a crisis or disaster is discussed, before the chapter outlines a classification of crises which consider threat level, time pressure and the intensity of specific incidents. The chapter also outlines the difficulty in predicting or responding to crises and disasters as each one has different characteristics and are often seen as impossible to control. Discussion is undertaken concerning chaos and complexity theory and various ways of viewing crisis and disaster management. However, this chapter concludes by suggesting that a strategic and integrated approach to crisis and disaster management can help limit the potential impact of shocks, crises and disasters and is particularly relevant for the tourism industry, despite the complexity of such incidents.

Nature and Impacts of Tourism Crises and Disasters

A number of authors have attempted to understand crises and disasters by (1) defining them (discussed in Chapter 1), (2) explaining the nature of crises and disaster and their lifecycle or anatomy to help improve our understanding of such phenomena, and (3) by stressing the complexity and chaotic nature of incidents which pose challenges in managing or preventing crises or disasters. Crises can range, according to Coombs (1999), from small-scale organisational issues ranging from staff illness, staff challenges/breakdowns, malevolence, and organisational misdeeds to external factors such as natural disasters (earthquakes, floods, fires), often a result of global environmental change as well as terrorist incidents. As Beeton (2001: 422) notes:

crises occur at all levels of tourism operations with varying degrees of severity, from much publicised environmental, economic and political disasters through to internally generated crisis such as accidents and sudden illness.

This book will focus on large-scale crises or disasters that have the ability to cause the most damage to tourism destinations and organisations. This is because dealing with staff illness and challenges are often a normal part of strategic management, unlike crisis and disaster management when management is concerned with dealing with incidents that can affect the viability of an organisation or destination. Furthermore, most of the literature in the crisis management and disaster management field is concerned with larger scale crises and disasters and their planning and management. Nevertheless, the way in which these crises or disasters are managed may provide insights for the management of smaller crises and disasters at an organisational level. It should also be noted that small-scale incidents can emerge into large-scale crises or disasters if they are handled ineffectively, dramatically impacting the reputation of an organisation or destination and its future viability. As Wiik (2003) noted while researching crisis management in the tour operators sector in the UK, it is often the smaller more obscure incidents that are more difficult for tour operators to manage as they are less common than the larger scale incidents or issues (such as political instability), that operators may be better prepared for.

Table 2.1 illustrates some of the types of crises and disasters, their characteristics and provides some examples. The table includes incidents that meet the core requirements of either being a crisis or disaster as they all involve sudden change, can create severe social and economic damage and all require urgency and quick action by organisations and destinations.

However, as can be seen from the table, some of the examples can clearly be self-inflicted (such as organisational misdeeds) and may be defined as crises, while others are clearly not self-inflicted per se (such as natural disasters) although some human processes and action may be partly responsible (such as building resorts close to the sea or in environmentally sensitive areas such as mountain regions). Furthermore, some natural disasters may lead to economic crises and vice versa (as they become linked) while crises and disasters may be international, supraregional, national, regional, local, or organisational in scope. Some crises and disasters can also be considered long running (such as civil wars or political instability) while others are short duration (such as airline strikes). This is reflected in the view of Seymour and Moore (2000) who believed that crises could be classified as either 'the cobra' that strike suddenly with no warning or the much slower 'python' which gradually grows over time. Similarly, Parsons (1996) suggests three types of crises:

Table 2.1 Typology of disasters and crises, their characteristics and some examples

Type of crises/disasters	Characteristics	Examples
Natural or physical disasters	• When an organisation or destination is damaged as a result of the weather, 'acts of God', human influence or a combination of the above. Examples include earthquakes, tornadoes, floods, hurricanes, avalanches, fires, bad storms or biosecurity threats or technological hazards. • May be as a result of natural processes such as climate change or the result of human processes or action such as deforestation, forest burning, pollution.	• UK Foot and Mouth Outbreak in 2001 • SARS epidemic • Hurricane Hugo • Asian fires and smog haze in 1997 • Kobe earthquake 1995 • European floods 2002 • Katherine flood (Australia) • Forest fires in southern France 2003 • Austrian Alps avalanche
Political crises/disasters	• The tourism industry and tourists are often an indirect victim but can be specifically targeted in some cases. Examples can range from within international tourism such as international wars, civil war, coups, terrorism, riots and political and social unrest.	• Gulf War 1991 and Iraq War 2003 • Sri Lanka, Yugoslavia • Fiji coups • British handover of Hong Kong to China in 1997 • Opposition by locals toward tourism development
Economic crises	• Ranging from international recessions, regional currency crises to national recession or monetary crises.	• Stock market crash 1987 and slow down after September 11, 2001 • Asian economic crisis 1997–1998
Malevolence	• When some outside actor or opponent employs extreme tactics to express anger toward the organisation or destination to force the organisation or destination to change. Examples include product tampering, kidnapping, terrorism and espionage.	• Basque separatist group ETA bombing campaigns in Spanish resorts • Muslim extremist attacks in Egypt in the 1990s to force change in government

Table 2.1 (*Continued*)

Type of crises/disasters	Characteristics	Examples
Challenges	• When the organisation or destination is confronted by discontented stakeholders. The stakeholders challenge the organisation because they believe it is not operating in an appropriate manner and does not meet their expectations. Examples include boycotts, strikes, lawsuits, government penalties and protests.	• Unofficial strike by British Airway check-in staff in July 2003 • Domestic air pilot strike in Australia in 1989
Megadamage	• When an accident causes significant environmental damage. Examples include oil spills and radioactive contamination.	• Chernobyl • Exxon Valdez
Organisational misdeeds	• When management takes actions, it knows will harm or serve to discredit or disgrace the organisation in some way. Examples include favouring short-term economic gain over social values, deliberate deception of stakeholders and illegal acts by management.	• Bribery or price fixing • Enron, Wordcom
Workplace violence	• When an employee or former employee commits violence against other employees on organisational grounds. Examples include killing or injuring co-workers.	• Sexual harassment by staff • Rape or violence against hotel guests
Rumours	• When false information is spread about an organisation or its products. The false information hurts the organisation's reputation by putting the organisation in an unfavourable light. Examples include rumours linking the organisation to radical groups or stories that their products are contaminated.	• Rumours of second terrorist attack after American Airlines plane crashes after September 11, 2001

Source: Modified after Coombs (1999: 61–62) and Hall and O'Sullivan (1996).

(1) *Immediate crises:* where little or no warning exists, therefore, organisations are unable to research the problem or prepare a plan before the crisis hits.
(2) *Emerging crises:* these are slower in developing and may be able to be stopped or limited by organisational action.
(3) *Sustained crises:* that may last for weeks, months or even years.

Moreira (2007) differentiates between catastrophic risks (such as sudden negative impacts such as airplane crashes, disasters of extreme events) which have short-term consequences and stealth risks (such as a gradual increase in negative or natural conditions such as crime, and the gradual degradation of neutral or positive conditions such as environmental quality). Strategies to deal with these different crisis situations will vary depending on time pressure, the extent of control, the magnitude of these incidents, and whether management perceive this situation to be a crisis or simply an issue which should be dealt with as a normal part of the strategic management function.

Crises can be divided into those caused by internal forces and those caused by external influences. The nature of the crisis for organisations can be divided into either technical/economic failures, or failures in the human/organisational/social processes. Figure 2.1, from Shrivastava and Mitroff (1987: 7), illustrates how various incidents may be classified,

	Technical/Economic	
Internal	*Cell 1* Major industrial accidents Product injuries Computer breakdown Defective, undisclosed information	*Cell 2* Widespread environmental destruction Natural disasters Societal crises (civil or political) Large scale systems failure	**External**
	Cell 3 Failure to adapt/change Sabotage by insiders Organizational breakdown Communication breakdown On-site products tampering Illegal activities Occupational health diseases	*Cell 4* Symbolic projection Sabotage by outsiders Terrorism, executive kidnapping Off-site product tampering Counterfeiting	
	Human/Organizational/Social	

Figure 2.1 Crisis classification matrix
Source: Reprinted from *Columbia Journal of World Business*, Spring, Shrivastava, P. and Mitroff, I., Strategic Management of Corparate Crises, pp. 5–11, copyright (1987), with permission of Elsevier.

although it is not an exhaustive list. Cell 1 includes technical and or economic failure in the internal environment (within a specific organisation) such as the Chernobyl nuclear disaster, while Cell 2 consists of technical and economic failure in the external environment such as political instability, natural disasters or hostile takeovers. Cell 3 includes factors as a result of human error which occur within an organisation such as organisational misdeeds, communication breakdowns and internal sabotage. Finally, Cell 4 includes incidents that occur from outside the organisation including external sabotage, product tampering and terrorism or kidnapping.

Although other crises and disasters can cause disruption and cause social and economic problems for organisations and destinations, it is natural, political and economic crises and disasters that are often longer lasting and have more substantial impacts on tourism organisations and destinations. The following section explores some of the characteristics and examples from each of these areas to highlight their potential impact on the tourism system.

Natural and technical disasters

Climate change, forest fires and pollution are often interrelated global environment issues that can impact upon tourism demand or create natural disasters or trigger crises (Gössling & Hall, 2006). In particular, climate change and pollution can have an impact on tourism demand, as demonstrated by the smoke haze over several countries in Asia in 1997. Changing weather patterns, particularly the 'El Niño' weather patterns caused drought in several countries in 1997 in the Asia-Pacific region. Leiper and Hing (1998) note that this, in combination with burning undergrowth to facilitate access to rainforest timber in Sumatra and Borneo, led to vast forest fires and smoke clouds which spread over West Malaysia, Thailand, Singapore, Sulawesi and Java. There was also evidence of the haze spreading as far as Darwin in Australia (Henderson, 1999b). This caused illness amongst residents and visitors and led to a decline in visitation to South-east Asia. A number of regional airports were closed and there was further negative publicity following a Garuda Indonesian Airbus-300 crash in north Sumatra which killed all passengers and crew after the pilot complained of poor visibility (Henderson, 1999b; Leiper & Hing, 1998).

A study by the Economy and Environment Program for South-east Asia calculated the total cost to Singapore of the environmental pollution alone to be S$104 million in 1997 with the tourism industry losing S$81.8 million and the airline sector S$9.7 million (Henderson, 1999b: 112). Forest fires have also occurred more recently in national parks in North America, Europe and Australia. Nearly 1000 visitors were evacuated from parks in the south of France in July 2003 as forest fires spread, while Australia has experienced forest fires which have dramatically affected the tourism industry (Armstrong & Ritchie, 2007; Cioccio & Michael, 2007). In Victoria, Australia fires affected an area equivalent to 5% of the State land area, with 1100 tourism businesses seriously affected with an estimated A\$20 million lost in the first month alone (Cioccio & Michael, 2007). In Canberra, Australia, the 2003 bushfires affected businesses that were not part of the tourism industry and reduced tourism business levels by approximately 50% below normal levels, while ancillary services such as restaurants struggled in the weeks after the bushfire (Armstrong & Ritchie, 2007).

The impact on transport and communications infrastructure resulting from natural disasters can dissuade tourists from visiting because of physical access issues resulting from a loss of infrastructure (Huang & Min, 2002). In Taiwan, an earthquake in September 1999 resulted in more than 2400 people being killed, over 13,000 people were injured, in excess of 10,000 were left homeless, many buildings were destroyed, and roadways, water, sewage, gas and power systems were cut. The tourism-related impacts, as outlined by Huang and Min (2002), resulted in a 15% drop in inbound tourists compared to the same time previous year, while international airline reservation cancellations soared to 210,000 for the September–December period of 1999.

A powerful earthquake of magnitude 9 on the Richter scale struck on 26th December 2004 off the coast of the Indonesian island of Sumatra triggering a tsunami, impacting on coastal regions and low lying islands in the Indian Ocean area killing an estimated 250,000 people, with many tourists killed. The impact on the Maldives was severe, with 82 persons dead, 1313 injured, 26 missing and some 10,500 people displaced by the tsunami (Carlsen, 2006). Estimates suggested a reduction in tourist arrivals for the Maldives between 28 and 36% from the previous year, while a reduction of GDP to between 1 and 1.5% compared to an estimate of between 5.5 and 7.6% (in Carlsen, 2006). The impact on tourism infrastructure varied amongst affected destinations with the majority of infrastructure in the Maldives destroyed, while in Thailand, Khao Lak and Phi Phi island lost 6000 and 4000 hotel rooms, respectively (Cheung & Law, 2006; Henderson, 2005).

Another issue related to climate change are changing weather patterns (such as that of La Niña) creating high levels of rainfall, which can lead to subsequent flooding. Faulkner and Vikulov (2001: 331) discuss the floods in Katherine in Australia which they note that for the Katherine community and its tourism industry, the Australia Day Flood in 1998 was a disaster of huge proportions, with half of the resident's homes, the whole of the town's Central Business District (CBD) and most of its tourism business premises being inundated, and extensively damaged or destroyed. A total of over A$60 million worth of damage was done to public sector infrastructure while the cost for the private sector was tens of millions (Reed, 1998 in Faulkner & Vikulov, 2001). Floods in Saxony, Germany in August 2002 created £6196 million worth of direct tangible damage, while damage-specific recreation and tourism infrastructure was estimated at £183 million (Bernsdorf, 2004). The Prague floods from the same period reduced visitor numbers by one-third with 30,000 passengers on Czech airlines cancelling flights in the two days after the floods (Field, 2003).

In sensitive mountain environments, infrastructure development coupled with changing weather patterns can lead to landslides and avalanches as well as increased exposure to extreme weather events for both resorts and visitors (Becken & Hay, 2007; Nöthiger *et al.*, 2006). As climatic conditions vary, an increase in rain has occurred in mountain areas leading to increased susceptibility towards landslides and avalanches (Becken & Hay, 2007). In the winter of 1998/1999 in the Austrian region of Tyrol, a number of avalanches occurred (Beritelli & Gotsch, 1999; Peters & Pikkemaat, 2005) causing damage and disruption to the local tourism industry. Furthermore, a total of 40 Swiss alpine resorts were cut off from the world for 14 days, resulting in a direct loss of US$1216 million and an indirect loss of US$215 million to the tourism industry (Nöthiger *et al.*, 2006). According to Stafford *et al.* (2002), hurricanes have always been a problem for the tourism industry located in Hawaii and the Caribbean. Examples include Hurricane Luis and Hurricane Marilyn on St. Thomas, St. John, and St. Croix which hit in September 1995. The economic impact of the 1999 hurricanes Dennis, Floyd, and Irene on North Carolina's Lodging Industry was between US$96 million and US$125 million for two months alone (Chandler, 2004), while Hurricane Katrina which dramatically hit New Orleans in 2005, effectively brought the tourism industry to a standstill.

Increased temperatures as a result of climate change may not only create more forest fires but also affect visitors by increasing the risk of heat stress and infectious diseases. For instance, Becken and Hay (2007) outlined that Western Europe could experience a 10°C increase in temperature due to Greenhouse-induced warming. This can increase heat stress for both locals and visitors and may increase the likelihood of respiratory disease, allergic reactions and even malaria which may develop as some destinations become warmer and tropical or subtropical. Furthermore, increased temperature is predicted to increase sea levels by between 0.1 and 0.6 metres in the 21st Century (IPCC, 2001), creating elevated sea levels and increased high wave incidents, which may increase coastal erosion and for small island states.

Biosecurity or biological disasters have also had a recent impact on the tourism industry and are expected to increase in the future due to increased human mobility (Hall, 2005, 2006). The Foot and Mouth

Outbreak in the UK in 2001 had a major impact upon the tourism industry in the UK and especially in London (although London had no outbreaks of the disease). A total of 2030 cases of the disease were identified and over four million animals were culled during the crisis with worldwide media broadcasts showing burning carcasses. The English Tourism Council (ETC) predicted that losses to English tourism in 2001 would be £5 billion, while in 2002 and 2003, reductions would total £2.5 billion and £1 billion, respectively (ETC, 2001). Cumbria was one of the worst affected regions of England, due to its location in the Lakes District National Park, and suffered an estimated fall in tourism expenditure of around £198 million (Blake *et al.*, 2001), 31% of the value of receipts. The recent emergence of a possible Foot and Mouth Outbreak in 2007 also concerned the tourism industry, although this small outbreak was declared over soon after it was first discovered. Horse or equine influenza also severely disrupted racing events and competitions throughout Australia in 2007, and was described as the biggest crisis the horse racing industry had ever faced. The role of tourists as vectors for plant and animal disease has not been widely discussed in the tourism crisis and disaster literature, but are one risk that may affect agricultural industries such as wine production (Hall, 2005).

The outbreak of the Severe Acute Respiratory Syndrome (SARS) also hit the world hard. The new infectious disease is caused by a corona virus, that is believed to have crossed from animals to humans in South China's Guangdong province (Yew, 2003) where it was first discovered in mid-November 2003 (BBC News, 2003a, 2003b). SARS was then brought by a human host from China to Hong Kong. From Hong Kong's *Metropole Hotel* where the infected spread the virus among guests, and was carried by air travel further to Canada, Singapore and Taiwan (BBC News, 2003a). The WHO has described SARS as a 'worldwide health threat' (BBC News, 2003b) and put travel warnings on a number of affected countries and regions in Asia and North America. Worldwide, 8437 people in and around 30 countries in Asia, North and South America, Europe and Africa became infected, and more than 800 died of the virus (CDC, 2003a; Layfield, 2003). The SARS outbreak might confirm the fear of infectious disease specialists that 'the increase in global air travel could assist a disastrous spread of a new and lethal infection' (BBC News, 2003b: n.p.). The director of the Centers for Disease Control and Prevention (CDC) in Atlanta mentioned in this context that the SARS epidemic 'reminds us that an emerging problem in one part of the world will soon be a problem for all of us' (Harder, 2003: 198), making it important to find effective strategies of managing such biosecurity and health threats.

Due to the significant reduction in foreign exchange earnings in certain countries, the SARS virus has not only hit the travel and tourism industry itself, but also the national economy as a whole. Asian countries were especially seriously affected (Xinghua News Agency, 2003). The World Travel and Tourism Council's (WTTC) Vice President for Research and Economics, Richard Miller, said at the '3rd *Global Travel and Tourism Summit'* in Vilamoura, Portugal that:

> the SARS crisis in China, Hong Kong, Singapore and Vietnam is perhaps the most dramatic prolonged shutdown of the industry on record. Only the 9/11 events in the United States can serve as a point of reference and the SARS impact is 5 times greater. Although we do not expect the impact to be permanent, and in fact expect a return to normal levels of business by 2005, the short-term impact is unprecedented. (WTTC, 2003: n.p.)

In their *'Tourism Satellite Accounting Research 2003'*, the WTTC and Oxford Economic Forecasting (OEF, 2001) published figures that express the estimated economic impact of the SARS virus on the travel and tourism industry of China, Hong Kong, Singapore and Vietnam (Table 2.2). According to Huimin and Wall (2006), the impact of SARS in China was a reduction of 30% from the same period the year before and a 49% drop in receipts from reduced length of stay and spend, although arrivals bounced back five months later. Japanese outbound travel dropped 24.3% during the three-month SARS crisis and 19.5% for the year (Cooper, 2005). Singapore hotels reported a 21% hotel occupancy rate for the second quarter of 2003, compared with 74.5% the previous year, while room rates were reduced by 18.8%. Evidence was collected that hotels were expecting to lose 50% of earnings for 2003 (Henderson & Ng, 2004).

The potential of future biological threats to animals as well as humans is a very real threat that has largely been ignored. As Hall (2006: 174) states, 'there is very little to suggest that the tourism industry is

Table 2.2 Estimated economic impact of the SARS virus on four Asian destinations in 2003

The WTTC/OEF has estimated that in 2003:
China: 25% of travel and tourism GDP will be lost and a total of 2.8 million industry jobs, or one-fifth of total industry employment.
Hong Kong: 41% of tourism GDP will be lost, as well as 27,000 industry jobs, representing 38% of total industry jobs in Hong Kong.
Singapore: 43% of tourism GDP and 17,500 industry jobs will be lost.
Vietnam: 15% of tourism GDP and 62,000 industry jobs will be lost.

Source: Based on WTTC (2003).

concerned or even aware of many [pandemics] such global health and disease issues'. The potential for bioterrorists to contaminate the food chain through the use of biological agents or spread diseases such as smallpox or even foot and mouth could have a catastrophic impact upon industry and society including the tourism system, and are only recently being highlighted by industry and tourism researchers (Hall, 2006). Such crises and disasters will maintain the interest of health and food officials and have the potential to dramatically influence the tourism industry. In some cases, such as SARS, the process of globalisation and the tourism industry itself has facilitated the spread of such disease impacting upon global security. More recently, the potential outbreak of bird flu and/or a global influenza pandemic have caused some concern amongst the tourism industry (Page *et al.*, 2006), while Hall (2006) suggests that these health risks are occurring at the same time as increased global mobility and travel.

Finally, blackouts caused by hurricanes, storms, flooding or human error (or a combination of these factors), have also impacted upon the tourism industry. The most recent is the big American blackout of 2003, the largest in North American history, which affected over 50 million people in seven American states, resulting in a loss of US$6 billion (Goodrich, 2005). The cause for these blackouts was human error, outdated procedures and shortcomings at an energy company and a regional grid monitoring centre. Every part of the tourism system was affected. The airlines cancelled flights to and from affected areas until electricity was restored; cruises were delayed; hotels were in darkness; cultural attractions, museums and sports facilities were closed; restaurants had to operate in the dark or close; retail, banks and other ancillary services were also closed. According to a study conducted by Kwortnik (2006), hotels were without electricity for 16 hours on average, with 90% losing air conditioning and guest lighting, while two out of three hotels lost power in rooms and bathroom facilities.

Political crises/disasters

As Hall and O'Sullivan (1996: 105) note, 'issues of political stability are and political relations within and between states are extremely important in determining the image of destinations in tourist-generating regions and, or course, the real and perceived safety of tourists'. Examples such as protests, violence, civil and international war as well as political coups or incidents of terrorism can have a major impact on image, perceptions of safety and ultimately tourism demand, plunging destinations into tourism crises. Political crises and instability can erupt into violence, war or terrorist activity. Beirman (2002) notes that political disasters can potentially have longer and further-reaching consequences on the marketing of a tourist destination compared to natural disasters. As Beirman (2002: 168) elaborates:

> while a natural crisis can initially get substantial media attention, it is often for a relatively short but intensive period of time. By contrast, the effect of continued and sustained media exposure to riots, killings and political stand-offs can carry on for a much longer period of time. Potentially, it can have a more sustained impact on the perceived tourism image of a destination.

Tourists can be direct or indirect victims of political instability. They may be targeted by terrorists in their pursuit to create political change and part of tactical, strategic or longer term ideological objectives (Hall, 1994). Tactical use of the tourism industry or tourists could be part of a short-term objective to gain money to fund further terrorist activity through kidnapping or robbing tourists. However, ideological objectives may be part of a long-term struggle such as that found in civil wars in Rwanda or the ongoing Arab/Israeli conflict. Actions to create political instability are usually for two main reasons according to Soñmez (1998):

(1) for *revolutionary goals* (to oppose or overthrow the current government or those in power) such as in coups and civil wars; and
(2) for *sub-revolutionary goals* (to create change or specific policy changes by the government or those in power) such as the call by Egyptian extremists for the government to resign in the 1990s.

In both the types, there is a need for political, economic and social power. Similar, to the discussion above on the nature of crises and disasters, political instability and its impact on tourism can lead to an immediate, emerging or a sustained crisis. Immediate crises include acts of terrorism or malevolence which impact either directly or indirectly on tourism and travel. Recently, it appears that tourists and the tourism industry are becoming targets of the terrorists as such targets can help them meet their goals (Soñmez, 1998; Wall, 1996) in the following ways:

- they generate more publicity for terrorist causes because the focus moves from national to international media;
- they can cause economic disruption as tourism is often highly important to economies; and
- tourists are ambassadors for specific countries and 'soft' targets (easy to identify and target).

Examples where tourists or tourism have been direct victims of terrorism include the al Jihad terrorist group that attacked and killed 16 Greek tourists in front of an Egyptian hotel in April 1996. Islamic militants at the 4000-year-old temple of Hatshepsut in Luxor killed another 58 international tourists in late 1997 (Soñmez, 1998; Stafford *et al.*, 2002) as they attempted to replace the government. However, Aziz (1995) suggests that the targeting of tourists is due to the sociocultural differences between westerners and their actions on holiday which are at odds against Islamic culture and tradition. Whatever the reasons, the attacks between 1993 and 1995 caused a 22% drop in international visitors, a 30% drop in tourist nights and a 43% decline in tourism receipts (Aziz, 1995; Wahab, 1996).

The Bali bombings of 2002 and 2005 are another direct examples where western tourists were specifically targeted because they were ideologically opposed to tourism and what tourists represent. A total of 202 people were killed in the 2002 Bali bomb blasts with the majority of them being British or Australian citizens. In 2005, a series of suicide backpack bombings were initiated in Jimberan Bay and the popular shopping district of Kuta Square. The impact on tourism in Bali in 2002 was devastating, with the hotel occupancy rate in Bali dropping from 69% in September 2002 (one month before the bomb blasts) to the lowest level of 18% in November 2002 (one month after the bomb blasts), and remained low through July 2003 (Toh *et al.*, 2004: 219). The contribution of tourism to Bali's Gross Domestic Regional Product dropped from 60 to 49%. According to Hitchcock and Putra (2005), despite widespread unemployment and a collapse in living standards, Bali did not experience widespread strife or retribution from ethnic minorities, which was rumoured to probably occur after the incident.

Over a two-year period from January 2000 to June 2002, a 34% downturn was experienced in domestic air passengers and 23% for international travel as a result of the September 11, 2001 terrorist attacks (Blake & Sinclair, 2003). The economic impacts of September 11 on the national economy of the United States were assessed by Blake and Sinclair (2003) using a computer general equilibrium (CGE) model, the first time one has been applied in the tourism crisis management field. Their research discovered that in the absence of offsetting policies, the terrorist attacks would have decreased GDP by almost US$30 billion with the majority of the impacts felt in the airline and accommodation sector and half a million jobs lost. However, the research illustrated the effectiveness of government subsides and assistance for the airline sector, as opposed to the suggestion by the Travel Industry Recovery Coalition for government tax credits for all trips. The later measures were considered by the authors as less effective in reducing the impact on GDP and reducing costs to government (Blake & Sinclair, 2003). As Blake and Sinclair (2003: 829) state, '[t]he overall conclusion is that directing subsides to the sector that is most severely affected by the crisis is the most efficient policy response in terms of both GDP and the number of jobs saved'. This point is discussed in more detail in Chapter 6.

Longer term political instability can also have an impact on tourism demand and flows. Beirman (2002) provides the example of the Israeli-Palestinian dispute as an example of a sustained or prolonged crisis which is well known. Despite a growth of tourist arrivals to the area in recent years and 2000 seeing the best inbound tourism to date for Israel (23% up on 1999 arrivals), the conflict and bombings reoccurred in September 2000 and numbers for October–December 2000 were down by 50% compared with 1999 and an estimated 15,000 Israelis lost their jobs. Nevertheless, it did not stop there, as the tourism industry in Jordan and the Palestinian territories were also impacted due to travel warnings, cancellations and restricted access to areas by Israeli authorities. Another example of a sustained or prolonged political crisis is Northern Ireland where past targets of bombing and violence have been British military, police and government officials. Visitor numbers fell from over 1 million in 1967 to over 300,000 in 1976 as a result of a poor image and perceptions of risk by potential tourists (Wall, 1996). After a ceasefire in 1994, visitor numbers rose by 59% compared with the previous year (O'Neil & Fitz, 1996) as political stability began to improve.

Soñmez (1998: 417) provides an excellent overview of terrorism and political instability impacts on the tourism industry and notes:

> well publicized examples of terrorism or political conflict involving the tourism industry are frequently referred to by studies which – although useful in chronicling the relationship – offer few solutions. Important questions remain: how do destinations burdened with political challenges deal with negative images? How does the industry manage the crisis of terrorism or political strife? How can it become immune to the effects of terrorism and political problems?

Some ideas and suggestions on how to deal with political instability and terrorist crises are illustrated in subsequent chapters through an analysis of crisis management theory and practice.

Economic crises/disasters

Tourism is extremely susceptible to changes in economic patterns including exchange rates and levels of disposable income. In times of recession or global down turn patterns of outbound, tourism may decline and destinations and organisations may have to deal with a drop in demand and visitation. In particular, the Asian Economic Crisis of 1997–1998 had a major impact on previous growth rates for tourism. As Leiper and Hing (1998) noted, the economic crisis may have not greatly affected the countries with respect to total numbers (which were down slightly) but reduced their growth partly because of the high level of intra-regional travel and interdependence in the Asia-Pacific region. Leiper and Hing (1998) note for instance, that outbound tourism from Korea to Australia was down by 80% in early 1998 compared with the same time in 1997. Furthermore, transit destinations such as Singapore were also impacted more than other destinations with a 17% reduction (Leiper & Hing, 1998). However, travellers from USA, Canada and Europe increased to the Asia-Pacific region because of better value for money based on exchange rates as the currency in Asia-Pacific countries dramatically fell. This illustrates the chaotic nature of crises and that they also provide advantages as well as disadvantages, which has been noted earlier in discussing the definitions of crisis.

Obviously with a decline in visitation, businesses suffered as a result in a drop of expenditures and airlines in the Asia-Pacific region were severely impacted with many cutting back routes, retrenching staff and reduced the size of their fleets. For example, Philippines Airlines announced that 5000 of its flight crew and other workers, about a third of the total were being retrenched (Lenthan, 1995). A sharp downturn in investment and property development was noted by Leiper and Hing (1998), as well as a number of mergers and acquisitions amongst tourism and hospitality companies. The global 'credit crunch' of 2007 and possible worldwide recession could have a major impact upon consumer consumption and may dramatically affect tourism demand patterns. Furthermore, fuel price rises and concern over levels of oil production could dramatically increase the cost of travel and may affect travel demand. O'Mahony *et al.* (2006) illustrated, early on during fuel price rises in late 2005 in Australia, that although the increase in fuel prices did not significantly affect travel propensity, it did affect travel decision-making with a significant proportion of travellers modifying the distance travelled, type of accommodation used and type of holiday.

Organisational collapses can also severely impact the tourism industry either direct or indirectly. The collapse of Ansett Airlines in Australia, as it accumulated losses of A$50 million and was placed into receivership, led to a loss of tourists from New Zealand, disruption of services to rural areas and reduced ability for customers of Star Alliance partners to use their frequent flyer points for travel to and within Australia (Prideaux, 2003: 288). Furthermore, in the same article, Prideaux (2003) notes that indirectly the collapse of HIH insurance in Australia, responsible for nearly 40% of the public liability insurance market, led to an increase in insurance premiums substantially affecting tourism attractions and the cancellation of many events.

Table 2.3 illustrates how some of these major crises and shocks can have linked impacts that may be both negative and positive providing an example of Indonesia. Political unrest led to ethnic and religious violence and rebellions in East Timor and Ache, while the Asian economic crisis

Table 2.3 Changed influences on tourist flows to Indonesia, 1997–2002

Origin pushes	Indonesia became more competitive as the value of the rupiah fell during the Asian financial crisis.
Destination pull factors	Asian financial crisis results in falling value of rupiah giving tourists greater buying power.
Repellents	Smoke haze Political unrest Ethnic violence Religious violence Rebellions in East Timor and Ache Bali terrorist attack in 2002

Source: Reprinted from *Tourism Management*, 24, Prideaux, B., Laws, E. and Faulkner, B., Events is Indonesia: exploring the limits to formal tourism trend forecasting methods in complex crisis situations., pp. 475–487, copyright (2003), with permission of Elsevier.

may not only have impacted upon outbound tourism but also provided better value for money for inbound tourists, as discussed previously.

Differentiating Between Incidents or Natural Events and Crises or Disasters

As with the definition of a crisis, it is the threat, time pressure, and intensity of incidents that perhaps lead to a crisis. A combination of these factors can lead to the development of a crisis continuum to help classify and understand such incidents, and more importantly, illustrate to managers when an 'issue' or a 'problem' can develop into a 'crisis'. Burnett (1998) outlines a crisis classification matrix (Figure 2.2), which uses a 16-cell matrix based on threat level (high versus low), response options (many versus few), time pressure (intense versus minimal), and degree of control (high versus low).

Burnett (1998) suggests that problems or issues found in the level 1 or 0 cell would not be classified as a crisis but would enable general strategic management responses as part of the normal management function. The most challenging problems are found in the only level 4 cell as the time pressure is intense, the degree of control is low, and the threat level high and response options are few in number. Several of level 2 or 3 cells could develop or be classified as crises, although Burnett (1998) does not state which ones specifically.

Billings *et al.* (1980) propose a model to help managers and planners understand when a problem becomes a crisis. The model has elements that explore the perceived value of the possible loss to an organisation, compared with the perceived probability of loss and the perceived time pressure. In other words, a threat level will be high because of the

Time pressure		Intense		Minimal	
Degree of control		*Low*	*High*	*Low*	*High*
Threat Level	Response options				
Low	*Many*	(4) Level 2	(3) Level 1	(2) Level 1	(1) Level 0
	Few	(8) Level 3	(7) Level 2	(6) Level 2	(5) Level 1
High	*Many*	(12) Level 3	(11) Level 2	(10) Level 2	(9) Level 1
	Few	(16) Level 4	(15) Level 3	(14) Level 3	(13) Level 2

Figure 2.2 A crisis classification matrix
Source: Reprinted from *Public Relations Review*, 24(4), Burnett, J.J., A strategic approach to managing crises, pp. 475–488, copyright (1998), with permission of Elsevier.

perceived loss and probability of loss combined with the time pressure. Perception of a potential crisis and the probability of loss suggests that a crisis may not occur, but also that if ignored it could be perception of publics and media which turn it into a real crisis rather than a potential crisis. Organisational decision-makers may perceive that there is nothing wrong with their actions or inactions, yet the media and various publics may see it differently. The influence of the media is discussed in Chapter 7 in more detail, while discussion of prevention and planning measures to help identify potential crises and their signals are outlined in Chapters 4 and 5.

Hazards, which if occur can create disasters, are commonly classified as depending on their probability or likelihood of occurrence and their potential impacts on humans or their welfare. The relationship between severity of the environmental hazard, probability and risk illustrates that hazards to human life are rated more highly (in this model), than damage to economic goods or the environment combining to create levels of low, medium and high risk (Smith, 1995). According to Hills (1998) and Heath (1995), most emergency management planning and policy focuses on highly probable but low impact events at the expense of low probability/high impact events, and ignore the potency of disasters to create other linked incidents. Magnitude, according to Heath (1995), can be viewed by the following six attributes:

(1) the degree to which impact damage seems random in occurrence;
(2) the size of the impact area;

(3) the severity of impact;
(4) the ratio of visible to invisible damage;
(5) the number of major sub-event crises triggered by the impact of the event; and
(6) the degree of psychological distortion caused by (or accelerated by) the impact of the event.

As discussed in the Section 'Crisis and Disaster Definitions' (Chapter 1), disasters are related to the concepts of vulnerability and risk. Risk is the probability or likelihood of a certain level of loss due to a hazard impact, while vulnerability is the potential for losses or other adverse impacts (Alexander, 2000). Risk is therefore concerned with the probable size and magnitude of a natural hazard. However, as Alexander (2000) notes, the two are interrelated as vulnerability in the light of known hazard produces a risk, while taking a risk creates vulnerability to a hazard. A tourism example could be the building of an unprotected tourist resort next to a river system that is known to flood. This creates a situation of risk (probable flood damage) and an element of vulnerability (threatened property). This example could be seen to be a medium level risk if the flood occurs and only damaged property, but if it threatens the life of tourists and staff at the resort, then it could be a high risk.

Furthermore, natural hazards are extreme natural events that can cause death or damage to humans (Smith, 1995). A severe earthquake that occurs in a remote part of the world would be considered an extreme natural event but not a natural hazard. Therefore, it is the location of people or humans and their property that creates a hazard through either risk taking or vulnerability. In other situations, Smith (1995) notes that natural events may be considered beneficial, in the case of floods providing silt for agriculture but not impacting upon human settlements. Consequently, there is a degree of socioeconomic tolerance of environmental or natural events, which determines whether events are seen as resources or perceived as hazards if they pass beyond damage thresholds. If damage progresses above or below a band of tolerance and affects humans, then it breaches the damage threshold and is seen as a hazard rather than a resource. Smith (1995) provides the example of snow, which is considered a resource for the activity of skiing and the business of ski resorts. If snow falls on the slopes then it may be considered a resource, but if it blocks access, then it will constitute a hazard and could result in a disaster if the resort is inaccessible by tourists or if tourists are caught in a snow storm. It is the human location, actions and perceptions that identify hazards within the range of natural events (Burton *et al.*, 1978).

In the tourism field, little discussion has been undertaken on the scale of crises and disasters and the development of typologies or classifications. Prideaux *et al.* (2003) are one of the few pieces of work

Table 2.4 Classification of shocks

Scale	Probability	Example of event
S4	Not anticipated	September 11 terrorist attack in the USA, 1991 Gulf War, Asian financial crisis
S3	Unlikely but just possible	Pre-existing conditions cause disruption (i.e. earthquakes, terrorist attacks, coups)
S2	The possible based on worst-case scenario of past trading conditions	Upper limit of variables normally used in forecasting (i.e. rapid rise in exchange rates)
S1	The expected based on recent past trading conditions	Within the range of expected movements in exchange rates and inflation

Source: Modified after Prideaux *et al.* (2003: 484).

that propose a four-scale classification of 'shocks' and provide examples of types of shock events. They note that shocks S3 or S4 have the ability to cause the greatest disruption to tourism (see Table 2.4) because they have low probability but high scale of impacts. The classification criteria used by the authors is somewhat similar to our previous discussions as it combines both the scale and probability of these incidents to form a classification model. Unfortunately, as noted earlier, agencies to date have been concerned more with the prevention of high probability and low impact incidents (Hills, 1998). Perhaps this view may change after the low probability and high impact of September 11, 2001 and the Boxing Day Tsunami in 2004? Certainly such incidents have meant a reassessment of terrorist activity and earthquake preparedness and perhaps make them more probable incidents.

Models for Understanding Crisis and Disaster Lifecycles

In both crisis and disaster definitions there is a belief that disasters and crises are temporary and that they have certain lifecycles which could last hours, days, months or even years. Although crisis management models and concepts will be discussed in detail in the next chapter, this section will briefly highlight the main models that assist our understanding and classification of crisis and disaster lifecycles. This will help provide a basis for the following chapters. Conceptual and theoretical models for helping managers and planners understand crises and disasters more effectively can generally be identified as being either prescriptive or descriptive models.

Prescriptive models or checklists have both general- and industry-specific applicability in that they provide useful prescriptions concerning crisis identification, response and resolution (Burnett, 1998). They provide managers with ideas on how to plan and attempt to manage crises or disasters. However, as with many prescriptive planning approaches, they may offer little new information or do not provide comprehensive strategies. This is partly because they only tell us what to do to solve problems before we actually experience them for ourselves. Previous crisis management research has also focused on producing prescriptive models concerning the stages of crises to assist understanding and future proactive and strategic management of crises (see Richardson, 1994, 1995). In some cases, these models or frameworks have been applied to real life case studies providing descriptive models, which are useful for examining how prescriptive measures worked in real life. Because descriptive models are historic, they are able to provide insights based on hindsight that can be useful for the future management of crises and disasters that affect the tourism industry. They are able to actually describe how plans or policies actually worked in relation to crisis or disaster situations. These models are discussed in more detail in the subsequent chapters; however, the focus of this section of the chapter will be to identify those conceptual or theoretical models that have helped understand the crisis and disaster lifecycle, and in so doing assist our understanding of the nature of crises and disasters.

A number of generic models have been developed to help managers and researchers understand the lifecycle of a crisis or disaster. In discussing organisational crisis management, Coombs (1999) developed a three-stage model, which included pre-crisis, crisis event and post-crisis. According to Coombs (1999: 14), restricting the model to three phases was to provide '... the appropriate macro-level generality for constructing the comprehensive framework necessary for analysing the crisis management literature'. Although it is easy to understand and random events can be placed in this model, it lacks the detail for fully understanding the lifecycle of crises and the response of individuals and organisations. Gonzalez-Herrero and Pratt's (1995) four-stage model is a more useful model, and it takes a more preventative approach to crisis management by having two of the four stages related to what they term 'issues management' and prevention and planning (which are discussed in more detail in Chapter 4), followed by the crisis event itself and then the post-crisis stage. In the hazards field, Smith (1995: 21) provides a four-phase model, often called PPRR or RRRR (Heath, 1998), ranging from:

(1) *Pre-disaster planning* (where land-use planning coupled with the creation and dissemination of evacuation plans or construction of

defensive engineering works could be undertaken to reduce the likelihood of a natural hazard).

(2) *Preparedness* (such as preparation of emergency warnings and the degree of alertness of officials to implement an evacuation plan).

(3) *Response* (dealing with events immediately before and after they have happened including reaction to warnings and emergency relief actions).

(4) *Recovery and reconstruction* (longer term activities to return an area back to normality after devastation).

Fink (1986, 2000) and Roberts (1994) both developed slightly different models to explain the lifecycle of crises (see Table 2.5) suggesting that crises and disasters go through a series of progressive linear stages. Fink (1986, 2000) described four distinct stages, while Roberts suggested five stages. Both were combined by Faulkner (2001) into a six-stage model to develop the first tourism-specific disaster management framework which was subsequently applied to the Katherine Floods in Australia (see Faulkner & Vikulov, 2001). This classification based on the lifecycle or anatomy of crises and disasters is useful as it suggests to managers what strategies could be considered or developed at the various stages of a crisis or disaster, and how to stop crises moving into the next stage. Application of lifecycle and disaster frameworks to specific case studies is important in order to refine such frameworks and ensure that they are more useful for managers in the tourism industry. Miller and Ritchie (2003) applied Faulkner's (2001) disaster framework to the 2001 Foot and Mouth Outbreak in the UK and noted a general agreement to the stages, although the crisis was complicated by the fact that, at a national level progression through the stages occurred, but at a regional or local level some areas were totally unaffected and thus were impacted by national level policy and perceptions of tourists. Prideaux (2003), referring to Australia's response to major tourism disasters in 2001, suggested changes to Faulkner's (2001) Tourism Disaster Management Framework, to include a forecasting element to help identify risks and develop contingency plans, as well as a suggestion to increase activities at the review stage. Further testing and the development and application of theoretical frameworks for tourism crisis and disaster management are required.

Fink (1986, 2000) believes that a crisis has many characteristics in common with an illness and thus termed his crisis lifecycle model with phrases such as acute, chronic, and resolution. He notes that 'a crisis is a fluid, unstable, dynamic situation ... must be ministered to in much the same way. With both an illness and a crisis, things are in a state of constant flux' (Fink, 1986: 20). According to Fink (1986, 2000), the prodromal stage is when the symptoms of the crisis begin to show, and it is at this stage that action can be undertaken to cure, prevent or

Table 2.5 The crisis and disaster lifecycle

Faulkner's (2001) stages	*Fink's (1986, 2000) stages*	*Robert's (1994) stages*
1. Pre-event	Proaction	Pre-event: where action can be taken to prevent disasters (e.g. growth management planning or plans aimed at mitigating the effects of potential disasters)
2. Prodromal	Prodromal stage: when it becomes apparent that the crisis is inevitable	
3. Emergency	Acute stage: the point of no return when the crisis has hit and damage limitation is the main objective	Emergency phase: when the effects of the disaster has been felt and action has to be taken to rescue people and property
4. Intermediate	Reaction	Intermediate phase: when the short-term needs of the people must be dealt with – restoring utilities and essential services. The objective at this point being to restore the community to normality as quickly as possible
5. Long-term (recovery)	Chronic stage: clean-up, post-mortem, self-analysis and healing	Long-term phase: continuation of the previous phase, but items that could not be addressed quickly are attended to at this point (repair of damaged infrastructure, correcting environmental problems, counselling victims, reinvestment strategies, debriefings to provide input to revisions of disaster strategies)
6. Resolution	Resolution: routine restored or new improved state	

Source: Modified after Faulkner (2001: 140).

plan to deal with the crisis. However, Roberts (1994) believes that before the symptoms show or a crisis hits action can be taken, through the development of crisis management strategies and plans in a similar way to Gonzalez-Herrero and Pratt (1995), and this is discussed in Chapters 4 and 5 of this book. Furthermore, although there is often an element of warning with a natural disaster (this may be ignored), whereas technological disasters are often preceded with very little warning. Whether or not organisations or destinations are aware or prepared, a triggering event occurs which may propel an issue into a disaster or crisis (such as a landslide which produces a natural disaster or media interest in an issue). A sustained or emerging crisis may turn into an immediate crisis due to the level of threat, potential or actual damage, or the need for an organisation to respond quickly (Keown-McMullan, 1997). As discussed earlier in this chapter, the triggering event can be established by perceptions of potential damage and a perceived ability by the organisation or destination to cope with the situation (Burnett, 1998) rather than actual objective facts. In fact, Kasperson *et al.* (1988 in Smallman & Weir, 1999) emphasised the nature of risk as a social construct rather than a physical phenomenon, which fits well with the previous discussion of natural events and hazards.

The proactive stages of a disaster or crisis lifecycle ends when the emergency phase termed by Faulkner (2001) and Roberts (1994) of the crisis or disaster begins and action is required through the development (if this has not occurred previously) and implementation of strategies to limit the damage (whether it is tangible damage such as flood or earthquake damage or intangible damage such as damage to image or reputation). This stage may occur suddenly in the case of immediate crises and disasters or move directly on from the prodromal stage if prodromes were ignored. Often termed 'the point of no return' when the speed and intensity and potential impact of the incident or 'shock' transforms a normal management process into crisis or disaster management. Here, inappropriate decisions and actions could result in the re-emergence of a crisis or the development of a new secondary crises or disasters (Heath, 1998; Seymour & Moore, 2000). This stage leads onto the intermediate phase where continued repairs and rebuilding occurs under a slightly less chaotic and complex situation. The focus for destinations and organisations at this stage is on the medium term needs of the affected parties through restoring services and trying to regain normality. The long-term (recovery) phase is a continuation of this phase of a crisis or disaster and here more long-term needs are dealt with such as the rebuilding of infrastructure and reinvesting in tourist destinations or embarking on recovery marketing. This may include the installation of a warning system or construction of a flood control reservoir, if there was a flood at a destination, for example.

The final stage of the crisis and disaster lifecycle is that of resolution where a routine is established or a new and improved state developed. This is because, as discussed earlier, crises and disasters are often seen as turning points and provide opportunities as well as threats for tourism destinations and managers. The pulling together of tourism enterprises alongside emergency or disaster managers to restore and rebuild tourism destinations affected by crises or disasters provides an opportunity for change and transformation which can be viewed as positive. Furthermore, a feedback loop can occur from the resolution stage back to the pre-event stage where destinations and organisations may learn from the crisis and disaster and improve their crisis and disaster management strategies for the future. This is also an important element of adaptive hazard management as this stage '... operate[s] as a closed loop because a major aim of hazard management is to learn from experience and feedback' (Smith, 1995: 21). These issues are discussed in the final part of the book.

A less linear model of the main steps in developing a crisis management policy was outlined by de Sauusmarez (2004), who advocates a continuous and dynamic process where evaluation occurs at each stage of the model. The model is outlined in Figure 2.3. In particular, the model provides more explicit emphasis on key steps often ignored by other authors, such as (1) evaluating the importance of tourism, (3) identifying and monitoring indicators, (4) resolving the issue of implementation and (6) exploring the potential for regional cooperation. These steps make explicit the importance of coordination and the involvement of a range of tourism and non-tourism stakeholders in the development of crisis management policy. As Hystad and Keller (2008) suggest, the primary stakeholders in tourism disasters are often emergency organisations, with tourism organisations and businesses taking a secondary or tertiary role. The concepts of stakeholders, collaboration and control in responding to tourism crises and disasters are discussed in detail in Chapter 6 of this book.

The timing of each stage differs depending on the nature of the crisis and disaster, its severity and the actions undertaken to contain it. For instance, an unofficial strike (like which British Airways suffered in July 2003) could be over quickly, but the long-term recovery and resolution stage could last much longer as airline staff contact customers to implement strategies to maintain customer loyalty. Furthermore, a biosecurity threat could be identified relatively early, but it could take months or years before the all clear could be given, such was the case of the Foot and Mouth in the UK, which took 11 months for the UK to be declared officially 'disease free'. As Ren (2000) notes, the resolution phase is often the longest stage of a crisis, while most research and emphasis has been on the response and recovery of disasters rather than their reduction (Hills, 1998).

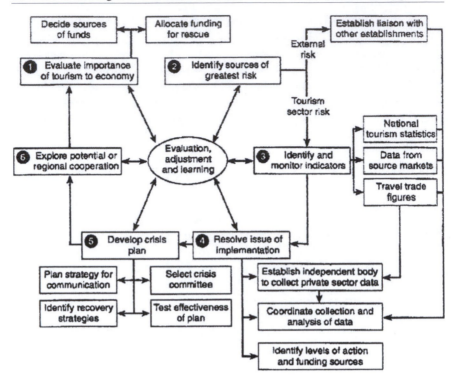

Figure 2.3 Main steps in developing a crisis management policy
Source: Crisis Management for the Tourism Sector: Preliminary Considerations in Policy Development. De Sausmarez, N., Tourism & Hospitality: Planning & Development, 1(2), 157–172, reprinted by permission of the publisher (Taylor & Francis Group, http://www.informaworld.com).

Understanding crises and disasters, their lifecycle and potential impacts and actions can help in the development of strategies by organisations to deal with such incidents. By understanding these phenomena, more effective strategies can be developed to stop or reduce the severity of their impacts on business and society, despite their complexity. However, crises are very individual situations and models have tended to be broad reducing their ability to relate directly to some industry sectors and specific types of crises or disasters. The difficulty is that, complex and chaotic situations are often difficult to research, understand and prepare for.

Dealing with Complexity: Chaos, Complexity and Interdependence

Despite the obvious need to understand and control the impacts of such incidents, this is not simple for managers because of the chaotic nature of crises and disasters and the uncertainty and lack of information that surrounds them. As Burnett (1998: 476) notes, crises are difficult to resolve due to time pressure constraints, limited control and high uncertainty. Previous research has illustrated the difficulty in identifying the stages of a crisis, particularly for those that are long running or sustained, as in the case of political instability in Israel (see Beirman, 2002) and general acknowledgement that they are dynamic (de Sausmarez, 2004).

Furthermore, identifying stages of a crisis is difficult when the crisis or disaster is spread geographically over a large area, as was the case with the Foot and Mouth Outbreak in the UK. Different regions were simultaneously in the emergency, intermediate and resolution stage of a crises while others were totally unaffected by the disease complicating management of the outbreak (see Miller & Ritchie, 2003). In addition, the prodromes of the next crisis can occur at any time, not necessarily after the resolution stage of the first crisis. This is particularly relevant for the tourism industry as actions by destinations to reduce a tourism disaster could trigger other crises or disasters. Furthermore, disasters or crises in other industry sectors (such as agriculture or manufacturing) could have an impact on the tourism system due to its interdependence and linkage to those industry sectors. An oil spill or biosecurity threat can have a massive impact on a tourist destination and enterprises. At an organisational level, triggers can also move a 'simple crisis' to a major disaster due to interactive complexity creating a chain reaction within an open system (Davies & Walters, 1998).

Many authors have noted this linkage between crisis and disaster occurrences with phrases such as 'escalation' (Heath, 1995; Hills, 1998) and the 'ripple effect' (Heath, 1998; Robert & Lajtha, 2002) or linked events referring to interdependence. Hills (1998) suggests that escalation can occur when a series of factors react in a chain, which she believes has implications for the strategic management of crises and disasters. Hills (1998: 163) suggests 'this concept [escalation] introduces an important new emphasis because it is concerned essentially with strategic planning, rather than with operational or tactical planning currently dominating disaster management'. Heath (1998) noted that linked crisis events seem to fan outward severely impacting other systems through their interdependence. Heath (1998) also believed that effective and well planned crisis management strategies were needed to prevent or limit the 'ripple effect' or outward chaos associated with crisis incidents, not only between organisations, but also across different industrial sectors.

The reasons why very little research has been conducted on the impact of linked crisis events is, as Ren (2000: 12) states, because 'there are hundreds of potential permutations in linkage between crises that can easily overwhelm a researcher'. Conceptually the idea of linked crisis events is important as society leaders and decision-makers usually only consider one crisis or disaster at a time, and at the resolution stage they simply see the resolution of one disaster or crisis rather than the series of linked crises or disasters which actually occurred, which has implications for learning from such incidents and future preparation. Ren (2000) suggests that this is dangerous in light of the growing interdependence of society as a whole and outlines the need for more research on linked crisis or disaster incidents.

Friedman (1999 in Prideaux *et al.*, 2003) suggested that the vulnerability of individual countries to shocks has increased exponentially as a consequence of the increase in interlocking systems associated with globalisation, political alliances and modern communication technology. A crisis or a disaster may make an organisation or destination more susceptible to a second or third incident which could hamper recovery efforts through harming recovery strategies or emergency personnel, resulting in a non-linear cumulative impact (Hills, 1998; Ren, 2000) as the second or third incident exploits vulnerability. Similarly, as McEntire (2001) notes, disaster management strategies may also contribute to increased vulnerability such as the case of dams which can exacerbate flooding or disaster relief which may subsidise risk taking and encourage external dependence.

Both Ren (2000) and Hills (1998) in the disaster area, and Fink (1986) and Heath (1998) in the crisis management area, note the chaotic and non-linear nature of crises and disasters which have obvious implications for their management and reduction. While Becken and Hay (2007) note the non-linear complex system of tourism and climate, in discussing climate change and tourism. Hills (1998) believes that because crises and disasters are non-linear, suggesting that disasters follow a series of stages to recovery is a weakness as it ignores the complexity and linked nature of crises and disasters. The comprehensive and linear PPRR approach to disaster has been adopted by policy-makers in many countries who organise disaster management plans around central elements linked to the disaster lifecycle. However, as Crondstedt (n.d.) suggests in his criticism of PPRR, a sequential approach to dealing with disasters and emergencies does not always entail responses that follow the same order. He also suggests that integration of PPRR into a broader risk management model may help develop innovative ways of treating risks. Discussions of the non-linear nature of crises and disasters make connections to complexity and chaos theory important, which is discussed in the remainder of this chapter.

Complexity and chaos theory may provide some insights into crisis and disaster management for organisations in the tourism industry as well as for those in the broader field of disaster management (Pelling, 2003). These theories have emerged as a school of thought to describe how complex systems function (McKercher, 1999) and may provide a framework for pulling together diverse elements and approaches to disaster management, according to Pelling (2003). Crises and disasters illustrate chaotic situations and illustrate the complex interrelationships between human and natural systems (Faulkner, 2001). Understanding the relationship between cause and effect and the implications of decisions and actions is a complicated process. This is illustrated in the case of the Foot and Mouth Outbreak, which started out as a farming crisis and ended up as a disaster for the tourism industry because of the way that it was handled (see Miller & Ritchie, 2003).

Similarly, the SARS virus and its spread throughout the world also illustrates the complex relationship between human and natural systems, and the impact of decisions of the World Health Organisation on tourist destinations, such as Toronto in Canada. The boundaries between human action or inaction and the development of disaster/crisis phenomena are difficult to distinguish because of this increasing complexity. Many systems can be influenced by small changes that can impact upon their stability. Changing weather patterns coupled by human action can cause major forest fires such as those experienced in France, Portugal and Australia in 2003. Similarly, changing weather patterns creating more rain in alpine areas can cause landslides, natural hazards and ultimately natural disasters if they impact upon humans or property. Global change researchers as well as mathematicians, physicists, biologists, chemists, ecologists and economists have been studying chaos since the 1970s (Gleick, 1987), yet tourism academics are well behind (McKercher, 1999), despite the obvious complexity and interdependence of the tourism system.

Chaos theory is the study of complexity, which explores non-linear complex systems. Linear systems are closed systems such as computers and aircrafts, while non-linear open systems can interact and intermingle between each other such as humans, weather systems and nature. They are unpredictable, dynamic and the future is not determined by the past, which makes future prediction of natural disasters, especially due to climate change, difficult (Becken & Hay, 2007). As Faulkner and Russell (2000) note, although a Newtonian paradigm has been mostly used in tourism research, this research philosophy is more attuned to stable systems and therefore may not be so useful in explaining turbulence and the underlying dynamics of change, such is that in tourism crises and disasters. According to Faulkner and Russell (2000: 329–330):

> the Newtonian/Cartesian approaches propagated a reductionist world view, whereby objects and events are understood in terms of their constituent parts and these are assumed to fit together like cogs in a clockwork machine. Every event is therefore determined by

initial conditions that are, at least in principle, predictable with some degree of precision owing to the predominance of linear or quasi-linear relationships.

Therefore, chaos and complexity perspective appreciates systems that are inherently complex and unstable (Russell & Faulkner, 1999). Although the tourism system can be considered linear it is also often non-linear and chaotic, particularly as a result of crises and disasters and their subsequent impacts. Small changes to a system can create a butterfly effect which can change the structure of the tourism system creating linked crisis events, escalation and ripples. A minor incident can trigger a crisis or disaster, which can have a major impact on the tourism system of a destination or organisation, and as the system attempts to adjust, it leaps from the 'edge of chaos' into chaos itself. As Fink (1986) suggests all organisations, and perhaps even tourism destinations, are on the edge of chaos, where any small change can create a loss of equilibrium resulting in a destination or organisation plunging into 'chaos' or 'phase shifts' as a result of crises and disasters (Faulkner & Russell, 2000).

Fink (1986: 20) also points to crises being 'fluid, unstable and dynamic situations' as discussed earlier which fits with chaos and complexity perspectives. Turning points of crises and disasters and the concept of recovery are consistent with chaos and complexity perspectives, which see chaos as a creative process. Chaos realises periods instability are part of the operation and essential for change to complex systems (Ditto & Manukata, 1995) such as tourism, which evolve abruptly rather than evolving slowly from one state to another (McKercher, 1999). However, chaos theory may be considered as disorderly but it has underlying order (Gleick, 1987) as the system will regenerate or reconfigure itself. The complex system can adapt because of the ability to self-organise and to respond to external stimuli without external coercion, thus regulating itself (Pelling, 2003).

To view crises and disasters as an element of chaos means a fundamental shift in how we view such incidents and brings into question whether crises and disasters can be managed effectively due to their chaotic and complex nature. It suggests the need for interdisciplinary research and an integrated approach to disaster and emergency management. However, it also suggests that tourism systems and crisis management research in tourism should consider new conceptual and methodological tools to help analyse turbulence more effectively, as the tourism system appears to be in a constant state of chaos. The traditional Newtonian paradigm dismisses chaos as being noise in the system while chaos theory appreciates upheaval as an intrinsic element of complex systems (McKercher, 1999: 429). This discussion of complexity and chaos suggests that, tourism managers and planners should consider taking a more strategic approach to such incidents, dealing with crises and disasters in a flexible but yet holistic manner, and that they should not be afraid of change which is inherent within an open tourism system which should breed transformation and long-term stability and vitality. As McKercher (1999: 433) nicely describes it:

> it [chaos and complexity theory] appreciates that turbulence and periods of intense upheaval are both an intrinsic element of the system and an essential element to promote rapid change in tourism communities ... a chaos approach to tourism explains, at a conceptual level, much of the variability noted in tourism that confounds the ability of tourism policy makers to control tourism and of strategic planners to predict accurately future tourism flows ... the role of public sector players in a chaotic tourism system becomes one of trying to influence the direction of growth within broad parameters rather than trying to exert covert control over it. At a micro, or operational level, the role of tourism enterprises becomes one of ensuring their niche in the rapidly evolving living tourism community by responding to or anticipating change, protecting its habitat and by continuing to evolve at least as rapidly as the system is evolving to secure a preferred habitat position.

To date, few researchers have used a chaos or complexity perspectives in the crisis or disaster field, mostly to help understand natural disasters (Comfort, 1999) or crisis communications (Murphy, 1996). Only Paraskevas (2006) has used a complexity perspective in the context of tourism, where he examined the responses of a hotel chain to a major food poisoning crisis.

Conclusion

This chapter has focused on the need to both define and understand crises and disasters in order to develop more effective responses with respect to the planning and management of tourism crises and disasters. It has explained the difference between crisis and disaster definitions, the interrelationship between the two and how the 'ripple effect' can turn a crisis into a disaster or vice versa. It then outlined the type of crises and disasters that exist and can impact upon the tourism industry through the use of examples on the size and scope of their impacts on the tourism industry, with particular focus on large-scale natural/technical disasters, political and economic crises. The chapter noted that an increase in biosecurity, health scares and global environmental change could pose serious challenges to the tourism industry, with their spread exacerbated by the tourism industry and greater levels of mobility.

An anatomy of a crisis or disaster was presented and the lifecycle of such incidents were identified and discussed. Understanding when an 'issue' becomes a crisis or disaster was discussed with the use of appropriate models. The chapter also outlined the difficulty in predicting or responding to crises and disasters as each one has different characteristics and are often seen as impossible to control. Discussion was undertaken concerning chaos and complexity theory and various ways of viewing crisis and disaster management. However, this chapter concludes by suggesting that a strategic and integrated approach to crisis and disaster management can help limit the potential impact of crises and disasters and is particularly relevant for the tourism industry, despite the complexity of such incidents. The use of chaos and complexity perspectives in future tourism crisis and disaster research could help understand the anatomy of these incidents as well as assist future management of crises and disasters.

Chapter 3
Strategic Crisis and Disaster Planning and Management

Crisis =
threat + opportunity

The two Chinese characters, which together form the word crisis, separately
mean threat and opportunity. An etymology like this is a reminder that
as conditions change, so can attitudes. In a world in which things
seem sure to get worse, there is increasing incentive to make
sure they do not.
ISDR (2004: 334)

Introduction

This chapter begins by defining the terms 'planning' and 'management' before focusing on strategic planning and management. As Elliot (2006) notes, there is a parallel between strategic management and crisis management. The concept of strategic planning and management from an organisational perspective is outlined and the elements of a strategic planning and management approach, such as strategic analysis, choice, implementation and control are discussed. Different perspectives on the approach of strategic planning and management are considered, which may impact upon how crises and disasters are viewed and dealt with by tourism managers.

This overview provides an important context for the book, as the final half of this chapter outlines a rationale for a strategic approach to both planning for, and managing, tourism crises and disasters. In particular, this section suggests that there are a growing number of crises and disasters that impact upon tourism and organisations need to think more strategically and proactively about the impact of potential crises and disasters. It also notes that planning and management are both sides of the same coin and should be integrated. An overview of crisis and disaster planning and management models is provided before a proposed strategic framework is presented which is linked to the structure of the book. The framework notes that the crisis and disaster lifecycle has a clear similarity to the strategic management framework. The chapter ends with a discussion of the main sections of the framework, and the book chapters.

Planning and Management

Planning has been defined as the design of a desired future and effective ways of bringing it about (Richardson & Richardson, 1992). In short, it is about gathering information and drawing up a plan of action. However, it is not actually the process of implementing these plans, but it is part of the 'planning–decision–action process' (Hall *et al.*, 1997). As Richardson and Richardson (1992) note, planning is therefore something which:

- designs and precedes action;
- attempts to fit appropriate actions to something we have to make sense of before it happens (have to be entirely certain);
- is directed at achieving the desired results (objectives); and
- is a response to the pessimistic belief that unless something is done, a desired future state will not occur, and to the optimistic belief that we can do things to improve our chances of achieving the desired state.

Planning is essentially required because as a business, and for society in general, we have limited physical and financial resources and need to be more effective and efficient in how we use those resources. Information has to be gathered and decisions made over the allocation of those resources and policies or plans created on how they can be best used. From a business point of view, planning is vital for staying in touch with the 'external operating environment' including competitors, trends and of course the impact of external change including shocks, crises and disasters. However, although planning is a process, Hall (2000: 7) notes that the various activities in the planning process are difficult to isolate as they may include such things as bargaining and negotiation, compromise, coercion, values, choice and politics.

As Gunn (1977: 85) observed, because of the fragmented growth of the tourism industry and its nature as a system 'the overall planning of the total tourism system is long overdue ... there is no overall policy, philosophy or coordinating force that brings the many pieces of tourism into harmony and assures their continued harmonious function'. Getz (1987: 3) defines tourism planning as 'a process, based on research and evaluation, which seeks to optimise the potential contribution of tourism to human welfare and environmental quality'. Similarly, Murphy (1985: 156) observes, 'planning is concerned with anticipating and regulating change in a system, to promote orderly development so as to increase the social, economic, and environmental benefits of the development process'. In this case the system is the tourism system and the potential outputs from that system can have either positive or negative economic, social and/or environmental impacts. The role of tourism planning is therefore to promote orderly development and regulation and attempt to increase the positive benefits through planning. However, this process is difficult because of the nature of the tourism system, the fact that most tourism planning is undertaken by a variety of different government agencies and questions remain over whether the future can really be predicted.

Hall (2000) notes that most tourism planning has tended to focus on destination planning rather than business planning and is based around land use planning at a regional, local or site level. Hall (2000: 12) notes the broad scope of planning by suggesting that tourism planning occurs in:

- a number of forms (e.g. development infrastructure, land and resource use, organisation, human resource, promotion and marketing);
- a number of structures (e.g. different government, quasi-government and non-government organisations);
- a number of scales (e.g. international, transnational, national, regional, local, site and sectoral); and
- a number of different time scales (e.g. for development, implementation, evaluation and satisfactory fulfilment of planning objectives).

The link between the development of plans and policies and their implementation is often made through managers who provide leadership with the operationalisation and coordination of more tactical and operational strategies and plans. Leadership tasks are more concerned with planning and vision of a destination or organisation, while management tasks focus on execution and control of tactical and operational plans and strategies. Management is essentially the coordination, implementation and monitoring of various plans, policies or strategies. As Cole (1996) suggests, management is about planning, organising, motivating and controlling (the so-called POMC approach). It involves managing human and financial resources, developing and coordinating organisational structures. Cole (1996) suggests that the strategic importance of management has grown significantly in recent years. From the management issues that Cole (1996) lists, this book is specifically interested in understanding and responding to the external environment and managing change, which are both vital for crisis and disaster management. However, in later chapters concerning tourism crisis and disaster management, discussion will centre around some of the other issues or central aspects of management, namely, the development of structures and systems for crisis and disaster management, developing and empowering employees in crisis and disaster management and developing a responsive organisational culture to help deal with such incidents.

Strategic Planning and Management

The concept

The development of strategy and strategic planning and management in organisations has grown since the 1960s as organisations attempt to take a more longer term view and consider the impact of the external operating environment. According to Chaffee (1985), definitions of strategy can be considered linear, adaptive or interpretive. Phillips and Moutinho (1998: 42) provide examples of definitions for all three types of models that Chaffee (1985) proposes. A linear example of strategy is where planning is used to fight competition and to achieve organisational goals. They use Chandler's (1962: 13) definition to illustrate the linear example that believes strategy to be the '... determination of the basic long-term goals of an enterprise, and the adoption of courses of action and the allocation of resources necessary carrying out these goals'. An adaptive example of a definition is given by Hofer (1973: 3) suggesting that strategy is '... concerned with the development of a viable match between the opportunities and risks present in the external environment and the organisation's capabilities and resources for exploiting those opportunities'.

Here, an adaptive strategy is concerned with an organisation realigning itself with its external environment (both industry or micro and the wider macro environment). Finally, Phillips and Moutinho (1998) provide an example of the third type of strategy, an interpretive approach that is concerned with the motivation of organisational stakeholders. Chaffee (1985: 93) provides an example by stating that strategy here is 'orientating metaphors constructed for the purpose of conceptualising and guiding individual attitudes of organisational participants'. The quote by Johnson and Scoles (1993) seems to integrate these three areas as they state strategy is 'the direction and scope of an organisation over the long term: ideally, which matches its resources to its changing environment, and in particular, its markets, customers or clients to meet stakeholder expectations'.

One of the most widely cited authors on strategy, Mintzberg (1987), suggested that the term 'strategy' could be used in a number of different ways and can be viewed as:

- a plan (whereby an organisation creates a strategic plan which may include different elements such as a marketing plan, a financial plan or a strategic plan for expansion into new markets);

- a ploy (or a short-term strategy with tactical aims such as threatening to lower prices to influence competitors);
- a pattern of behaviour (where an organisation through consistent behaviour emerges into success rather than actually formulating a strategic plan. This is considered an emergent strategy.);
- a position (such as a low-cost leader similar to airlines EasyJet and Ryan Air, or those airlines that compete on service and reputation such as British Airways rather than price); and
- a perspective (which may be to change the culture of an organisation to be more customer focused or more flexible in dealing with a changing environment).

Mintzberg's (1987) five elements of strategy illustrate that strategy can be both planned, through a deliberate 'plan' or emergent, through developing consistent 'patterns of behaviour' and that strategies can exist in relation to the organisation itself, its competitors or its customers. Strategy is about thinking medium to long term and can be developed at a general strategic, tactical or an operational level connected through specific measurable goals, objectives or targets. As Evans *et al.* (2003) note, decisions at the strategic level are often made by senior managers and are long term in focus, whereas tactical objectives deal with corporate objectives made by heads of business units, which are often called business strategy (Phillips & Moutinho, 1998). Finally, operational decisions are made on a more tactical level and are less complex than strategies at the tactical or strategic level. Nevertheless, operational and tactical strategies are set within the context of the organisation's long term strategic plans, forming an interrelated coherent as a whole.

The terms 'strategic management' or 'planning' are often used with similar terms such as 'business planning', 'management policy', organisational strategy' and 'corporate strategy' (Tribe, 1997). However, despite this, Tribe (1997: 3) notes that all these terms involve decisions which:

- are complex rather than simple;
- are integrated rather than isolated;
- are long term rather than short term;
- are proactive rather than reactive;
- have an impact on the whole, rather than a part of the organisation;
- involve major rather than minor change;
- involve grand design rather than marginal tinkering; and
- are made by those in positions of power in the organisation rather than subordinates.

Elements of strategic planning and management

Strategic planning and management is usually concerned with four main elements according to prescriptive theory (Johnson & Scholes, 1993; Richardson & Richardson, 1992; Viljoen, 1994):

(1) *strategic analysis:* examining the macro or micro operating environment;
(2) *strategic direction and choice:* developing and selecting strategic directions and specific generic strategies to achieve organisational goals;
(3) *strategy implementation and control:* developing suitable organisational structures, human and financial resource strategies, providing leadership to control and allow for the implementation of specific strategies; and
(4) *strategic evaluation and feedback.* continuous improvement is an important part of strategic planning and management and organisations learn how to improve the effectiveness of strategies through evaluation, monitoring and adaptive management.

These elements of strategic planning and management are illustrated in Figure 3.1 which demonstrate the key stages and tasks for planners and managers, as well as key considerations and techniques that are used by strategic managers. The figure shows that the strategic analysis and direction/choice stages are considered strategic planning, as they are concerned with the collection and analysis of data pertaining to the organisation and its external operating environment as well as identifying and selecting strategic directions and alternatives to implement, as strategic, tactical or operational strategies. The final two stages are concerned with the actual implementation, control and evaluation of the strategies and plans that were decided upon in the planning stage and are thus considered management functions (Phillips & Moutinho, 1998), similar to the earlier discussion on the definitions between planning and management. The different stages will now be elaborated in this section of the chapter.

The strategic analysis stage is where the internal resources of an organisation or destination, including tangible resources including physical resources such as buildings and fixtures, human resources, financial resources and also intangible resources such as goodwill and corporate image, are examined and compared to the external industry environment (often called the micro environment) and the remote environment (called the macro environment). Here, a competitor analysis using Porter's (1980) five forces model is often undertaken, coupled with an examination of any direct and indirect competition or substitute products. The macro environment is often analysed through a variation

Stages of process	Key planning tasks	Key considerations/techniques
Strategic Analysis	Examining the macro or micro operating environment	SWOT analysis Strengths and Weaknesses from internal analysis and Opportunities and Threats from external analysis
	Internal resource analysis including resource audit for both tangible and intangible resources	
	External analysis including competitor and SCEPTICAL analysis	Porter's (1980) Five force analysis
Strategic Direction and Choice	Brainstorming to select strategic directions and choices that will overcome threats and weaknesses using strengths and opportunities	Consideration of suitability, feasibility, acceptability.
	Consideration and selection of generic strategies (price based, differentiation, zone x, hybrid) and strategic directions (market development and product development etc)	Cash flow forecasting, investment appraisal, cost-benefit analysis, impact analysis
	Consideration and choice of strategic methods (such as internal growth, mergers, joint development, strategic alliances)	Ranking options and selecting
Strategic Implementation and Control	Developing suitable organisational structures and cultures to implement strategies	Redesigning structure and culture of organization through reward system, skills and training need analysis, recruitment and selection of staff, project logistics and operations management, changes to management style
	Implementing human and financial resources to address the strategies	
	Providing leadership to control and allow for the implementation of specific strategies	
Strategic Evaluation and Feedback	Continuous improvement is an important part of strategic planning and management	Avoidance of strategic drift, implementation of plans and strategies, increase in market share, increase in share price, return on investment, performance indicators
	Evaluation of operational, tactical and strategic strategies through targets and performance indicators	
	Feedback loop back to strategic analysis and strategic decision-making	Meetings and debriefings on strategy design and implementation

strategic planning   strategic management

Figure 3.1 Strategic planning and management stages, tasks and considerations
Source: Modified after Viljoen (1994), Tribe (1997), Evans *et al.* (2003).

of the PEST analysis, or as Peattie and Moutinho (2000) term it a SCEPTICAL analysis (noted earlier in Chapter 1). The goal of strategic planning is to match the internal strengths of the organisation with opportunities in the industry and remote environment, and limit the weaknesses and threats facing the organisation or destination to form strengths, weaknesses, opportunities and threats (SWOT) analysis. Although this analysis can be applied to destinations, Porter's (1990) diamond analysis has been used to determine the competitive advantage of nations by assessing the degree to which a country or region has a competitive advantage through assessing the strengths and weaknesses of four factors including:

- factor conditions (physical resources, human resources, capital resources, infrastructure and knowledge resources);
- market structures, organisation and strategies;
- demand conditions; and
- related and supporting industry.

As Evans *et al.* (2003: 185) note, Porter identified two other factors: government (which can influence any of the four factors) and chance events (which can shift competitive advantage in unpredictable ways). Crises and disasters may impact upon region's and nation's competitiveness depending on how such chance events or incidents are managed. Strategic direction or choices are often concerned with the organisation's scope or domain (Phillips & Moutinho, 1998). From the strategic analysis, an organisation should develop a mission statement and a set of goals and strategies. It is within this context that strategic directions and choices/alternatives are considered. Porter (1980) argued that, to achieve a sustainable competitive advantage, organisations would have to pursue one of his generic strategies such as:

- overall cost leadership where an organisation becomes the lowest cost provider in an industry;
- differentiation where customers would pay a premium price through actual or perceived uniqueness; or
- a focus strategy where business focuses on a market niche using cost leadership or differentiation.

Nevertheless, although an important theory, Porter (1980) has been criticised by other authors in the management and tourism management field. As Tribe (1997) notes, cost leadership may be elusive as competitors can often quickly be the low-cost leader, and as Phillips and Moutinho (1998) suggest, cost leadership and low prices are the same, whereas cost reduction does not necessarily lead to low prices for consumers. Organisations do not need to follow only one of Porter's generic strategies and may offer a differentiated product at the same price as their competitors, following what is termed a hybrid strategy. Kotler (1988) and Bowman (1992) have reworked Porter's generic strategies to take into consideration these issues and apply his work to service industries. They came up with four generic strategies including:

- a price-based strategy (similar to cost leadership, but emphasises low-cost savings are passed on as low prices);
- differentiation;
- hybrid (which tries to provide quality products at low prices), and zone x (comprising low quality and high prices); and
- price based or differentiation strategies can be focused to specific target market segments.

Strategic directions can include internal growth, withdrawal from markets or products, consolidation, market penetration or development, as well as product development or diversification (Tribe, 1997). In particular, the number of strategies incorporating strategic alliances has increased in the tourism system to help organisations expand into new markets or offer new products. The most widely known example is that of airline alliances where airlines work together in order to provide access to a greater number of routes, reduce the costs of marketing and pool the use of resources such as facilities, airline lounges and the like. In a globalised world, strategic alliances allow tourism businesses to expand their reach and reduce their costs with limited risk, compared with other options such as mergers and acquisitions.

Both these generic strategies and directions need to be evaluated by organisations in light of their mission statements and goals/objectives, as well as through considering their feasibility (can it be done?), suitability (does it fit our situation?) and acceptability (do we want to do it?) analysis which will allow an informed strategic choice (Tribe, 1997). After deliberation of these key considerations and questions, managers may have to screen and rank choices before selecting the most appropriate generic strategies, directions and options. Once selected, then the implementation of these strategies moves the organisation from strategic planning to strategic management through developing systems, allocating resources and controlling the management strategies at a tactical and operational level.

As part of the strategic management and implementation process, managers may have to make changes to both the organisational structure and organisational culture in order to assist with the implementation of the chosen strategies. For instance, the height of organisational structures may have to be reduced so that fewer management layers exist to successfully implement strategies, or in the case of complex environments as an organisation expands its height and organisational structure will grow adding new layers of management (Evans *et al.*, 2003).

Organisational culture of organisations can be a major barrier or facilitator of change. Defender cultures are those that are found in organisations that exist in well-defined markets areas which tend to improve or penetrate into their markets as a strategic option. Defenders would feel out of place expanding into new markets or developing new products because of their values (Miles & Snow, 1978). However, Tribe (1997) goes further and describes defenders as conservative, inflexible, reactive, set in their ways and cultures that avoid change as opposed to prospectors who are outward looking, flexible, proactive, adaptive and opportunistic. These organisations are often seeking new markets or developing new products and so their cultural norms are more aligned to change and uncertainty.

Miles and Snow (1978) also developed two other types of organisational cultures: analysers and reactors. Analysers are able to act like either defenders or prospectors and can handle both stability and instability, whereas reactor cultures can often lack strategic focus and can be more susceptible to changes in the environment and are less innovative. Thompson (1998: 40) suggested a number of characteristics which he believed indicated crisis proneness in an organisation, including:

- specialist functions and businesses which fail to think and act holistically;
- a tendency to look inwards rather than outwards with internal rivalry replacing external competitiveness;
- a strong and rigid belief in present, or event past, competitive paradigms – which might be reflected in a focus on content as distinct from awareness and learning competencies;
- a reluctance or inability to manage change;
- inadequate communications – an over reliance on either vertical or horizontal communications and an inability to handle both simultaneously;
- an inability to interpret environmental signals adequately; and
- a readiness to break rules and procedures for short-term results.

During strategy implementation, new budgets may need to be established and resources allocated to the implementation of new strategies. For instance, a new product development strategy would require resources for the product development and market testing prior to the incorporation of that product as part of the organisation's portfolio of products. Training or retraining for staff or the recruitment and selection of new staff could also occur as a result of the implementation of new strategies. Implementation may mean a reduction in resources for one department and an increase in others, specifically to implement strategies. For instance, more resources may be provided for the product development and marketing division of an organisation if they intend to develop a new product or expand into a new market. Many authors note the need for effective communication and leadership from the strategic and tactical level to the operational or frontline level. Communication may be democratic (where stakeholders including staff are encouraged to participate), educative (where managers at the strategic level make decisions but staff at the lower levels may be involved to help refine the strategy) or autocratic (where decisions are made and handed down from the 'top' to the 'bottom' of an organisation). Rewards or punishments may have to be designed to create compliance with the new strategic directions through the use of incentive schemes, perks, bonuses and the like. Subsequently, these incentive schemes are often linked to performance indicators or goals that relate to targets which help monitor the implementation of strategies.

The final stage of the strategic planning/management process is then the evaluation and feedback stage. The process of strategic planning/management involves a feedback process, whereby modification can be made back into future strategic planning based on the actual degree of success during implementation based on performance targets or indicators which could include (depending on the strategies implemented) market share, profitability or increase in share price.

The rationale approach contested

Strategic planning and management is important for all types of organisations (including public sector organisations) because the lack of strategic planning can lead to strategic drift (Johnson, 1988) when an organisation has failed to monitor and keep pace with its changing external environment. Without a strategic view, an organisation is likely to replicate existing policy without change, which is fine when the environment is stable, but if it changes (which it most certainly does), strategic drift can occur. Changes to the external operating environment or even changes to the organisation itself can all create strategic drift and should be monitored. Old strategies should be revised and new ones created so that the organisation operates more effectively and efficiently. New strategies can be implemented in either a step change (where change occurs rapidly) or incremental change (where change occurs over a period of time in a series of stages). Evans *et al.* (2003) note that the distinction between the two will depend upon how urgent the need for change is, with a market crisis bringing about an urgent step change. However, an organisation with a culture that is resistant to change may be best suited to an incremental implementation of strategies with periods of rest after each stage of change, a concept supported by Quinn (1978).

In fact, some authors believe that the classical approach, the prescriptive 'design school' or 'visionary prescriptive' approach towards strategic planning is flawed and that other approaches should be considered. The classical approach includes authors such as Ansoff and Porter who suggest the importance of strategy formulation, implementation and evaluation. However, the evolutionary school of thought sees organisations in a similar way to biology, with only those organisations surviving that can adapt to changing conditions (with the fittest surviving). Prosessualists also disagree with a classical approach as they believe that humans can only process a certain amount of information, so cannot possibly compose a whole strategic picture and challenge the implementation of strategy due to the wide range of factors that motivate staff. The systematic school believes in the social context and cultural differences between organisations and individuals within an organisation. Therefore, different types of strategies are more suitable for different parts of the world and managers should consider the social/cultural system of planning.

Others believe that strategy is emergent and not formed deliberately (Mintzberg, 1987) and that planning often does not link to strategy formulation with the descriptive of strategy making is not very helpful in turbulent conditions (Phillips & Moutinho, 1998; Richardson, 1995). Emergent strategy may occur where it is difficult to develop a medium–long-term strategy, in the case of an unpredictable environment. Managers may then have to react, according to Phillips and Moutinho (1998: 56), 'in a flexible, opportunistic, and accidental manner to unpredicted events and muddle through'. This approach sees strategy development as more spontaneous, incremental and adaptive, which is perhaps more useful in contexts of high environmental uncertainty. Finally, Johnson and Scholes (1993) suggest a political view or perspective of strategy where strategy emerges after a variety of internal battles, in which managers, individuals and other groups bargain and trade their interests and information.

Richardson (1994) suggests that strategic planning and management theory simply sees the turbulent environment a 'force which is out there' which has been called by Buchanan and Huczynski (1985) as 'environmental determinism'. The idea of managers being able to control the environment is a Newtonian concept and does not fit with a chaos or complexity perspective of crises and disaster management. As Richardson (1994) notes, it ignores the interdependence of interactive systems (such as tourism) as organisations can affect their environments and create crises and disasters. The problem with strategic management, as Richardson (1994) sees it, is associated with single-loop learning and feedback in dealing with crisis situations. He suggests that organisations should remove themselves from the 'current organisational/environment context back to a slower moving, less interactively linked, more bureaucratic, less exploitative, and safer type of context which seemed to characterise our not too distant past' (Richardson, 1994: 74). Simply put, a move towards simplicity and stability is required if managers are to reduce the likelihood of chaotic and catastrophic impacts (Richardson, 1995: 15).

Strategic Planning and Management of Crises and Disasters

A rationale

Although this book partly agrees that it is impossible to consider every scenario or future development and so undertake a full classical or rational approach to crisis planning and management (and in fact chaos and complexity suggests that this may be difficult), the book suggests that managers of tourism destinations and organisations should consider, understand and respond to crises and disasters in a more strategic and comprehensive way in the future. As Elliot (2006) suggests, there are strong parallels between strategic and crisis management, and there are several reasons why strategic management should be better integrated with tourism crisis and disaster management. First, as mentioned in the introduction of this book, there appears to be a growing number of crises and disasters occurring because of the current state of the world which impact upon tourism systems. We live in uncertain times, and with current development models and patterns of globalisation and environmental change, tourism organisations and destinations may be more susceptible to crises and disasters than ever before.

Second, as discussed in Chapter 2, there is a need for a more holistic and integrated approach towards crisis and disaster management in tourism systems for both enterprises and destinations ranging from site, local, regional, national, transnational and international levels. Third, there is a need for organisations and destinations to move away from responding or 'managing' crisis or disaster incidents towards identification and reduction. In other words, a movement is required away from management of such incidents (or responding to them) towards planning for such incidents (or reducing their likelihood of occurring), which Richardson (1994, 1995) effectively suggests. This requires a paradigm shift away from 'this won't happen to me or us' to 'it probably will happen so what should I do about it'. Authors such as Kash and Darling (1998) believe that although crisis management is a requirement for organisations, many do not undertake productive steps to address crisis situations. Managers who do take productive steps will be in a much better position to respond when a crisis or disaster effects an organisation or destination. This step is actually often the least expensive, but often overlooked. As Kash and Darling (1998: 180) note:

> making decisions while under stress, excitement and danger of a crisis situation is much harder than having to react to a crisis in terms of a preapproved framework. Proactive planning helps managers to control and resolve a crisis. Ignoring the possibility of a crisis, on the other hand, could lead to the crisis taking a life of its own.

Finally, taking a more strategic or holistic approach to crisis management may reduce the likelihood of linked events, 'escalation' or the 'ripple effect' occurring due to the chaotic and complex interrelationships within an open tourism system (which was discussed previously in Chapter 2). Perhaps, Richardson (1994, 1995) points about going back to more stable and simpler times could lessen the complexity and chaos surrounding the world and reduce the chances of linked crises or the 'ripple effect'. However, with the current world dominated by the Western free market paradigm, globalisation and increasing global mobility, it is unlikely that this will happen, especially in a system as open, international and interconnected as tourism. Nevertheless, some pre-planned or thought through strategy that can be modified in light of the type of crisis or disaster encountered, can perhaps limit hasty and ineffective decisions leading to escalation or the creation of new crises and disasters.

From response and management to reduction and planning

The aim of this book is for tourism managers and destinations to consider crisis and disaster planning and management as both sides of the same coin, which need to be integrated together. Planning can help avoid crises or disasters or at the very least can help reduce the damage to businesses and societies when a crisis or disaster hits. This is why this book includes sections on both the identification of crises and disasters, crisis and disaster prevention and planning, but also discusses crisis and disaster management strategies if incidents do occur. It proposes a strategic and integrated approach to crisis and disaster management in the following section of this chapter. However, before this, the current section examines literature concerning a more strategic and integrated approach to both organisational crisis management and destination disaster management (with an emphasis on natural hazards and disasters).

The UN has attempted through their publications and decade of disaster reduction to bring to the fore the concept of reduction rather than response. The ISDR (2004) has illustrated that past focus on emergency management and crisis management should move towards disaster risk reduction strategies. As they state (ISDR, 2004: 38):

> Despite the progress achieved, much more is required to implement institutional changes favouring the evolution of a disaster reduction culture. The processes conditioning the emergence of disaster reduction need to be conducive to risk and vulnerability under-standing, awareness and management, leading to long term safe development planning based on anticipation rather than cure.

As outlined in Chapter 2, examining the lifecycle or anatomy of crises and disasters at the pre-event stage can help organisations undertake activities prior to a crisis or disaster by searching for certain signals or prodromes. However, as the IPCC (2007) note, those industry sectors that are located in high-risk climate affected locations are often those with little adaptive capacities. There are also ways in which risk and vulnerability can be reduced (see Chapter 4) by using technologies such as hazard mapping and early warning emergency systems. In their definition of key terms for climate change, the IPCC (2007: 21) suggest that '[a]daptive capacity is the ability of a system to adjust to climate change (including climate variability and extremes) to moderate potential damages, to take advantage of opportunities, or to cope with the consequences'.

Heath (1998) identified two major approaches concerning the manage-ment of crises: the traditional crisis management approach and the risk management approach. The traditional crisis management approach involves no initial (pre-crisis) planning or management as the approach begins when the crisis starts (see Figure 3.2). The approach of the risk management tradition or paradigm is to respond to the crisis and

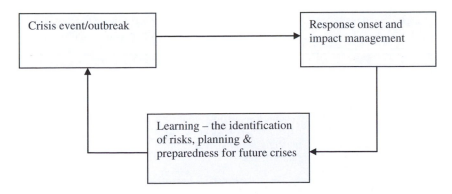

Figure 3.2 A traditional approach to a crisis
Source: Heath (1998).

manage the impacts effectively and efficiently. The evaluation, risk assessment and crisis planning does not occur until after the crisis event (post-crisis) and the findings are then kept for future reference. The risk management approach follows on from the traditional crisis manage- ment approach as it starts where the other finishes and is concerned with assessing and managing risk before a crisis begins (pre-crisis). It is then in the position to implement appropriate response and recovery plans as the crisis emerges (see Figure 3.3). Again, similar to the first approach, learning and feedback are crucial requirements for the development of future crisis management planning. Heath (1998) states that authors and authorities often overlook reduction for two major reasons: because of the reactive mindset of individuals, and that reduction and preparedness activities lack the excitement and challenge of response and recovery management. He suggests a four-stage model to deal with crises in a strategic way (see Figure 3.4) using principles related to strategic planning and management.

Heath's (1998) model suggests that reduction can occur before a crisis hits through undertaking risk management strategies (which are discussed in Chapters 4 and 5) as part of the strategic planning function. He considers Readiness, Response and Recovery to be part of strategic management, although he notes that Readiness is somewhat different to the other two categories as it requires awareness, training and tests/ exercises (which one could assume to be part of the planning function). Training is important to reduce human response errors to crises and improve the time taken to deal with crisis incidents. Response and Recovery both include the development of impact analysis, plans, skills acquisition and audits which are all part of the strategic management function. However, Heath (1998: 270) notes that:

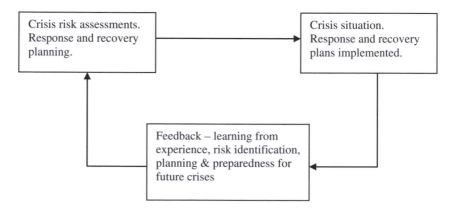

Figure 3.3 A risk management approach to a crisis
Source: Heath (1998).

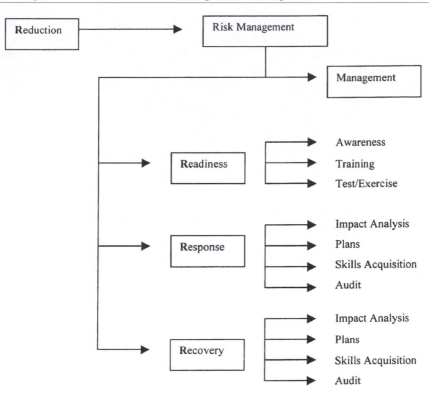

Figure 3.4 Heath's 4 R model for crisis planning/management
Source: Heath (1998).

Response and Recovery management is likely to be slow, costly, inefficient and potentially unsafe for those involved if planning is not adequate and up to date, if training is rarely done and erratic, or when crisis situations are not somehow made familiar to those people.

Heath (1998) believes that crisis reduction and crisis management should be built into the surrounding organisational environment, structures, systems and people and part of the strategic process for organisations, which is especially important for the tourism industry in today's turbulent environment. Gonzalez-Herrero and Pratt's (1995) four-stage model (mentioned in Chapter 2) also emphases a prevention and reduction approach to crisis management, with two of the four stages related to what they term 'issues management' and prevention and planning. Other researchers have also provided some discussion of the pre-disaster or pre-crisis phase of tourism crisis and disaster management. Hystad and Keller (2006) suggest a four-phase model for tourism and disaster management (pre-disaster, disaster, post-disaster and resolution), while de Sausmarez (2004) and Santana (2003) suggest three phases in the proactive crisis management (signal detection, preparation, prevention) and two stages after the crisis hits (damage limitation and recovery) with learning occurring at all stages. In the tourism disaster management arena, Faulkner (2001) proposed a framework for dealing with tourism disasters which emphases reduction and takes a more strategic and integrated perspective concerning tourism disaster management (see Figure 3.5). This framework model sets out elements of the tourism disaster response as well as principal ingredients of disaster management strategies for each stage of the disaster lifecycle.

A Proposed Strategic Framework for Tourism Crises/Disasters

Figure 3.6 sets out a strategic framework for the planning and management of crises and disasters for public or private sector organisations, and also identified the structure of this book. The model suggests that a strategic management and planning approach to crisis and disaster management can be beneficial for tourism planners and managers, despite the criticism over rational strategic planning and management approaches. In particular, the model outlines three main stages in managing such incidents strategically: prevention and planning, implementation, evaluation and feedback. Within each stage, various management tasks or activities are identified. For the purposes of this book, the aspects illustrated in the model are considered by the author as the most common attributes in managing crises and disasters and act as discussion points within this book in subsequent chapters. Due to space restrictions, the book is unable to cover every element within each part of the model. However, the main themes in the model are elaborated in more detail with examples from the management and tourism field later in the relevant sections of the book, with equal attention provided for all three main stages of the crisis or disaster lifecycle.

Understanding and classifying crises and disasters, including the type of incident, its scale and magnitude (discussed in the previous chapter) will impact upon strategy development and implementation. Specific strategies will have to be developed to deal with an evolving crisis or disaster as it progresses through its lifecycle. A crisis with a long drawn out emergency phase may require quite different strategies than a crisis which quickly progresses through the intermediate, long term and finally to the resolution stage. A sustained crisis will require different strategies than an immediate crisis. Nevertheless, there are clear similarities between the lifecycle of a crisis and disaster and the strategic planning/management framework including:

Phase in disaster process	Elements of the disaster management responses	Principal ingredients of the disaster management strategies
1. *Pre-event* When action can be taken to prevent or mitigate the effects of potential disasters	***Precursors*** • Appoint a disaster management team (DMT) leader and establish DMT • Identify relevant public/private sector agencies/organisations • Establish coordination/consultative framework and communication systems • Develop, document and communicate disaster management strategy • Education of industry stakeholders, employees, customers and community • Agreement on, and commitment to, activation protocols	***Risk assessment*** • Assessment of potential disasters and their probability of occurrence • Development of scenarios on the genesis and impacts of potential disasters • Develop disaster contingency plans

2. *Prodromal*
 When it is apparent that a disaster is imminent
	Mobilisation
	 • Warning systems (including general mass media)
	 • Establish disaster management command centre
	 • Secure facilities
		Disaster contingency plans
		 • Identify likely impacts and groups at risk
		 • Assess community and visitor capabilities to cope with impacts
		 • Articulate the objectives of individual (disaster specific) contingency plans
		 • Identify actions necessary to avoid or minimise impacts at each stage
		 • Devise strategic priority (action) profiles for each phase
		   o *Prodromal*
		   o *Emergency*
		   o *Intermediate*
		   o *Long-term recovery*
		 • On-going review and revision in the light of
		   o *Experience*
		   o *Changes in organisational structures and personnel*
		   o *Changes in the environment*

3. *Emergency* The effect of the disaster is felt and action is necessary to protect people and property	***Action*** • Rescue/evacuation procedures • Emergency accommodation and food supplies • Medical/health services • Monitoring and communication systems	
4. *Intermediate* A point where the short-term needs of people have been addressed and the main focus of activity is to restore services and the community to normal	***Recovery*** • Damage audit/monitoring system • Clean-up and restoration • Media communication strategy	
5. *Long-term (recovery)* Continuation of previous phase, but items that could not be attended to quickly are attended to at this stage. Post-mortem, self-analysis, healing	***Reconstruction and reassessment*** • Repair of damaged infrastructure • Rehabilitation of environmentally damaged areas • Counselling victims • Restoration of business/consumer confidence and development of investment plans • Debriefing to promote input to revisions of disaster strategies	
6. *Resolution* Routine restored or new improved state establishment	***Review***	

Figure 3.5 A tourism disaster management framework
Source: Reprinted from *Tourism Management* 22, Faulkner, B., Towards a framework for tourism disaster management, pp. 135–147, copyright (2001), with permission of Elsevier.

- a pre-event stage crisis or disaster stage allowing the development of strategy, preparation and plans;
- a stage immediately before or after a crisis or disaster occurs which requires the implementation of strategies to deal with its impacts;
- continued implementation of strategies to control or reduce the severity of the crisis/disaster; and

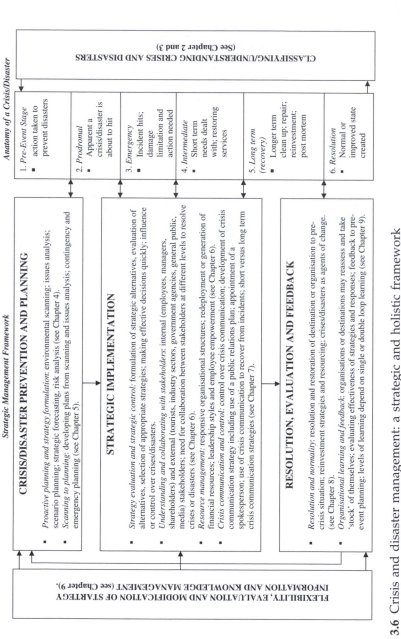

Figure 3.6 Crisis and disaster management: a strategic and holistic framework
Source: Reprinted from *Tourism Management* 25, Ritchie, B. W., Chaos, Crises and Disasters: A Strategic Approach to Crisis Management in the Tourism Industry, pp. 669–683, copyright (2004), with permission of Elsevier.

- a long-term recovery or resolution phase allowing for evaluation and feedback into future prevention and planning strategies for destinations and businesses.

However, at all stages of the strategic planning/management process, there needs to be flexibility, evaluation and potential modification to strategy development and implementation depending on the nature of the crisis/disaster (its magnitude, scale, time pressure), information acquisition and knowledge management. This is especially important as crises and disasters are inherently complex and chaotic. It is impossible to be aware of all of the potential implications of strategies used to deal with crises or disasters, although through historical analysis and hindsight it is possible to gain some understanding. However, as discussed in Chapter 2, as society becomes increasingly complex and interdependent, linked events can cause further crises and disasters, and organisations may in responding to a natural disaster create a crisis through the handling of the situation. Therefore, within the strategic planning and management process, flexibility, adaptation and a fluid response is needed through the use of information and knowledge, which fits in with the emergent, adaptive and incremental views on strategic management and planning, as well as adaptive perspectives on the climate and tourism system (Becken & Hay, 2007).

At the *pre-event and prodromal stage* of a crisis or disaster, activities can be undertaken by public and private sector organisations and managers to develop strategies and plans to stop or limit the impacts of a crisis or disaster. Although organisations are able to design pre-crisis strategies to help with crisis management, they are often unable to prevent a crisis from occurring. However, the real challenge is to recognise crises in a timely fashion and implementing strategies to limit the damage (Darling *et al.*, 1996). Authors such as Burnett (1998) and Kash and Darling (1998) note that decisions undertaken before a crisis occurs will enable more effective management of the crisis, rather than organisations being managed by the crisis and making hasty and ineffective decisions. Proactive planning through the use of strategic planning and issues management will help reduce risk, time wastage, poor resource management to reduce the impacts of those that do arise (Gonzalez-Herrero & Pratt, 1995; Heath, 1998). Techniques such as strategic forecasting, contingency planning, issues analysis and management, scenario analysis, hazard mapping, risk analysis and hazard adjustment are all available to managers and decision-makers, and are useful tools to prevent or reduce crises and disasters or increase the ability of society to increase its resilience to vulnerabilities. These are all discussed in Chapters 4 and 5.

These techniques signify the need for managers and planners to gather information, develop and test knowledge on potential issues or problems and consider plans or strategies they would implement if a crisis or disaster occurs. Understanding the type of disaster or crisis a destination or organisation is susceptible to, and the nature of such an incident is invaluable to the creation of suitable plans and strategies which can prevent or limit the impact of such an incident. In short, moving from simply 'scanning to planning' is required through developing contingency and integrated emergency plans and systems. If a potential crisis or disaster is identified, then strategies may be implemented to detect signals and perhaps stop it from occurring. However, if this cannot occur, then the crisis or disaster enters the prodromal stage and into the next phase of strategic crisis management: the *implementation* of strategies and plans to deal with the impacts.

However, the implementation phase can also be complex and chaotic and complicate any specific strategy implementation. Implementation therefore requires flexibility, use of good quality information and knowledge, as well as constant monitoring concerning:

- the evaluation, selection and implementation of appropriate strategies;
- implementing an effective crisis communication and control strategy;
- controlling or reallocating resources to deal effectively with such incidents; and
- identifying and working collaboratively with key stakeholders in the tourism and other associated sectors.

Regular meetings (perhaps even daily) are required to assess the effectiveness of strategies, the response of various stakeholders to strategies, and to review the development of the crisis or disaster as it evolves over its lifecycle. The most important elements of this stage are combined in Chapter 6, which examines coordination, control and resource allocation. Chapter 7 focuses on crisis communication and recovery marketing, very important for dealing with tourism crises and disasters.

The final stage of dealing with crises and disasters more strategically and holistically is the *evaluation and feedback stage* as a destination or organisation begins to recover from a crisis and normality begins to occur. The main goal of an organisation or destination is to control the crisis or disaster and reduce its severity or to stop it completely. However, as discussed previously, crises and disasters are chaotic and complex and their impacts can make long lasting changes to systems, and these changes can be positive or negative. Burnett (1998) suggests that crises create heroes or leaders who emerge to help direct a destination or organisation facing such crises back to normality or an improved state. An improved state is possible because of the ability of an organisation or destination to learn from crises and disasters, make policy changes, and adapt and modify strategies that did not work effectively. Furthermore, as discussed in Chapter 2, natural hazards and disasters can bring about resources for the host community if the threat to humanity is gone or reduced, and the climate system is a self-regulating system. Therefore, at the resolution stage of crisis and disaster management, a feedback loop back to proactive planning and prevention is possible through managing knowledge and organisational learning. However, there is debate about the degree of learning from crises and disasters and these issues are discussed in Chapters 8 and 9 of the book. The final chapter (Chapter 10) concludes the book and examines future research issues or topics for investigation in this particular field.

Conclusion

This chapter suggests that an understanding of planning, management and strategic planning/management are crucial for the effective management of tourism crises and disasters. The concept of strategic planning and management was outlined, debates presented by divergent perspectives on strategic planning and management. The elements of a strategic planning and management approach were outlined and discussed, including strategic analysis, choice, implementation and control, and the link between planning and management functions. Key concepts in strategic management were introduced including understanding the internal and external operating environment, organisational culture and the allocation of resources (all important in managing tourism crises and disasters and discussed in the following chapters). The rationale perspective on strategy was contested, however, due to the complexity of tourism crises and disaster events and the view from many authors that strategy is not formed deliberately (Mintzberg, 1987).

The final half of this chapter outlined a rationale for a strategic approach to both planning for, and managing, tourism crises and disasters. In particular, this section suggested that there are a growing number of crises and disasters that impact upon tourism and organisations need to think more strategically in both planning for, and managing, tourism crises and disasters. An overview of crisis and disaster planning and management models was provided before a proposed strategic framework was presented, linked to the structure of the book. The framework noted that the crisis and disaster lifecycle has a clear similarity to the strategic management framework. The final section ended with a discussion of the main sections of the framework, and the subsequent book chapters.

Part 2

Tourism Crisis and Disaster Prevention and Planning

Chapter 4

Tourism Crisis Prevention and Disaster Mitigation

> *Proactive planning helps managers to control and resolve a crisis. Ignoring the possibility of a crisis, on the other hand, could lead the crisis taking a life of its own.*
>
> Kash and Darling (1998: 180)

Introduction

Tourism crisis and disaster prevention and mitigation is a central factor in crisis and disaster management. Reducing the risks, time wastage and poor resource management, fewer crisis situations arise and those that do will likely to be handled more effectively (Heath, 1998). As discussed in Chapter 2, disasters are a function of the relationship between risk and vulnerability, therefore any disaster planning or prevention measures should be directed to addressing both risk and vulnerability. A change of thinking by disaster planners and managers has seen a move toward reduction rather than simply responding to natural disasters after they occur. However, despite some discussion of reduction mechanisms in the literature, there is still a lack of action to reduce risk and vulnerability for specific tourism destinations.

This chapter is divided into two distinct elements. First, the chapter outlines organisational strategic planning to prevent or reduce the chances of crisis through the use of scanning and planning. The use of quantitative or qualitative forecasting techniques and brainstorming by organisation staff can improve understanding of the types of risks and possible response strategies. The second part outlines pre-disaster mitigation or prevention steps to alleviate or prevent a hazardous event and its possible impacts. These include structural and non-structural mitigation techniques. Both parts of the chapter identify the need for information gathering and interpretation to understand potential vulner-abilities to the organisation, industry or community and assess risks. Such information can then assist prevention through reducing exposure to risks, increasing resilience or improving signal detection to reduce the likelihood of a crisis or disaster occurring.

Organisational Crisis Prevention

The challenge for organisations is to monitor both the external and internal operating environment in order to predict possible issues and deal with those issues before they turn into crises. There are a number of business systems and techniques suitable to help provide early identification and warning of possible issues, shocks and crises in the political, economic, social and technological area. The aim of this section of the book is not to cover all of these techniques, but to provide some information on those that may be of more interest to tourism organisations. In particular, it should be noted that tourism organisations are often small and medium-sized enterprises that do not necessarily have vast amounts of resources to put into strategic planning systems.

However, some of the techniques listed below, do not require much investment and require more of a change of mindset away from ignoring potential events to actually acknowledging such events and considering ways to deal with them. As Rousaki and Alcott (2007: 28) state, readiness is a state of mind and 'crisis readiness can ... be broadly defined as the readiness to cope with the uncertainty caused by a crisis'. Furthermore, one of the major problems in responding to crises is a lack of information, experience and preparedness coupled with the intensity and speed of such events. The development and use of systems and techniques such as forecasting to gather information and check for crisis and natural disaster signals, coupled with the development of crisis and disaster management plans and strategies (outlined in Chapter 5), may reduce the vulnerability amongst tourism managers and improve their capacity to deal with incidents if they do eventuate. This can build valuable time into response actions helping to buffer the demands on resources (Reilly, 1987). However, this section also notes that current forecasting techniques are based on the Newtonian paradigm and are not as useful for projecting immediate shocks such as crises or disasters, which may be triggered by incidents outside of the tourism system.

There are a number of interrelated steps in the development of crisis planning and preparation including:

- scanning for issues or signals that could turn into potential crises through using specific indicators (political, economic, social, technological) and information sources;
- examining potential risks, forecasts and scenarios of such crises and their likely impacts; and
- creating preventive and contingency plans which could include a strategic crisis management system including a crisis management team, suitable staff training and resources.

The third point in this list is covered in the next chapter on crisis and disaster planning and preparedness, although these three steps are difficult to separate in reality.

Scanning the environment

As Ansoff and McDonnell (1990) note, since the 1950s the organisational environment has become less predictable, leading to a growth within strategic planning and management called strategic issue management, or sometimes referred to as issues management. A strategic issue is 'a forthcoming development, either inside or outside of the organisation, which is likely to have an important impact on the ability of an enterprise [or organisation] to meet its objectives' (Ansoff & McDonnell, 1990: 369). Although the authors note that a strategic issue can be a strength or opportunity, it can also be an external threat or an internal weakness which could occur in between annual planning cycles, and therefore may be missed by managers. Ansoff and McDonnell (1990) and Heath (1997) believe that strategic issues management is important and should be separated from the normal planning cycle for businesses when the environment is turbulent and if organisations cannot afford to, or do not need to, undertake annual strategic planning. This fits well with the tourism system, which is comprised of many small enterprises, which cannot afford to undertake regular strategic planning, and is often susceptible to a turbulent environment.

A strategic issue management system (SIM) is a systematic procedure that can be used for early identification and fast response to surprising challenges from both within and outside the organisation. SIM has been described as a 'real time' strategic planning tool that can be used on a periodic review (monthly) and updating of a key strategic issue list (Ansoff & McDonnell, 1990). Fast response to issues can occur in the following ways, according to Ansoff and McDonnell (1990: 370):

- the responsibility for managing the system is assumed by a senior management group who has resources and authority to initiate prompt action;
- SIM can cut across organisational structures and units best placed to deal with issues can be assigned responsibility, or, ad hoc committee can be created across business units which reports directly to senior management; and
- responsibilities including not only planning but also attempting to resolve the issue, therefore the separation between planning and implementation is not visible in an SIM.

Mobilising general management, specific issue management staff and general workers is a key part of the strategic issues management system.

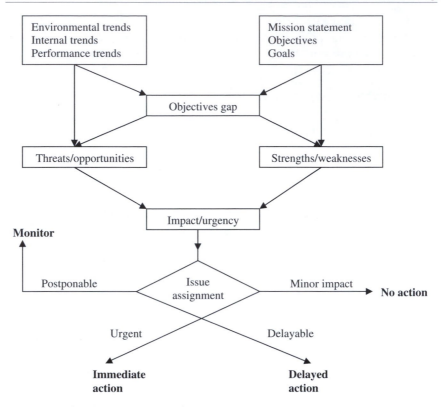

Figure 4.1 Strategic issues analysis stages
Source: Modified after Ansoff and McDonnell (1990: 372).

Issues may range from political, economic, social or technological issues. Three major steps are required and are illustrated in Figure 4.1 adapted from Ansoff and McDonell (1990).

(1) The first step after systems and people have been dedicated to the task of strategic issues management is issue identification from a number of sources of information including the external environment, trends in the enterprise and trends in its performance. Issues should be developed that are related to the organisation (including breakthroughs in technology) through scanning the internal and external environment.

(2) Issues should be examined in relation to the attainment of the organisations objectives; however, this is difficult and managers often have to use judgement by assigning an impact number (from + 10 to −10 for instance) based on manager's judgement and the collection and use of information from outside of the organisation

(through the use of experts for instance). Here, it is important to examine the probability of the event or issue occurring and its impact strength. Burnett's (1998) crisis classification matrix, discussed in Chapter 2, may be useful for differentiating potential issues (which could be dealt with later or simply monitored) with that of impending crises. According to Burnett (1998) and Billings *et al.* (1980), it is the perceived loss and probability that combine to create a threat. Coupled with a lack of information, time pressure and a lack of control, this perceived loss and probability could propel an issue into a crisis. A minor impact would drop the issue from the issue list according to Ansoff and McDonnell (1990), whereas a major impact coupled with an urgent need would constitute the need for immediate action by an organisation because a quick response is vital. If the response can be delayed until the next planning cycle than it can be labelled delayable. If, according to estimates, the response can de delayed indefinitely until better estimates of the impact can be made, the event is labelled postponable.

(3) Key threats and opportunities are noted down and prioritised according to their expected impact and the key issue list is updated as issues are resolved, become minor or new ones are added through issue analysis.

(4) Although this is useful for analysing the potential impact and urgency of single events, it fails to examine the impact of interrelated trends and events and their interdependence, which was noted in Chapter 2 as a key component of crises and disasters.

Business cross-impact analysis may be a better tool as it examines the impact that a range of events may have on the strategic directions and fields that the organisation is involved with. According to Witt and Moutinho (2000: 298), cross-impact analysis is a less known technique but is useful for examining inhibiting events and unfolding relationships between events which may initially appear unrelated. It is useful for environmental scanning in order for organisations to view the likely impact of trends. It involves selecting a small number of people (top decision-makers and outside consultants) to specify critical events relating to the project subject, while each event is placed in matrix and the impact of each event on every other event is examined (Witt & Moutinho, 2000). High threat events are provided with a high negative value, whereas opportunities are provided with a positive value, and these may be given numeric values by the participants. Members of the decision-making team may be involved in more than one round of scoring or voting related to the issues, and the review of the matrix provides managers with an understanding of those events which are strong actors and significant reactors that are important for strategic planning and strategy development (Witt & Moutinho, 2000). The cross-impact analysis indicates the complexity of events which may provide crises for some fields and units within a business and yet provide opportunities for others, and has been identified as an important tool for crisis management (Elliot, 2006).

Interaction matrices are also useful tools in that they examine the strength of causality between causes and effects. Glaesser (2003, 2006) notes that the interaction matrix can be used to examine the dependability between areas and events and is able to reduce complexity through a range of possibilities. This matrix examines the active and passive relationship between a number of events or areas and scores these using a range from 0 (or no influence) to 3 (strong influence). The bottom row of the matrix adds the columns to produce a passive sum, while the right-hand column produces an active sum with the quotient being a function of the active sum divided by the passive sum. The higher the quotient the more influence the event or area has over others, while the lower the quotient, the more exposed or weaker it is to other influences or events (Glaesser, 2003: 110). However, as Glaesser (2003, 2006) notes, both types of analysis are only useful for pre-selected events and are dependant on the information of experts, both of which may not be useful for immediate crises, but may be more useful for emerging or sustained crisis situations.

Forecasting techniques and information gathering

Along with general issues management and impact analysis, there are more specific indicators and techniques that can be used to help forecast or assess the likely impact of incidents and events that could develop, if not dealt with, into crises. In the politics and economics field, exists the political risk analysis and business environment risk analysis which often use strategic forecasting tools including quantitative modelling techniques and qualitative techniques. Forecasting often involves using a range of analytical tools to assist tourism mangers with decision-making and should be integrated with organisational planning (Witt & Moutinho, 2000). Forecasting at a strategic level can be undertaken, according to Cole (1994: 68) under two main headings:

(1) *Quantitative* (i.e. where projections are based on numerical data, such as statistics and accounting data, often analysed by computer-based models). This approach uses 'hard' data and techniques such as budget forecasts, simple projections, computer modelling including econometrics and is a rational/deterministic approach.

(2) *Qualitative* (i.e. basing projections on explicit assumptions and individual judgements about them). This approach uses 'soft' data

and techniques such as PEST, SWOT, scenario development, Delphi technique and brainstorming and is an intuitive/judgmental approach to forecasting.

Although it is not the role of this section of the chapter to explore in depth forecasting techniques in detail, it is important to outline the types of forecasting tools that could be used by the tourism industry to avoid or reduce the impact of economic, political or social crises. Calantone *et al.* (1987) note that there are several different types of forecasting:

- *Exploratory forecasting* extrapolates past trends using regression or time-series analysis based on assumptions about relationships between variables.
- *Normative forecasting* incorporates discussion of the methods needed to attain a desired future outcome.
- *Integrative forecasting* relies on a variety of methods to determine the underlying relationships amongst a variety of forecasts, integrating these to maximise the forecasts.
- *Speculative forecasting* uses qualitative techniques such as scenario writing or the judgement of experts such as in the Delphi or expert approach. This approach has been used within the tourism industry repeatedly since the 1970s. The Delphi technique belongs to a set of qualitative research methods that rely on the judgement of individuals presumed to be experts in the subject under consideration. Other 'judgmental' research techniques include juries of executive opinion, subjective probability assessments, and consumer intentions surveys (Frechtling, 1996). The Delphi approach is often used for technological and specific event occurrence. Lloyd *et al.* (2000), for instance used the Delphi technique to predict changes in the Hong Kong hotel industry as a result of the transfer of sovereignty from Britain to China in 1997.

There is an obvious divide between rational/deterministic use of exploratory and normative forecasting techniques which use quantitative data analysis and those that are more intuitive/judgmental and use speculative forecasting techniques. However, integrative techniques combine both types in order to maximise forecasts. Scenario planning can be useful for 'sensitizing decision makers to the potential outcomes of events and trends' (Grewe *et al.*, 1989: 112). Scenario planning can be useful for brainstorming tourism futures and may provide worst and best case scenarios concerning future trends and events. However, as Joyce (1999) notes, if there are a small number of variables that are under review in scenario planning then this technique can be effective, but if there are a large number of variables then scenario planning may become unwieldy. Scenario planning has been used by some tourism researchers to help brainstorm potential approaches to dealing with crises or disasters (see Page *et al.*, 2006; Yeoman *et al.*, 2005b).

All of these forecasting techniques rely on previous experience or past history and perhaps rely on stability in order to produce accurate forecasts for the tourism industry. Although the limitations of forecasting have been acknowledged by some (Turner & Witt, 2001; Witt & Song, 2001), the incorporation of shocks, disasters or crises in forecasting have been limited. As Leiper and Hing (1998: 250) note with respect to the Asian Economic Crisis of 1997–1998, 'despite sophisticated monitoring of trends and environmental conditions by apparent experts in the business world, academia and in governments, nobody predicted that the APR [Asian Pacific Region] economy would plunge into crisis and depression'.

Political risk analysis is discussed in the context of tourism multinational companies and less developed countries by Poirier (1997) who suggests that companies who are considering investing in tourism development in foreign countries should consider some form of political risk analysis to assist decision-making. Traditionally the focus of multinational companies has been on economic, rather than political risk (Poirier, 1997: 676); however, political instability and the global expansion of tourism, opens the industry up to potential global risks. As Poirier (1997: 676) states, 'although the boundaries between economic and political risk cannot be determined precisely, PRA attempts to consider various political threats to MNE [multinational enterprises] arising from predictable or spontaneous events taking place within a specific environment'.

Although problems have been acknowledged concerning political stability and whether some organisations are likely to benefit from instability, tourism organisations are more likely to lose out due to consumer perceptions of risk. Furthermore, Poirier (1997) comments that political instability as such may not impact upon tourism, but specific events can create risk to an organisation's operation and achievement of its goals. Schmidt (1986) noted the difference between a risk event and a risk effect, with a risk event posing potential problems for organisations, whereas a risk effect impacts can effect organisational goals or profitability. Some events and effects are undertaken by government and have a degree of predictability, while others occur within society and may be less predictable (Poirier, 1997: 678). Some analysts, such as the World Political Risk Forecasts (WPRF), use quantitative and qualitative data from 150 political scientists, government officials and country experts to generate 18 month and 5-year forecasts.

Another forecasting information source is the Business Environment Risk Index (BERI), which attempts to predict political climate and business stability in approximately 130 states. The index comprises three major elements, according to Glaesser (2003: 127–128) and BERIs (2003):

(1) *The Operations Risk Index (ORI):* which evaluates business climate through 15 factors that impede affects investment climate and involves experts from banks, industry and government (with 5–10 experts evaluating a country according to set criteria). The scoring of factors ranges from 0 (unacceptable conditions) to 4 (very favourable conditions).

(2) *The Political Risk Index (PRI):* which assesses political stability in a country covering 10 criteria ranging from the causes and symptoms of instability and involves political scientists and sociologists. Rating is conducted from 0 (extraordinary problems) to 7 (no problems), with a further 30 points that can be allocated to criteria of particular importance. Both the ORI and PRI totals are derived from adding the mean score of experts to provide classes of risk ranging from low risk (100–70 points), moderate risk (69–55 points), high risk (54–40 points) and unacceptable risk (39–0 points).

(3) *The Remittance and Repatriation Factor (R factor):* which examines the ability of a country and its obligation to pay and considers its ability to convert capital and profits into other currencies. This is based more on quantitative data as opposed to the ORI and PRI which are based on more subjective expert opinion.

The overall result from these three analyses is one of four categories, which are published three times a year:

(1) Business transactions not recommended. Advise against all business relationships.

(2) Suitable for trade only and no investments. Only short-term transactions without capital movements are recommended.

(3) Suitable for profit-independent payments only. Realisation of profit via the transfer of know-how or licences only is to be recommended.

(4) Suitable for investment and investment of capital recommended. Problems related to the conversion of currency or transfer of dividends are not expected.

Although these tools are useful for examining the political and economic environment and monitoring political and economic changes, they may be less useful for spontaneous and unpredictable events (including crisis situations such as coups, terrorists attacks and so forth). These kinds of events are less able to be predicted by analysts and may create immediate crises for organisations. Another potential issue noted by Poirier (1997) is that political risk can be created by the organisation itself through its actions or inactions (such as unethical or questionable behaviour). This is discussed by Aziz (1995) who suggested that terrorist attacks on the tourism industry in Egypt were due to cultural differences between Western actions and Muslim traditions and inappropriate tourism development undertaken by the tourism industry.

The techniques noted above have been criticised because of the difficulty of transferring important and completed information to end users (such as business decision-makers). Problems, as Poirier (1997) notes, relate to simplification of data and production of understandable assessments for decision-makers in business. Furthermore, as described above, these reports are produced three times a year in the case of BERI and every 18 months with respect to the WPRF, so such information may become rapidly outdated as things can change quickly due to spontaneous events (such as protests, political unrest, etc.).

There are a number of private companies offering similar services for risk assessment including the World Markets Research Centre who have a Political & Economic Forecasting Unit responsible for a range of country intelligence services. It assesses and forecasts political, economic, regulatory and business conditions in 186 countries through their Same-day Analysis and Special Reports, Country Reports and Five-Year Economic Forecasts, FDI and Sovereign Risk Rating Models. The World Markets Research Centre (2003) in August 2003 ranked the US as the country with the fourth-highest risk of terrorism with the UK facing the greatest risk from terrorism of any European state ranked 10th overall. According to the report, the motivation for such an attack among Islamist extremist groups is very high owing to the UK's close alliance with the US, while sophisticated militant networks are known to be present within the country.

Regionally, the Middle East and North Africa have the highest risk rating with Israel rated second in specific countries after Colombia. Their client survey showed that 84% of respondents thought that the risk of terrorist attacks against the US and the UK had increased as a result of the war in Iraq. These figures throw into question the likely effectiveness of the war on terror in successfully reducing risk, at least in the short term. Almost three-quarters of those polled thought terrorism posed a greater risk to their operations now than five years ago. A similar amount, 72%, revealed that they had included this risk in their decision-making process. However, a surprising 56% of those polled revealed that their company had never conducted a safety drill or business continuity exercise. Transferring the strategic decisions to address risk into tangible operational management tactics seems difficult for those surveyed.

In the tourism industry travel advice from Foreign Offices (FO) are one of the most influential information sources for potential travellers and the tourism industry, and should be seen as part of an information system for tourism organisations and businesses (Glaesser, 2003, 2006). The FO of countries provide a regular update on the political and economic situation of countries and provide advisories to travellers based on political stability, threat of terrorism, health and medical facilities, etc. Information is provided in FO fact sheets and on web pages. If travel to certain countries is deemed a risk, then travel advisories and announcements are often made against travel to certain destinations. Although systems vary between countries, the British Foreign and Commonwealth Office classify warnings as either a warning against all travel or all travel unless on essential business with further information about why these advisories have been provided. Glaesser (2003, 2006) notes that information from FO is often more useful to consumers than BERI or other country risk information, as it is more in tune to travellers and takes their origins into account. FO have a network of consular representatives who can provide advice and information that are used in the development of travel advice, advisories or warnings for citizens of countries.

However, Calder (2003) suggests that although the Foreign and Commonwealth Office (FCO) of the UK may provide information concerning the current risk of terrorism, it does not alert potential travellers to other risks, such as motor vehicle accidents, which Calder (2003) notes in New Zealand are 150% higher than in Britain. He concludes by suggesting that for backpackers, the FO travel advice is about as much use as a 1971 edition of the Hitchhiker's Guide to Europe! Furthermore, travel advice differs between countries depending on the interrelationship between both countries (the one advising and the one being advised for). The WHO described the Severe Acute Respiratory Syndrome (SARS) as a 'worldwide health threat' (BBC News, 2003b) and put travel warnings on a number of affected countries and regions in Asia and North America. An overview of the of travel warnings including travel advisories ('Postpone all but essential travel to these area') and travel alerts ('A health concern exists; take precautions when travelling to these areas') for SARS is given in Table 4.1. After Toronto had been removed from the WHO's list of SARS-affected regions on 20 May 2003, there was dispute about restarting the travel alert after a second outbreak of the deadly virus which became officially known a few days later (Kondro, 2003).

Another example which shows the importance placed on travel advice and its role in warning travellers about possible risks of terrorism is related to the 2002 Bali bombing. The FCO (Foreign and Commonwealth Office), UK has been criticised 'for failing to give, or being late with, sufficient warnings of terrorist activity' in connection with the Bali bombing (Templeton, 2003: 4). After a public outcry following the Bali bombing, the FCO has changed the way it gives travel advice: now the terrorist threat to UK travellers in each country (whether considerable or non-existent) is the first item on each page, vague bureaucratic language has been abandoned, links to other countries' travel advice websites are

Table 4.1 Travel advisories and travel alerts related to the SARS outbreak

Region	*Advisory started*	*Advisory stopped*	*Alert started*	*Alert stopped*
Mainland China	3/13/03	6/17/03	6/17/03	7/3/03
Beijing, China	6/17/03	6/25/03	6/25/03	7/11/03
Taiwan	6/25/03	6/25/03	6/25/03	7/15/03
Hong Kong	5/1/03	6/25/03	6/25/03	7/1/03*
Hanoi, Vietnam	3/13/03	4/29/03	4/29/03	5/15/03
Toronto	Never had an advisory	Never had an advisory	4/23/03 restarted: 5/23/03	5/20/03 restopped: 7/8/03
Singapore	3/13/03	5/4/03	5/4/03	6/4/03

*This change was posted on 7/9/03, retroactive to 7/1/03.
Source: Modified CDC (2003b).

available as well as a page of tips on how to keep safe within each country (Templeton, 2003: 4). Yet, the FCO warns travellers that 'it could not always take final responsibility for whether trips should be made' (Templeton, 2003: 4). Many of the changes made have been appreciated by the travel and tourism industry; however, there are concerns among some tour operators regarding the increasing political influence on the travel advice unit (Templeton, 2003: 4). Stuart Britton, managing director of Somak Holidays (in Templeton, 2003: 4) argues that 'there is more political bias in our Government's advice than in the advice of others. There's a danger that, on entering the page for any given country, the consumer would be scared witless when immediately confronted by a paragraph on terrorism'.

Beirman (2002: 169) agrees and suggests that travel warnings may be highly politicised and also inaccurate, significantly damaging tourism destination. With respect to the reduction of visitors to Israel in 2000, he notes that the impact:

> was exacerbated by the actions of certain governments, notably the USA, which took the extreme (by world standards) measure of advising its citizens to avoid travel to Israel. Most Western governments advised their citizens to avoid travel to Palestinian Authority areas and specific parts of Israel and to take extra precautions, but fell short of a ban on travel.

The downgrading of travel advisories with respect to the Fiji coups were extremely important, coupled with investment in marketing and promotional activities implemented only after travel advisories were downgraded in key markets (Berno & King, 2001).

Pressure on overseas diplomatic representatives and a consistent media strategy were also useful in influencing the travel advisories provided by key source markets.

A Critique of Forecasting

Although Prideaux *et al.* (2003) suggested that these risk assessment reports (and possibly travel advice) may be useful for forecasting change or crises, they still note that traditional approaches have problems in predicting shocks including crises and disasters. Generally forecasting is used to predict future tourism activity and is useful in times of normality or stability, but in times of uncertainty predicting future tourism flows is problematic (Prideaux *et al.*, 2003). Accuracy of forecasts is a critical ingredient of forecasting enabling decisions to be made more effectively and efficiently.

However, similar to political analysis, although these can be useful for organisational decision-making, the use and forecasting of such indicators may not predict economic or financial crises, such as the Asian Economic Crisis of 1997–1998. It seems as though such techniques and tools are flawed when it comes to providing warning systems for shocks and incidents like economic crises. According to Prideaux *et al.* (2003) such forecasting tools may be flawed simply because they operate in a Newtonian paradigm which sees change events such as shocks and crises in the same way. As discussed in Chapter 2, complexity and chaos may be a better way to view such incidents; however, forecasters need to consider and incorporate a broader range of shocks or disruptions which may impact upon organisations or destinations into their forecasts.

Prideaux *et al.* (2003) note the wide use of scenarios as the basis for predicting shocks such as crises and disasters in the risk management field. Yet as they suggest:

> the tourism literature has not begun to investigate the rich range of techniques developed in the risk management literature, yet this literature has the potential to yield models, frameworks and theories that will assist tourism forecasters and planners to cope with a arrange of disasters and crises. (Prideaux *et al.*, 2003: 477)

They argue that forecasting, using current techniques, could be based upon risk specification, identification and management using revised variables from forward-looking scenarios or risk analysis. Risks that are ranked or prioritised can provide data which could be used in forecasting. Forecasting or scenario building can then be linked to the development of contingency or crisis management plans (which is discussed in Chapter 5). Ultimately, the above discussion is concerned with gathering information and data to understand the context and possibly identify the signals of a potential crisis. Many authors suggest that this is just one part of the risk management process (Tarlow, 2006; Then & Loosemore, 2006), with the need to use this information to develop action plans to treat risks. The Risk Management Process created by Standards Australia and Standards New Zealand provide a generic framework for establishing the context, identifying and evaluating risks and considering the treatment, monitoring and communication of risk. Analysis of the impact of risk can use some of the tools highlighted in the above section, in conjunction with questions over the potential likelihood and impact of certain risks occurring. A crisis profile matrix (Arbel & Bargur, 1980) or shock classification system (Prideaux *et al.*, 2003) can help identify the range of potential crises and their possible responses and return for investment.

Table 4.2 outlines the range of forecasting tools and their certainty of forecast based on the level of shock (which was discussed in Chapter 2). S1 and S2 events such as changes in exchange rates and inflation should be picked up by current econometric forecasting techniques. However, S3

Table 4.2 Shock classification, forecasting tools and level of certainty of forecast

Scale	Forecasting tools	Level of certainty of forecast
S4	Scenarios, risk assessment, Delphi forecasting and historical research may be used to identify risks of this nature and develop estimates of post-shock travel demand and supply conditions. At this point, new parameters are established allowing employment of standard forecasting techniques.	Very low
S3	Scenarios determine possible boundaries of the impact of shock allowing employment of standard forecasting techniques to test tourism responses for a range of possible outcomes.	Beyond current range of acceptability
S2	Existing forecasting techniques with allowance for sudden changes in demand and supply conditions.	Medium to low
S1	Standard forecasting methods.	High for the near term, lower in the medium term

Source: Modified after Prideaux *et al.* (2003: 484).

and S4 are more severe with S3 shocks (such as earthquakes and terrorist attacks) beyond normal forecasting tools but could be included in forecasts through the use of scenarios or risk analysis to determine the extent of the problem and applying standard forecasting techniques to examine low, medium and high probable impacts. S4 incidents may be the result of an unseen disaster or crisis such as an economic crisis. An extended use of techniques used in S3 incidents could be used to provide information for standard forecasting techniques. Prideaux *et al.* (2003) note that the likelihood of terrorist attacks for some countries may move into S3 or S2, which is supported by recent studies on terrorist risk outlined above, which may have a great impact upon the tourism system. The use of scenarios can provide certain advantages to aid organisational learning of potential crises/disasters and helps systems thinking (Miller & Waller, 2003). Table 4.3 outlines some of the strengths and weaknesses of using scenario planning in business management.

As the discussion above indicates, the main reason for examining the external environment through analysing issues, risks, strengths and weaknesses as well as the potential for shocks or crises is to detect signals (Pauchant & Mitroff, 1992). Signals may first appear weak but if information can be gathered then courses of action will become clearer helping to stop or delay a potential crisis situation. As Ansoff and McDonnell (1990) note, as the information becomes more precise, so will the firm's response to such change induced by a crisis. Over time as information is gathered and risk analysis or business cross-impact analysis is undertaken, the organisation will begin to form a response and develop suitable strategies and actions to deal with impending threats.

Disaster Prevention, Reduction and Mitigation

Considering risk and vulnerability

Risk cannot be completely eliminated; however, it can be better managed so that vulnerability to such risk is reduced. According to Smith (1995), this often involves some form of risk assessment and management so as to reduce the element of risk or vulnerability to human property or lives as a result of a natural hazard. As Salter (1997) notes, this social element related to vulnerability has shifted the emphasis from hazards as physical events to social products. Australia's National Emergency Management Competency Standards define vulnerability as 'the degree of susceptibility and resilience of the community and environment to hazards' (in Emergency Management Australia, 1995). As Alexander (2000) suggests, if the level of risk or vulnerability is significantly greater than the frequency or magnitude of a hazard, then hazard mitigation as a strategy has potential.

Table 4.3 Strengths and weaknesses of scenario planning

Strengths	*Weaknesses*
Participative – insights are drawn from many different sources, thereby adding rich details to envisioned futures and enhancing knowledge.	*Practically unwieldy* – without logical consistency and rigorous examination, scenarios can be nothing more than imaginative speculations.
Detail rich – reaches beyond the constraints or mechanistic models and incorporates contingencies that are difficult to quantify.	*Non-quantifiable* – as many of the inputs to a scenario planning process are not quantifiable, the output is likewise not quantifiable.
Narrative – produces a series of stories about plausible future states that take into account the dynamic interactions of key stakeholders and the organisation's role in creating the future.	*Biases* – envisioned scenarios may reflect current circumstances rather than future possibilities dominant personalities or group think can limit the possibilities considered.
Broad scope – considers multiple plausible scenarios, covering a range of possible contingencies and outcomes; it facilitates diverse perspectives and helps uncover blind spots.	*Lack of consensus* – because scenario planning allows for divergent perspectives, participants may not converge on shared understanding or a common strategy.
Systems thinking – encourages learning about the interrelations (including feedback effects) among key environmental variables.	
Externally focused – provides a framework to envision long-range opportunities and uncertainties in the organisation's environment.	

Source: Reprinted from Long Range Planning, 36(1), Miller, K. and Waller, G. Scenarios, real options and integrated risk management, pp. 93–107, copyright (2003), with permission of Elsevier.

Although the number of associated disasters has increased in recent decades and the number of the population threatened by such incidents has grown, the death rate has nearly halved (ISDR, 2004) because of disaster and risk mitigation or prevention strategies. However, more can be done in the mitigation and prevention of disasters, and particularly their impact on tourism destinations. Conditions related to populations can create a greater susceptibility and risk of a natural hazard becoming a natural disaster. People who are more vulnerable to such hazards create greater risks that they may encounter a disaster in the future. The ISDR (2004: 15) describe well the challenge for risk and disaster reduction:

'disaster reduction policies and measures need to be implemented, with a twofold aim: to enable societies to be resilient to natural hazards while ensuring that development efforts do not increase vulnerability to these hazards'. Anticipating disasters through previous experience, knowledge and awareness are vital for communities to reduce their risk and vulnerability to natural hazards. The *International Decade for Natural Disaster Reduction* (IDNDR) proclaimed by the General Assembly of the United Nations from 1990 to 1999 and its programmes are one way to raise awareness of disaster and risk reduction amongst members of the scientific community but also local communities, who should be communicated with in partnership with scientists and government (Salter, 1997).

Disaster reduction programmes are investments to reduce the likely impact of a disaster and need to be developed by government departments and sectors (such as finance, environment, agriculture, health, education, construction, industry, social protection and community services) as well as scientists, non-government organisations and the general public. As Christoplos (2003) suggests, government are not often interested in disaster mitigation or preparedness unless the threat of disaster is imminent, perhaps in a similar vein to organisational managers. The ISDR (2004) has developed a disaster risk reduction framework (see Figure 4.2), which sets out the core components of risk reduction. As discussed earlier, the context for disaster planning and management is associated with the concept of *sustainable development*, which in a broad and holistic sense encompasses economic, socio-cultural, political, and environmental elements.

From a tourism disaster perspective, there is a need to consider reducing disasters to save tourism businesses or destination's substantial economic costs if vulnerability or risk can be reduced or managed. Furthermore, a disaster which impacts upon a destination (especially a developing country) could have a major sociocultural impact if the local community are perhaps reliant on income from tourism activities. Politically, government need to be aware of the impacts and tools available to sustain their residents in the long term and should act, while the environment also should be sustained and not impacted negatively through human activity. If local populations, or indeed tourists, can be more respectful of the environment, then hazards and disasters may be reduced. These are the more long-term aspects that can impact on vulnerability. Environmentally unsound practices, global environmental changes, population growth, urbanisation, social injustice, poverty, and short-term economic vision are all attributes that can create more vulnerable societies.

Natural disasters are providing a real threat to poverty reduction and sustainable development as relief funding is required, diverting financial resources away from poverty alleviation unless relief funding is directed at improving livelihood outcomes (see Chapter 8). In particular,

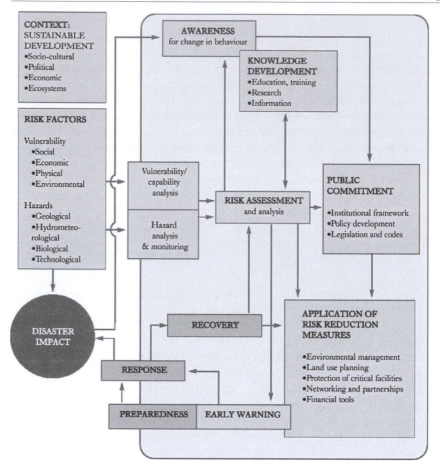

Figure 4.2 Framework for disaster risk reduction
Source: ISDR (2004: 15).

in developing countries including small islands, natural disasters are having a large impact upon their environmental resources and also their tourism industry, severely impacting upon their livelihoods. Furthermore, as Christoplos (2003: 97) notes, 'efforts to understand how poor people perceive and deal with their poverty have highlighted how their livelihood strategies are often more about addressing vulnerability and handling shocks than about "escaping" from poverty *per se*'. Therefore, the debate about disaster (and tourism disaster) prevention and reduction should be considered in the broader context and framework of development and sustainable development.

Risk factors relate to both vulnerability and the likely frequency and magnitude of hazards in a particular destination. Risks can be both involuntary (which most hazards are classified as) or voluntary (such as human-induced hazards like pollution), with involuntary risks tolerated more by the public, according to Smith (1995). Kates and Kasperson (1983) suggest that *risk assessment*, similar to an organisational risk management framework, consists of three distinct steps:

(1) An identification of hazards likely to result in disasters. For instance, what hazardous events may occur?
(2) An estimation of the risks of such events. For instance, what is the probability of each event?
(3) An evaluation of the social consequences of the derived risk. For instance, what is the loss created by each event?

However, as Smith (1995) notes, very few questions occur after risk assessment to assess the actual impact of mitigation or protective measures, which constrains our understanding of hazard reduction and its value. Furthermore, the WTO (1998) suggest that any risk analysis and assessment should include the indirect impacts of a disaster including secondary losses from death and injury, loss of function of essential services, loss of markets and interruption to tourism. Smith (1995) suggests a risk equation based on the three questions outlined above:

$$R \text{ (risk)} = P \text{ (probability)} \times L \text{ (loss)}$$

However, risk assessment involves not only identification, estimation and evaluation of risk but also should consider the ability of the population to cope or deal with such risks and should therefore include this capacity element in any risk assessment equation, such as the following from the ISDR (2004):

$$\text{Risk} = \text{Hazard (H)} \times \text{Vulnerability (V)}/\text{Capacity (C)}$$

or

$$\text{Risk} = \text{function of (H and V/C)}$$

Vulnerability can be related to both the vulnerability to the hazard, and also a concept called underlying vulnerability (Allen, 2003) that relates to a contextual weakness or susceptibility underpinning daily life (such as market forces and policy trends like globalisation), which create the vulnerable situation. Vulnerability can include the following four main types:

(1) *Physical vulnerability* includes aspects such as location, density of population, and design of physical infrastructure. Examples of physical vulnerability include businesses or populations located in flood plains or houses/businesses built without earthquake-resistant building materials.

(2) *Economic vulnerability* includes the capacity of a destination of individual to respond to huge economic losses that often occur from disasters and is closely linked to debt levels and financial reserves of countries. Furthermore, a destination whose economy is not diversified and reliant on a small number of economic sectors could also be vulnerable to disasters on those sectors (such as tourism in the case of small island states). Ultimately, the poorer individuals or countries are less able to respond to disasters and therefore need economic assistance for response and recovery from disasters.

(3) *Ecological vulnerability* includes elements such as levels of environmental degradation, loss of biodiversity, loss of resilience of the ecological system which could create increased vulnerability to natural disasters.

(4) *Social vulnerability* includes organisational and governance structures which combined could cause a greater increase in vulnerability amongst groups such as women, those from ethnic minority groups and disabled people who are often more vulnerable groups of the population during disasters.

An understanding of vulnerability and risk are important in understanding how disasters may be mitigated or prevented, which is discussed in the following section. Risk assessment requires information concerning natural hazards, previous natural disasters and their responses and there is a direct link (as suggested in Figure 4.2) between *knowledge development* and risk assessment/analysis. Risk assessment and analysis, therefore is dependant upon an analysis of the risk likelihood, potential loss, vulnerability and the capacity of the local population to deal or cope with this loss or impact. Risk assessment and analysis may follow the following steps outlined in Figure 4.3. *Risk analysis* is concerned with two steps:

(1) Determining the location, intensity and probability of a hazard occurring. The WTO (1998) suggest regional hazard and microzoning maps for the area under study. For more details on techniques such as hazard mapping (through Geographical Information Systems), quantitative risk analysis and extreme event analysis, see Smith (1995).

(2) Determining susceptibilities/vulnerabilities and the capacity of society to cope with hazards.

Geipel (1982) ranked levels of community impact in a manner that implies a continuum between minimal effects and total collapse. Granot (1995) believes that there are few objective measures of resilience challenging Geipel's (1982) continuum by suggesting that the effect of

Identification of Risk Factors	
Hazard	*Vulnerability/Capacities*
Determines geographical location, intensity and probability through hazard mapping use of historical data to produce quantitative risk analysis and extreme event analysis.	Determines susceptibilities and capacities to cope through community-based mapping and risk perceptions analysis of economic, social, environmental and physical vulnerabilities.
Estimates levels of risk	
Evaluates risk	
Socio-economic cost/benefit analysis Establishment of priorities Establishment of acceptable levels of risk Elaboration of scenarios and measures	

RISK ANALYSIS

RISK ASSESSMENT

Figure 4.3 Stages of risk analysis and assessment
Source: Modified after ISDR (2004) and Smith (1995).

a disaster on a community might be more similar to the percolation principle, which sees changing states as being non-linear. He suggests that, once a certain threshold is crossed in a sufficient number of constituent subsystems, a basic change takes place in the community system as a whole, affecting its overall capacity to cope (Granot, 1995: 6). Factors affecting a community's capacity to cope can include:

- community background factors (relevant demographic, socio-economic, political, cultural, organisational and resource level characteristics);
- event factors (objective factors precipitating the cause or causes of the incident); and
- impact factors (immediate discernible outcome, as reflected in such factors as number of casualties, property damage, etc.).

Gathering information on hazard risks and vulnerability requires the collection of data to assist in the development of policies and plans by national governments and insurance organisations. For instance, in New Zealand they use a six-point risk evaluation strategy (in Salter, 1997: 63) which:

(1) Determines the significance of estimated risks (in absolute and comparative terms).
(2) Considers acceptability (in terms of individual and societal tolerance).
(3) Examines economic impact and funding options for response and recovery.

(4) Examines costs and benefits of control for the most serious risks.
(5) Assesses cost–risk–benefit balance.
(6) Decides whether to accept, reduce or transfer risk.

However, data on risk analysis and assessment is often not widely disseminated and although hazard mapping is common, it is less common to map the susceptibilities or vulnerabilities of the local community or a tourism destination. For instance, a project in the 1980s which integrated both hazard mapping and vulnerabilities, noted that the main airports of Guatemala are located near high-intensity seismic areas (in ISDR, 2004). Cairns, Australia is one of the few tourism destinations to have produced risk maps using GIS to understand landslide risk (Michael-Leiba *et al.*, 2000). Becken and Hay (2007) and the IPCC (2007) propose a risk-based approach to dealing with the challenges and opportunities of climate change. In particular, Becken and Hay (2007) consider the risks associated with climate change on: (1) appeal of the destination by tourists, (2) impact on both transport infrastructure and operations (including investment in new attractions infrastructure and reinvestment in existing infrastructure), (3) human and natural resource base, (4) tourist health, safety and satisfaction, and (5) sustainability of facilities and the destination.

The development of cost/benefit analysis based on community and government priorities and interests develops acceptable limits of risk. However, risks are dependant upon risk perception and the level of threat anticipated by decision-makers (Smith, 1995), often founded on Newtonian science which searches for interrelationships between variables. These techniques described in the crisis prevention section, including forecasting techniques such as the expert judgement or Delphi approach. As Robert and Lajtha (2002) note, risk analysis uses a rational approach considering probability and severity, whereas low probability events do occur creating huge damage to society. They suggest the need for more unconventional techniques in the planning for crises and disasters. Local communities can provide their levels of perceived risk, which combined with more objective statistics and data can provide a more accurate information to base decisions upon. The final area of *risk assessment* is concerned with the development of scenarios and measures which can help government and communities consider the variety of risk reduction measures available to help with the mitigation or reduction of hazards and disasters, which is the subject of the next section.

Considering mitigation measures

Mitigation and reduction of hazards and potential disasters is required at an international, national, regional, local and individual level. These different levels indicate that the concepts of vulnerability, risk and capacity could be viewed on many different scales from international to individual. McEntire (1999, 2001), considering the concept of vulnerability, suggests the need for invulnerable development which is broadly defined as vulnerability management. In this context, McEntire (2001: 193) suggests that the concept of invulnerable development is an attempt to:

- link development activities to vulnerability reduction;
- formulate a culture of safety, prevention and preparedness amongst all individuals, families, groups, businesses, organisations, communities, and nations around the world; and
- increase the capacities, cooperation, coordination and effectiveness of all public, private and non-profit organisations and agencies involved or related to disaster management and vulnerability reduction (building disaster management institutions).

Strategies need to be developed to address previous and potential vulnerabilities through a combination of structural and non-structural measures. Mitigation attempts to reduce vulnerability to climate change impacts and build resilience and capacity (Becken & Hay, 2007; IPCC, 2007). Although authors such as Allen (2003) believe that reducing vulnerability to natural disasters (or single events) may not help minimise underlying vulnerability (such as economic needs). This emphasises again that the context of disaster reduction and prevention should be given in the broader context of development and sustainable development. As Christoplos (2003: 96) suggests, development actors downplay vulnerability and tend to emphasis economic development as they link poverty to a lack on income, not human suffering as a result of a variety of vulnerabilities. Invulnerable development is about the planning and implementation of safer development practices, beliefs and behaviour which can act as triggering agents for natural disasters. The focus on vulnerability is because, as McEntire (2001: 194) observes, '... humans are able to control vulnerabilities, not natural hazards'. Breaking out of vulnerability may require not only new development paradigms but also new ways of conceptualising vulnerability which take into consideration broader social and economic vulnerability, not just vulnerability to specific events or natural hazards. As discussed in Chapter 2, vulnerability to natural hazards can leave some communities more vulnerable to further disasters or crises indicating more emphasis on reducing vulnerability through long-term planning and development measures.

Community, industry and tourist altitudes toward natural hazards and risk are important to consider. For instance, the public plays an important role in prevention and preparedness and should understand how to manage if a natural disaster hits. However, as Larsson and Enander (1997) suggest, people tend not to be interested in preparedness and believe that they are less vulnerable than others. The role of social norms and values and the level of preparedness are under researched, especially with respect to tourism, yet vital to help formulate strategies to encourage preparation and response of tourists and locals in vulnerable locations. Different messages and information may be required for the local community, tourism industry and tourists themselves as well as specific segments from all groups.

According to Hoogenraad *et al.* (2004), independent travellers and tourists are more vulnerable to natural hazards as they travel outside of formal groups and some may take more risks, while Murphy and Bayley (1989) suggested that tourists tend to ignore risk and show a low level of natural disaster awareness. Yet, tourists are widely regarded as being more vulnerable towards natural disasters as they are unfamiliar with local conditions and resources (Buckle *et al.*, 2001; WTO, 1998). Research in the US suggested that 46% of visitors were unaware of tsunami warning systems compared to 28% of locals and only 19% of visitors had seen tsunami hazard maps (Johnston *et al.*, 2002 in Johnston *et al.*, 2007). A study of backpackers in North Queensland, Australia suggests that backpackers have a low awareness of cyclones and only 30% received information concerning cyclones during their trip, with main information sources including word of mouth and the television (Hoogenraad *et al.*, 2004). The vast majority surveyed did not understand the level of storms or what key characteristics of cyclones were (a storm surge, likelihood of occurrence, etc.). The researchers suggested the need to provide destination cyclone information in pamphlets and the internet, while information on cyclones could be provided in backpacker media (such as guidebooks and backpacker magazines).

Visitors to Northern Queensland after Cyclone Larry hit in 2007 were asked about their information sources about Tropical Cyclone Larry, with over 43% noting information on the cyclone came through television, followed by other information sources including newspapers (19.9%) and friends or relatives in North Queensland (13%), according to Prideaux *et al.* (2007). However, domestic visitors had a high propensity to use the television while international visitors used the internet in greater numbers. A total of 57.9% of respondents outlined that the cyclone did not affect their satisfaction with their trip, or had impacted very little (33.5%) on their satisfaction. Only 8.6% indicated that the cyclone had a strong impact on their satisfaction. These respondents were more likely to be first time visitors to the region than repeat visitors (Prideaux *et al.*, 2007).

Smith (1995: 66) notes three major intentional adjustments to hazards: modifying the loss burden, adjusting damaging events to people, and finally, adjusting people to hazard events. In all of these instances, both structural (through engineering and other physical protective measures) and non-structural (through legislation, codes and urban planning) measures can be used by, or imposed on the tourism industry.

Modifying the loss

Modifying the loss burden by spreading the financial burden as widely as possible through relief and insurance schemes. These are loss-sharing or risk-transfer rather than loss-reduction and are perhaps a reactive and limited response to disasters. However, as Smith (1995) notes, disaster aid and insurance can be used to a limited extent to encourage future loss reduction. For instance, there is some possibility of insurance not covering some countries or regions if mitigation does not occur according to Salt (2003) who provides examples of hurricanes, volcanic explosions and floods where the insurance industry has demanded action to reduce vulnerability and risk. For instance, the UK insurance industry demanded after a recent series of floods that the government spend more on flood defences or they would deny cover in various parts of the UK. Salt (2003) suggests that due to current changes to climate the insurance industry could, in the future, refuse to claim parts of the world most susceptible to disasters. As Becken and Hay (2007: 59) suggest, '[i]nsurance is critical for tourism. In many cases it allows the tourism industry to spread the residual climate-related risks that cannot be avoided by other adaptation measures'.

Furthermore, the ISDR (2004) observed how international and regional development banks (such as the World Bank), who have provided many of the funds for post-disaster recovery, are promoting investment in disaster reduction strategies and plans to assist countries with their economic and social development. Insurance companies may also provide reduction in premiums if businesses engage in hazard mitigation strategies, especially if building codes or land-use planning regulations are adhered to. This may work in developed countries where the insurance industry is well developed but may be difficult to implement in less developed countries. Such measures are required to deal with issues concerning economic vulnerability to natural disasters, which have created severe economic problems for those countries tourism industries.

Event modification

A more proactive response to hazards and natural disasters is to reduce losses by adjusting damaging events to people. Some natural hazards can be suppressed at the source through some kind of environmental control engineering. Furthermore, hazard-resistant design and emergency measures can safeguard human life and property in high-risk areas. However, as Smith (1995) notes, controlling the environment is extremely difficult and can only successfully occur if human prevention can ensure that the hazard is contained. Hazard mapping and knowledge on types of hazards can be used to modify the hazard event itself through creating rock walls in coastal areas, setting off controlled avalanches in mountains, creating dams and flood control reservoirs to prevent river flooding and so forth. This approach is concerned with preventing hazards becoming natural disasters. However, such work may only be effective if begun years in advance of the hazard event, and human interference can exacerbate or cause subsequent future problems by contributing towards vulnerability and the increased incidence of natural disasters such as floods (Mileti, 1999). For instance, huge hydraulic projects may change landscape references of communities and their perception of risk, thereby increasing vulnerability by reducing the people's capacity to assess and anticipate hazard-related threats. The construction of engineering works on a river may offer protection from floods and encourage invasion of the floodplain with an increase in risk because of pressures on land for tourism development (WTO, 1998).

For reducing physical vulnerability, important facilities or infrastructure for tourism (such as roads, airports, accommodation stock and communications infrastructure) can be better designed to withstand hazards in the future, while mechanisms can be implemented to make current infrastructure more hazard resistant, although not all can be protected against hazards in high-risk areas (Mileti, 1999). For instance, Switzerland has recognised the value of forests in protecting important economic assets (roads, industries, infrastructure, tourism) as well as human settlements and people against avalanches and landslides. The economy provided by the protection afforded by forests was estimated between US$2 billion and US$3.5 billion per year (OFEFP, 1999). The infrastructure such as roads and hotels can be made more hazard resistant in high-risk areas, dramatically reducing potential losses. As Mèheux and Parker (2006) note, cyclone shutters and anchoring structures can be used in cyclone-prone tourism destinations. The aim of planning, according to the WTO (1998), is to prevent the triggering of hazards and regulate its impact through changes to the physical site of tourism infrastructure reducing the likelihood of a hazard becoming a disaster. Furthermore, low-density tourism development in areas vulnerable to flood (such as rivers, lakes and coasts) are more likely to require a reduction in risk (WTO, 1998). The use of information such as hazard maps or past histories of natural hazards can be used to provide better building codes and design to protect key tourism infrastructure from hazards.

However, hazard-resistant techniques can not only be applied to new buildings, but also by modifying existing buildings through retrofitting to better protect it or its contents from an event. Walls that may be susceptible to earthquake damage can be reinforced or braced, while heavy furniture can be strapped to walls to protect it from damage, by making walls watertight and fitting flood-resistant doors and windows

(Smith, 1995). Rock walls on coastal areas may be created to limit beach erosion and sand dune loss, which may be necessary in tourist destinations, which are prone to natural hazards. However, as Smith (1995) rightly notes, the majority of the costs of retrofitting (and mitigation of potential disaster) are borne by property owners and not the government. Incentives may be able to be provided by government to assist those living or working in hazardous locations to implement better design for future constructions (through tax incentives) and for retro-fitting for current developments (through some funding schemes to help property owners protect themselves). Local government is also respon-sible in enforcing building codes, which was noted by Kouzmin *et al.* (1995) as lacking prior to Australia's Newcastle earthquake which caused more than A$3 billion of damage.

Other mechanisms that may be used to reduce the likelihood of ecological disasters could include the development of programmes by government or non-governmental organisations to facilitate good envir-onmental practices in both developed and developing countries. For instance, conservation projects involving better wetland management or water treatment may help communities to sustain the environment which they are a part of and reduce the likelihood of future environ-mental disasters and global environmental change which may impact upon the tourism appeal of a destination.

Vulnerability modification

The largest group of responses is concerned with modifying human vulnerability by adjusting people to damaging events. This can be through legislation, voluntary acts and raising awareness of hazard-prone locations. Land-use planning is one of the largest methods of modifying and reducing vulnerability of humans to hazards. Land-use plans enable local governments to gather and analyse information about the suitability of land for development, so that the limitations of hazard-prone areas are understood by policy-makers, potential investors and community residents. Physical and spatial planning has a vital role to play to detect areas that are prone to hazards and restrict their use to reduce vulnerability to disasters. Human settlement planning systems have a major in modifying vulnerability (Skertchly & Skertchly, 2001). This form of planning is usually undertaken at a local governmental level and is vital as population growth expands into areas that are more susceptible to hazards for living or recreational/tourism purposes. Examples include the growth of populations to coastal areas and the construction of development and ski resorts into mountain areas. By their very nature, mountain and coastal areas can be hazardous locations for residents and visitors. Land-use planners need to first identify and evaluate high-risk areas (through risk analysis/assessment and hazard mapping) before a number of measures can be used to reduce the vulnerability associated with the land-use area. Smith (1995: 98–99) notes a number of measures that can be used to reduce vulnerability through land-use planning:

(1)   Public acquisition of hazard-prone land and management of an area for public safety or low-density development, or if this is too costly, local government may purchase land and either sell it with certain conditions, or lease it for low-intensity use or it may exchange hazardous land for safer land elsewhere, if businesses are willing to relocate.

(2)   Land zoning can develop zones through regulations and ordinances to again use vulnerable areas (such as areas susceptible to landslides or earthquakes) for low-density development or open spaces for parks or grazing. However, this land may appear attractive to developers who may perceive the local government as being overly cautious.

(3)   Public education and voluntary methods which may include guidelines or laws where builders, developers and the like disclose existence of hazards to prospective buyers. Other education tools could include signage, posters, conferences and community work-shops to raise awareness of hazards and disaster mitigation.

(4)   Financial measures such as tax incentives, loans, insurance or grants or the like can be used to provide an incentive to public and private organisations to use land located in hazard-prone areas.

Smith (1995) alludes to the potential conflict amongst stakeholders concerning land-use planning and perceptions of land value. This is one of the major issues in using land-use planning to reduce vulnerability to tourism disasters, especially as tourists and the tourism industry may be attracted to areas which are vulnerable to natural hazards (such as beaches, riverside camping areas, mountains, etc.). For instance, on the Gold Coast of Australia (which is a 40 km long and 3 km wide stretch of land on the Queensland coast) many hotels have been allowed to build on the sand dune with little in the way of planning regulations or a buffer zone between the sea and the dunes. The increasing pressure for ocean views have led to the encroachment on the dune ridge and affected dune regeneration and vegetation. Furthermore, tourism development has facilitated urbanisation resulting in the dredging of the river and coastal flood plains to create a network of canals (for housing development) with the soil deposited on the flood plain. During wet weather, the flood plains can no longer accommodate excess water and this creates flooding problems up stream leading to serious flooding in recent years. The over reliance on tourism in the Gold Coast has meant that planning regulations have been lax so as to encourage investment and continued economic growth from tourism. Certain countries are heavily dependent upon specific economic sectors and perhaps need to diversify economically to reduce their vulnerability if their major or only economic activity is destroyed through a natural disaster. For instance, small island states located in the Pacific Islands and in the Caribbean rely heavily on tourism and are also susceptible to hurricanes and cyclones impacting negatively upon the tourism industry. Other countries may be more reliant on other economic sectors such as agriculture, and therefore should diversify into other sectors (possibly even tourism) to limit their economic vulnerability.

Allen (2003) for instance, noted in the case of Tigabo in the Philippines that although dredging and diverting a flood-prone stream helped with reducing event-centred vulnerability, the underlying economic vulnerability to farmers was not addressed. Allen (2003) suggested diversification through the development of a livelihood scheme to provide extra sources of revenue to fall back on if further flooding or other incidents occurred. In the Havana Province of Cuba, a project has recommended that in order to reduce disaster risk for coastal settlements in this area, a number of direct and indirect measures were required. Direct measures included to:

- prohibit the construction of vacation houses in existing settlements;
- relocate the population vulnerable to disasters;
- regulate and supervise the construction of new homes in the settlements;
- retrofit and build homes adapted to flood conditions;
- improve the drainage systems in and around the settlements;
- improve the adequacy of potable water supplies and sanitation systems;
- improve health and transportation services; and
- create employment opportunities.

Indirect measures included to:

- improve the natural resilience of beaches;
- improve the water irrigation systems near the coast; and
- rehabilitate the wetlands.

Although this may occur in an industry such as farming or agriculture, these sort of schemes or proposals are often not suggested for tourism-reliant destinations or the tourism industry.

Conclusion

This chapter has outlined the role of organisational strategic planning to prevent or reduce the chance of crisis and the role of disaster reduction and mitigation. Although forecasting techniques can signify the like-lihood of emerging crises and disasters, they are limited with respect to their forecasting of immediate shocks including economic and political crises. As this chapter has argued, despite the growing threat of global environmental change and natural disasters to tourism businesses and destinations, few tourism businesses are prepared to handle the impacts of such threats, yet crisis and disaster planning should be a core competency of tourism managers. The chapter also outlined key literature from the hazards, natural disasters and emergency manage-ment field to consider ways that environmental risks and natural disasters may be reduced or mitigated. Understanding risk and vulner-ability and their broader links to sustainable development and sustain-able tourism are vital and suggest the need for long-term reduction of global environmental change and natural disasters. The concept of 'invulnerable development' should be considered in combination with structural and non-structural mitigation measures.

If prevention or mitigation of crises and disasters are not possible, then contingency plans have to be developed and tested for dealing with these incidents at an organisational and destination level. Chapter 5 outlines crisis and disaster planning and preparedness for tourism organisations and destinations.

Chapter 5

Tourism Disaster and Crisis Preparedness and Planning

Introduction

There are two major interrelated stages related to disaster planning and prevention according to Kim and Lee (1998: 191), prevention and mitigation (outlined in the previous chapter) and pre-disaster preparedness (outlined in this chapter). Pre-disaster preparedness involves the development of emergency plans, warning systems and other activities adopted in advance of a disaster to aid in its management. At an organisational level crises, contingency plans should be developed which include the formulation of a Crisis Management Team (CMT), the development of manuals and procedures, staff training and simulation exercises. All of these activities can help ensure an organisation is prepared and able to respond more effectively to incidents. The chapter concludes by discussing the level of tourism crisis and disaster planning and the need for such planning in a crisis/disaster-prone and vulnerable industry.

Disaster Preparedness: Emergency Planning

In conjunction with risk analysis and assessment and the development of reduction or mitigation strategies, comes the development of preparedness strategies or emergency plans that can help if a disaster or emergency occurs. This preparation is a key area for providing strength and resilience to disasters and therefore can reduce the vulnerability of communities (Blaikie *et al.*, 1994). As Alexander (2000) notes, emergency planning and emergency management need to be viewed as linked activities as planning creates the structure for managing disasters. However, as Quarantelli (1988) suggests, the management of disasters does not automatically follow from planning because there is often a gap between planning and actual response to a major disaster. Two main reasons for this gap are noted by Quarantelli (1988):

(1) Disaster preparedness may be poor in the first instance. If plans are too specific or segmented, then implementation will simply be of poor confused planning.
(2) That crisis management (of disasters) and disaster planning follow different principles. Disaster planning may assume that management will automatically occur through the implementation of plans.

> Good disaster preparedness involves the formulation of plans or strategies to deal with disasters and emergencies, but disaster or emergency management is based on tactics, which may follow the general strategy or plan with changes due to the situation or context of the disaster.

The statement above is confirmed by Alexander (2000: 163) who suggests that good emergency planning consists of a combination of prior preparedness and ad hoc improvisation, with planning and education central to preparation.

In this chapter, only disaster and emergency planning will be discussed, along with crisis planning and preparation. Discussion concerning disaster and emergency management or response (as with crisis management or response) will occur in the following section of this book (Part 3). However, the two are obviously linked and there needs to be both attempts at prevention and planning as well as the management of incidents. If disasters cannot be prevented or mitigated and do hit and cause damage, then these strategies and systems can be used to try and limit the damage to society and business. In the emergency phase, disaster management will most likely use modified tactics and plans devised during the disaster preparation phase. As Robert and Lajtha (2002: 184) note, emergency response and disaster plans have many problems and can be worse than having no plans at all. The major problems noted include that they:

- are written as compliance gestures rather than realistic operating guidelines;
- are often out of date by the time that they are published and are not updated;
- are often not in appropriate formats;
- remain unknown to key persons who are likely to be involved in any response; and
- contain elements of useless information.

As Turner (1994), Quarantelli (1984), Cassedy (1991) and Drabek (1995) note, there is a need for strategy development and the testing of disaster strategy (see Table 5.1). Faulkner (2001) in his proposed tourism disaster framework connects planning and strategy to specific stages of the tourism disaster lifecycle (discussed in Chapter 2). He notes a series of precursors which connect to risk assessment and the creation of contingency plans as well as factors which help the destination mobilise at the prodromal stage when it becomes apparent that the hazard is about to hit (see Figure 3.5). The following sections examine these factors in more detail with regards to disaster preparation and strategic planning.

Table 5.1 Potential ingredients of a disaster and tourism disaster strategy

Strategy development	*Implementation*
• Form disaster recovery committee and convene meetings for the purpose of sharing information • Risk assessment (identify possible threats/disasters and prioritise in terms of probability of occurrence – real, likely and historical threats. Perhaps stimulated by a definition and classification of potential disasters) • Analysis of anticipated short- and long-term impacts • Identification of strategies for avoiding/minimising impacts, critical actions necessary, chain of command for coordination, responsibilities and resources • Prepare and disseminate manual and secure commitment from responsible parties and relevant agencies. Relevant contact information must be included.	• Holding disaster drills, rehearsals and simulations • Developing techniques for training, knowledge transfer and assessments • Formulating memoranda of understanding and mutual aid agreements • Educating the public and others involved in the planning process • Obtaining, positioning and maintaining relevant material resources • Undertaking public educational activities • Establishing informal linkages between involved groups • Thinking and communicating information about future dangers and hazards • Drawing up organisational disaster plans and integrating them with overall community mass emergency plans • Continually updating obsolete materials/strategies

Tourism disaster strategy ingredients

• *Selection of a team leader:* a senior person with authority and ability to command respect (ability to communicate effectively, prioritise and manage multiple tasks, delegate, coordinate and control, work cohesively with a crisis management team, and make decisions quickly)
• *Team development:* permanent and integral feature of strategic planning; able to identify and analyse possible crises and develop contingency plans
• *Contingency plan:* including mechanism for activating the plan, possible crisis, objectives, worst-case scenario, trigger mechanism
• *Actions:* strategic actions including gathering information and developing relations with other agencies and stakeholders internal and external to the tourism industry. But also tactical or operational action plan of assigned tasks including warning, confirmation, mobilisation, providing customer information and shelters, dealing with employee concerns, transportation, looting and pre-entry issues
• *Crisis management command centre:* a specific location and facility with relevant communication and other resources for the crisis management team

Source: Turner (1994), Quarantelli (1984), Cassedy (1991), Drabek (1995) modified after Faulkner (2001: 141–143).

Disaster Preparedness: Precursors

Faulkner (2001) proposes a series of precursors which should occur at the pre-event stage of a disaster for more effective tourism disaster management. First, because of the range of private and public sector organisations that are directly and indirectly involved in the tourism system, the development and implementation of a tourism disaster strategy requires a coordinated team-based approach. A designated tourism Disaster Management Team (DMT) should be established to work in conjunction with various other public sector planning agencies and providers of emergency services in order to ensure that the tourism industry's action plan dovetails with that of these other parties. Second, consultation both within the tourism sector and between tourism and the broader community should be integrated with other strategic planning processes (such as land-use planning and broader economic development plans). Third, Faulkner (2001: 145) stresses the need for commitment between stakeholders and states:

> no matter how thoroughly and skillfully the disaster management plan may be developed, and regardless of the level of consultation that takes place in the process, it will be of limited value if the various parties involved are not committed to it and all individuals who are required to take action are not aware of it.

Therefore, any plan should also include clear protocols regarding the activation of the strategy and a communication/education programme aimed at ensuring that all parties understand what is expected of them, which is especially important for those organisations and staff involved directly with tourists. In particular, tour operators and resort managers should be involved in strategy development, contingency planning and testing to ensure that their staff and individual tourists are properly informed and/or evacuated in any disaster or emergency situation. Risk analysis and assessment as well as a community capabilities audit should be carried out, as discussed in the previous chapter (Chapter 4), to examine the likely scenarios and impacts of disasters and during the pre-event stage of the disaster lifecycle. This risk analysis and assessment should also be linked to disaster or scenario-specific contingency plans for the management of tourism disasters (discussed below).

Disaster Preparedness: Mobilisation and Warning Systems

Forecasts attempt to detect and evaluate an event as it evolves and attempts to specify the timing, location and magnitude of an impending event. However, the lead time for such warnings are usually short and forecasts are generally limited to warnings given to the general public (Smith, 1995). According to Smith (1995), combined forecasting and warning systems can be effective in averting disaster through short-term response, often involving evacuation. Smith (1995) notes three main stages of warning and mobilisation:

(1) *Evaluation.* This stage involves detecting the hazard, examining the scale and intensity and then issuing a warning if there is risk involved to people or property. The evaluation task is usually associated with a national agency such as a meteorological agency or geological service if the hazard poses a risk at a regional or national level. The accuracy of the forecast and the lead time between the warning and onset is crucial for the community to take effective action. However, forecasters often have to make difficult decisions in short periods of time, and if they suggest evacuation when no threat occurs, then they may be liable for civil action by affected tourism businesses.

(2) *Dissemination.* This requires transmitting the warning from the specialist agency to the hazard zone occupants usually through media communications (such as TV or radio) or through personnel (such as police, emergency services or neighbours). The WTO (1998) for instance, suggest that tour operators should be involved in destination contingency planning and should be involved in the dissemination of, and response to, warnings and any required response.

(3) *Response:* Those in the hazard-prone area should undertake loss-reducing actions. This may include securing facilities, evacuating staff and guests or leaving the hazard area.

Technology has helped improve the detection and warning of natural hazards, although technological failure can result in disaster. Many natural hazards can be warned against through warning systems with the most important way to mitigate risks associated with cyclones through effective warning systems (WTO, 1998). However, smaller localised hazard warning and mobilisation may rest with tour guides or operators, particularly for adventure tourism activities. One example is the Swiss Cannoning river disaster in Interlaken where 21 people died as a result of a heavy thunderstorm which sent a torrent of water and rocks down the river canyon. Although the thunderstorm had been forecast in weather reports and could be seen from the start point of the trip, the trips down the river were not cancelled. The thunderstorm sent a wall of water through the group which killed 18 tourists and three tour guides. The company, Adventure World, were found guilty of man-slaughter through culpable negligence. Evidence from the trial suggested a lack of training for tour guides to detect and monitor river conditions and a lack of knowledge of where forecasts could be found. This example suggests the need for adventure tourism operators to carefully consider staff training in accessing timely information and forecasts and detecting possible risks as a result of natural hazards. This is especially important for commercial tour operations as tourists place their trust in tour operators to assess risk and vulnerability on their behalf.

Disaster Preparedness: Contingency Plans and Simulation Exercises

The effectiveness of disaster plans will be limited unless those who are required to implement them are directly involved in their development and testing (Quarantelli, 1984). Pforr and Hosie (2007) argued that Human Resource Development (HRD) is an important aspect of any well conceived and executed preparation for crisis management. Contingency plans can be developed in advance of a natural hazard or disaster, and in conjunction with risk analysis and assessment, can be useful for targeting vulnerable groups and areas of a tourism destination. According to Faulkner (2001), contingency plans can identify specific actions required at each stage of the disaster lifecycle and devise tactical actions (which may be revised in the light of experience, changes to the organisational structures and personnel or changes in the environment).

According to the WTO (1998), contingency plans for tourism disasters could include the following five areas:

(1) *Employee coordination.* Employees should be aware of their roles and responsibilities in a tourism disaster and resort managers should be aware of what staff members they need and which ones are immediately able to make preparations with their respective families (which may live in the affected area).

(2) *Protecting and assisting guests and staff.* Guests look to staff for advice and assistance in times of trouble and so in room information should include hazard checklists (such as earthquakes and fire information) in guest rooms. When it is apparent that a hazard will hit, resort managers or staff can distribute specific information packs related to the hazard. Previous experience suggests the need for resort managers and staff to keep guest records to alert the authorities to who is in residence, who has departed and where visitors intended to go. The resort staff should also be trained on dealing with guests who specifically check in or out prior to the onset of a hazard. Evacuating tourists during a hazard has advantages and disadvantages. First, they have a place of origin that they can return to if appropriate and are more responsive to evacuation arrangements. However, they often have little experience of a natural disaster, have limited familiarity with the area, local practices and maybe even the language. All of these factors may require special attention from

tour operators and resort managers. This uniqueness of tourists involved in disasters is further elaborated by Faulkner and Vikulov (2001: 334) in discussing the Katherine Floods in Australia in 1998, 'it might be argued that visitors to Katherine at the time were potentially more vulnerable when the disaster hit because they were in a strange and unfamiliar environment, and less independent in terms of the action necessary to ensure their personal safety. On the other hand, it may have been a less traumatic experience for them, because they did not have the same emotional attachment to the place (Katherine) as the residents, and they were not witnessing the destruction of everything they owned'. Furthermore, staff should also consider those guests who are more vulnerable to the impact of a disaster such as the young, elderly or disabled people, and consider specific strategies to deal with their vulnerability. This was also noted by Drabek (2000) whose research suggested the need for specific strategies to deal with non-English speaking guests and guests with pets during a disaster.

(3) *Travel assistance and transport coordination.* According to Drabek (2000), the high level of uncertainty that guests may face as a result of perhaps being less aware of the area may affect their ability to make wise personnel choices. Tourists will look to resort managers or tour operators for information about the status of transport infrastructure such as road, rail and airport facilities and the tourism industry should be able to provide information of travel assistance or transportation.

(4) *Emergency shelter coordination.* Large resorts or even attractions such as museums may serve as emergency shelter either before or immediately after a disaster. Areas of the resort or attraction that are lower in risk should be designated as places suitable for shelter from hazards. Logistical planning of food, sanitary facilities, blankets and space must be identified and prepared prior to any disaster. Furthermore, guests should be made aware of shelter locations.

(5) *Advertising and press communication preparation.* Resorts or industry groups may need to prepare advertising and press communication strategy prior to any disaster. For instance, Caribbean resorts and councils have a stock of advertising copy, which need minor alterations to be used as an advertising tool in the recovery process. Similarly, the media will require certain facts and information regarding any disaster and a list of contact people to talk with. Identifying key individuals to talk to including a spokesperson from the DMT is a vital part of preparation.

Tourism Disaster Planning Research

To date, most research concerned with tourism disasters has focused on response and recovery, and not preparation, mitigation or readiness. Few studies have been carried out concerning tourists or the effectiveness of tourism disaster planning at a regional or organisational level, with the exception of Drabek (1995, 1996, 1999, 2000), Murphy and Bayley (1989), Faulkner and Vikulov (2001) and Johnston et al. (2007). More recent studies have been undertaken which include industry perceptions of natural hazards (Mèheux & Parker, 2006), or research which includes some focus on preparation alongside general research on response and recovery to tourism disasters (see Cioccio & Michael, 2007; Hystad & Keller, 2006, 2008).

Understanding perceptions of risk are important as a precursor to developing tourism disaster planning, according to Mèheux and Parker (2006), with higher risk perceptions leading to more advanced planning, mitigation and preparedness. Primary research, comparing tourism industry perceptions of natural hazards with secondary data, illustrated that the majority of respondents in an island destination accurately perceived the likelihood of damaging hazard events, with the exception of volcanic hazards which were overestimated, while 27%, respectively, overestimated the likelihood of a tsunami or sea level rise, perhaps due to previous experience and history with these types of hazards (Mèheux & Parker, 2006).

However, as Cioccio and Michael (2007) note, business owners located in bush fire-prone locations who were affected by bush fires in 2003 in northeast Victoria, Australia, were not necessarily well prepared for a bush fire disaster. Respondents to research did not consider any scenario planning and were consumed with day-to-day operations. Although insurance was widely used and considered as the main method of hazard mitigation, many operators were not covered for loss of business unless their properties were destroyed or specifically affected. The researchers also noted that actions to reduce the risks were part of mandatory obligations related to their leases, suggesting the role of legislation as a non-structural mitigation strategy. Similar responses were discovered by Hystad and Keller (2008) who found that despite the location of tourism businesses in an area with a high likelihood of experiencing a bushfire in Canada, only 4% of businesses recognised bush fires as a major disaster threat. Only 27% of surveyed businesses were aware of the regional emergency plan and less than 5% were part of that plan, while 26% had their own emergency plan. Furthermore, the local tourism agency (Tourism Kelowna) did not have any disaster management plans in place prior to the bush fire. Confirming previous studies, the authors found that larger businesses were more likely to have disaster plans and procedures.

A repeat of this study in 2006 using the same location, found that only 38% of businesses had a disaster management plan (only an 11% increase) and those that were aware of the regional emergency plan rose from 5% to 32% of the sample (Hystad & Keller, 2008). Most respondents felt that it was the responsibility of emergency organisations and tourism organisations to prepare for disasters and to respond to such incidents, whereas tourism businesses felt that they had a more secondary role in post-disaster recovery activities. However, as discussed above, post-disaster advertising and marketing materials can be developed before a natural hazard becomes a natural disaster. One possible reason for a lack of action could be what Drabek (2000) suggests is a perceived lack of responsibility by tourism managers for dealing with natural disasters. As Hystad and Killer (2008) suggest, emergency management agencies are the main stakeholders involved in dealing with tourism disasters, with tourism stakeholders involved more in the recovery stage of tourism disaster management. Managers may perceive that dealing with such events are beyond their control and this may affect the propensity of the tourism industry to effectively prepare for such incidents.

Drabek (2000) undertook a study to compare the perceptions of tourist business managers and guests who were involved in tourism disasters between 1991 and 1994. Drabek (2000), over this time period undertook interviews with 603 tourists who were affected by a disaster and 185 executives responsible for a tourism business during a disaster. The results indicated that tourists often received less knowledge of the disaster from the general media and more warning from lodging firm operators and neighbours and also had less warning than local residents before the event actually occurred, limiting their ability to seek shelter. A total of 40% of tourists surveyed, claimed that warnings lacked precise information and they therefore sought confirmation from tourism staff, other tourists or relatives in assessing the risk. As Drabek (2000) outlines, unlike people evacuating from their homes who may shelter with friends and relatives, 23% went to public shelters, or returned to their home residence (20%), booked into other accommodation (18%), while 39% became trapped in heavy traffic and slept in cars, roadside restaurants and other places. Those who found shelter in public shelters were less satisfied with the arrangement (43% of the sample) compared to those who made it to other commercial accommodation outside the county (82%), those stayed with friends and relative in another county (87%) or made it to other commercial accommodation in the same county as the disaster (65%).

Most interesting, Drabek's (2000) research showed a large gap between the perceptions of the tourism industry and tourists regarding disaster planning. As Table 5.2 illustrates, these differences existed with respect to the locus of responsibility for disaster planning and policy options for disaster planning. In particular, 50% of tourists surveyed either agreed or strongly agreed that managers had little or no commitment to disaster-evacuation planning and 91% agreed or strongly agreed that local government should require accommodation operators to have written disaster-evacuation plans, compared to only 23% and 50% of managers, respectively. The results indicate that tourists place a high level of responsibility on tourist businesses and local government to protect their interests in a disaster situation suggesting that simply evacuating guests from their properties is not enough on its own. This is echoed in questions that asked tourist for recommendations in policies after the disaster, and over half of respondents provided suggestions. As illustrated in Table 5.3, improvements were suggested with respect to evacuation planning (61% of the sample) and warning procedures (57%) followed by aspects such as information flow and threat information (56% each). It appears from this research that tourists place responsibility for disaster preparedness on tourism managers, who in turn place this responsibility elsewhere with emergency management or government authorities as they may not perceive it to be their responsibility.

In the case of Katherine, Faulkner and Vikulov (2001) noted that there was no destination-wide disaster plan in place prior to the floods and no tourism-specific plan in place, while little coordination occurred between the tourism industry and emergency services. The researchers also noted that in the prodromal stage, the community-wide early-warning system needed to be supplemented by a tourism-sector system based on a communication tree, to provide messages and instructions through a predetermined sequence of tourism agencies and operators, with cross-checks and alternative media contingencies in the event of system failures.

A total of 49% of tourists from Drabek's (2000) study indicated the need for more staff training, suggested that simulation exercises or drills could be useful for staff. Simulations and drills are useful for individual organisations in the tourism industry as well as local and regional tourism organisations. However, as Johnston *et al.* (2007) discovered, only 22% of accommodation establishments in Ocean Shores, Washington, USA, were exposed to training on how to respond to hazard events, and only one establishment from 18 had tsunami training programmes. Only one establishment had signage in rooms on tsunami, although all had the legally required signage for fire hazards. Despite the costs associated with preparing and undertaking a simulation exercise or training, the

Table 5.2 Locus of responsibility and policy options – customers' versus managers' perceptions (%)

Locus of responsibility statements	Strongly disagree	Disagree	Neither agree nor disagree	Agree	Strongly agree
Despite some public relations efforts, I suspect that managers of most business firms have little or no commitment to disaster-evacuation planning.	3% (27%)	24% (36%)	23% (14%)	41% (22%)	9% (1%)
Unless we were directly ordered by the local government through a mandatory evacuation notice, we probably would not evacuate because we've seen too many false alarms.	26% (19%)	41% (29%)	17% (16%)	14% (22%)	3% (15%)
The role of businesses ends with getting customers off property; they certainly are not obligated to provide guests with evacuation-route information, shelter options, or transportation assistance.	47% (38%)	41% (40%)	5% (12%)	6% (7%)	1% (3%)
Local governments should provide more disaster-evacuation training for private-sector tourist executives.	2% (3%)	5% (19%)	30% (16%)	45% (52%)	19% (10%)
Tourist business associations (e.g. hotel and motel trade associations) should demonstrate more interest in disaster-evacuation planning.	1% (3%)	2% (15%)	14% (20%)	48% (45%)	36% (17%)
A major priority for local government following any disaster should be a media-awareness campaign to ensure that prospective tourists know the community has recovered and businesses are open.	2% (1%)	7% (1%)	11% (5%)	50% (41%)	30% (52%)

Table 5.2 (*Continued*)

Locus of responsibility statements	Strongly disagree	Disagree	Neither agree nor disagree	Agree	Strongly agree
Policy option statements					
Local governments should require all firms providing lodging, including RV parks and campgrounds, to have written disaster-evacuation plans.	3% (8%)	1% (8%)	4% (14%)	45% (26%)	46% (24%)
Disaster planning by private firms should include provision to ensure effective evacuation of special populations (e.g. Non-English speaking, individuals with some disability). Note: this item was worded behaviourally in the managerial survey (i.e. 'Our planning had provisions to ensure ...')	1% (2%)	2% (29%)	6% (37%)	49% (25%)	42% (7%)
The effectiveness of future evacuations could be enhanced if lodging establishments participated in a disaster-evacuation exercise each year.	1% (8%)	7% (21%)	16% (18%)	43% (37%)	34% (15%)
Local governments should do more to promote vertical evacuation (e.g. to upper floors of multi-storey hotels) in appropriate structures within the community rather than solely urging people to evacuate elsewhere.	7% (13%)	20% (21%)	38% (35%)	27% (26%)	9% (6%)

Note: Managers' perception responses are in brackets alongside customer perceptions. All responses are significantly different between customers and managers, except for the last statement in the table.
Source: Modified after Drabek (2000: 53).

Table 5.3 Customers' perceptions of disaster-planning improvements

Statement	Strongly disagree	Disagree	Neither agree nor disagree	Agree	Strongly agree
Lodging establishments should provide all guests with a brochure that outlines their disaster-evacuation procedures.	4%	3%	5%	33%	55%
If I ever found a hazard-awareness brochure (e.g. hurricane information and response procedures) in my hotel room, I would not feel comfortable staying there.	52%	41%	4%	2%	1%
Staff from lodging establishments should be prepared to provide disaster-evacuation road information to all guests requesting it.	1%	1%	3%	39%	56%
Since some people travel with their pets, disaster planners should make some type of arrangement for them when evacuations are required.	3%	8%	22%	46%	22%
Lodging establishments should have policies that permit a full refund of pre-paid deposits and penalty-free cancellations when their local government has issued any type of a disaster-evacuation advisory.	2%	6%	7%	40%	46%
If the managers of lodging establishments expect to keep tourists coming back to the area we were visiting, they must modify their refund and cancellation policies related to disaster evacuation.	3%	13%	29%	36%	20%

Source: Modified after Drabek (2000: 56).

lessons learned can be invaluable as there is often a difference between disaster planning and management (Quarantelli, 1984, 1988).

The tourism industry (including businesses, travel and tourism trade or industry groups and government) should perhaps work together to plan and develop simulations based on scenarios to help train staff on disaster management principles and practice. Faulkner and Vikulov (2001) note how prior to the 1998 Katherine Floods in Australia, the Katherine Region Counter-Disaster planning group had only recently (November 1997) conducted exercises in which the disaster scenario was a major flood, which helped their response to the actual flood in January 1998. Van Biema (1995) noted that although prior to the Kobe earthquake in 1995, Tokyo army and civilian officials conducted yearly drills to test their coordination, military officials reluctantly admit that in the Kobe area they did not under take drills. However, more research is required into the barriers and impediments to tourism disaster planning.

Barriers or impediments to disaster planning by tourism businesses found by Hystad and Keller (2008) included lack of money (68% of the sample), lack of knowledge on what a disaster management plan entails (48%), inability to make changes due to the small size of their businesses (23%) and a perceived lack of cohesiveness in the tourism industry (14%). Johnston *et al.* (2007) suggest training needs analysis should be under-taken on disaster preparation and planning for the tourism industry, to understand current knowledge levels, barriers to implementing mitiga-tion measures as well as training opportunities. Training could be conducted with sectors of the tourism industry to reduce costs and improve coordination and control. As Johnston *et al.* (2007: 211) suggest, '[g]iven most tourism ventures are privately owned firms, there is a need to establish relationships with owners and operators to convey the importance of emergency plan g for their employees (tourism personnel) and their clients (tourists)'. Mèheux and Parker (2006) propose an awareness strategy based on persuasive communication for the tourism industry. They suggest five key considerations in developing such a strategy (Mèheux & Parker, 2006: 79):

(1) *Source of the communication.* Credibility, trustworthiness, attractive-ness, liking, similarity, power.
(2) *Message characteristics.* Style, clarity, forcefulness, speed, ordering, amount of material, repetition, number of arguments, extremity of position.
(3) *Channel* variables. Media type, verbal versus non-verbal commu-nication, context of channel.
(4) *Receiver variables.* Age, intelligence, gender, self-esteem, level of active participation, incentives for participation.

(5) *Target or destination variables*. Attitudes versus behaviour, decay of induced change, delayed-action effects, resistance to persuasion.

Perhaps the blame lies with National Tourist Organisations (NTOs), Destination Marketing Organisations (DMOs), or even industry associations, who may be in a better position to develop awareness amongst their stakeholders, collect data and information on possible disasters and provide training and support for the broader industry. Ritchie and Crouch (2003) observed that DMOs are an important stakeholder in responding to crises and ensuring a competitive and sustainable tourism destination. As Page *et al.* (2006: 361) note with regards to NTOs and tourism shocks, they have a remit '... to undertake a leadership role to understand, analyse, plan and manage crises and disasters', and should prepare contingency and disaster plans. In the same article, the attempt by Visit Scotland to consider the impact and possible initiatives to prepare for a potential influenza pandemic was discussed. Furthermore, industry associations can take a proactive role in developing risk and disaster prevention strategies. For instance, Beeton (2001) illustrates that measures can be undertaken to reduce the likelihood of a crisis and also reduce insurance premiums for tourism businesses.

However, Mèheux and Parker (2006) also suggest that a complex range of factors influence disaster preparedness, and may be responsible for a lack of reduction and readiness planning for tourism. Figure 5.1 illustrates the stage, outcomes, potential indicators and broad influencers on disaster preparedness. This model is useful as it provides some indicators that could be examined in future tourism disaster research on preparedness, and suggests possible future research topics on tourism disaster preparedness. Exploring the influence of variables presented in the model, such as experience, values and beliefs, messages, personal attributes and sociocultural norms would be an important step in better understanding tourism disaster preparedness. As discussed earlier in this chapter, experience may influence preparation, as could values and beliefs about the likelihood and response to tourism disasters. More research and focus should be placed on understanding tourism industry attitudes and perceptions concerning disaster preparedness and planning, to complement the already growing research which focuses on response and recovery of tourism organisations to natural disasters.

Integrating Crisis Scanning with Planning: Development of Crisis Plans

It is obvious that scanning the operating environment and considering the impact of risks such as crises and shocks may enable managers (through an established issues analysis system, risk analysis, or forecasting techniques) to predict crises and disasters and implement coping

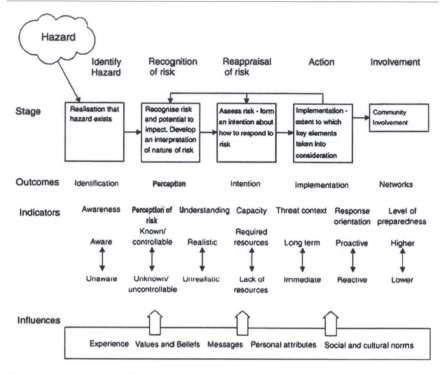

Figure 5.1 A preparedness model
Source: Reprinted from Tourism Management, 27(1), Méheux, K and Parker, E., Tourist sector perceptions of natural hazards in Vanuatu and the implications for a small island developing state, pp. 69–85, copyright (2006), with permission of Elsevier.

mechanisms before a crisis hits. The development of scenarios, forecasts and risk analyses should be integrated into strategic planning so that if an issue does develop into a crisis that hits an organisation or destination, contingency plans can be enacted. Contingency plans are alternative plans that can be implemented if a crisis or disaster hits and impacts upon the strategic direction of an organisation. These are helpful for less certain situations and can help resolve crisis situations quickly if they were to occur, but their usefulness may not be useful for high shock and immediate crises. Examples include contingency plans for impending war or the possible striking of key workers within an organisation. Plans may include removing some destinations from tour operator itineraries or moving tasks from frontline to management staff for the duration of the strike. As Smith (1993: 150 in Joyce, 1999) notes:

> the contingency plans that the organisation has in place prior to the event will be of critical importance in determining its initial response

in setting up chains of command, organisational structures and decision making procedures to cope with the high level of demand that is inevitably generated by a crisis event.

As discussed above, managers may create an issues or CMT who may not only scan the environment but also be involved in the development of contingency plans in case issues develop into crises for the organisation. This may help the organisation deal with the crisis under less intense pressure. A core characteristic of crises is their lack of information, so inevitably an information gathering system should be put into place to gather as much information as possible on the impending crisis, so that alternative sources of action can be evaluated (using forecasting and information gathering techniques discussed in Chapter 4). The development of crisis management training for staff and simulation exercises and drills are also important preparations for organisations. Obviously, as outlined in Figure 3.6, flexibility will be important in implementing developed contingency plans if an actual crisis hits an organisation, when responses move from strategic and tactical plans to actual operational management in the context of a crisis.

Crisis management systems and tools

A number of specialist arrangement and decision-making procedures need to be established to deal effectively with crises. Many authors note the need for an establishment of a CMT or crisis committee which may be directly involved in the scanning of issues and risk, training and development of crisis strategies and techniques. They may also be involved in coordinating simulation exercises or conducting safety audits and inspections, as well as assigning specific tasks to other staff, gathering and disseminating information, developing liaisons with other organisations and establishing a crisis management command centre (Cassedy, 1991; de Sausmarez, 2004). However, as Robert and Lajtha (2002) note, usually the key top executives do not participate in the CMT despite their inevitable involvement if a crisis does occur. They believe that entrusting the creation of a crisis management system to consultants can cause crisis management policies to be ineffective.

In house teams of individuals are needed to develop customised tools (such as impact analysis or risk analysis relevant to their organisation), develop suitable information systems and undertake management training and testing. Cassedy (1991) suggests the need for a team leader to coordinate and control a CMT, which should help identify and develop crisis management strategies to deal with incidents. They should meet regularly to reflect and redesign the strategy as the environment changes and a pre-planned team can also respond to crises quickly and implement strategies more effectively. Essentially the team should be cross-functional providing input from all parts of a respective business, industry or destination to more effectively cover issues and problems likely to be encountered. Parsons (1996) suggests at an organisational level a steering group of senior executives should be involved but only one, preferably a senior director, should be nominated as a spokesperson. Yet as Robert and Lajtha (2002: 185) state with respect to senior management perceptions of crisis management:

> why then are such people generally unprepared? What levers can be used to make them see the importance of such preparation? Why do many top managers devote so little time to crisis management planning and training when the return on the small investment may be huge and even commercially life-saving?

As the quote notes, it is not only the strategic level planning that is required, but also the training of staff to operate under a crisis situation. In particular, staff should be trained in how to deal with the time pressure and lack of information that often occurs in crisis situations. Because crisis create psychological pressure, staff may have to undertake counselling and training to deal with stress, fatigue and fear-all elements of crises management. Furthermore, public relations personnel should also be trained in the area of crisis communication, which is an important element in the crisis management stage (and which is discussed in Chapter 7 in detail). General staff should be made aware of risk and evacuation policies and procedures. Senior management may also need to carry out simulation exercises or role-plays based on scenarios identified in the issues or risk analysis planning stage. Simulations have been considered by some people to be superior to scenario planning (Timmins, 1997 in Joyce, 1999) because it actually involves implementing plans and learning from the operational success or failure of such plans. Simulations may be viewed by external observers (sometimes consultants), who may produce reports to help the organisation in its future planning and response. Although the production of company manuals and procedures is important, Bland (1995) considers training more important as manuals are often inflexible and often not used in crisis situations. Bland (1995: 29) provides six major components of crisis management training for organisations, which provide a good framework for crisis management training for organisations:

(1) *Theoretical training:* to get management to consider about crises and what a crisis is defined as. This helps to form the skeleton of the crisis plan.
(2) *Brainstorming:* of the various types of crises that could hit and how they could respond to them. Asking questions concerning what

could hit? Who the audience would be and how would they react? How do we communicate to them?

(3) *Planning:* Any written plans are now drawn up in a crisis manual.
(4) *Media training:* Any media spokespeople must be trained in crisis interview techniques.
(5) *Simulations:* Crisis simulations are a useful way of assessing the strengths and weaknesses of the team and keeping them crisis-aware.
(6) *Audits:* A crisis auditor can check individual awareness of crisis procedures and ensure data and manuals are kept up to date.

Lee and Harrald (1999) report that a study conducted on Fortune 1000 companies in the US found that 71% of companies had a crisis management plan, with 82% noting crisis communication as part of that plan, 79% noted security, 75% business continuity/disaster recovery, 70% health/environment/safety and 66% had plans related to risk management or loss control. In their own smaller separate study, the authors discovered that only 29% of their sample used Business Area Impact Analysis in their crisis planning strategies. In Hong Kong, Chong and Nyaw (2002) discovered that from their small sample of businesses, only 23% had a crisis management plan for an average duration of 6.95 years. Those that did have a crisis management plan perceived that it helped them continue their business during difficult times but also recognised the potential damage to people and property resulting from disasters and the need for preparation.

Consistent with the crisis management plan, the majority of crisis management plans had reactive contingency plans (see Table 5.4). The

Table 5.4 Type of contingency plan

Type of contingency plan	Percent of sample
Continued servicing of existing markets	71.4
Alternative sourcing	28.6
Product recalls	19.0
Replacing key vendors	14.3
Alternative markets	9.5
Subcontracting	9.5
Replacing key management	4.8
Immediate withdrawal of scheduled advertisements	4.8

Note: Multiple responses allowed so numbers do not add up to 100%
Source: Modified from Chong and Nyaw (2002: 14).

Table 5.5 Crisis management team members

Function area represented	Percent of sample
Corporate safety/security	76.2
Production/operation	71.4
Public/media relations	61.9
Personnel	57.1
Finance	47.6
Marketing/sales	38.1
Data processing	33.3
Land/property development	19.0
Legal	19.0
Insurance	9.5

Note: Multiple responses allowed so numbers do not add up to 100%
Source: Modified from Chong and Nyaw (2002: 14).

average group size of members of the CMT was 12.33 for respondents averaging 2168 employees (less than 1% of the workforce). The list of CMT members can be found on Table 5.5, which illustrates a wide representation from corporate security/safety, production/operation and public/media relations areas involved in crisis planning. However, elements related to training were limited to group reviews amongst 57% of those with crisis management plans, while drills and simulations were only undertaken by 52% and 33%, respectively. This is despite nearly all of those with plans stating that a continuous review of the plan was the most important factor for improving it, and 43% noted the frequent testing of the plan as important. In both these cases, few studies have been undertaken. In the tourism area, there has also been a lack of research concerning crisis planning and preparation. Robert and Lajtha (2002) provide a 10-point list which they call the crisis management platform – an essential mental action plan to change the attitude and mindset of managers and executives, which could be applied to tourism managers at all levels.

Tourism Crisis Planning and Preparation

Despite the importance of proactive planning for crises in the tourism system, the number of studies related to the travel and tourism industry is limited and unexpected considering the characteristics of the system and its vulnerability (Henderson, 1999b). The perceptions of risk amongst travellers and the decision-making process is also high (Pizam & Mansfield, 1996), suggesting the need for some consideration of crisis management and risk reduction. A Pacific Asia Travel Association (PATA) survey conducted in 1991 discovered that few members included crisis management in their strategic planning, although the chances of a crisis occurring were as high as 40%, while only four of the NTOs in the region had crisis management plans (in Henderson, 1999b: 108). More recently, crisis management groups at a national level have been formulated, but they often don't have a tourism-specific remit (de Sausmarez, 2004), suggesting that good communication between government departments and from national down to local levels are required.

At the destination level there are examples of teams or crisis management units that have been developed to deal with tourism crises and disasters. The team should comprise representatives from local government, travel and tourism industry professionals and community leaders. Soñmez *et al.* (1998) suggest that any group can be divided into teams to share tasks including:

- a *communications/public relations team* to represent the destination and provide accurate information to the media and public;
- a *marketing/promotional team* to manage the recovery marketing process including any required re-imaging or branding activities;
- an *information coordination team* to gather information on the crisis or disaster and to assess the damage done to help aid recovery; and
- a *financial or fund raising team* to estimate the cost of recovery and develop strategies for fund raising or lobbying government to fund ongoing crisis management and recovery marketing activities.

The development of Fiji's Tourism Action Group (TAG) during the military coups illustrates the advantages of forming such a group. Fiji's tourist industry responded faster than expected during the most recent coup in 2000 because of the implementation of a task force which was established in 1987 after the first coup. As Berno and King (2001) suggest, although the circumstances of the second coup were not exactly the same as the first coup, it was relatively easy to respond to the incident and restore consumer confidence in Fiji as a tourist destination. Within one week of the second coup in 2000, the task force was formed and allowed for a quick and coordinated response. The authors suggest that Fiji's history of political instability and vulnerability to natural disasters, ensured that a tourism crisis plan was adopted by the tourism industry.

Task forces or groups are important because they can establish specific strategies and documents to be enacted by personnel to manage the incident and move towards crisis recovery at a national, regional, local or organisational level. However, not all responses have been praised. For instance, during the 2001 Foot and Mouth Disease (FMD) outbreak in the UK, national level tourism industry representatives believed that the British Tourist Authority (the then NTO) failed to react sufficiently and effectively, as they did not appear to have a crisis management strategy in place prior to the outbreak. Nevertheless, the British Hospitality Association (BTA) stressed that they did have a 'fairly basic crisis management strategy in place' although the BTA believed that it was too little too late (Cotton, 2001).

The BTA excused the insufficiency by explaining that the intensity of the FMD could not be forecast despite a previous outbreak in 1967. Nevertheless, they acknowledged that the FMD has taught them 'how to have an even better crisis response strategy in the future' (in Ritchie *et al.*, 2003). The Tourism Industry Emergency Response (TIER), comprised of senior industry partners, was formed soon after to create an effective network to develop and disseminate information and strategies in the event of future crises (Frisby, 2002). According to Paraskevas and Arendell (2007), this group has a major role to play in the formation of a destination anti-terrorism group and partnering with law enforcement officials. The Bali bombing has also influenced the Asia-Pacific region to place crisis management at the top of the agenda. Malaysia soon began the development of a tourism crisis management plan following the action of the PATA region-wide crisis management plan (in Anon, 2003), and after it experienced a drop of visitors of approximately one million to nearly half of that after the Bali bombing in 2002, shocking them into a reactive approach to crisis management.

However, more recently NTOs are starting to take a leadership role in crisis preparation and planning. Page *et al.* (2006) outline substantial work by Visit Scotland in conducting a thorough issues and risk analysis, followed by scenario planning related to a potential outbreak of influenza as well as potential oil depletion (Yeoman *et al.*, 2007). This followed previous research related to the war in Iraq (Yeoman *et al.*, 2005a) and a reoccurrence of the FMD (Yeoman *et al.*, 2005b), which actually occurred in 2007. In developing scenarios concerning a potential influenza pandemic, Visit Scotland went through several phases:

(1) They used a scenario planning workshop to develop two realistic scenarios, which were previously tested by Visit Scotland staff, the Scottish Executive Department of Health and the research team.
(2) The scenarios were pre-circulated to workshop attendees.
(3) A Workshop was undertaken with 20 attendees where the coherence, content, validity, impact and suggestions on crisis management were provided. A scenario thinking methodology was undertaken.

(4)   The scenario responses were then put through the Moffat model (to examine the implications and the economic and tourism impact of possible actions or responses were assessed).

Based on the findings and workshops, a number of issues and actions required at each stage of the crisis were proposed and outlined in Table 5.6 and relate to the three main audiences in a tourism crisis (government, the tourism industry and visitors). The issues and actions, as Prideaux *et al.* (2003) suggest, can then be used to develop a crisis response model for an influenza pandemic specifically.

In Australia, the former Federal Government Department of Industry, Tourism and Resources has also taken a leadership role and developed in partnership with the industry a national tourism incident response plan to set out a coherent response framework and actions for government in cooperation with industry for national incidents (such as terrorism, war, disease outbreaks and natural disasters). A filter matrix is used to determine the activation level of the plan, which includes certain actions by groups such as the Tourism Ministers Council, Policy Advisory Group, Tourism Communicators Network, Monitoring Group and the Tourism Research Committee. The plan clearly sets out how these groups are convened (if not already convened), key outcomes, operational objectives, priorities and membership. Each group has detailed actions, responsibilities noted and timeline depending on the activation level. Interestingly, the plan includes suggested templates for information bulletins, possible policy responses, meeting agendas and the like. The different activation levels and filter matrix scores required for each activation level are:

- *Blue* (*low risk*), which is a score of 0–20 and represents a no or low threat.
- *Green* (*guarded risk*), which is a score of 21–40 and represents a watching brief.
- *Amber* (*medium risk*), which is a score of 41–70 and requires an incident response.
- *Red* (*high risk*), which is a score from 71 to 100 and requires a major incident response.

The scores of the filter matrix are derived through the potential impact of a crisis incident on six main aspects of tourism in Australia, according the plan (Federal Department of Industry, Tourism and Resources, 2007: 11), and an overall weighted score (see Figure 5.2).

With regard to tourist industry sectors and specific organisations, national research conducted by Gonzalez-Herrero (1997) discovered that tourist organisations in the US are better prepared to prevent and cope with business crises than comparable organisations in Spain. Only

Table 5.6 Issues and planning actions at each crisis stage

Stage	Issue	Action required	Who?
Stage on: pre-crisis	Planning required to cope in the event of a flu pandemic	Develop contingency plans	Individual businesses: Visit Scotland
Stage two: 'It's out there!'	Monitoring of tourism trends and data	Monitoring of bookings	Individual businesses: Visit Scotland
	React to changing situation	Implementation of contingency plans	Individual businesses: Visit Scotland
	Ensure effective communications	Use trusted sources and communicate with staff and customers	Individual businesses
	Restriction on normal supply chains	Develop links with alternative local suppliers	Individual businesses
	Implement contingency plans	Convene 'Joint Action Group' (JAG)	Visit Scotland
	Assess situation for tourism	Monitor reaction of markets through business advisors	Visit Scotland
	Changes in markets	Implement revised marketing initiatives	Visit Scotland
	Ensure situation is portrayed accurately	Implement communications strategy	Visit Scotland

Table 5.6 (*Continued*)

Stage	Issue	Action required	Who?
Stage three: 'It's here!'	Survival of crisis	Instigate lending agreements with banks	Individual businesses
	Curtailing of expenditure	Reduce or suspend marketing activities	Individual businesses: Visit Scotland
		Lay-off staff/temporarily close business or sections of business	Individual businesses
	Provision of leadership	Communicate and act as point of contact for tourism industry	Visit Scotland
	Assist tourism industry recovery	Develop recovery plans to deal with the aftermath of the pandemic	Visit Scotland
Stage four: 'It's over!' (post-crisis)	Adaptation to new market situation	Review marketing strategies to account for new opportunities	Individual businesses: Visit Scotland

Source: Reprinted from *Tourism Management*, 27, Page, S., Yeoman, I., Munro, C., Connell, J. and Walker, L., A case study of best practice—Visit Scotland's prepared response to an influenza pandemic, pp. 361–393, copyright (2006), with permission of Elsevier.

ISSUE		WHERE 2 IS MEDIUM IMPACT	WHERE 1 IS LOW IMPACT	WHERE 0 IS NO IMPACT		
Evaluation Criteria:		Score (0 - 3)			Weight	Weighted Score
Anticipated impact on Brand Australia				÷ 3	x 25 =	
Anticipated impact on international travel patterns				÷ 3	x 15 =	
Anticipated impact on domestic travel patterns				÷ 3	x 15 =	
Anticipated impact on industry profitability				÷ 3	x 20 =	
Anticipated impact on industry's ability to recover				÷ 3	x 20 =	
Anticipated impact on government financial support				÷ 3	x 5 =	
TOTAL WEIGHTED SCORE (refer this score to the Activation System in Appendix 2)						

Figure 5.2 Australian tourism industry crisis response filter matrix
Source: Federal Department of Industry, Tourism and Resources (2007: 43).

around 29% of Spanish organisations had crisis plans compared with 78% in the US. Absence of formal planning was also discovered by Henderson (1999a, 1999b, 2002) in research concerning crisis management of the tourism industry in Asia. Barton (1994a) also noted the need for crisis management strategies in the hospitality sector, while facility managers could also benefit from crisis and disaster management (Barton & Hardigree, 1995; Then & Loosemore, 2006). Furthermore, adventure tourism operators also need to deal with crises and incidents often concerning risk management, as Beeton (2001) notes with respect to horseback adventure tourism, and can do so through developing safety risk management plans and policies.

However, research discussed by Ritchie *et al.* (2003) concerning the FMD response at the local level discovered a lack of updated crisis management planning. Furthermore, from industry representatives interviewed none had a crisis plan in place for their own business before the outbreak. Few people expressed an interest in developing a crisis management plan in the future, because crises were seen as infrequent and that little can be done to alter their impacts. The only contingency considered was setting aside money and resources to deal with unforeseen events. However, crisis management theory suggests that established plans can limit the severity of crises and disasters through proactive contingency planning (Heath, 1998; Kash & Darling, 1998).

In a study concerned with terrorism preparedness in built facilities, the authors found that hotels were perceived by managers as the third most vulnerable facility after government buildings and iconic buildings (Then & Loosemore, 2006). However, they felt that the chance of an attack was low while the authors suggested that '... [i]t would seem that our respondents are underestimating the current level of terrorism risks' (Then & Loosemore, 2006: 168). A total of 24% of respondents felt totally unprepared for a terrorist attack, while 76% considered the buildings to be unprepared and only 48% had a formal terrorism risk management system. From those that did exist, 69% had been developed in the five years since September 11, 2001 and the 2002 Bali bombing, and only 55% had been updated since their creation (Then & Loosemore, 2006).

The lack of crisis management preparedness and planning by the tourism industry may be partly explained by a feeling amongst tourism managers that they cannot control many of the external elements that may create crises (such as political instability and economic decline), and are more likely to be able to control specific events such as airline crashes or organisational failure (Henderson, 1999b). As Anderson (2006) noted in her interviews of tourism operators coping with crises in Australia in 2001, many felt helpless, unprepared, or tried to use plans that were not updated or useful. As Rousaki and Alcott (2007) suggest, tourism managers may also see themselves as incapable of failure, reducing their responsiveness to danger signals and scanning the environment for potential crises. Furthermore, hotel managers who were more likely to perceive a crisis occurring and those with crisis experience were more likely to consider themselves prepared (Rousaki & Alcott, 2007). No differences were found between size of hotel, and job level of respondents.

Crisis preparation may even be good for the bottom line. Barton (1994a) provides evidence of this with the example of a hotel in Nevada, USA, that was able to reduce its annual insurance premiums by 7% after developing a crisis plan. As Barton (1994a: 63) correctly suggests:

> insurance companies often find that their exposure to claims is aggravated by angry customers of hospitality properties that ignore

or delay a response during a fire accident or other catastrophe – something that could be mitigated by the presence of a crisis plan.

Because tourism is an industry that comprises many individual businesses from a wide range of sectors, and public sector organisations at the international, national, regional and local level, an integrated approach to crisis and disaster management is required. Within the tourism industry established and large companies may have such a CMT on permanent staff. However, the tourism and travel industry is characterised by a large number of small or micro businesses and may rely on industry organisations to provide support during a crisis or disaster who can promote crisis readiness and preparation. As Anderson (2006) suggests, tourism operators appear to rely on past experiences rather than formal plans in dealing with crises, and so tourism industry organisations and National Tourism Administrations (NTAs) have an important role to play in facilitating the communication and dissemination of this knowledge through sharing in meetings, seminars, promoting training and the development of materials such as handbooks and sector manuals.

For instance, the Federation of Tour Operators (FTO) in Britain have a designated CMT who help members deal with crises and disasters and use their experience to provide leadership to the industry. They also provide workshops with the Association of British Travel Agents (ABTA) on effective crisis management for industry members, specifically targeting newer members.

Staff training with scenarios can be useful for preparing for likely crises. As Barton (1994a) notes, training programmes should involve elements including decision-making, communication, avoiding panic and coordination of resources with the private sector, state or local tourism office, security consultants and crisis consultants. A role-play of how staff handle questions from reporters surrounding a specific crisis scenario can help managers critique their performance and practice crisis communication strategies and techniques in advance of an actual crisis occurrence. Gonzalez-Herrero and Pratt (1998) note that although 89% of tourist organisations surveyed in the US and 69% in Spain had a designated company representative to field questions from media in crises, only 74% in the US and 47% in Spain had been media trained.

Crisis management handbooks have been suggested by some authors as important for the tourism industry (Soñmez & Blackman, 1999; WTO, 1998). A study conducted on the crisis management strategies of tour operators (Wiik, 2003) showed that from the tour operators studied, many had handbooks or manuals which classified the scope of the crisis and what action plans were required for each type of crisis. The handbook covers crashes, hijackings, terrorist activity, riots, rapes, floods, hurricanes, etc. One respondent noted with respect to manuals and procedures that:

> it is very difficult when dealing with a crisis to remember everything that you need to do. You focus on the safety of your clients, but there are other bits and pieces that are less important but still important for you to carry out. When you have plans, manuals and procedures in place it is easier to remember everything. We keep those manuals updated and we read through them. (Wiik, 2003: 40)

Furthermore, the FTO suggested that major disasters are relatively easy to control as they are more frequent, whereas unusual or unique incidents may be more problematic as they are new. The respondent suggested a bus crash in Turkey that killed one person was more difficult to deal with than the Bali bombing because the media were at the site immediately and the FTO had a lack of information to respond to media questions. Both tour operators and the FTO who were interviewed in this research suggested that they reviewed their plans after each incident, if it was different than previous incidents, or if they could improve their strategies in managing the crisis. They also noted that the effectiveness of their response was determined by quick mobilisation of relevant staff who were trained in using the manual and enacting procedures developed by the CMT (Wiik, 2003).

Conclusion

This chapter commenced by discussing preparedness measures for dealing with tourism disasters if prevention is not possible, including an understanding of emergency planning, the nature of precursors and warning systems, and finally, the development of training and simulations for emergency and tourism managers. Limited academic attention by tourism researchers and tourism managers has explored tourism disaster preparation. Due to the nature of the tourism industry comprising a large number of small businesses, this chapter has argued that NTOs, DMOs or industry associations have an important role to play in assisting their stakeholders to change their reactive mindset and develop readiness strategies and initiatives. Recent efforts by such organisations, such as Visit Scotland are promising, but more effort is required.

This chapter has also identified that tourism organisations and destinations should set up a system to identify emerging issues and potential crises consisting of a core number of staff from various functional areas and even from related organisations (such as tourist associations and law enforcement officials). This group should undertake scenario brainstorming to improve their understanding of the types of risks and possible response strategies and their impacts. Contingency plans should be developed which include the development of manuals and procedures, staff training and simulation exercises. All of these activities can help ensure an organisation is prepared and able to respond more effectively to both emerging incidents and unpredictable shocks. To date, the evidence suggests that the tourism industry has had less formal planning than other industries, possibly because of its nature (many small enterprises and interconnected with many sectors).

Tourism Crisis and Disaster Response, Implementation and Management

Chapter 6

Coordination, Control and Resource Allocation

Introduction

This chapter outlines the implementation of strategic management strategies and tactics to deal with crises and disasters within public and private tourism organisations. Such organisations need to be flexible in how they source, administer systems and control resources for effective crisis and disaster management throughout the response and recovery phases. The allocation of resources requires coordination within organisations, between stakeholders, both within the tourism industry and between the tourism industry and external stakeholders, such as emergency services personnel. An understanding of stakeholders and the development of an integrated tourism crisis and disaster response are required. Leadership is required at a local, regional, national, and perhaps even international level depending on the size and scale of the tourism crisis or disaster. Cultural backgrounds may influence leadership and tourism crisis or disaster management, while there is debate about the characteristics that make effective leaders in these situations, the nature of decision-making, and the degree to which leadership should be (de)centralised.

For large-scale tourism crises and disasters, the government may be lobbied by the tourism industry for resources to be allocated towards reassurance and recovery marketing activities as well as tax relief for tourism-related businesses, while developing countries may become reliant on general aid and tourism development projects to assist their response and recovery. At an organisational level, resources may have to be (re)deployed to communication and information activities, activities to stimulate tourism demand (through marketing, price cuts, value adding, targeting new markets). In conjunction with these activities, organisations may need to diversify their businesses away from tourism to reduce their vulnerability and impact, while implementing cost control measures including reducing costs, postponing payments to creditors, reducing operations and reallocating human resources.

This chapter outlines the coordination, control and allocation of resources to deal with tourism crises and disasters during the strategic implementation phase of response and recovery. Chapter 7 provides more detail concerning crisis communication and recovery marketing efforts, which are an important part of tourism crisis and disaster response and recovery.

Coordination, Collaboration and Leadership

Stakeholder coordination and control

Understanding and working, with key internal and external stakeholders is a major requirement in managing crises and disasters successfully. According to Freeman (1984: 46), 'stakeholders are those group(s) or organization(s) that can affect or are affected by the achievement of an organization's objectives'. Sautter and Leisen (1999: 326) note, 'if [tourism] players proactively consider the interests of all other stakeholders, the industry as a whole stands to gain significant returns in the long term'. In the case of crisis and disaster management, understanding the impact of a crisis or disaster on internal (business units, staff, managers, shareholders) and external (other agencies and organisations, general public, media, tourists) stakeholders is critical. As Pearson and Mitroff (1993: 50) explain the three key questions regarding stakeholders in crisis management are:

(1) Which stakeholders affect crisis management?
(2) Which stakeholders are affected by crisis management?
(3) How can the stakeholders be systematically analysed and anticipated for any crisis?

Stakeholder relations are a two-way process with stakeholders able to influence crisis and disaster policy either explicitly or implicitly by their potential actions toward such policy. In this respect, they both can affect tourism crisis policy and be affected by such policy. Figure 6.1 by Pearson and Mitroff (1993) outlines the two-way process and the range of possible internal and external stakeholders. Crisis policy-makers need to consider the likely response of stakeholders to policy measures or strategies, and if possible, use stakeholder responses to previous crises or disasters as a learning tool in formulating their responses (see Chapter 9 for more detail on organisational learning and the role of stakeholders). The type of crisis or disaster and its magnitude will impact upon stakeholders in different ways.

For example, airline strike action that will obviously impact upon the day-to-day management of a tourism organisation and could impact on consumers (such as tourists) and suppliers (such as catering services and tour operators). However, other incidents may only impact upon internal stakeholders within an organisation such as other departments or managers. For large-scale disasters and crises, the impacts will be felt by external stakeholders such as the general public, tourists, and other sectors of the tourism industry, special interest groups and possibly even

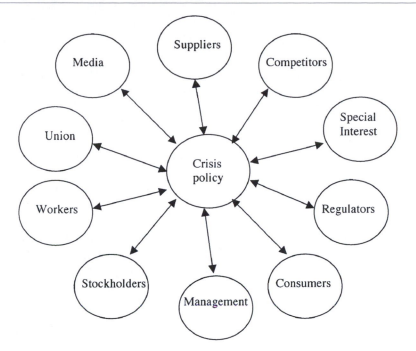

Figure 6.1 Functional organisational stakeholders
Source: Modified after Pearson and Mitroff (1993: 56).

stakeholders in other industries. The media are an important stakeholder in communicating information concerning a crisis or disaster to various publics (including tourists) and are also important in restoring confidence in an organisation or destination when a crisis or disaster is entering the long-term recovery or resolution phase (they are discussed in more detail in Chapter 7).

Furthermore, understanding the complex relationship between these stakeholders and how they influence the implementation of crisis or disaster management strategies is important, but nevertheless has largely been ignored to date. The importance of understanding stakeholders in tourism crisis and disaster management becomes clear when one considers the interrelationship and dependency between these groups within the tourism system. As Hystad and Keller (2008: 159) state, '[u]nderstanding the roles of various stakeholders throughout the stages of a disaster is a significant step to improving tourism disaster management'. The fragmented nature of the tourism system, coupled with the need for integration within emergency management organisations suggests collaboration and coordination between tourism and emergency management agencies is crucial. Furthermore, border security agencies, their engagement with the tourism industry and their respective policies before and at the border of countries, has not been explored to date (Hall, 2006).

However, as Hystad and Keller (2008: 159) suggest with respect to a forest fire disaster, the lack of collaboration between tourism agencies and emergency response organisations was surprising. Because of the nature of tourism, it is especially important that crisis or emergency management plans are integrated. Collaboration is required between different organisations, government departments, emergency personnel, media organisations, and other stakeholders. Collaboration towards an integrated approach for tourism crisis and disaster management is vital in a number of different scales: local, regional, national and international (if the crisis or disaster crosses borders).

In discussing the government and industry response to SARS, McKercher and Chon (2004) highlight the need for stronger international collaboration and coordination amongst tourism departments to develop more effective responses to crises that cross borders. A lack of central coordination was blamed for the over reaction of the impact of SARS and the role, and restrictions, placed on travel. De Sausmarez (2005) agrees that cooperation is required between stakeholders in tourism, with Chapter 7 outlining cooperation in crisis communication and recovery marketing in detail, and the use of already established regional government agencies (such as ASEAN) and industry associations (such as PATA) to coordinate activities related to crises in the Asia-Pacific area. Internationally there are a range of governmental and non-governmental organisations which are able to assist destinations in disaster response, and are able to provide aid and logistical assistance including the Red Cross, CARE and OXFAM, as well as to provide financial assistance in the case of banks and governments to help response and recovery after a disaster. The scale of natural disasters can pose problems for the coordination, transportation and distribution of aid, such as that experienced during the Indian Ocean tsunami in 2004. Systems, such as the United Nations Joint Logistics Centre, can help facilitate air traffic control and manage logistics assets, creating more efficiency and effective use of assets, while coordination amongst relief organisations is crucial for planning, damage assessment, public information management, appeals and donations management (Oloruntoba, 2005).

At a national level, the role of Destination Marketing Organisations (DMOs) should not be under-estimated as way to coordinate the crisis or disaster response and recovery. As Ritchie and Crouch (2003: 63) state, the 'M' in DMO should be more about management than marketing, with a DMO being responsible for visitor management, inflow and outflow of information, human resources development, resource stewardship, access to finance and venture capital, and crisis management. However, as Paraskevas and Arendell (2007: 1564) note, in the ...

> emergency and intermediary recovery stages apart from its vital crisis communication role, the DMO has the responsibility to manage and ensure safe visitor flows within the destination (by relocating them for example to safer accommodation) and the business continuity (restoration of mission-critical operations) for both the organisation and the destination stakeholders. Finally, in the long-term recovery and resolution stages, apart from the well-discussed in the extant literature media management and image recovery roles, the DMO also has the role of advocating a 'no fault learning' culture with the destination.

Furthermore, the DMO provides the important coordinating role between industry associations, industry stakeholders and the central government. At the national level, policy structures are usually in place not only to restrict vulnerability through land-use planning and legislation, but also through the development of plans to facilitate response and recovery if disasters occur. As Schneider (1995) argues, government should be involved in disaster situations for a number of reasons:

(1) Disasters can cause severe and obvious social problems.
(2) They can become highly politicised issues, for which public figures are willing and able to respond to citizens' needs.
(3) In many situations, the disaster victims have little control over the scope or severity of the event and require help.

Added to this, many governments have sufficient resources, manpower and technical expertise to cope with disasters (Kim & Lee, 1998). Previously, governments have seen disaster and emergency planning as the role of law enforcement and fire departments, supported by public health and civil defence organisation (Cigler, 1988) but as the number of incidents increase, there has been increased calls for a more holistic approach to reduction rather than response leaving national government in a position to only help and act as a facilitator. The World Tourism Organisation (1998) suggests a national policy or committee which integrates the National Tourism Administration with other relevant government agencies (such as health, police, customs, civil defence) as well as tourism industry operators, through representatives from relevant tourism industry associations.

In particular, all destinations should have a multi-disciplinary or multi-agency approach to crisis and disaster management for tourism. Gurtner (2006) also suggests that integration is important in tourism disaster management, noting that after the tsunami the well-resourced and experienced Thai government Department of Disaster Prevention and Mitigation was deployed in the region, quickly establishing a centralised operational centre and coordinating emergency response efforts. As Heath (1995) noted with regard to the Kobe earthquake, poor interaction between civil and military authorities and a lack of integration between ministries and divisions within those ministries contributed to a loss of time in responding to the impact of the earthquake.

Kim and Lee (1998) note that, in South Korea government, policy and legislation is in force for man-made, natural and civil defence disasters. They have the Natural Hazards Act (for natural disasters), the Disaster Management Act (for man-made and technological disasters) and the Civil Defence Act (for civil defence affairs). Each has a number of tiers or levels ranging from the legislative body that propose laws and budgets to deal with disasters, to executives who are particularly concerned with response and recovery (the actual management phases). However, Kim and Lee (1998) note that division of responsibilities based on the type of disaster experienced, does not occur and that further integration and coordination is required. In Australia, the Commonwealth government Disaster Response Plan is led by Emergency Management Australia (EMA), although State and Territories have their own responsibility (and plans) for their jurisdiction, unless the State cannot cope with the needs of the situation and can seek assistance from the Commonwealth government. The Department of Homeland Security in the USA now has responsibility for many different government agencies and activities, including the coast guard, border security, the Transportation Security Administration and the Federal Emergency Management Agency, who deal with emergency preparedness and response.

Coordination is also needed at the regional level, as Kouzmin *et al.* (1995: 23) stressed levels of government in Australia were not productive towards coordination in a disaster situation. They note large levels of intergovernmental fragmentation and disputation with state government coordinating local government and state agencies coordinating local ones. In some state governments, police forces are the dominant forces in managing disasters, while in others professional disaster managers control affairs. However, things have improved more recently with a Council of Australian Governments' (COAG) investigation into disaster management in Australia in 2005. COAG noted the importance of a consistent and coordinated response by Australian, State, Territory and Local Governments at the onset of any national emergency. Leaders noted that the current arrangements have the capacity to manage any substantial emergencies and agreed to develop a protocol to ensure effective coordination and communication in the unlikely event of an emergency of greater magnitude. The National Emergency Protocol (NEP) describes the communication arrangements between the Prime

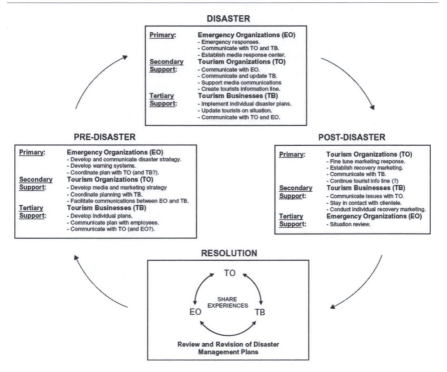

Figure 6.2 Stakeholder roles within a destination tourism disaster management cycle
Source: Reprinted from *Tourism Management*, 39(1), Hystad, P. and Keller, P., Towards a destination tourism disaster management framework: Long-term lessons from a forest fire disaster, pp. 151–162, copyright (2008), with permission of Elsevier.

Minister, Premiers, Chief Ministers and the President of the Australian Local Government Association (ALGA) during a national emergency.

At a local level, coordination is required between disaster management agencies and specific units of fire and civil defence agencies, as well as affected industries (including tourism). Figure 6.2 outlines the roles of stakeholders at a local destination level, based on longitudinal research undertaken by Hystad and Keller (2008). The model illustrates the importance of coordination between primary, secondary and tertiary stakeholders before, during or after a disaster. In particular, collaboration is required not only between tourist organisations (including NTAs, DMOs and industry associations) and tourism businesses, but also between these groups and emergency organisations, with emergency organisations considered primary stakeholders before and during a disaster, while tourism organisations and businesses are suggested to take the lead role after the disaster. Nevertheless, the important point from Figure 6.2 is that coordination and collaboration is required between all three types of stakeholders for planning and response/recovery efforts. Accommodation establishments often play an important role in housing and feeding people (both survivors and emergency workers) during a natural disaster should be integrated into emergency management plans. However, as Quarantelli (1988) states, coordination as a concept has different meanings with some organisations viewing coordination as merely informing other groups what they will be doing, while others will see it as the centralisation of decision-making in a particular agency or among key officials.

The following section outlines the resources that are needed to help key leaders to make decisions on how to effectively and efficiently allocate resources to manage tourism crises and disasters.

Decision-making, leadership and resource allocation

As discussed in Part 2 of the book, both organisations and destinations should have a pre-arranged crisis or disaster management group either at an organisational, local, regional or national level. This group should have a clear idea of the types of crises and disasters that can occur due to risk and vulnerability of the organisation or destination and have a pre-planned response drafted. However, the actual implementation of such plans and the response to a crisis or disaster can be substantially different to pre-event planning. Managing crises and disasters in the heat of the moment with little information, time pressure and the psychological nature of such incidents require fast thinking and response. Furthermore, because of interdependence and the complexity associated with such incidents, responses can generate subsequent crises or disasters. One of the most vital components of a response to a crisis or disaster is the emergence of leadership from either an individual or organisation representing the destination or company impacted. This person must provide leadership in managing the incident by operationalising or overseeing crisis or disaster management strategies. In reality, few organisations and destinations have an established crisis or disaster management team (as outlined in Chapter 4). Therefore, one of the first responses, after a crisis or disaster is imminent or occurs, is to create such a structure to gather information and respond to the threat.

The emergency manager, according to Alexander (2000) has to be able to make sense of rapidly conflicting information, and need to cope with high risk levels, fluid and ill-defined situations, competition and conflict amongst emergency workers, and urgent situations where time is scare (Drabek, 1990 in Alexander, 2000). The basic model of emergency management systems follows a rigid chain of command

and a structured hierarchy with clearly defined responsibilities. In the basic model, centralisation ensures that duplication does not occur and that information is used where it is best needed. However, as Alexander (2000) remarks, this model has been criticised for being too rigid and mechanistic, and for allowing bottlenecks to occur in the flow of decisions and information. As Quarantelli (1988) suggests, coordination, not control, is what is required and is achievable, since loosening up command structures may actually be better in the response phase of a disaster. As Williams and Ferguson (2005) note with respect to the foot and mouth outbreak in the UK, centralisation (via the national Ministry of Agriculture, Farming and Fisheries) did not help the information flow, with the department labelled insular by industry stakeholders.

The alternative to a centralised model is known under a series of different names such as incident command system (ICS), emergency-resources coordination model, matrix organisational structure, multiple-agency coordinating system or integrated emergency management system. In the alternative model, coordination occurs through consultation and flexibility with task forces set up as problems arise. The reconciliation of roles and responsibilities, especially amongst multiple agencies, is through common elements of procedure, terminology and structure to improve collaboration (Alexander, 2000). A good ICS should be linked to the procedures and systems of existing agencies and should be able to be used as a range of destination-wide disasters or crises including smaller and larger incidents. One of the major roles of an ICS is to facilitate and delegate tasks and activities that need to occur in order to respond effectively to the crisis or disaster.

Models such as the cascaded strategic priority profile (CSPP) and operational management triage (OMT) can be used to more effectively communicate and undertake response to control the crisis or disaster situation (Heath, 1995). CSPPs create priorities, tasks and activities that need to be undertaken from the highest to the lowest priority, and can cut across local and overall affected areas. The three main areas of response management are included in CSPPs and include, according to Heath (1995: 18):

(1)   Sources and sites of resource demand.
(2)   Tasks that facilitate and enhance response operations.
(3)   Containment of sub-event threats to life and property.

CSPP sites may include priority attention areas such as hospitals, schools, sporting stadia, power generators, etc. (locations where vulnerability and risk may be high), while priority tasks may include facility access and clearing major sites, creating evacuation centres and removing threats to life and property. Each allocated priority is checked in turn from the highest to lowest priority using tactical response units or information scouts, and thus resources can be allocated effectively. Priorities that do not need resource allocation can be marked off and resources can be deployed to other priority areas.

OMT uses similar principles to emergency medical triage to help allocate resources in the emergency phase of a crisis or disaster. Modern triage actually uses four classifications, suggested by Grant *et al.* (1989):

(1) *Highest priority:* immediate treatment and evacuation; severe injuries requiring urgent attention; often colour-coded red.
(2) *High priority:* secondary treatment; moderate injuries requiring attention; often colour-coded yellow.
(3) *Low priority:* tertiary treatment (including first aid); mild injured; often colour-coded green.
(4) *The dead:* no treatment beyond mortality check; often colour-coded grey or black.

OMT uses data on operational sites in terms of resources required, the number of victims, and urgency of action to determine priorities, map out specific sites that need resources on a priority basis using a comparison table. The table enables managers to make decisions based on information and data, suggesting that gaining this data before decisions are made and communicating with suitable agencies who can, provided that data is critical. Numbers can be allocated to three main areas:

(1) Adding resource costs (2 = minimal, 1 = moderate, 0 = heavy).
(2) Numbers of people needing attention (2 = many, 1 = some, 0 = one).
(3) The four category medical triage (4 = class 1, 3 = class 2, 2 = class 3, 1 = class 4).

Those sites that have high urgency and numbers requiring attention will often have a higher priority and thus resources will be deployed to those sites first. For instance, consider a tourist resort that has had major earthquake damage. A situation where one hotel has a high number of people needed attention (two points) with many in the class 1 emergency triage (four points), and would require heavy resource costs (zero points) would score higher, and be of a higher priority than a hotel with less people (one point) with lower medical needs (one point), even if resource costs were minimal (two points). However, the use of the OMT needs to be flexible as linked crisis or disaster events may create situations where human lives are more at risk, including emergency workers (through a landslide event after an earthquake for instance). Therefore, response managers may have to adapt their scores; priorities and therefore resource deployment may change.

In the case of disaster aid, damage and needs assessments are required by governments and aid agencies to ensure that livelihoods are not destroyed in the short term and that support is provided promptly to those who really need it. It is also important that donors and aid agencies consider whether relief is given according to the level of need or loss and not simply on the basis of social justice and equity (Oloruntoba, 2005). According to Oloruntoba (2005), calls to get the tourism industry in Phuket back to operation quickly to attract tourists have meant that those who need help may have been marginalised if they were not involved in the tourism industry. Assessing priorities, needs and involving the local community in decision-making are all considered important in tourism disaster management.

Furthermore, the creation of an emergency operations centre (EOC) where communication is centred to government, media, the general public as well as the participating organisations is vital. Such a centre should be located in an area which is not vulnerable to natural hazards or if it is impacted physically by a disaster than this will slow information communication, collaboration and ultimately response to the incident. Payne (1994) outlined how the borough of Bexley in London deals with emergency planning and strategy in two separate but connected levels in the Borough Emergency Control Centre. First, there is a strategic level, where control is left to a decision-making team comprising the borough controller (often the chief executive), and an emergency operations director supported by a planning officer. At the tactical level, planning is vested in the support team who process information into intelligence, advise and implement actions and facilitate liaison with other utilities (such as the emergency services). This team, according to Payne (1994) consists of an information publicity manager, a communications officer, a management information coordinator and other senior support officers. However, Alexander (2000) notes that requiring workers to perform different tasks in an emergency situation could put extreme pressure on these individuals, unlike full-time professional emergency managers. Heath (1995: 15) notes that:

> where response management is not professional, or when such management relies heavily on guidance from central authority, adaptivity will be low. Difficulties and impediments from within a crisis or disaster environment are likely to drain resources and slow respondents in completing their assigned tasks.

Delays in response to destination crises or disasters are often blamed on lack of communication, slow response and a lack of resource deployment. As Allinson (1994: 43) suggests, crises or disasters often strike at the weakest links of an organisation, which are often those links which may limit or constrict information flow. This flow of information may be stopped or blocked because of differences between the terminology, knowledge and equipment of the agencies involved

(Alexander, 2000; Heath, 1995). This may partly be because individuals are not used to working together, which was noted by Heath (1995) as a problem with the Kobe earthquake where emergency organisations seldom dealt with each other before the earthquake. This suggests the value of pre-event planning, simulation and drills to encourage consistency in communication and terminology between stakeholders. Furthermore, emergent groups, with their own norms, social and communication structure may be formed to deal with the incident. Examples include relief communities that may only exist for a limited period of time. These communities may create new relationships between emergency management organisations and could even challenge the views of full-time emergency managers, for instance, by handing out relief supplies, burying the dead or putting up temporary shelters. According to Oloruntoba (2005), such actions could be another obstacle to effective disaster management, due in part to cultural differences.

Cultural differences can also impact upon communication and therefore the ability of organisations or destinations to respond to crises or disasters at a national, regional, or local level. Differences in cultural norms and behaviours may influence tourism crisis and disaster responses. For instance, Hofstede's (1984, 2001) research into motivations and leadership suggest that cultural differences may be partly responsible for differences in decision-making at a national or regional level. Hofstede (2001: xix) outlined five dimensions on which country cultures differ through both theoretical reasoning and statistical analysis:

(1) *Power distance.* This is the extent to which the less powerful members of organisations and institutions accept and expect that power is distributed unequally. The basic problem involved is the degree of human inequality that underlies the functioning of each particular society, with countries that downplay wealth and power differences is classified as a low-power distance country, while one that has institutionalised differences in wealth and power as justified and not to be challenged is classified as a high-power distance culture. In organisations, power distance refers to the degree of centralisation of authority, leadership and decision-making.

(2) *Uncertainty avoidance.* This is the extent to which a culture programmes its members to feel either uncomfortable or comfortable in unstructured situations. Unstructured situations are novel, unknown, surprising, different from usual. The basic problem involved is the degree to which a society tries to control the uncontrollable. Some societies socialise their members into thinking that there is uncertainty in life and there is little one can do to change the situation, while others socialise their members into

thinking that they can beat, influence or control the future. Organisations with strong uncertainty avoidance will be more likely to create rules, regulations and policy documents and be relatively task orientated, whereas when uncertainty avoidance is weak, employees will be expected to spend less time devoted to work policies, procedures and a greater emphasis will be placed on ambiguity and less control.

(3) *Individualism versus collectivism.* This is the degree to which individuals are supposed to look after themselves or remain integrated into groups, usually around the family. Positioning itself between these poles is a very basic problem all societies face. Some societies value individualism positively where people value their individual freedom, while others are expected to have extended families and expected to look after other members of society. This translates into organisations, with those from a collectivist society more likely to view the organisations success with their own, whereas in countries where individualism is likely to produce less bond or commitment where staff prefer extrinsic rewards.

(4) *Masculinity versus femininity.* This refers to the distribution of emotional roles between the genders, which is another fundamental problem for any society to which a range of solutions are found; it opposes 'tough' masculine to 'tender' feminine societies, and societies may maximise or minimise the social and sex-role defini- tions. Masculine societies stress values such as assertiveness, acquisition of money and disregard for others. This may influence an individual attachment to rewards, recognition, achievement and challenge, which may affect an organisation's reward system and management style.

(5) *Long-term versus short-term orientation.* This refers to the extent to which a culture programmes its members to accept delayed gratification of their material, social, and emotional needs. This dimension was added to the 2001 second edition of Hofestede's book, as a result of research from a Chinese Value Survey. This tends to suggest that residents of countries with long-term orientation include characteristics such as persistence, personal adaptability and think about the future.

The implications of this are that countries vary on these five dimensions which have implications for the functioning of organisa- tions. A better understanding of a culture's values and attitudes can help understand organisational behaviour in a particular cultural setting. As Heath (1995) explains, Hofestede's research found that the Japanese culture is likely to be collectivist in nature, with a strong accent of large power distance and a high need to avoid uncertainty.

The Kobe earthquake of 1995 is an example of how delayed response can limit the management of crises and disasters. Heath (1995) and Van Biema (1995) believed that response by the government to the earthquake was slow because of the slow decisions made concerning cordoning off of roads, the delay of police and emergency vehicles and the delayed decision to use armed forces to assist emergency organisations. However, the authors note that this delay could be partly explained by a lack of information on which to base decisions (which are often a problem in crisis or disaster situations), com-pounded by the Japanese culture and organisational structure, which is often bottom-up. This consensus-driven approach reduced the ability for quick decisions to be made and strong leadership to be shown by government leaders. Furthermore, the characteristics of a country's national culture were also acknowledged as a possible reason for a failure to plan for crises in Turkey despite having previous crisis experience (Okumus & Karamustafa, 2005), as well as in Bali concerning the implementation of a national tourism crisis management plan, despite having experienced two terrorist attacks on the tourism industry (Andrai, 2007).

Leadership in dealing with a crisis or disaster has been mentioned by a number of key authors (Cassedy, 1991; Faulkner, 2001; Turner, 1994). Leadership is required within a specific organisation, within an industry sector, and at a destination level to provide direction and guidance in dealing with incidents as well as a spokesperson to deal with the media. Wilks and Moore (2004: 47) suggest five main points in regards to leadership in a crisis or disaster:

(1) Immediately dispatching a senior, responsible individual to the scene of a problem sends two important messages: I care and I am accountable.
(2) It is important to make sure there is a plan in place where senior government officials and industry leaders are among the first to know about the crisis.
(3) Organisations should identify a primary media spokesperson with the authority to be very open with the media (this is discussed more in Chapter 7).
(4) Effective leaders must be able to tolerate confusion and hostility and separate what is important and what is background noise in a chaotic atmosphere.
(5) Effective leadership in the midst of a crisis can be easily provided for in the continuity plan and contingency plan prepared in readiness for a crisis.

According to Heath (1995: 13), 'in crisis and disaster response management ... time is too limited for consensus driven decision-making processes that include all those involved'. Heath (1995) suggests that quick thinking leadership and the ability to make fast but effective decisions is needed. This is easier to do if there is a pre-crisis unit or management team at an organisation, industry or destination level. However, if decisions are centralised and therefore limited to management, Heath (1998) believes that this can lead to resentment and conflict if the needs and desires of stakeholders for consultation increase and are compromised. As previously discussed, such a response may be in part due to country and/or organisational culture. Barnett and Pratt (2000) suggest that opening up communication processes and decentralising control processes in crises results in greater organisational flexibility and long-term viability. Cosgrave (1996) provides a list of problem characteristics and their possible responses based on leadership and decision-making, with the three problem characteristics of quality, acceptance and urgency being used as a tool for analysing decision-making in emergencies.

Few studies have been undertaken on decision-making processes or leadership in tourism crises and disasters. Bonn and Rundle-Thiele (2007) suggest that following a shock event, decision-making often moves from consultative and comprehensive towards limited consultation and a more simplified process. Table 6.1 also illustrates other decision-making processes following a shock event compared to decision-making in a stable environment. In particular, Bonn and Rundle-Thiele (2007) suggest from their research that shock events lead to greater board involvement in setting and approving strategy and faster decision-making, compared to during stable environments. Martín-Consuegra *et al.* (2007) found in a study of airlines after September 11, 2001, that internal factors, such as top management involvement, department relationships and organisational systems played an important role in the implementation of market-oriented activities in an airline after a crisis. Their results also indicated that top mangers should place more emphasis on being market oriented and being less averse to risk after a post-crisis stage.

According to Quarantelli (1988: 380–381), there are at least four problem areas involving organisational decision-making in community disasters:

(1) *Personnel burnout.* Key decision-makers should be rested and/or replaced so they do not burnout and become inefficient in decision-making. This may be achieved by operating shifts and replacing staff with others.
(2) *Organisational authority conflicts.* New disaster-related tasks may have to be undertaken in an *ad hoc* fashion by the key decision-makers.

Table 6.1 Decision-making processes under different conditions

	In a stable environment	*Following a shock event*
Use of analysis	In depth analysis of data, broad range of alternatives considered	Little analysis of data, small number of alternatives considered
Use of intuition	Limited use of intuition	Greater use of intuition and 'gut feeling'
Management involvement	CEO and senior management team	CEO and selected members of senior management team
Board involvement	Predominately strategy approval, limited involvement in setting strategy	Heavily involved in setting strategy, responsible for strategy approval
Decision-making approach	Consultation	Limited consultation
Decision-making processes	Comprehensive	Simplified
Speed of decision-making	Slow	Fast
Role of regulations	Major drawback	Can be quickly overcome

Source: Reprinted from *Tourism Management*, 28, Bonn,I. and Rundle-Thiele, S., Do or die–Strategic decision-making following a shock event, pp. 615–620, copyright (2007), with permission of Elsevier.

(3) *Organisational domain conflicts.* Disputes may emerge as a result of conflict or a lack of organisation over who has responsibility for a particular problem or issue amongst established organisations and emergent groups (aid agencies or community groups).

(4) *Organisational jurisdictional differences.* Conflicts are possible if a disaster crosses jurisdictional boundaries of local organisations. A good solution is to obtain a temporary consensus on areas of responsibility with the understanding that there will be no formal carryover into the recovery period.

Government Resource Allocation

According to an extensive literature review, Israeli and Reichel (2003) constructed four categories of crisis management practices (see Table 6.2): (1) human resources, (2) marketing, (3) infrastructure maintenance and

Table 6.2 Importance and usage of tourism crisis management practices by Israeli hotel managers

Category	Practice	*Mean importance score*	*Mean usage score*
Human resources	Firing employees to reduce labour force	5.43	4.77
	Using unpaid vacation to reduce labour force	5.39	3.34
	Decreasing number of working days per week	5.50	4.92
	Freezing pay rates	4.88	5.06
	Replacing high tenure employees with new employees	2.79	2.44
	Increased reliance on outsourcing	4.47	3.61
Marketing	Marketing to domestic tourists in joint campaigns with local merchants (such as Visa, MasterCard)	5.46	4.68
	Marketing to domestic tourists with focus on specific attributes of the location	5.93	5.51
	Price drop on special offers	5.14	5.77
	Reducing list price	4.86	5.07
	Marketing to foreign tourists with specific focus on the location's distinctive features and relative safety	3.55	2.97
	Marketing and promoting new products and services (family events, catering)	4.89	4.05
	Marketing to new segments (such as the ultra orthodox)	5.32	4.69
Maintenance	Cost cuts by limiting hotel services	4.27	3.90
	Cost cuts by postponing maintenance of the building (cosmetics)	4.11	4.07
	Cost cuts by postponing maintenance of the engineering systems	3.26	3.36
	Extending credit or postponing scheduled payments	4.92	4.68

Table 6.2 (*Continued*)

Category	Practice	Mean importance score	Mean usage score
Government	Organised protest against lack of government support	4.01	2.38
	Industry-wide demand for government assistance with current expenses	5.83	4.40
	Industry-wide demand for a grace period of tax payments	5.46	3.82
	Industry-wide demand for a grace period on local tax (municipality) payments	6.45	5.74

Note: Scales used were a seven-point scale for importance ratings ranging from 1 (least important) to 7 (most important). Actual usage ranged from 1 (extensively used) to 7 (rarely used).
Source: Modified after Israeli and Reichel (2003).

(4) governmental assistance. The remainder of this chapter examines these themes commencing with government assistance and resource allocation followed by an exploration of organisational resource allocation including communication resource deployment, pull-based resource allocation and marketing, diversification of business or target markets, cost reduction measures and finally, human resource deployment. The creation of destination-specific crisis or disaster management action groups often lobby government to provide funding to respond to a tourism crisis or disaster. The ability to fund resources has been noted by Heath (1995) as an important factor in dealing more effectively with natural disasters.

Because government agencies rarely provide pre-event resources for major crises and disasters, there is a need when they do occur to deploy such resources quickly. The higher the magnitude of the crisis or disaster, the more of a drain it will be on resources and the slower the response time by agencies and organisations (Heath, 1995). Therefore, in high magnitude crises or disasters, the tourism industry needs to lobby government and the private sector for resources to deal with such incidents quickly. As Carlsen (2006) suggests, a funding submission may have to be presented to treasury, while other funding sources from development banks may be used to help a destination affected by a crisis or disaster to restore and recover. Government agencies may also have to work together through inter-departmental task forces to assess the likely impact of a crisis or disaster prior to developing and implementing policy decisions. As Blake and Sinclair (2003: 814) note, there are three main issues for government to consider:

(1) Whether the downturn in tourism activity is sufficiently large to merit offsetting measures. This will require information on the impact of a crisis on tourism and the economy at large.
(2) The duration of the downturn, whereby policy-makers may concentrate on minimising adjustment costs as the economy moves to a new equilibrium, if a shock is likely to be long lasting. If it is temporary, then policy should try and insulate the economy from adverse effects.
(3) What policies are the best and most cost effective in raising income and limiting adjustment costs.

The major role of the action group, developed by the British Tourist Authority during the foot and mouth outbreak was to source funding to aid in the recovery marketing and communication effort from both public and private sector sources. Over two weeks in March 2001, the action group prepared a bid for special funding from the government (Firsby, 2002). The action group succeeded in gaining additional funding to provide recovery marketing and branding initiatives throughout the crisis, which are outlined in Chapter 7. As Frisby (2002) notes, the BTA had already held back £2.1 million of its own grant-in-aid from the 2000/2001 financial year to support its emergency response phase, specifically new media initiatives and the World Travel Leaders' Summit. On 6 April 2001, the government awarded the BTA additional funding of £2.2 million, followed by £12 million in May, with £2 million of this additional funding allocated for press and public relations work. As discussed in Chapter 7, the Irish Tourist Board provided extra funding for a reassurance and recovery marketing campaign in the US (Tiernan *et al.*, 2007) after lobbying by industry. Israeli hotel managers emphasised the importance and use of lobbying for a grace period on local government tax payments (Israeli & Reichel, 2003), whilst research showed 'reliance on government and marketing' as the most important factor in crisis management practices. Lobbying by the services sector in Hong Kong after SARS, led to a HK$1.8 billion package that included tax rebates, lower rent for shops in public shopping malls and reduced water and sewage charges for restaurants (Tse *et al.*, 2006).

As Sharpley and Craven (2001: 533) noted, early on during the foot and mouth outbreak, a number of policy measures were introduced for local rural tourism businesses, not just support for reassurance and marketing campaigns, including the ability to:

• claim rate (i.e. local tax) relief from the local authority;

- apply to the Inland Revenue and Customs and Excise for the deferral of tax and national insurance payments;
- apply to bank managers for extended lines of credit or capital repayment holidays;
- apply for loans, guaranteed by the government, of up to £250,000 on Small Business Service helpline; and
- seek advice on employment issues from local job centres.

However, these measures were perceived by Sharpley and Craven (2001) as confusing and insubstantial, particularly as businesses were expected to seek advice from a variety of sources and the support was short term. Only 10% of British Chamber of Commerce members affected by the outbreak had applied for business rate relief or deferral of tax and national insurance payments, due to the perceived complexity in applying for such relief (in Sharpley & Craven, 2001). Rate relief was only available to businesses with a rateable value of £12,000 or less, with Williams and Ferguson (2005) noting that even small guesthouses earned more than that. Research with respect to the 2003 Canberra Bushfires, suggests the importance of a 'one-stop-shop' of government services and support for disaster victims provided by a government-run recovery centre (Nicholls & Glenny, 2005) which could reduce the complexity in accessing support services and funding.

After September 11, 2001, the Travel Industry Recovery Coalition, comprising 25 tourism organisations, proposed a six-point plan to restore tourism demand in America. Their plan included policy measures such as tourist and workforce tax credits, business loan programmes, the extension of allowances for net operating losses and government and private sector funding for recovery marketing (Blake & Sinclair, 2003). As Blake and Sinclair (2003) note, 11 days after the September 11 attacks, the congress passed the Air Transportation Safety and System Stabilisation Act, which provided:

- federal credit to airlines totalling $10 billion;
- compensation to airlines totalling $5 billion;
- compensation for airlines facing increasing insurance premiums;
- limitation of the extent of liability by airlines for the results of terrorist acts;
- allowances for airlines to make late payment of excise taxes;
- compensation for individuals killed or injured in the attacks; and
- a total of US$3 billion on airline safety.

These measures were designed to keep the airlines operating and to compensate those who were harmed as a result of the attacks. The major differences between government measures and those proposed by the

Travel Industry Recovery Coalition were that the government did not provide compensation to other tourism-related businesses (only airlines).

The Singapore government during the SARS outbreak developed several assistance programmes, with the most prominent, according to Henderson and Ng (2004: 414) was a S$230 million relief package comprising:

- property tax rebates and bridging loans for small and medium enterprises facing cash difficulties;
- halving of the unskilled foreign worker levy for hotels;
- waiving television license fees for hotels;
- fixed interest rate financing scheme for short-term funds; and
- the development of a SARS Relief Tourism Training Assistance programme to retrain workers and minimise redundancies.

At a regional level, the South West Regional Development Agency in conjunction with the DETR made £14 million available to support businesses affected by the foot and mouth outbreak, including tourism businesses (Rodway-Dyer & Shaw, 2005), to ensure business continuity. Tourism Kelowna and the BC Wine Institute contributed C$155,0000 towards an advertising campaign following their bushfire disaster, while the federal and provincial governments and tourism partners provided C$600,000 to enhance promotional efforts and to help offset the effects of the summer wildfires (Hystad & Keller, 2006). The Malaysian government provided a four-fold increase in funding after the Asian-Economic crisis of approximately US$39.5 million for a recovery marketing campaign (de Sausmarez, 2004).

Although there are examples of public and private investment and allocation of funds, for mostly marketing or reassurance campaigns, there is often no research underpinning or comparing various policy approaches. As Blake and Sinclair (2003: 814) suggest, 'they [governments] have operated in an environment where very little research into the merits of offsetting policy responses has been conducted'. As de Sausmarez (2004) suggests, an evaluation of the importance of tourism to the economy compared with other sectors is an important first step in order to prepare a government response, while indicators from statistics, source markets and the travel trade are required to be established and used to determine an appropriate plan. The importance of background information is also identified by Sharpley and Craven (2001), who suggested that the favouritism towards the agricultural sector by the government during the foot and mouth outbreak was due to a lack of data and understanding on the importance of rural tourism. Furthermore, as de Sausmarez (2004) discovered in regards to the Malaysian governments funding of the recovery marketing campaign in 2000, the treasury had been reluctant to allocate funds for promotional efforts as there was no concrete evidence of any potential return on this funding. This evidence or data is particularly important for countries, which have competing demands for government funds. For instance, in order to cover the costs of covering worker's entitlements after the collapse of Ansett Airlines, the Australian government implemented an AU$10 levy on all domestic air travel (Prideaux, 2003) in response to concerns about the burden of their policy to financially assist workers after the collapse of Ansett Airlines.

Data may be required on impact of a crisis or disaster not only to lobby for funding and resource allocation, but also to ensure that resources are allocated effectively and efficiently. Research is lacking on the direct link between recovery marketing campaigns and increases in visitor numbers, perhaps making government uncertain about committing resources to recovery marketing campaigns. Therefore, research should be undertaken not only to track arrivals, visitor satisfaction but also specifically conversion studies of recovery marketing campaigns (Carlsen, 2006). Furthermore, Prideaux (2003) noted that a survey of 5000 tourism businesses in Australia was used to assess the economic impact of the collapse of HIH insurance and Ansett Airlines, so that government could consider effective support measures.

Blake and Sinclair (2003) modelled the impact of government measures discussed earlier in this chapter, and discovered that the absence of offsetting policies would have decreased GDP by US$30 billion, with the airline sector the worst affected followed by the accommodation sector, with half a million jobs lost. However, the research found that policies directed to the airlines sector were the most effective in reducing the impact of September 11, while subsidies to travel (especially business travel) were effective, but less compared to assistance directly to the sector itself. The Tourism Industry Response Coalitions proposal for an individual tax credit for tourism expenditures was deemed relatively ineffective in light of their research (Blake & Sinclair, 2003). The research provides useful information and a model, which can be used by other destinations and policy-makers in designing policies to help destinations respond and recover from tourism crises or disasters.

Not all countries will be able to recover from a crisis or disaster using their own resources and may require international aid to assist with response and recovery. According to Gurtner (2006), after the tsunami, Thailand did not only require money or material donations, but required foreign skills, knowledge, and expertise to restore the damaged regions. The aid agencies of developed countries (such as USAid in America or AusAID in Australia), either alone or with charitable organisations, provides assistance to governments when a major disaster hits. Resources include relief supplies, medical teams, transportation or equipment. As Smith (1995: 70) notes, 'aid is the inevitable outcome of humanitarian concern following a serious event, usually involving the loss of life. As such, it is usually applauded on moral grounds'. Disaster aid is usually used for two main purposes, according to Smith (1995):

(1) *Relief.* Most aid is provided immediately after a disaster through providing medical supplies, clothing and emergency shelter to assist victims.
(2) *Rehabilitation and reconstruction.* Aid is used to help reconstruct the destination, restore major services, and assist construction of new permanent structures and homes. This may take up to 10 years in the case of large disasters.

Organisation and Business Resource Deployment

Heath (1998) suggests the conservation and deployment of resources during a crisis or disaster is vital. Managers should first try and save resources threatened by the crisis/disaster. Second, they should try to conserve those resources used to resolve the crisis and crisis impacts, and third, they should deploy resources to help resolve the crisis and its resultant impacts. Heath (1995: 11) states, 'unrealistic goals and task allocations mean that response management slows as resources diminish without a corresponding goal and task achievement rate'.

The first task of saving resources threatened by a crisis or disaster could refer to tourists and potential travellers. Pull-related initiatives and incentives are needed to address perception of risk and the possible vulnerability of tourists. In some situations this is mainly concerned with perceptions management and providing accurate information for potential travellers (as outlined in detail in Chapter 7). In other instances, reactive and defensive strategies are needed to cut costs, increase cash flow and redistribute human and financial resources to effectively deal with the impacts of a crisis or disaster. These are covered in the remainder of this chapter, with relevant examples provided from the tourism crisis and disaster literature.

Communication and information resource deployment

The establishment of phone information lines is a well-known strategy for dealing with crises and disasters (Ashcroft, 1997), and one that is fairly cost effective. These are often developed to provide consistent and accurate information to public during the response and recovery phase of a crisis or disaster. Phone lines can provide assistance and information for the general public, media but also the tourism industry itself. Many examples of their use are provided in the tourism crisis and disaster field. Beirman (2002) outlined details on a 'situation hotline' for travellers and Israeli operators where consumers and travel agents can be advised of the security situation in places they are visiting or booking. The use of Internet sites including real-time video news updates were also used to instil consumer confidence and counter negative perceptions generated by sensationalist media reporting.

The use of DMO websites are also a useful tool and one that was used by the British Tourist Authority to aid in the recovery throughout the foot and mouth outbreak. It provided information to consumers that the majority of the countryside was open, but also provided information for the tourism industry on government policy concerning the outbreak and recovery and compensation packages. Furthermore, e-mail can be used to communicate recovery marketing efforts and actions directly to individual tourism operators (such as the case of the Kelowna bushfires), although there are questions raised about the use of e-mail as a crisis communication tool (Ritchie *et al.*, 2003). Frisby (2002: 92) notes that the British Tourist Authority already had an established website for the UK's tourism trade, which during the crisis was developed to be a ready source of up-to-date information for the industry. Businesses were asked to provide details of any special deals or offers they were running to promote their product overseas, and these were entered into a database on the website and used for positive stories at home and overseas. The allocation of resources for information sharing amongst key internal and external stakeholders is very important.

Pull-based resource allocation

As demand for visiting the destination declines due to a crisis or disaster, resource allocation will be required to generate incentives to positively influence tourist decision-making. As demand dropped, competitive pressures have forced the national carrier El Al and many hotel chains to advance selective price cuts and introduce marketing incentives, while the Israel Ministry of Tourism increased levels of subsidy to operators marketing Israel programmes as a direct response to the political crisis (Beirman, 2002: 17). Cutting room rates was more pronounced in mid-tier and low-tier hotels in Hong Kong after SARS, rather than top-tier hotels, while those that reduced their rates extended this rate into the peak season for their corporate clients (Lo *et al.*, 2006). Research by Enz and Canina (2002) on US hotel performance after September 11, suggested that the average percentage drop in revenue per available room (RevPAR) was 11% for the third quarter of 2001, 14% for the fourth quarter, while the second quarter of 2002 was a 4% drop. Destinations, which suffered the greatest drop in revenue, were those with the largest population centres. This was partly because they offered favourable conditions during good times, and so had a larger fall in bad times, with San Jose, San Fransisco and New York facing a decline of

26.71%, 23.48% and 20.36%, respectively, in the second quarter of 2002 (Enz & Canina, 2002: 52).

Marketing incentives were introduced in Prague to attract tourists back to the city after severe floods. In November 2002, low cost airlines, such as Easyjet, offered reduced cost flights and Czech airlines also offered discounts (Independent News Travel, 2002 in Field, 2003). Furthermore, accommodation and flight packages are often offered to stimulate demand in combination with reassurance and marketing campaigns (Beirman, 2003). In the case of the Maldives, individual resorts offered additional accommodation nights, complimentary meals, free transfers, tours, activities and welcome back gifts to encourage visitation and a perception of value (Carlsen, 2006). As discussed later in Chapter 7, perception of value is particularly important for some groups of potential visitors, and it may be a better strategy to add amenities or value to the product rather than just discount. In response to SARS, restaurants offered 'anti-SARS' menus that claimed to boost customers immune system, advertised their sanitation procedures or provided take-away meal services (Tse *et al.*, 2006). The provision of travel insurance cover for travellers who may not be covered due to source market travel advisories can also be used as an incentive to encourage visitation. Beirman (2002) noted that the Israeli government, during times of political instability, extended insurance cover to all international travellers within Israel, helping to combat the negative influence of travel advisories.

Diversification of business or target markets

Hystad and Keller (2006) suggested that only 17.3% of businesses surveyed after the forest fire expected the nature of their business to change because of the bushfire, with a higher proportion of accommodation and entertainment businesses suggesting changes (22.2%, respectively) compared to 6.3% of businesses in the food sector. The second largest response strategy for bushfire affected businesses, after recovery marketing, in Hystad and Keller's (2006) study was diversification of the target market followed by reduction in prices and discounts. Stimulating the market by introducing new global brands may help offset reduced demand due to a crisis. According to Evans and Elphick (2005), major UK tour operators started to promote new destinations in the aftermath of September 11, 2001. In discussing the response to a decline in the MICE market due to external crises in Thailand, Campiranon and Arcodia (2007: 159) identified the importance of targeting resilient market segments and noted that 'as a short-term strategy, organizations will be able to temporarily compensate the loss of revenue while it is recommended that medium-term and long-term strategies are to target regional and long haul markets, respectively'.

After the foot and mouth outbreak in Keswick, England, a newly formed partnership company, Rural Regeneration, rebranded Keswick as 'Hi-Energy' by promoting extreme sports experiences and constructing the first mountain bike trail in England (Williams & Ferguson, 2005). This was seen as an important step towards long-term recovery and prosperity for the local tourism industry. In the case of Hong Kong hotels dealing with SARS, some hotels offered cleaning services for their clients at a reasonable cost and turned guest rooms into temporary offices to rent to corporate clients, while many tapped into video conferencing market to limit the impact of declining business travel (Lo *et al.*, 2006). However, in the case of small-scale businesses in developing countries diversification may not be possible. For instance, Cushnahan (2003) outlines 16% of small businesses in an Indonesian island had no alternative income sources to call upon after the 2002 Bali bombing, while approximately 14% turned to fishing, 11% farming and 5% boating. Nevertheless, because of the poor state of the economy and large interest rates, several operators had to borrow funds from banks to sustain themselves.

In the case of September 11, Taylor and Enz (2002) noted how upscale hotels relied on marketing strategies to attract new customers, whereas budget ones offered discounts to try and stimulate demand. Some segments may be more vulnerable to the negative perceptions associated with a tourism crisis or disaster. For instance, the seniors market and school groups were the most affected segment of the motorcoach industry in the US after September 11, 2001 (Ready & Dobbie, 2003). Despite the schools segment comprising 70% of the market for respondents prior to September 11, it dropped 57% in the first quarter of 2002, with 30% of those losing money indicating a loss in excess of $50,000, 30% lost less than $50,000, while 40% did not lose any revenue (Ready & Dobbie, 2003). Targeting the domestic or local market is a well-known strategy (discussed in more detail in Chapter 7) and one that was used in the case of some Hong Kong hotels after SARS (Lo *et al.*, 2006). However, this may work for some countries but destinations such as Singapore may find this strategy difficult to implement due to their geographic size and small domestic market (Henderson & Ng, 2004).

Cost control measures

Any loss in demand from visitors will require tourism operators to reduce their capacity or reduce costs in order to protect the long-term viability of their business. Airlines are often the first to reduce their capacity in a crisis or disaster situation due to a lack of demand. After the Boxing Day tsunami, 26 charter flights were cancelled to the Maldives (with charter flights representing 20% of all arrivals), having a profound affect on visitor flows (Carlsen, 2006). While after the SARS outbreak, Hong Kong-based Dragonair cut its passenger capacity by 50% (Pine & McKercher, 2004), tour operators responding to September 11, 2001, cut their capacity and reduced their product offerings. For instance, First Choice reduced their capacity for the next winter by 15% and the next summer by 20%, while cutting aircraft fleet from 32 to 26 (Evans & Elphick, 2005). In China, during the first six months of 2003, research suggested that 46.2% of residents in three main regions cancelled their holidays (Zeng *et al.*, 2005). An over reliance on package tour groups can lead to block cancellations and a significant down turn in business. This obviously has a flow on affect throughout the tourism industry, illustrated by 53% of accommodation operators in the South West of England recording a loss of turnover between 20% and 60% due to the foot and mouth outbreak (Coles, 2003). During SARS, some Hong Kong hotel floors and/or restaurants were closed to reduce costs, while others reduced the number of elevators to save power and maintenance costs (Lo *et al.*, 2006), similar to the response of Korean hotels (Kim *et al.*, 2005).

Resources may be required to negotiate with these operators and lobby governments in the source markets to lift any travel advisories to stimulate demand. As Carlsen (2006: 77) suggests with regard to the Maldives tsunami 'Asian visitors from Japan, China and Korea were being discouraged from visiting the Maldives and a high-level government-to-government lobbying campaign was needed to restore these markets'. This may require diverting resources to regional destination marketing offices, which are more cost effective and, because of the nature of tourism, are able to directly provide information to travel agencies and tour operators (Beirman, 2002: 170). DMO staff may need to work with foreign offices in order to establish adequate crisis communication processes and gather information for formulating such strategies.

Another strategy to reduce costs is reducing the actual cost of marketing or other activities. For instance, non-urgent expenditures may be limited and luxuries reduced. Evans and Elphick (2005) provide some useful examples from the response of major tour operators in the UK post-September 11, 2001:

- staff parties and educational trips in the brochure production section were stopped;
- the quality of the paper used for the brochure was down graded to save costs;
- non-essential adverts at airports and overseas were cut; and
- press trips were stopped and public relations activities were cut for three months.

Okumus and Karamustafa (2005) outlined how after the 2001 economic crisis in Turkey, tourism hoteliers from the one to three star properties were most affected with respect to increased costs, and were most likely to have reduced their budget for staff training. The third-most perceived short-term negative impact was postponing future investment projects, while the second-most important factor was maintenance cost cuts which included limiting services in the hotel, postponing maintenance of the building or engineering systems similar to research in Israel (Israeli & Reichel, 2003). Furthermore, the research also suggested the practice of postponing payments to creditors, postponing scheduled payments or outsourcing as important ways to reduce costs in the short term whilst the crisis is being dealt with. For instance, the national carrier Ryanair delayed the delivery of two new aircraft due to SARS (Pine & McKercher, 2004). Such practices are perhaps better than going out of business all together which are often the effect of crises (Kash & Darling, 1998). Williams and Ferguson (2005) noted that sole traders were the worst affected by the effect of the foot and mouth outbreak in Keswick, England, with several businesses having to cease trading altogether, as many were not insured for their losses and simply could not reduce their costs to create cash flow and continue operating.

Human resource deployment

According to Soñmez and Backman (1992), the effect of Hurricane Hugo in South Carolina led to one-third of the hotels closing leaving 20,000 people unemployed. While Dwyer *et al.* (2006), in modelling the economic impacts of 2003 crises on Australian tourism, suggest that the impacts were not as severe as predicted. They note that the impact on travel may be affected initially, but travel through the use of consumer savings, substitution of outbound to domestic tourism and 'pent-up' demand after the crisis reduced the effects and job losses. A loss of between 692 and a high of 1642 jobs were estimated by the authors (Dwyer *et al.*, 2006). In the UK, after September 11, 2001, the major four tour operators cut capacity and made staff redundant (Evans & Elphick, 2005). Over the space of one year, the following job cuts were estimated by the major four tour operators, and reported in Evans and Elphick (2005):

- job losses ranging from 350 jobs by MyTravel to 1930 jobs lost at Thomas Cook;
- staff were offered unpaid leave, reduced hours or voluntary redundancy; and

- Thomas Cook introduced pay cuts up to 10% for remaining staff and 15% for senior staff and closed 100 agencies after a 12% fall in bookings.

In Devon, England, the foot and mouth outbreak led to approximately 900 job losses with 34% of Dartmoor accommodation operators making staff redundant losing an estimated £331,699 in Dartmoor and nearly £1 million in other locations (Coles, 2003). In some cases, staff may be asked to take leave without pay or a break from employment while the organisation copes with the crisis. Israeli hotel managers were very hesitant to replace older staff with new staff at lower rates (Israeli & Reichel, 2003), and this was also found to be the case for Singapore hotels after the SARS outbreak (Henderson & Ng, 2004). However, in the case of Singapore hotels, contract workers were often terminated while salaries were reduced and employees were often requested to take unpaid leave or took training taking advantage of the SARS Relief Tourism Training Assistance programme (Henderson & Ng, 2004). One hotel in Hong Kong dismissed 130 employees or 22% of its workforce in order to stay in business (Lo *et al.*, 2006), while Cathay Pacific Airways asked all employees to take four weeks unpaid leave for four months after the crisis with 99% of ground staff accepted this, saving the company HK$300 million (Pine & McKercher, 2004). However, hotels and hospitality businesses in Washington, DC, which was one of the worst affected cities after September 11, had to lay off 75,000 employees several weeks after the attacks (Stafford *et al.*, 2002).

A redeployment of human and financial resources may also be needed. In some instances staff may be asked to perform different tasks or multiple tasks to reduce costs (Henderson & Ng, 2004; Lo *et al.*, 2006), while other staff may have been relocated to other sites, for instance to other hotel properties (Lo *et al.*, 2006). Extra staffing and financial resources may need to be deployed to the public relations function of an organisation or to commission an outside public relations company. Staff may be required to perform visitor safety and health activities to reassure guests and deal with government regulations, such as hotels dealing with SARS who had to check staff and customer body temperatures and increase their cleaning of hotels (Lo *et al.*, 2006; Pine & McKercher, 2004). Furthermore, some effort and resourcing may be required for the sales team to communicate directly to travel agents and tour operators in major markets to reassure their clients that there is no need to cancel, if appropriate.

Conclusion

This chapter outlines the implementation of strategies and their need to be flexible in how they source, administer and control resources and systems for effective crisis and disaster management. The chapter has emphasised the importance of coordination between stakeholders, both within the tourism industry and between the tourism industry and external stakeholders such as emergency services personnel in order to effectively and efficiently allocate resources. Furthermore, leadership is required at a local, regional, national, and perhaps even international level depending on the size and scale of the tourism crisis or disaster. As outlined in this chapter, an understanding of the influence of cultural backgrounds in tourism crisis or disaster management decision-making and resource allocation are important. The debate about the characteristics that make effective leaders in crisis and disaster situations, effective decision-making, and the degree to which leadership should be (de)centralised were all outlined in this chapter as significant issues in the strategic implementation phase to deal with tourism crises and disasters.

Government may have to provide substantial resources not only towards reassurance and recovery marketing activities to assist the recovery of the tourism industry, but provide measures such as tax relief or tax credits to help businesses to continue operations. As Blake and Sinclair (2003) suggest, there is limited research on the policy measures that should be supported by government in large-scale tourism crises. At an organisational level, resources may have to be (re)deployed to communication and information strategies and to develop appropriate activities to stimulate tourism demand. In conjunction with these activities, organisations may need to diversify their businesses away from tourism to reduce their vulnerability and increase their resilience (applying adaptive management techniques). Other organisations will need to implement cost control measures such as reducing costs, postponing payments to creditors, reducing operations and reallocating human resources. In some aspects, staff will be asked to undertake unpaid leave or may lose their jobs completely due to a tourism crisis or disaster. Chapter 7 discusses crisis communication and recovery marketing responses, which are often part of the medium-to-long-term response to restore confidence in a tourism destination or organisation to assist with a quick resolution to the incident.

Chapter 7
Crisis and Disaster Communication and Recovery Marketing

Introduction

One of the most important elements of dealing effectively with a crisis or disaster is the concept of crisis communication. Effective crisis communication is needed to deal with internal stakeholders and externally for external stakeholders. Control over communication and the messages on the nature, impacts and outcomes of a crisis or disaster are vital. The media can encourage the flow and the intensity of a crisis or disaster or even help turn an incident or issue into a crisis due to negative media coverage. Subsequently, organisations need to work with the media to ensure that a consistent and accurate message is transmitted to the various public and stakeholders. A crisis or disaster communication plan should be part of the pre-event strategy, but also needs to be flexible depending on the nature of the crisis and the response of stakeholders. Key target audiences should be identified and a communication and public relations plan developed and implemented. Poor communication strategies can often make the crisis worse as a deluge of questions is often asked from a wide range of stakeholders including reporters, employees, stockholders, government officials and public residents.

This chapter examines crisis and disaster communications and public relations by integrating theory from the crisis communications field, with that from the tourism crisis and disaster field. In particular, this chapter outlines public relations and communication efforts that tourism managers can implement in the emergency and intermediate stage of a crisis or disaster. Finally, this chapter discusses the role of crisis marketing as part of the long-term recovery process providing examples from the literature. However, first the chapter begins by outlining the importance of perceptions and image for the tourism industry and the effect crises and disasters can have on image and destination choice, illustrating the media effect and importance of crisis communication and recovery marketing for tourism.

Perceptions of Risk: Understanding Destination Choice

Moreira (2007) noted that risk perception is an element of the general perceived image of products or services and is found to have a critical impact on organisational results. As noted in various studies, it is often the perception of risk of a crisis or disaster that has the most impact on tourism. McKercher and Pine (2005) suggested that SARS only affected 0.2% of the Hong Kong population, yet greatly affected the lifestyle and travel behaviour of most Hong Kong residents. Sensationalist media reporting coupled with consumer perceptions of risk can have a huge impact on tourism demand patterns at source and receiver destinations. Furthermore, as Woodside and Sherrell (1977) suggest in their destination choice model, choice destinations are based on awareness, availability and positively perceived destinations. Awareness is a direct result of destination image, while availability is determined by decision or constraint factors, such as available time, money, distance, availability of travel companions and the like. Finally, positive perceptions create a small group of possible destinations in the evoked set, which the tourist chooses from.

Negative destination images can occur as a direct result of a crisis or disaster, which ultimately affects consumer confidence, the decision-making process and ultimately destination choice and behaviour. Hall and O'Sullivan (1996) suggest three main elements that create destination images. First, returning tourists through word of mouth reporting on their return. Second, the media through their reporting and image making, and finally, government through their policies and strategies. All of these three elements can have an affect on tourist image, decision-making and behaviour. The negative impact surrounded by a lack of perceived safety and security can '...damage the tourism and travel industry due to its unavoidable nature through the negative word-of-mouth communication...' (Kozak *et al.*, 2007: 234). However, as Kozak *et al.* (2007) observed, overall perceptions of visitors may be dependent on external factors, difficult for destination management or local tourism businesses to influence.

A crisis or disaster at either the receiving or originating country can severely influence visitor perceptions and behaviour, creating a challenge in dealing with consumer perceptions of risk. In a study undertaken after September 11 in the US, 58% of respondents reported travelling less as a result of September 11 (Vlahav *et al.*, 2002 cited in Chen & Noriega, 2003). Government policies to reduce the likelihood of terrorist attacks through safety and security measures, may not necessarily reduce perceptions of risk, but may reduce the likelihood of future successful terrorist attacks. For instance, research on tourism faculty and students, by Chen and Noriega (2003) demonstrated that faculty staff were more likely to experience changes to their life, travel decisions and activity choice than students, and also believed that terrorist attacks were more likely to happen again. However, the students felt less comfortable going through increased security measures at airports than staff and perceived that American businesses over reacted to September 11.

Soñmez and Graefe (1998) discovered in their study that favourable attitudes toward international travel and risk seeking, along with higher income levels, best predicted he likelihood of travel during periods of political instability and terrorism. Floyd *et al.* (2003) in November 2001 research with New York residents discovered that 62.4% rated the risk of terrorism associated with pleasure travel as low or very low. Safety concerns, social risk, air travel experience and income were the best predictors of travel intentions in their survey, helping to better understand the link between risk perceptions and travel intentions. Simpson and Siguaw (2008), in a comprehensive study on perceived travel risks, identified health-related risks as the highest perceived risk, followed by the travel and destination environment, and perceived criminal harm which included sub-categories of safety/security and terrorism.

Soñmez (1998) suggests that tourists tend to change travel behaviours due to terrorism, by substituting risky destinations with safer alternatives during the decision choice process, placing safe destinations in their evoked choice set. Other researchers, have noted how negative perceptions can affect entire regions, such as the Middle East due to political instability (Beirman, 2002) or Asia after SARS and the Boxing Day tsunami (Kozak *et al.*, 2007), drastically affecting destination choice, suggesting that image management is an important aspect of tourism crisis communication.

Image

Image is an important con pt in the tourism literature and an important component of reputation. Crompton (1979: 18) defines an image as 'the sum of beliefs, ideas, and impressions that a person has of a destination'. Leiper (2000) believes that destination image depends upon the tourists' perception of its ability to satisfy their needs. Gartner (1996) indicates that a destination's image is important in the set of variables that influence destination choice and the travel process. If this image is negative then it may significantly impact a destination's competitiveness as destination image has been shown to be a significant factor in determining visitor choice (Konecnik, 2004; Lee *et al.*, 2002), while a loss of reputation due to poor image can affect purchasing decisions in tourism (Callander & Page, 2002 in Stanbury *et al.*, 2005). Gartner (1996) suggests that the image of a place as a potential destination comprises cognitive, affective, and conative components. The cognitive is what is known, or perceived to be known about the potential destination (based upon knowledge and beliefs). The affective is the weighting of what is known by the consumer's value system, which is influenced by individuals' feelings toward the destination. The conative stage of destination image is the 'choice' stage. It refers to the process of making a decision on whether or not to travel to a destination based on the cognitive and affective stages of image development.

In this decision-making theory, the cognitive stage of image building may contain false or inaccurate facts/beliefs about the destination, which may be partly as a result of consumer perceptions or attitudes formed by a crisis or disaster at a destination location. However, modifications to the image can occur as a result of crisis communication and public relations, helping to develop a positive destination image to restore develop positive images and increase visit intentions, followed by recovery marketing efforts to capture actual visitation during the conative stage of the decision-making process. This is in part related to Gunn's (1972) concepts of 'organic' image and 'induced' image, whereby 'organic' images are developed through a lifetime of socialisation and include agents such as popular culture, the media, literature and education. 'Induced' images are those that directly try to influence consumer perceptions of a destination, mostly through official tourist organisations brochures, websites and marketing materials. Gartner (1993) outlined a number of different image formation agents, which range from:

(1) *Induced images* that which are under the control of the destination with differences in control level and credibility. For instance, covert-induced 1 refers to traditional advertising, which is highly controlled but has low credibility. However, covert-induced 2 would consist of lower control levels but higher credibility as consumers source information from the tourist industry. Covert-induced 1 could keep control and credibility high, such as the use of a celebrity, while information provided to the travel industry or media through promotional programmes and travel writing are included in covert-induced 2.

(2) *Autonomous images* include those from the mass media through broadcasting news, documentaries, films and television shows. Such images are perceived as credible and independent from the control of a destination.

(3) *Organic (unbiased) images* are from 'unbiased sources' as a result of word-of-mouth by knowledgeable others and can be either solicited or unsolicited.

(4) *Organic (own experience) images* as a result of tourists own visitation experiences.

These theories and concepts are useful for mangers who may want to reinstate confidence in a destination or an organisation after a crisis or disaster, as they illustrate what methods are the most credible and what influence they may have in changing consumer perceptions. Certainly, the above discussion suggests the difficulty in dealing with the mass media and the importance of crisis communications and public relations as an important precursor to recovery marketing efforts.

The Media Effect

As Gartner and Shen (1992: 47) state, 'the only agent capable of changing an area's image dramatically in a short period of time is the media' due to its high credibility and market penetration. The mass media have also been acknowledged as having an important role in destination pre-selection by helping to stimulate awareness and interest in travel and destinations (Hall, 2002; Nielson, 2001). Crisis management literature emphasises the need to have a detailed communication strategy as the media can encourage the flow and the intensity of a crisis or even turn an incident into a crisis (Keown-McMullan, 1997). Barton (1994a) believes that the implementation of a strategic crisis communication plan can help limit the damage from a crisis and allow an organisation to concentrate on dealing with the crisis at hand. Marra (1998: 461) notes that poor communication strategies can often make the crisis worse as a deluge of questions are often asked from a wide range of stakeholders including reporters, employees, stockholders, government officials and public residents. Media coverage of disasters is often controversial, sensationalist and can even be misleading (Baxter & Bowen, 2004; Faulkner, 2001; Murphy & Bayley, 1989; Soñmez *et al.*, 1999; Tarlow, 1999). As Young and Montgomery (1998: 4) observed 'a crisis has the potential to be detrimental to the marketability of any tourism destination, particularly if it is dramatised and distorted through rumours and the media'.

Responding quickly to demands of the media and public are important as the media have deadlines to work to and are looking for quick sources of information. If the crisis team does not fill the void, someone else will (Coombs, 1999). Zerman (1995: 25) agrees stating 'the mass media has the power to make a break a business'. Sensationalist media coverage of the 1980 Mt St Helens disaster and the 1985 East Kootenay forest fires were noted as contributing to confusion during the emergency phase as the media were blamed for misleading public opinion concerning the severity of the disasters. This also impacted upon the long-term recovery phase for the destination (Murphy & Bayley, 1989). Beirman (2002: 169) notes that the media reporting of the more recent Palestinian–Israeli conflict has given the false impression that Israel is enmeshed in violence, severely damaging the tourism industry at an important time for pilgrimage tourism in 2000/2001. In the Foot and Mouth Outbreak, the British Tourist Authority (BTA) felt that the media was very intense for the first three months and at times their reporting was hostile, sometimes neutral but rarely friendly leading to misinformation and a severe decline in tourism (BTA, 2001). Britton (2003) argued that American Airlines encountered media hostility towards the airline sector prior to September 11, 2001, which perhaps influenced the way that American Airlines handled crisis communication.

A lack of attention to details on the crisis or disaster location can lead to confusion among tourists and potential tourist about safe destinations and can delay the recovery period (Cavlek, 2002; Faulkner, 2001). However, over-time interest in the crisis or disaster from the media will decline as the media begin to focus on new stories, suggesting an issue–attention cycle may dominate crisis and disaster media reporting of crises and disasters. Hall (2002) notes that the media, through the issue–attention cycle can bring issues to the attention of government and policy-makers because of the power and influence they have over public opinion, can help speed up the response and recovery process. Hall (2002: 459) suggests that the issue–attention cycle is 'one of the most significant concepts in understanding the relationship between the media and how important certain issues are to consumers'. Initially developed by Downs (1972) to help understand why social issues are given attention by the media, and how long this attention will last, it has been applied to the influence of the media after September 11, 2001, by Hall (2002). The issue–attention cycle is divided into five stages, which may vary in duration but occur in the same sequence:

(1)   the pre-problem stage;
(2)   alarmed discovery and euphoric enthusiasm;
(3)   realising the cost of significant progress;
(4)   gradual decline of intense public interest; and
(5)   the post-problem stage.

The issue–attention cycle can be seen to follow the crisis lifecycle over time, indicating that although the destination may be undergoing recovery for quite some time, the media and public may lose interest in this issue as another crisis or issue then emerges replacing the new issue in terms of media coverage. Such a decline of interest, according to Hall (2002), could also result in a decline in political interest or impetus to bring about change or investment in recovery strategies. The media's interest, particularly during anniversaries of a crisis or disaster, such as that over delays by the government over rebuilding New Orleans is an example of the issue–attention cycle at work, as is the waning interest in political instability in Nepal in 1999–2001 (Baral *et al.*, 2004). Further evidence of an issue–attention cycle was provided by Beirman (2003: 165), who in discussing the effect of the 1999 Izmit earthquake in Turkey, stated that although...

there was intense media interest in the Izmit earthquake at the time of the event, media coverage ran its course and waned within one month... [o]ther stories such as the onset of the millennium and the great scare of the 'Y2K Bug' rapidly replaced the Izmit earthquake in Western media headlines.

Organisational Crisis Communication and Control

Communication is a key component of strategic planning and management, along with planning, leading, organising and controlling. Crisis communication and public relations are mainly concerned with providing correct and consistent information to both internal and external stakeholders and enhancing the image of the organisation or industry sector faced with a crisis or disaster. The aim of this is to manage negative perceptions and restore consumer confidence, at the same time as undertake recovery marketing to increase tourist activity. This is because, as Cavlek (2002) observes, a crisis usually outlives the physical damage and so the tourism destination and industry need to find ways to manage its affects. Soñmez *et al.* (1999) agree that the media are important agents in rebuilding the image and restoring confidence in a destination or organisation. Nevertheless, despite the importance of dealing with the media difficulties have been noted in managing them as it is unlikely that there will be a time delay between the start of any crisis and media coverage (Ashcroft, 1997). Furthermore, poor media relations during a crisis can severely damage the long-term viability of the industry to recover (Cavlek, 2002) Sensationalist and misleading reporting can significantly affect crisis communication and recovery marketing efforts.

An emphasis on communication and public relations is required to limit harm to an organisation in an emergency that could ultimately create irreparable damage. Cooperation with the media is considered vital because the media provides information to the general public (Berry, 1999), illustrating the need to keep the media briefed frequently so that misinformation is reduced. Regular two-way communication is the best way of developing a favourable relationship with publics (Coombs, 1999). However, Britton (2003) noted that internal public relations and communication is just as important in the context of organisational crises, as staff morale may suffer if cutbacks and job losses occur in the aftermath of a crisis (see Chapter 6 for details on resource allocation and employment). In this respect, American Airlines embarked on a company-wide public relations exercise to improve morale and developed reward programmes for staff continuing after September 11.

Henderson (1999b: 108) states that 'National Tourist Organisations with their responsibility for general destination marketing, research and development have an important role to play in the process of travel and tourism crisis management, representing and acting on behalf of the industry as a whole'. However, Henderson (1999b) found that in the case of the Asian Economic Crisis, the Singapore Tourist Board implemented reactive strategies which took time to implement reducing their effectiveness. Gonzalez-Herrero (1999) explains how numerous tourist enterprises and organisations have managed to reduce the negative impact of crisis situations, thanks to the previous design of a communications plan. Soñmez *et al.* (1999) noted the importance for marketers to have a prepared crisis communication and marketing plan, as the cost of this will be far less than the costs associated with a downturn in visitor confidence and visitation due to a slow response.

As Soñmez *et al.* (1999: 8) suggest 'it is imperative for destinations to augment their crisis management plans with marketing efforts, to recover lost tourism by rebuilding a positive image'. Table 7.1 outlines planning efforts that can be undertaken prior to a crisis or disaster hitting. Situational theory is a way of researching and segmenting an organisation's publics or stakeholders in order to understand them more effectively, and is an important part of developing symmetrical two-way communication (Dozier *et al.*, 1995). According to Gonzalez-Herrero and Pratt (1996: 83), situational theory looks for key traits in publics such as problem recognition, constraint recognition, level of involvement, information seeking and information processing. To date, few researchers have examined the role of situational theory in tourism crisis communication (see Fall, 2004 for an exception). Using these variables, key publics are divided into four segments:

(1) *Non-publics:* groups of individuals or organisations in the environment not affected by an organisation's behaviour.
(2) *Latent publics:* affected by an organisation's behaviour, but they are not aware of it.
(3) *Aware publics:* are affected by an organisation and are aware of it.
(4) *Active publics:* are affected, aware of it and organise to do something about it.

Tourism publics can be divided into four main groups. First, an external group consisting of potential travellers. Second, an internal group comprising travel agents and media representatives. Third, an intervening audience of people who live in work in a tourism destination, and finally, visitors to a tourism destination. All of these publics will need crisis communication strategies implemented by tourism organisations to communicate, help restore confidence and assist with recovery marketing efforts. Strategies work best when communication is two-way and symmetrical. According to Dozier *et al.* (1995), one-way communication emphasises flow of information out from an organisation's management to publics, often through press agencies. In two-way

Table 7.1 Crisis communication theory and crisis communication planning

Lifecycle of a crisis/ disaster	*Situational theory*	*Two-way symmetrical communications*
Pre-event planning/ issues management or reduction	• Define publics • Identify potential problem relationships with stakeholders • Segment publics by difference in response to crisis and by linkage to organisation • Assess level of problem recognition, constraint recognition, involvement, information seeking, information processing among strategic publics • Assess the impact of latent, aware and active publics • Estimate pattern in which issue may evolve, based on preceding assessment • Identify objectives of communications planning.	• Search proactively for potential problem areas • Engage in long-term mutually beneficial, dialogic, socially responsible activities • Conduct symmetrical communications to avert development of issue • Re-emphasise balanced relationships with publics
Readiness and preparation	• Conduct research to ensure plan demonstrates cognisance of public attitudes • Segment publics according to their characteristics *vis a vis* the issue • Develop communication strategies based on characteristics of publics • Identify actions for improving or resolving the situation	• User negotiation, dialogue and bargaining to establish relationships with public • Use dialogue, negotiation, conflict management and shared meanings to develop crisis communication plans • Inform internal public about symmetrical communications with external audiences

Source: Adapted from Gonzalez-Herrero and Pratt (1996).

symmetrical communication, information is gathered about the publics to aid management decision-making, resulting in an organisation sending messages to try and persuade or alter the public's behaviour. Two-way symmetrical differs from this in that communication uses this gathered information to promote mutual understanding, manage conflict and support both sides. As Coombs (1999: 134) states, regular two-way communication is the best way of developing a favourable relationship with publics. Barton (1994a) believes that many issues within crisis communication are often overlooked, such as focusing on identifying the audience, developing goals for communicating effectively and creating strong positive messages, possibly because these take time to develop and implement.

As Figure 7.1 suggests, organisational culture and public relations autonomy may have an influence on crisis prevention and planning, as well as crisis communication processes and practices (Marra, 1998). Research suggests that excellent crisis public relations do not occur without a supportive organisational communication ideology that facilitates communication, with 'closed' or 'defensive' organisational culture not conducive to the development and implementation of effective crisis communication strategies (Marra, 1998). Moreover, Marra (1998) suggests that the amount of power and responsibility an organisation gives its public relations staff predicts excellent crisis communications better than the presence or absence of a plan. Without a supportive organisation, the effectiveness of crisis communication strategies could be limited. Decision-making autonomy in crisis and disaster situations is vital for crisis communication and was outlined in detail in the first part of Chapter 6.

These concepts from the crisis communications field are important in developing more effective tourism crisis communication strategies. First, they illustrate the need to understand the need of key publics, to develop suitable communication and public relations strategies with their needs in mind, and to ensure two-way information flow with publics in order

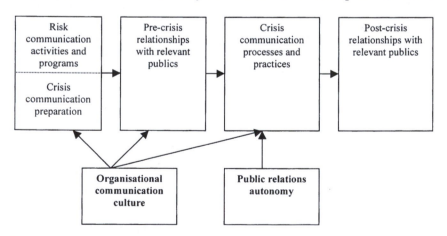

Figure 7.1 A crisis communication model
Source: Reprinted from *Public Relations Review*, 24(4), Marra, F.J., Crisis communication plans: Poor predictors of excellent crisis public relations, pp. 461–474, copyright (1998), with permission of Elsevier.

to improve crisis communication activities. As Dozier *et al.* (1995: 13) suggest, '...communicators practicing a two-way symmetrical model seek win-win solutions to conflicts with publics'. Furthermore, they suggest that organisational culture and providing autonomy for public relations departments are crucial factors that influence the success of crisis communication practice. This suggests that crisis communication planning and the development of a responsive 'outward looking' culture is a priority for the tourism industry.

Crisis Communication in the Emergency and Intermediate Stage

Table 7.2 provides an outline of crisis communication 'dos' and 'don'ts' from Nielsen (2001) in dealing with the media, who are the most important publics as they are able to transmit information to a range of stakeholders, including tourists, potential tourists, tourism businesses and government. Press handling during a crisis is a key factor in how news is presented and can contribute to the final outcome of the crisis (Pen, 2000 in Stanbury *et al.*, 2005) and help develop credibility. As Taylor (2006: 172) notes, '[t]he various media messages convey an image, this image impacts on the attitude of the potential tourist'. Key issues in an effective crisis communication strategy have been summarised by Coombs (1999) and Berry (1999) as:

- existence of a crisis communication plan including a recovery marketing plan;
- rapidity of development and implementation of the marketing campaign;
- access to funding for marketing activities;
- consultation with stakeholders;
- consistency of messages;
- use of messages to correct destination image perceptions; and
- honesty and openness (willingness to disclose information).

Some of these points will be discussed in the remainder of this section, including a discussion of crisis communication strategies for other publics (such as potential travellers and the tourism industry). In particular, this section will focus on crisis communication in the emergency and intermediate stage of a crisis or disaster by focusing on the key themes of quickness in response, consistency, openness and honesty, and providing access to information to reduce the impact of a crisis or disaster. In essence, these activities constitute public relations, which attempt to create a positive image and influence public opinion, often through a third party (such as the media). Fall's (2004) research with convention and visitor bureau managers in the US, found that some

Table 7.2 Crisis communication 'Do' and 'Don'ts'

Do	*Don't*
Do have a crisis plan that includes natural disasters, security breaches, safety issues, strikes and so on	Don't wait for a crisis to design a plan
Do update the plan often	Don't assume that the plan will cater for changing circumstances
Do train tourism participants to handle crisis and do attend to the injured immediately	Don't wait for a crisis to train tourism staff; don't treat the injured as liabilities
Do be aware of legal issues; do document training of staff and the updated crisis plan	Don't admit fault until an investigation and don't offer to pay injured parties' medical costs or compensation until all of the facts are in
Do cooperate fully with government authorities	Don't appear difficult or defensive
Do have one spokesperson (and only one) available at all times to discuss the crisis	Don't let anyone but the spokesperson answer questions; don't speak off the record to anyone
Do speak truthfully, authoritatively, and factually	Don't speak in tourism industry jargon; don't provide lurid descriptions
Do provide facts to the media and respect their deadlines and job functions; do say 'I don't have that information yet'	Don't frustrate the media by lack of cooperation; don't answer reporters with 'no comment'
Do deal equally with all media	Don't favour one reporter over another
Do keep tourists informed	Don't put up a defensive wall of silence
Do show concern for tourism workers also affected by the crisis	Don't appear indifferent to the wider economic consequences on others
Do be prepared for possible questions; tackle negative issues	Don't freeze when interviewed on the television; don't become defensive when asked questions; don't fail to respond to all questions; don't leave a negative impression without making a response
Do verify all callers asking for statements	Don't respond to anonymous enquiries

Table 7.2 (*Continued*)

Do	Don't
Do increase security if necessary, making it highly visible at tourist sites if advisable	Don't appear inactive or incompetent
Do respect privacy	Don't release the names of any victims
Do keep detailed notes of disclosed information	Don't inadvertently contradict what has been previously said
Do initiate information/press updates	Don't be cast in the defensive role of being pursued – initiate contact with media
Do thank a reporter if information has been reported accurately	Don't assume that accurate reporting will happen automatically
Do show concern for tourists, stressing past safety records and actions	Don't assume that others know what has been done in the past
Do create a positive follow-up campaign	Don't allow matters to take their own course
Do review crisis policy after an event	Don't assume that everything worked well

Source: Modified after Nielsen (2001).

eight months after September 11, respondents had increased their use of public relations tactics and decreased advertising tactics, emphasising the importance of public relations after a major tourism crisis.

Quick response

Without a crisis communication plan, the response to a crisis or disaster is likely to be slower, as was the case with the UK foot and mouth outbreak in 2001 where the first response was well into the emergency phase of the disaster (Ritchie *et al.*, 2003). A quick response is often required to deal with negative perceptions associated with a tourism crisis or disaster. Evidence from the Fiji Coups suggest that the development of a Tourism Action Group (TAG) allowed the tourist industry to respond faster than expected after the second coup because the group was prepared and experienced in crisis communication (Berno & King, 2001). Furthermore, some tourism industry associations in hurricane-prone regions in the Caribbean hold templates for press releases ready for release if a natural disaster should occur, while

Stanbury *et al.* (2005) suggest that press release templates would be invaluable in the initial media surge. Having up to date press contact details and maintaining press relations are also suggested as useful tools for proactive crisis communication, and should improve press reporting from the initial start of the crisis or disaster through to recovery and restoration (Beirman, 2003).

In regards to the foot and mouth outbreak, industry representatives at the national level agreed that the response of the tourism sector generally had been slow and the power and effect of the media had been under-evaluated. However, the response of the BTA was to attempt to market and improve the image of the UK to target markets but this process was hampered by the ongoing outbreak and continued spread of the disease throughout the UK. The BTA in their media releases noted this in a statement issued by the head of EU Affairs in Brussels which stated 'in dealing with the Belgian media, the current tactics are more reactive than proactive' (BTA, 2001). As Page *et al.* (2006) noted, the media will set the pace and agenda and it is therefore the role of tourism organisations to react quickly with prompt and consistent information. This requires suitable training of front line staff, which often has to provide such information to media, tourists, potential tourists and the industry itself.

Several authors suggest that specific expertise should be outsourced to public relations agencies, which have specific skills in this area (Stanbury *et al.*, 2005), particularly for smaller organisations. However, as Frisby (2002) suggests in the case of the BTA, who used a public relations agency during the foot and mouth outbreak, the agency was not aware of the tourism product and was therefore discarded after the emergency phase of the crisis.

Consistency

In dealing with the media, the consistency of response is a noted as a key element in crisis communication. The ability to provide a consistent message to all stakeholders will build credibility and preserve the image of an organisation instead of tarnishing reputations through providing inconsistent messages (Coombs, 1999).

As noted in Chapter 6, leadership is required within a specific organisation, within an industry sector, and at a destination level to provide direction and guidance in dealing with incidents as well as a spokesperson to deal with the media. The role of an official spokesperson is vital to control the flow of information and develop consistent messages during the emergency and intermediate stage. This may often be the chief executive officer of an organisation or director of public affairs. In the case of the Singapore Airlines flight SQ 006 crash, the Director of Public Affairs was the key spokesperson alongside the

Chairman and Deputy Chairman (Henderson, 2003). Research comparing US and Spanish tourism organisations suggested that 89% of US organisations had a designated company representative who acted as a spokesperson in crisis situations, compared to 63% in Spain, with only 47% of Spanish representatives undergoing media training compared to 4% in the US (Gonzalez-Herrero & Pratt, 1998). However, Spanish organisations were more likely to have their chief executive as one of the company representatives than their counterparts in the US. Having more than one spokesperson can cause problems due to an increased possibility for mixed messages and incorrect facts to be reported (Stanbury *et al.*, 2005). This was certainly the case in the aftermath of the 2002 Bali bombing where the coordination of press conferences and public statements were uncoordinated, and various individuals were portrayed as authoritative speakers (Gurtner, 2007).

Mechanisms to create consistency or provide access to information can be implemented during the crisis or disaster. For instance, during the foot and mouth outbreak in Ireland a letter of reassurance was sent to 5300 retail travel agents and other trade groups to reassure members of the North American travel trade that Ireland was not closed to tourism (Tiernan *et al.*, 2007). Furthermore, a reassurance letter signed by the Chief Executive of the Irish Tourist Board in New York was published in the travel section of *USA Today* (with a circulation of 2.6 million), while reassurance letters were sent to those who had enquired on the trade websites. These provided information to the tourism industry and potential travellers and enabled the tourist board to develop and implement a recovery marketing campaign once Ireland was declared disease free. After Hurricane Hugo devastated South Carolina in 1990, an official tourism advisory faxed letters to 4000 industry members, media, tourism offices and other relevant bodies (Soñmez & Backman, 1990). The London Tourist Board gave on average six broadcast interviews a week during the foot and mouth outbreak (Hopper, 2002) to deal with negative press coverage, while the 'WOW Philippines' reassurance campaign sought to disseminate a message that terrorist attacks that may happen on part of one island do not impact on the other 7000 islands (Beirman, 2006). The Regent Wall Street Hotel in New York, after September 11, wrote to every customer who had stayed in the hotel to reflect their feelings and situation and the hotel received 'many replies of support, which helped to strengthen our relationships with our guests' (Knable, 2002: 19).

Access to information

Frequent briefing of the media can reduce the amount of misinformation and help to reduce the likelihood of further crises or disasters

(Horsley & Barker, 2002). The very nature of crises and disasters is that they are often unexpected and lack immediate information. Therefore, the media who are looking for quick sources of information to meet deadlines may fill the information void that the crisis creates. As Coombs (1999: 114) states 'silence is a very passive response ... passiveness is the exact opposite perception an organisation should be attempting to create'. Minimising contact with the media in order to distance an organisation from a crisis is not suggested. Pan Am's decision to distance itself from the Lockerbie crash proved misguided (Regester & Larkin, 1998 in Henderson, 2003), while Frisby (2002) acknowledged that disseminating accurate information on a consistent basis was the key part of the BTA's response to the foot and mouth outbreak as well as September 11, 2001.

The role of the media can be argued to be pluralistic, in that they act as an informer, lobbyists and educators (Stanbury *et al.*, 2005). They can assist recovery by helping to make the community aware of potential risks, and in this respect the media can help emergency managers contain damage and raise awareness, acting as a potential agent of mitigation (Perez-Lugo, 2001). Regular press briefings and press releases are important for delivering an accurate and consistent message to the public via the mass media, and to assist with lobbying various stakeholders (such as governments) for recovery marketing funding. For instance, Chacko and Marcell (2007) noted the importance of the New Orleans media centre in providing a venue for updates to deal with 'myths' about the impacts of the hurricane. Websites can also be used by the industry or relevant government agencies to target-specific audiences (media, public, actual or potential tourists), however, the audience, a goal and message should be correctly identified for each stakeholder, as suggested by Barton (1994a) and discussed previously in this chapter. A 'back site' crisis website can be developed prior to a crisis and ready to launch (Page *et al.*, 2006). Coombs (1999) suggest the need for providing instructing information during the initial response, including:

- what, when, where and how information;
- precautions stakeholders should take to ensure safety to enhance business survival; and
- corrective action being undertaken by organisations with respon-sibility.

However, in the foot and mouth case, access to information was difficult initially due to uncertainty and slow response of the national government. Although the development of communication channels were created by the BTA as information and policy was developed, many industry operators were simply unable to access some of the information due to a lack of e-mail and internet facilities. For instance, in the South

East of England, only 60% of Tourist Information Centres had e-mail facilities and prior to the outbreak only six out of 10 Regional Tourist Boards had websites (DCMS, 2001). The website, however, was useful for providing information to potential overseas visitors. Sources of information followed a long chain of command from national government, regional tourist boards, county councils to the local level. At the local level, consistent messages were created by press and media contacts as well as briefing Tourist Information Centre staff regarding what attractions and footpaths were open (Ritchie *et al.*, 2003). Singapore Airlines, after the crash of flight SQ 006 in 2000, immediately provided information on passengers killed, crash survivors and summarised the steps that they undertook, and kept updating this information (Henderson, 2003). Fall (2004) notes how US convention and visitor bureaus increasingly used websites and media releases in the eight-month-period after September 11 compared to before this period, to get their messages out to key publics via the media, even though they are crisis communication methods which they have limited control over. Website feedback, by allowing individuals to submit questions, request further communication which are then used to develop frequently asked questions, and are a good example of two-way symmetrical crisis communication.

Massey (forthcoming) suggests that in the three months after September 11, airlines attempted to restore their image and the image of the industry as a whole by undertaking systematic crisis communication through print, online sources and television advertisements. E-mails were sent to customers, columns written in industry and in-flight magazines to reassure customers that airline travel is safe, with the airlines often aligning themselves with symbols of American freedom and determination (Massey, forthcoming). The Regent Wall Street Hotel in New York ran full page ads in key newspapers showing the façade of the hotel with the copy 'Stars and Stripes Forever', as a picture of unshakable strength (Knable, 2002: 19) after September 11. As Tiernan *et al.* (2007: 317) noted:

> one of the most dominate features concerning the negative publicity attached to the foot and mouth crisis in Ireland was that it occurred at a time when potential holiday makers are very impressionable and engaged in selecting holiday destinations.

The Irish Tourist Board implemented in America an 1-800 telephone number, provided exact precaution details on their websites indicating that Ireland was disease free (at this stage) and made a list of closed attractions available on the website, all which were updated daily (Tiernan *et al.*, 2007). Travel trade and 18,000 travel agents were also included in regular updates regarding both the disease outbreak and tourism in Ireland. Hong Kong hoteliers contacted their valuable corporate market to show that the hotels cared about them even in times of crisis (Lo *et al.*, 2006).

Openness, honesty and sympathy

According to Ray (1999 in Henderson, 2003) there are five crisis communication strategies available including: (1) denying responsibility, (2) hedging responsibility, (3) ingratiation, (4) making amends and (5) eliciting sympathy. Ingratiation strategies seek to increase or gain public approval for the organisation through public relations activities. This can be achieved through bolstering, or reminding people of the positive aspects of the organisation, transcendence to place the crisis in a larger and more positive context or finally through praising others to receive praise from the target (Coombs, 1995 in Massey, forthcoming). Henderson (2003) added to Ray's (1999) five strategies accepting responsibility and looking ahead, whilst noting that these strategies are not mutually exclusive or necessary linear. Henderson (2003) discovered in the aftermath of the Singapore Airlines crash of flight SQ 006 in 2000, that despite the legal consequences the Deputy Chairman of Singapore Airlines accepted responsibility for the accident and expressed his distress, sorrow and regret for the accident, with a minutes silence and company flags flying at half-mast to respect the 83 passengers and crew who lost their lives in the crash. Evidence of 'making amends' consisted of flying family members to funerals while relatives were linked to a staff member trained in counselling, and immediate assistance and compensation were proposed four days after the accident (Henderson, 2003). Reassurances were provided by the airline that a full investigation would be undertaken, and that actions would be undertaken to ensure that the accident would not happen again, showing that the company was looking towards the future.

Although apportioning blame can be contentious, especially as a spokesperson may not have all of the facts, honesty and sincerity are considered important in crisis communication. American Airlines were the only airline post-September 11 to try and elicit sympathy from key publics as a direct involvement of their status as a victim, while remediation were used by many including responding to victim families requests for financial and travel arrangements through to facilitating the donation of frequent flier miles to assist the Salvation Army in providing travel to victim family members (Massey, forthcoming). Furthermore, rectification strategies were widely used early after September 11, with airlines communicating the reinforcement of cockpit doors, even though they were not mandated to do so by federal agencies. Finally, ingratiation, only through the use of bolstering to remind the public that the airlines would now be stronger, to praising others, particularly the citizens of New York and the Department of Transportation's Rapid Response Team's proposal to increase security for airline travellers (Massey, forthcoming). During the emergency and intermediate stages of the crisis, spokespeople and senior management needed to be available and willing to be interviewed and needed to disclose as much information as possible to the media. However, in some cases this may be difficult, such as the case of September 11 where federal agencies were investigating the incident, placed controls on information that could be released by American Airlines complicating crisis communication activities (Britton, 2003).

Long-term Recovery Marketing Actions

The recovery phase of a tourism crisis starts when 'the image of security and pleasure... is shattered, and uncertainty about future conditions will affect bookings and economic prospects' (Murphy & Bayley, 1989: 38), and will depend on the impact of a crisis or disaster on infrastructure as well as image. As discussed above, the first stages of a crisis communication and recovery campaign require restoring confidence through the use of the mass media and public relations campaigns. A key component of a crisis communication plan is a recovery marketing campaign which is frequently used in the short to medium term to counteract negative media coverage, inform consumers and other stakeholders of the destination's status and regain consumer confidence (Ritchie *et al.*, 2003). Marketing recovery campaigns aimed at encouraging continuation of travel or formation of new travel plans are a significant feature of recovery, particularly if the economy is relatively dependent on tourism, and the description and analysis of recovery marketing is receiving considerable researcher and practitioner attention (see for example, Armstrong & Ritchie, 2007; Beirman, 2002, 2003, 2006; Faulkner & Vikulov, 2001; Frisby, 2002; Ritchie *et al.*, 2003).

The main aim of the recovery marketing campaign is to reverse the negative destination image and increase tourist flows and demand. Several techniques are used, including persuasive advertising and partnership marketing, the use of trade shows and visiting media programmes and the hosting of special events. However, the timing of the recovery marketing campaigns is critical. As Young and Montgomery (1998) indicate crises or disasters that damage essential infrastructure, services and facilities necessarily delay marketing recovery campaigns as the priority is on restoring those parts of the destination. In some situations where crises or disasters linger with no clear ending such as political conflict (Beirman, 2002) and diseases or biosecurity outbreaks (Ritchie *et al.*, 2003), it may be difficult to implement recovery marketing until the all clear is given so that public are not confused and resources are not wasted. However, as McKercher and Pine (2005) suggest, pent up demand from possible source markets affected by a crisis or disaster, may provide likely targets for well-timed marketing campaigns.

Consumer advertising and partnership marketing

According to Floyd *et al.* (2003), persuasive advertising is advertising which increases consumer's willingness to travel. But questions arise in understanding who can be influenced and how. As discussed earlier in the chapter, certain socio-demographic groups may be less risk adverse than others. Taylor (2006) believes that persuasive marketing needs to consider specific market segments which would be more likely to respond to such marketing. He outlines two key groups of consumers who have different information processing needs and level of involvement in processing information:

(1) *Centrally processing consumers.* These consumers form or change an attitude on the basis of a deliberate and concerted evaluation of facts. They respond well to two-sided messages outlining the benefits and risks, clear statistics and data. Those who are risk neutral and can be persuaded that safety and security measures have been undertaken, those consumers believe that a visit would provide value (Taylor, 2006). This group may be those people who are already considering a holiday destination which is in their choice set, and are thus highly involved in the decision-making process and seek a level of credible information.
(2) *Peripherally processing consumers.* These consumers are influenced by general messages and sources which express an opinion, rather than their personal evaluation based on facts and perception of value. Isolation marketing (Beirman, 2006) could be used to differentiate specific countries or parts of a country that are safe or totally unaffected by a crisis or disaster. Consistency in updating and reinforcing key messages are vital for this group. The use of opinion leaders, spokespeople, mass media and celebrities could be considered for this group, which has a low level of involvement, and perhaps are at the early stages of their decision-making process.

Fall (2004) suggests that in the eight months after the September 11 terrorist attacks, 48% of convention and visitor bureaus researched had redesigned their promotional message, with a focus on accessibility, safety and relaxation. However, only 33% had redirected their target publics with the most frequently reported changes including a renewed focus on drive markets, regional markets and families (Fall, 2004). Capturing the increased importance placed on family, friends and relationships post-September 11, some visitor bureaus in America also focused accessible domestic self-driven markets with taglines such as 'Fall back in Time: A short drive down the road. A million miles away' developed for Charleston (Litvin & Alderson, 2003) which extended its target markets from a six-hour drive to a 10-hour drive away. Charleston's reputation as a family-orientated destination became an advantage for those seeking safe and secure destinations. It is common after tourism crises or disasters for destination managers to focus on domestic tourism, especially after terrorist attacks or political instability (Soñmez, 1998). The largest changes by hotel managers in Washington, DC, after September 11 were focusing on regional business and redirecting their marketing efforts (see Figure 7.2), particularly those hotels reliant on business travel (Taylor & Enz, 2002). To help recovery of the tourism industry in New Orleans after Hurricane Katrina, the tourist bureau implemented a repositioning campaign directed at repeat visitors asking them to 'Come fall in love with New Orleans all over again' (Chacko & Marcell, 2007).

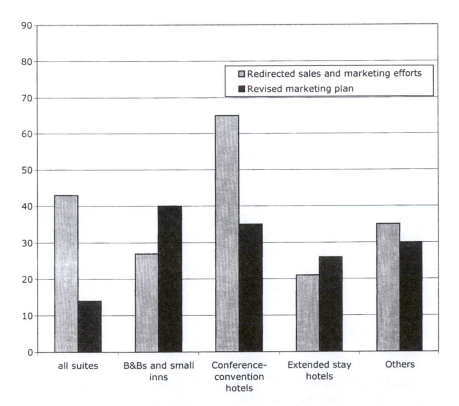

Figure 7.2 Percentages of general managers (by hotel type) who adopted new marketing strategies after 9/11
Source: Modified From Taylor and Enz (2002: 15).

Stafford *et al.* (2002) noted that dialogue and crisis communication strategies with government officials were vital in helping to raise funds for crisis recovery activities with respect to 9/11 in Washington, DC, but also government officials were an important part of strategies to encourage visitation through:

- issuing executive orders to encourage federal agencies to continue to visit and host conferences and conventions in Washington, DC;
- urging the State Department to communicate with embassies to encourage international travel to Washington, DC; and
- using the cast of the 'West Wing' television program, first-lady Laura Bush and other political leaders to promote tourism to the national capital.

Furthermore, George Bush was used in advertisements for the 'Travel Industry Recovery Campaign' to encourage Americans to resume travelling and to see America (Floyd *et al.*, 2003). The ads ran for four weeks and research suggested that more than two-thirds of the public saw the ads. The Irish President and tourism minister played a part in the Irish Tourist Board's recovery marketing campaign during the foot and mouth disease by attending receptions for travel trade, giving interviews to the media and meeting the Irish American community (Tiernan *et al.*, 2007). Furthermore, New Orleans after Hurricane Katrina used opinion leaders and celebrities to deliver credible information to the public about New Orleans, thanking the public for their support and suggesting they visit to help with the recovery effort (Chacko & Marcell, 2007). The use of credible and high-profile celebrities are examples of using biased third parties to endorse and encourage travel after a crisis or disaster.

Evidence on using unbiased third parties to market a destination after a disaster can be found in the case of Canberra, Australia which experienced a major bushfire in January 2003. The development of the Heart Recovery Marketing Campaign only five days after the state of emergency was removed, was smoothly integrated into the existing Autumn campaign in order to convey stability and a forward looking ethos. Armstrong and Ritchie (2007) noted that the print campaign was relatively easy to achieve, but that the television campaign took longer to develop with the first advertisements aired on 30 March (61 days after the state of emergency was lifted), due to the complexity in producing such media.

The print campaign comprised eight full colour advertisements carrying the line 'Our heart's still going strong', which appeared in Sydney metropolitan and New South Wales regional press between 2 and 10 February 2003 (see Figure 7.3). A similar advertisement was placed in the March 2003 edition of the TNT Backpackers Magazine in response to a drop in backpackers. The marketing spend was concentrated on

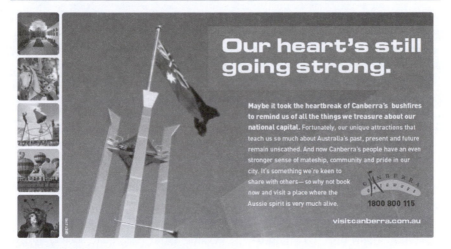

Figure 7.3 Print advertisement from the Heart Recovery Marketing Campaign
Source: Canberra Tourism and Events Corporation (2003), with permission.

reliable markets and there were five clear messages (see Table 7.3). A destination marketing representative mentioned that the print advertising served as a public thank you for the support that Canberra had received from other jurisdictions in addition to letting people know that 'we are still going, open for business and this is when we really need support, so if you were coming to Canberra really think about it before you cancel your holiday' (in Armstrong & Ritchie, 2007).

Although some funds for recovery marketing may come from internal reallocations such as diverting spending on international marketing to domestic marketing, or some small changes to promotional materials already near scheduled production, not all destinations have the resources or time to implement such actions. This requires fundraising or lobbying activities to take place, to ensure suitable resources for an integrated recovery marketing campaign, as discussed in Chapter 6 under discussion of government resource assistance. For instance, Tiernan *et al.* (2007) notes how the Irish Government provided US$2.2 million for both the reassurance and recovery campaign after the foot and mouth outbreak (see Table 7.4). Partnerships are vital between government, and the private sector in any recovery campaign in helping to establish consistency, cost sharing as well as for creating special product or offers to encourage visitation. As Litvin and Alderson (2003) note, the local Charleston convention and visitors bureau worked with hotels and operators to develop packaged vacation experiences directly linked to the recovery campaign. The figures on visitor arrivals and

Table 7.3 Messages from the Canberra Recovery Print Campaign

Direct quote from advertisement	*Implied message*
Our heart's still going strong.	The heart of Canberra (central Canberra) which contains the national attractions (for example, National Gallery, High Court, Old Parliament House, Parliament House, National Museum, National Library) was not damaged by the bushfires. They are still open. Canberra is still healthy – it's heart is still beating.
Maybe it took the heartbreak of Canberra's bushfires to remind us of all the things we treasure about our national capital.	With disaster comes reflection on what we value about Australian society and community. The capital contains many nationally significant monuments, museums and collections and the true value of these was not acknowledged until Australians were in danger of losing them.
Fortunately, our unique attractions that teach us so much about Australia's past, present and future remain unscathed.	The unique national capital attractions in Canberra were *not* damaged in the bushfires.
And now Canberra's people have an even stronger sense of mateship, community and pride in our city.	Canberra is often derided as the 'city without a soul' but the bushfires have shown that the city does have a strong sense of community as evident in the cooperative recovery effort.
It's something we're keen to share with others – so why not book now and visit a place where the Aussie spirit is very much alive.	When interacting with locals, visitors will encounter this Canberra spirit. Visit Canberra to experience the Aussie (slang for Australian) spirit.

Source: The Heart Recovery Marketing Campaign: Destination recovery after a major bushfire in Australia's national capital. Armstrong, E.K. and Ritchie, B.W. *Journal of Travel & Tourism Marketing*, 2007, 23 (2/3/4), 175–190, reprinted by permission of the publisher. (Taylor & Francis Group, http://www.informaworld.com).

average daily rate in accommodation suggested a year-on-year growth from November 2001 onwards and the single biggest April ever experienced, despite a gloomy picture for the USA as a whole (Litvin & Alderson, 2003).

Table 7.4 Irish government budget allocation to the reassurance and recovery campaign

Budget allocation	*Amount (US$)*
Advertising phase 1	1,600,000
Advertising phase 2	1,600,000
Ministers visit	60,000
Task force	60,000
Postcard mailing	300,000
Other direct mail	100,000
Public relations	85,000
Trade advertising	50,000
Radio advertising	60,000
Delta in-flight advertising	40,000
Travel	40,000
Total	3,995,000

Source: Tiernan, S., Igoe, J., Carroll, C. and O'Keefe, S. (2007) Crisis communication response strategies: A case study of the Irish Tourist Board's response to the 2001 European Foot and Mouth Scare. In E. Laws, B. Prideaux and K. Chon (eds) Crisis Management in Tourism (pp. 310–326). Wallingford: CAB International, reprinted by permission of the publisher.

This was attributed to the targeting of new markets, which have also been undertaken in many other crises (de Sausmarez, 2005), while flight and accommodation packages were offered to customers after the 1999 Taiwan earthquake (Huang & Min, 2002). Singapore, in response to the crisis events in the late 1990s targeted niche markets such as seniors, the young and honeymooners as well as providing discounts to friends or relatives of Singaporeans in their 'Friends of Singapore' scheme (Henderson, 1999b). However, 'ideally, the incentives should cover as wide a spread of tourism product as possible ... encouraging all elements to benefit from the recovery phase' (Beirman, 2003: 37). Hong Kong implemented the 'Be my guest' campaign after it was declared disease free, which had the support of 77 members of the Hong Kong Hotels Association (Pine & McKercher, 2004).

The English Tourism Council (ETC) was given £3.8 million to promote tourism to domestic audience in April 2001 due to the foot and mouth outbreak, which was spent on specific market campaigns, coupled with developing websites to inform potential visitors of the places safe to visit.

The ETC calculated that this financial aid generated 766,000 additional visits and produced a return on investment of £27 for each £1 spent (ETC, 2001). In May, a further £12 million was given to the BTA for international marketing, while no further finance was available for the ETC and the domestic market (ETC, 2001). The BTA started planning in September 2001 to re-brand and re-image Britain through a new £5 million campaign called 'UK OK' which was implemented in January 2002 to attract the visiting friends and relatives market. This was targeted at seven selected key markets (USA, Canada, Germany, France, Belgium, Netherlands, the Republic of Ireland). However, industry representatives believed that it was not enough for such a large target audience (Ritchie *et al.*, 2003). Further funding for marketing of Britain overseas was secured in April 2002 with £20 million contribution from the government, £5 million cash from industry and a further £15 million of collateral marketing by the campaign partners (BTA, 2002). This money was spent on the 'Only in Britain: Only in 2002' campaign which was expected to attract an extra one million visitors in 2002 and generate £0.5 billion for the national economy (BTA, 2002). Frisby (2002) noted the importance of private sector partners who could contribute cash and in kind for tactical marketing campaigns, as well as provide venues for press briefings.

Media partners were very important for PATA's 'Project Phoenix', the overall strategy used to coordinate tourism recovery for all destinations affected by the SARS outbreak in 2003. Working behind the scenes with their contacts at CNN, BBC World and CNBC PATA positioned itself as the authority they could turn to for information and received extensive press coverage. These media organisations were used to publicise positive messages that SARS was under control and that destinations were safe and ready to welcome tourists. According to Beirman (2006), this was one of the most effective models of perception management in tourism. PATA worked closely with National Tourist Authorities to secure US$350,000 in three weeks alone (de Jong, 2004). Using the media agencies, who relied on tourism advertising revenue, PATA along with CNN, TIME and Fortune developed a the 'Welcome Back', media campaign pitched at the hearts and minds of global travellers (see Figure 7.4). Furthermore, the role and influence of Non-Governmental Organisations (NGOs) in recovery marketing should not be under estimated. For instance, the Nepal Tourism Board (NTB) noted the importance of partnership marketing particularly, with the NTB working with the Nepal Mountaineering Association in promoting the 50th anniversary of the climbing of Mount Everest (Baral *et al.*, 2004). This was considered important for a small country with limited resources, helping to extend the reach of their marketing efforts after a period of political instability.

Figure 7.4 Welcome Back Campaign implemented by PATA 'Project Phoenix'
Source: PATA, with permission.

It is obvious that partnerships between DMOs, public sector, non-government sector and the private sector are important, however, for large-scale crises and disasters, regional cooperation and involvement in recovery marketing may be necessary As Beirman (2006) suggests, although a crisis may affect a specific location, it often has a regional impact. Regional recovery models or alliances may have to be developed. In the Asia-Pacific region organisations such as APEC and PATA play important coordination roles, as their 'independence from individual governments, strong ties with business stakeholders, and regional focus are valuable facilitators in recovery programs ranging from terrorism to SARS to the Indian Ocean tsunami' (Beirman, 2006: 13). Using existing government networks, such as ASEAN have also been suggested by some authors to deal with tourism crises and disasters together, although under normal circumstances are traditionally competing for the inbound tourism market (de Sausmarez, 2005).

However, although there are examples of 'good practice' and useful hints at alliances, there are few examples of recovery marketing campaigns that have been deemed unsuccessful or those that have failed. For instance, Gurtner (2007) suggests that although recovery marketing campaigns were conducted after the 2002 Bali bombing; they lacked coordination, were not developed quickly enough and lacked substantial resources. The initial campaigns 'Bali for the World' and 'Unified Diversity: United We Stand' were initially formulated to show the strength of the industry and community, while trying to capture interest in culture and heritage. However, they failed to capture significant media or consumer interest (Gurtner, 2007). There is a need for more research to examine the failure of recovery marketing campaigns and the underlying reasons for their failure, as well as their often slow response. In some instances this may be due to the time it takes in receiving financial support, aid or even drafting legislation to allow the use of government funds, as was the case with the 2002 and 2005 Bali bombings (Andari, 2007).

Industry and media roles in recovery marketing

Although visiting media programmes may be useful in some crisis or disaster situations, they may constitute a waste of resources unless they are well timed. The hosting of study trips for the travel trade and media, are useful to develop and promote messages to key target markets (Cavlek, 2002) and for industry representatives to see recovery at first hand and reduce negative media coverage. Potential clients rely heavily on 'organic' images created independently of local or national authorities, while induced' images given by travel trade will also be more credible than those from authorities (Cavlek, 2002), especially for those potential travellers who process information peripherally. The BTA in April 2001 brought a group of 40 travel industry leaders from Japan, Canada, the USA and across Europe to see for themselves the impact of the foot and mouth outbreak (Frisby, 2002). This combined with the hosting of the World Travel Leaders Summit covered by media coupled with television programmes, gala events and placement of advertorials were all part of an integrated marketing communication programme. The Maldives also hosted visiting media after the tsunami to explain that most of the resorts were operational and that tourism could help residents to rebuild their lives (Carlsen, 2006). In Taiwan, after the 1999 earthquake, more than 400 representatives of overseas media and major foreign tour wholesalers were invited for familiarisation tours of the earthquake-affected areas. The NTB undertook a major public relations exercise with media representatives while dealing with political insecurity and unrest from 1999 to 2001. This included familiarisation trips for operators and journalists in key source markets, particularly those closer to Nepal, which required fewer resources than the UK or USA markets (Baral *et al.*, 2004).

Henderson (1999b) notes the Singapore Tourism Board doubled the number of trade shows in the late 1990s to deal with combined crises and disasters. A three-year Global Meet 2000 initiative was launched costing

S$6 million and involving exhibitors, hoteliers and Singapore Airlines. Taipei International Travel Fair in November 2001 was used to help improve the image and restore the destination after the earthquake (Huang & Min, 2002). Chacko and Marcell (2007) explain how meeting planners were lured back to New Orleans after Hurricane Katrina through a public relations and advertising programme featuring testimonials. An advertising campaign featured the byline 'New Orleans, just as you remember it,' and as described by Chacko and Marcell (2007: 232) 'displayed photographic evidence of time-stamped French Quarter scenes before and after the storm (with no discernable difference). In addition, a direct e-mail campaign was mounted, also to travel intermediaries, showing images of the undamaged areas of New Orleans'. The World Travel Market, one the largest trade fair, was used by Indonesia after the first Bali bomb attack (Henderson, 2003). Furthermore, after the foot and mouth outbreak, Visit Britain used the Queen's silver jubilee anniversary in 2002 as a key promotional event (Frisby, 2002; Hooper, 2002), while anniversary events of terrorist attacks, such as those in Bali and Egypt have also offered an opportunity for destinations to develop positive media relations, while hosting important regional conferences and events also help the recovery marketing effort, especially for crises such as terrorism (Soñmez, 1998).

An event allows a positive focus and can help the public and private sector work together to provide marketing, incentives and discounts to stimulate visitation. Although not located in origin markets, there are opportunities to engage media and industry directly in source markets, although examples are limited. For instance, a week-long 'Agent Appreciation Week' which was undertaken in five American cities for the Irish Tourist Board foot and mouth recovery campaign, included an hour-long trade show followed by dinner and entertainment (Tiernan *et al.*, 2007).

Monitoring recovery marketing

As McKercher and Pine (2005) suggest, the timing of campaigns are crucial, not least because early campaigns may be deemed as insensitive. Market research throughout the response and recovery period can help track consumer and industry perceptions and willingness to respond to recovery marketing techniques. Research may include commissioning media monitoring agencies as in the case of the foot and mouth outbreak (Tiernan *et al.*, 2007) or research to help decision-making on campaign timings (Armstrong and Ritchie, 2007; Britton, 2003). In responding to the 2003 Canberra bushfires, Australian Capital Tourism (the DMO) commissioned research to gauge Sydney residents' perceptions of Canberra post-bushfires (Australian Capital Tourism Corporation, 2004). The research comprised a short telephone survey with a random sample of Sydney residents and found that 53% of respondents agreed with the statement 'the recent bushfires have made me see the human side to Canberra in a way I didn't before' and 25% with 'the recent bushfires in Canberra have made me realise the importance of Canberra as the national capital of Australia' and 'has given me a stronger sense of ownership and identification with Canberra as a national capital'. These findings contributed to the format and creative direction of the print and television recovery campaign in February and March 2003, after the state of emergency had been lifted.

Although some researchers have acknowledged that no conversion studies have been conducted on recovery marketing activities (Litvin & Alderson, 2003), others have clearly had the resources and foresight to conduct such activities to monitor the impact of recovery marketing campaigns. Research from the 2003 Canberra bushfires suggested that from those respondents who saw the advertisement, 68% expressed an interest in visiting Canberra for a short break holiday and 70% in visiting for cultural events or exhibitions, compared with 49% and 54%, respectively, for those who did not see the advertisement (Armstrong & Ritchie, 2007). The tracking and monitoring of recovery campaigns are vital to measure their success.

A media evaluation system was used by the BTA to assess the media coverage of their recovery campaigns during the foot and mouth outbreak, while other information from individual journalists was also collected. Research on five of the specific marketing campaigns were evaluated and suggested 216 million positive 'opportunities to see', generating £1.9 million in positive public relations value (Frisby, 2002). Research on PATAs 'Project Phoenix' campaigns illustrated that a total of US$1.4 million of advertising space with CNN, TIME and Fortune was undertaken with an estimated US$2.2 million worth of exposure generated taking into account all 'Project Phoenix' exposure (de Jong, 2004). As noted in Chapter 6, research on the value of such campaigns may help provide the evidence required to help lobby the government for resources for tourism crisis and disaster response and recovery activities.

Conclusion

This chapter outlined the importance of image and perceptions for the tourism industry and the effect crises and disasters can have on consumer destination choice. In particular, it suggests that the media have an important role to play in crisis communication, perceptions management and recovery marketing. The media can encourage the flow and the intensity of a crisis or disaster or even help turn an incident or issue into a crisis due to negative media coverage. Subsequently, organisations need to work with the media to ensure that a consistent and accurate message is transmitted to the various public and stakeholders.

A crisis or disaster communication plan should be part of the pre-event strategy but also needs to be flexible depending on the nature of the crisis and the response of stakeholders. Key target audiences should be identified and a communication and public relations plan developed and implemented paying particular attention to concepts such as the issue–attention cycle and understanding the information needs of key publics. Symmetrical two-way communication may be the best way to communicate to public during the emergency and intermediate stage of a crisis or disaster. Quick communication is required while destinations and organisations should develop a consistent set of messages through a spokesperson, provide access to information for stakeholders and should be open, honest and express sympathy to victims at all times.

In the long-term recovery phase, recovery marketing initiatives are often undertaken using integrated marketing communication pro-grammes that include persuasive consumer advertising as well as partnership marketing between government and industry stakeholders. The timing of marketing campaigns is crucial in order to limit wasting resources and misjudging consumer sentiment. The use of credible and unbiased third parties, such as celebrities, politicians and the like may be used to provide more credibility to marketing efforts, while the travel trade and media can be invited to take part in trade shows, events and familiarisations in order to increase positive exposure to the destination seeking to reverse negative images. Recovery marketing activities can be costly and fundraising and collaboration between the public and private sectors are often required. Finally, research is required to understand the information needs of publics, help establish when recovery marketing campaigns should start and should be used to evaluate their effectiveness. Such information is vital for the future support of recovery marketing campaigns by government and industry.

Part 4

Tourism Crisis and Disaster Recovery, Resolution and Feedback

Chapter 8
Long-term Recovery and Resolution

Introduction

This chapter discusses how destinations and organisations work towards the goal of resolving the crisis or disaster and finally a restoration back to normal conditions. However, it questions whether in some cases normality can ever be restored. Some crises, depending on their magnitude and nature, can have a dramatic impact upon individuals, organisations and destinations. In some cases, resolution or restoration is complicated as other towns or cities may be still suffering the impact of a crisis or disaster while others have entered into the resolution stage or may not have suffered at all. This chapter outlines community responses to crisis and considers reinvestment strategies in providing marketing support and changing practices that lead to crisis situations, and ensuring destination and business move towards what can be considered 'normal practice'.

This chapter also notes that crises and disasters can be a force for positive as well as negative change and several examples are provided where the community, or indeed the tourism and travel industry, has been strengthened through responding to such incidents. First, this chapter outlines key aspects of the long-term recovery and resolution phase, in order to provide the context for the remainder of the chapter.

Understanding the Long-term Recovery and Resolution Phase

The final stage of the crisis and disaster lifecycle is that of resolution, which occurs when recovery efforts are no longer required and have been finished. The resolution stage of a crisis or disaster is where a routine is restored or a new and improved state can be established. An improved state is possible, as discussed in Chapter 2, because crises and disasters are often seen as turning points and provide opportunities as well as threats for tourism destinations and managers. As Berman and Roel (1993: 82) note with respect to the 1985 Mexico City earthquake, '[c]rises bring about marked regressions as well as opportunities for creativity and new options. They are turning points in which regressive tendencies uncover discrimination (and) resentment about ethnic and socioeconomic differences... yet they also trigger progressive potentials and solidarity'. The collaboration of tourism enterprises alongside emergency or disaster managers to restore and rebuild tourism destinations affected by crises or disasters, provides an opportunity for change and transformation that can be viewed as positive in the long term, especially if learning results from such incidents (see Chapter 9 for more detail on organisational learning).

However, depending on the size and nature of the tourism crisis or disaster, it may take several months or even years for the destination and tourism businesses to reach the resolution stage of a crisis or disaster, if indeed victims ever fully recover. This is in part dependent on the resilience and vulnerability of an organisation, destination and community and the support provided for recovery efforts. According to Peters and Pikkemaat (2005), it took the community around one year to re-establish routines after the 1999 Avalanche disaster in Tyrol. Interestingly, in a longitudinal study on forest fires in Kelowna, British Columbia, Canada, conducted by Hystad and Heller (2008), the food and beverage sector was the fastest sector to recover in three months, compared to the accommodation sector (which took five months) and the entertainment-related sector (which took 10 months). In Phuket, after the 2004 tsunami, only 20% of hotel rooms were lost and 85% reopened after one week (Henderson, 2005).

At a destination and community scale, after the Croatian–Yugoslav war in 1995, it took several years of infrastructure investment on roads, communication and transport infrastructure resulting from government funds and international aid assistance. The World Heritage Listed port city Dubrovnik sustained considerable damage during the war, with damage to over 60% of the buildings in the city (Beirman, 2003), illustrated in Figure 8.1. Although Dubrovnik's recovery was slowed in 1999 due to the neighbouring Kosovo conflict, it reached pre-war visitor arrivals in 2000, some five years after the end of the war. As Ren (2000) noted, it is not uncommon for a second crisis to exploit underlying vulnerability caused by the first crisis, providing a negative cumulative effect, which can hinder the long-term process of recovery.

To understand when a destination or business is fully recovered and returns to 'normal' activities, it is important to highlight the multiple dimensions or criteria often used to comprehend when resolution occurs. Is a destination fully recovered if its tourism economy and visitor arrivals are back to or better than, pre-crisis or disaster levels? However, what if its inhabitants or workers still suffer psychological distress and have not been able to cope psychologically with a crisis or disaster? How important is community and human recovery to the tourism industry? These questions highlight the economic, social and human dimensions of recovery, and the need for longitudinal research on what constitutes the end of recovery and the final resolution of crises and disasters. Camilleri *et al.* (2007) from their study of recovery from the 2003 Canberra bushfires suggest that, '[w]hile many people did not experience lasting

Figure 8.1 Dubrovnik rebuilt
The walled port city of Dubrovnik, Croatia, which received substantial funds to rebuild the city as the tourist icon of Croatia. Note the different coloured roof tiles with the darker colour representing new tiles that replaced the roofs destroyed during the war.

negative psychological outcomes following the 2003 Canberra bushfire, a considerable number of individuals continue to encounter ongoing mental health and psychosocial problems'. Their research identified that 12.9% of respondents surveyed could meet the diagnostic criteria for post-traumatic stress disorder three years after the bushfire (Camilleri *et al.*, 2007). Furthermore, as Faulkner and Vikulov (2001: 344) state:

> the expectation of returning the destination to a situation that exactly replicates the pre-disaster equilibrium is therefore neither realistic, nor necessarily desirable. It is not realistic because some of the negative impacts (e.g. financial losses and downstream impacts on investment capacity) are unavoidable, while it is not desirable because there are positive impacts (e.g. improved cohesion of the tourism sector) that can contribute to the longer-term sustainability of the destination.

The question of resolution is also difficult to answer due to the complexity of such incidents and the scale and scope of some crises and disasters. As Miller and Ritchie (2003) note, the foot and mouth outbreak was a complex biosecurity disaster as the prodromal, emergency and recovery stages were all happening simultaneously at different locations and different industrial sectors at the same location. There was no turning point, such as a reopening of a business after a bushfire in which one could identify as the end of recovery and the resolution phase. Thus the end of recovery and the start of the resolution phase were only possible when the disease was completely eradicated and the whole country announced disease free in March 2002.

Further complexity on the end of recovery and the resolution phase may be because some elements of the tourism system may actually benefit from a tourism crisis or disaster, either with respect to particular sectors or locations. For instance, Wright (2003) noted an increase in tourist arrivals to England's South East coastal town of Eastbourne, at the expense of rural tourism, while Coles (2003) noted a similar pattern in the South West of England. After September 11, 2001, Enz and Canina (2002) noted that hotels located in five states actually improved their year-to-year performance in the fourth quarter of 2001, against the national trend. This was in part attributed to their lower population figures meaning that they had greater reliance on regional travel and less reliance on air travel.

In some cases tourism businesses may gain advantages from servicing people involved in the recovery and reconstruction efforts and may recover themselves quicker than other sectors. This may be through providing catering or accommodation facilities, with hotels an obvious example (Drabek, 2000). As Pottorff and Neal (1994: 117) state, 'if hotels survive the [disaster] impact their occupancy percentages may increase. The media, insurance adjusters, disaster works, victims, and even researchers converge to the site', perhaps helping to speed up recovery and resolution. Faulkner and Vikulov (2001) noted that despite the flood, the Katherine region had nearly 60,000 more guest nights in 1998, compared with 1997. This was attributed to the influx of trades-people drawn to the area in the reconstruction phase over the first two quarters of 1998. Furthermore, as identified in Chapter 6, some restaurants in Hong Kong benefited from SARS by promoting SARS immune meals and providing meal delivery services. Some tour operators may set up tours for visitors to inspect the damage of a natural disaster, while a company in America apparently sold the ash remains from the Mt St Helens disaster as souvenirs (Pottorff & Neal, 1994).

At a destination level, Bonham *et al.* (2006) illustrated an increase in travel by Americans post 9/11 to Hawaii as a substitute for foreign travel. However, the researchers also note that US government's policy requiring Americans to show passports when returning from Mexico, Canada and many destinations in the Caribbean could also be responsible for an increase in domestic travel to Hawaii. Other research on the effect of terrorist attacks suggests that the 'spillover effect' may taint destinations located in close proximity to political instability, while tourists chose safer locations (Soñmez, 1998). Another perspective is that the destination affected by a crisis or disaster may increase its appeal by using the media focus and interest to market itself to potential consumers once the crisis or disaster is over. For instance, Faulkner and Vikulov (2001) believed that the media exposure in Katherine after the floods enhanced its appeal as a destination. Bartlett (1993, cited in Field, 2003) highlighted the case of Kauai who promoted their beaches after Hurricane Iniki carried sand from the sea onto the shores. Hurricane Mitch in Honduras ended up cleaning the coral reefs, rather than destroying them, proving a valuable and marketable resource for the diving industry. While Armstrong (2008) noted that the 2003 Canberra bushfires produced a number of positive impacts for the tourism industry and for Canberra's destination image including boosting community spirit, humanising the city, increasing the region and city's profile and awareness, re-valuing the industry, and opportunities for product development. Some of these positive impacts are noted in the next section.

Long-term Transformation

As discussed in Chapters 1 and 2 and at the start of this chapter, the definition of crisis has an element of transformation associated with it. The two Chinese characters, which together form the word crisis, separately mean threat and opportunity. Furthermore, the turning points of crises and disasters and the concept of recovery are consistent with chaos and complexity perspectives, which see chaos as a creative process. Therefore, during the recovery phase and movement towards resolution, it is not surprising that transformation (both positive and negative) can be found within organisations, destinations and communities that have experienced such incidents. This section explores some of the ideas of transformation from these three perspectives, which indicate how crises and disasters can have profound changes at the long-term recovery and resolution stage.

Organisation transformation

As Barnett and Pratt (2000) suggest, crises and the organisational learning that occurs within an organisation (which is discussed in Chapter 9) can constitute organisational renewal through experimentation and adaptation. 'A seemingly life-threatening organisational crisis may ironically result in increased organisational vitality and longevity. In the end, crisis breeds stability' (Barnett & Pratt, 2000: 76). Miller and

Ritchie (2004) in their research on the impact of the foot and mouth outbreak on the Cheltenham Festival horse race, noted that although the event was cancelled in 2001 it enabled the event organisers to re-evaluate the relationship between the festival, its suppliers and stakeholders, particularly with regard to issues such as dependency and partnerships. The disaster forced recognition that there had been complacency with regard to the value of customers from Ireland as well as the 6500 members of Cheltenham who were not entitled to a refund on their membership because of the cancellation of one particular racing meet during the year, even though the festival represents the main attraction of membership. This caused great upset amongst some members and the managing director conceded the problems arose in describing a policy that was not well stated originally. However, as a result of the disaster he stated that, '... we will better state it (the policy) so that people know at the point of engagement what the deal is ... it is a very good example of how we have taken them for granted and therefore we haven't managed it well and so we now have a whole new re-design of how we are going to engage with our members' (in Miller & Ritchie, 2004).

Similarly, the cancellation of the festival meant local hoteliers, restaurateurs and others dependent on the three-day meet were forced to re-evaluate their relationship with the racecourse. There was evidence that suppliers had profited from the outbreak by being refunded after the decision to cancel, and then not passing this refund on to those who would supply the suppliers. Such practices have led to a revision of relationships and a tightening of the procedures for engagement with suppliers by the event organisers. Furthermore, attention has been drawn to the inappropriately low levels of insurance cover that many organisations had, weighing the likelihood that outbreak, or something similar, would not happen again.

The evaluation of relationships with stakeholders can also lead to opportunities to develop new products, new markets, programmes and ways to reduce costs (Okumus & Karamustafa, 2005), some of which were mentioned in Chapter 6 of this book, which may continue in the recovery phase. In the case of the 2001 economic crisis in Turkey, the short- and long-term positive impacts are outlined in Table 8.1. The table indicates that in the short-term hoteliers were able to increase prices in Turkish Lira, able to reduce costs and introduce new management techniques. In the longer term, respondents believed that more attention would be given to marketing, new markets would be expanded and they would employ more professional management techniques. However, due to the nature of the research no detailed information is available on what these professional management techniques are, and whether they include crisis planning and the use of appropriate prevention and planning techniques. Ready and Dobbie (2003) discovered in a survey

Table 8.1 Perceived short- and long-term positive impacts of the 2001 Turkish economic crisis

Short-term positive impacts		Long-term positive impacts	
Items	*Mean Score[1]*	*Items*	*Mean Score[1]*
Managed to increase our prices in Turkish Lira	1.98	More attention will be given to marketing	1.63
The crisis let us decrease our costs	2.09	The crisis will lead us to expand into new markets	1.80
Introduced new management techniques	2.70	Will employ more professional management techniques	1.81
We recognised some of our operational problems	2.81	Service quality will become more important	1.90
Introduced a restructuring process	2.83	The crisis will force us to develop new products	1.91
The crisis helped us to build our self-confidence	2.89	The crisis will facilitate mergers in the tourism industry	1.91
Foreign tourism demand has increased	2.93	We can put more pressure on the government for support	2.43
Realised our internal managerial inefficiencies	3.02		
Government support to the industry increased	3.28		

Source: Modified after Okumus and Karamustafa (2005).
[1]Scale values range from 1 (strongly agree) to 5 (strongly disagree).

of US motor coach-based operators that 42% were considering increasing part of their operations after September 11, 2001, with 43% indicating a focus on a different market segment. A total of 76% of operators were optimistic about their businesses, while 10% were uncertain and only 1% pessimistic (Ready & Dobbie, 2003).

Other studies have shown how a crisis can foster organisational team spirit and cohesion. For instance, Kwortnik (2006) outlined how hotel employees worked together to overcome the difficulties surrounding the 2003 electrical blackouts in the US. Some hotel managers suggested providing excellent levels of personal service due to the blackouts, hopefully providing positive impressions, gaining confidence and loyalty of guests. Two-thirds of managers who lost power anticipated a positive impact on hotel image (and loyalty) from the crisis, compared to only 22% of managers from hotels that did not lose power (Kwortnik, 2006). Thus the crisis was seen as a way to provide exceptional service with customers, build loyalty and team spirit amongst hotel workers and the community.

Destination transformation

From a tourism systems perspective, Scott *et al.* (2007) argued that destinations are networks of stakeholders which may be reconfigured into more efficient structures following a crisis. Crises may also lead to a more cohesive industry-wide or community-wide response mechanisms, better information flows and indeed the development of new organisa-tional structures. Details on improvements to government policies for tourism crises and disasters specifically, through organisational learning and feedback, are outlined in Chapter 9 in detail. However, new services and products may be developed during the resolution stage of a tourism crisis or disaster as a result of government agency policies, either directly or indirectly affecting tourism. As Hills (1998) notes, disasters may also become political events in themselves, prompting or accelerating change within an affected community. Many authors have commented on the more visible importance and role of tourism in rural communities in the UK after the foot and mouth outbreak (Coles, 2003; Miller & Ritchie, 2003; Sharpley & Craven, 2001; Williams & Ferguson, 2005). As Sharpley and Craven (2001: 535) stated:

> there is no doubt that, in a positive sense, the foot and mouth crisis in Britain has served to focus attention on the value, scope and importance of rural tourism and the extent to which it is an integral element of economic and social structures in rural areas.

Several key policy decisions were made at the national level after the crisis, including:

- the need for more cohesive marketing at local, regional and national levels and that funding levels should be commensurate with the contribution to the tourism economy;
- the creation of regional tourism satellite accounts to measure the economic impact of tourism at a regional level; and
- new national protocols on footpath closures to limit them in area and time, as contact between walkers and animals was deemed to very low.

The Thai government after the 2004 tsunami also committed to stronger regulation of structural standards and redevelopment activities close to the shoreline, according to Gurtner (2006), which is an important part of reducing future vulnerability through structural and non-structural mitigation measures. An increased emphasis on safety, security and emergency response capabilities in Bali has also been noted (Gurtner, 2006). At a regional level, Peters and Pikkemaat (2005: 16–17) note the following new mitigation programmes and tourism products created at the resolution stage of the Avalanche disaster in Tyrol in 1999:

- The 'Alpinarium', an avalanche barrier and multifunctional building informs tourists about avalanche disasters in the past. The institution systematically collects data about natural alpine disasters and fosters networking with other institutions in the field of catastrophe management (see www.alpinarium.at). On the one hand, this new building is an architectural and entertainment attraction for tourists, and on the other hand, it provides safety and security for the centre of Galtuer.
- A non-profit 'Alpine Safety and Information Centre' (ASI) was established to promote safety and security in the mountain environment (see www.alpinesicherheit.com). Its goal is to provide a communication bridge to all participating institutions and local organisations.
- A new internet platform pursuing the goal to overcome geographical barriers and to allow efficient communication among security and emergency units without time constraints. Furthermore, the public part of the platform allows targeted and controlled communication among the crisis management team members, media, and interested stakeholders (e.g. potential tourists). The system was first used at the Olympic winter games 2001 in St Anton, Austria, to support security management in the destination.
- Another product is emergency preparedness checklists, which are customised solutions and plans for organisations in mountain regions (e.g. checklists for avalanche accidents, search operations, aircraft accidents).

Some communities are able to rebuild their tourism infrastructure through financial assistance from aid agencies, government or insurance payouts. Furthermore, the government can stimulate new investment in tourism through providing tax incentives and adjust tourism planning and marketing plans. In Honduras, after Hurricane Mitch, the government was able to restructure the government tourism department and introduce new policies and programmes to support the development of tourism. A major programme of modernising hotel infrastructure was undertaken and the development of tourism was more widely dispersed throughout the country to reduce inequality (Field, 2003). In some cases, government may provide tax breaks to speed up the recovery phase, and in doing so encourage the development of private investment in tourism and the privatisation of tourism-related infrastructure, such as the case of Croatia (Beirman, 2003). The refurbishment and improvement of infrastructure was found to be the most positive outcome of the 2002 floods in Saxony, Germany, according to Bernsdorf (2004). While after the foot and mouth outbreak in Keswick, England, a newly formed partnership company, Rural Regeneration, rebranded Keswick as 'Hi-Energy' by promoting extreme sports experiences and constructing the first mountain bike trail in England (Williams & Ferguson, 2005). This was seen as an important step not only towards long-term recovery but also future prosperity for the local tourism industry by attracting 'better quality' tourism.

Faulkner and Vikulov (2001: 341–342) also noted a number of positive and negative transformations from the 1998 Katherine Flood, which are illustrated in Figure 8.2. In particular, additional positive transformations

	POSITIVE	NEGATIVE
MARKETING	• Media profile due to flood coverage; • Flood history a potential attraction in its own right.	• Focus on flood impacts delays market response beyond restoration of services; • Focus on recovery diverts attention/resources from strategic issues.
INFRASTRUCTURE AND INVESTMENT	• Refurbishment of infrastructure.	• Curtailment of investment in expansion of infrastructure.
IMPROVEMENT IN DISASTER PREPAREDNESS	• Development of tourism disaster management plan; • Upgrading of insurance policies to allow for flood damage.	• Losses incurred as a consequence of the flood represent a high price for a "wake-up call".
COHESION	• Team spirit and cooperativeness galvanised within tourism sector; • Improved community awareness of tourism benefit.	• Tensions between tourism sector and business community over allocation of resources.
HUMAN RESOURCES	• "Acid test" for staff.	• High staff turnover and loss of experienced staff.

Figure 8.2 Long-term positive and negative impacts of the 1998 Katherine floods
Source: Reprinted from *Tourism Management*, 22, Faulkner, B. and Vikulov, S., Katherine, washed out one day, back on track the next: a post-mortem of a tourism disaster, pp 331–344, copyright (2001), with permission of Elsevier.

from those outlined above included the use of more appropriate insurance policies as a mitigation measure and the development of disaster planning; improved attitudes towards tourism by the community and an 'acid test' for staff employed in tourism businesses. Negative transformations in additional to those noted above included a lack of long-term planning due to short-term recovery efforts, community tensions over the allocation of recovery funding, and the movement of people and staff outside of the destination due to trauma (which are discussed in more detail in the next section).

Human and community transformation

The recovery and resolution stage is an important part of having the community reflect on their past and plan their future. Debriefing of emergency workers, tourism operators and the broader community are an important part of the recovery and resolution phase, while debriefing itself should be considered an integral part of organisational learning and managed reflection outlined in Chapter 9. The initial impact of a crisis or disaster on the community is likely to increase psychological morbidity, such as non-specific psychological distress or post-traumatic stress symptoms, among both individuals and communities experiencing such a loss (Camilleri *et al.*, 2007). Decision-makers and emergency workers can also be placed under severe personal stress due to the time pressure and uncertainties in dealing with crises and events and the search for scapegoats. As Peters and Pikkemaat (2005) noted, the search for a culprit can lead to formal investigations and accusations of homicide, causing psychological pressure that lasts for years after the incident. Faulkner and Vikulov (2001: 340) also suggested, in reviewing the recovery efforts after the Katherine Flood in 1998, that:

> management and staff in both the KRTA [Katherine Region Tourism Association] and the tourism industry more generally observed how the challenge of the emergency and the subsequent clean-up required an extraordinary physical effort on everyone's part over an extended period of time. This, along with the psychological stress associated with exposure to the threatening conditions of the flood and the loss of businesses and personal belongings, meant that many of those involved reached a point of physical and mental exhaustion once the task of getting their lives and business operations back to some degree of normalcy was completed.

Psychological debriefing provides an opportunity to facilitate emotional disclosure of feelings and help participants to understand their reactions, although it is acknowledged that the timing of debriefing needs careful consideration so that it enhances and does not prolong recovery (Paton, 1997). The psychological impact of crises and disasters on tourism operators and destination managers, as well as emergency workers are not widely researched or reported. As Camilleri *et al.* (2007: 19) state:

> [l]ittle is known about how individuals and communities respond in the long-term and what assists recovery. Research into understanding how people deal with and recover from trauma may contribute to emergency management mitigation and our understanding of vulnerability and resilience.

The effect of social and organisational characteristics, such as family, peers, co-workers and the nature of the incident all interact to influence the nature and rate of recovery (Paton, 1997). Resources should be provided to the community in order to facilitate community recovery, although the question remains as to the exact timing of disaster-specific resources to help recovery and when these should be reduced as the community enters the resolution phase. Furthermore, the community should not be viewed as a homogenous group, but rather a number of sub-groups perhaps defined by their level of vulnerability and role in the crisis or disaster. In particular, those community groups (and tourists) that are most vulnerable to natural disasters could include children, the elderly as well as individuals with previous mental health problems, ongoing stress or limited social capacity or capital. Tourists and their ongoing psychological distress as a result of a natural disaster are often ignored, yet may require interventions and support in their home destinations.

The Role of Livelihood Assets and Capital in Long-term Recovery and Resolution

As discussed in Chapters 2 and 4, the concept of vulnerability, risk and resilience with respect to natural disasters should be considered within a broader sustainable development framework, while Chapter 6 noted that resources should be targeted based on needs and not simply relief. The Sustainable Livelihoods Approach (SLA) is an attempt to understand and reduce vulnerability to disasters taking vulnerability as the starting point and unifies poverty reduction strategies, sustainable development, and participation and empowerment processes into a framework for policy analysis and programming (Mubarak, 2007: 60). A number of aid agencies and NGOs use the concept of SLA along with a Sustainable Livelihoods Framework (SLF) to guide development intervention so that it contributes to livelihoods and sustainable development. Furthermore, it has had limited applicability in the tourism development field (Shen *et al.*, 2008). The SLF is identified in Figure 8.3 and comprises five main components, according to Mubarak (2007):

(1) *A vulnerability context:* this forms the environment in which people exist and which can impact upon livelihood assets through health shocks, natural hazards, economic shocks and political conflicts. Resilience to shocks is an important factor in livelihood sustainability.

(2) *Livelihood assets:* which is concerned with people and their assets or capital. Assets are used for people to achieve their goals. A list of assets and their descriptions are outlined in Table 8.2 and include physical assets, natural assets, human assets, financial and social assets.

(3) *Transforming structures and processes:* can feedback into the vulnerability context to reduce or exacerbate vulnerability and the impact of shocks and livelihoods. Structures are the 'hardware' that set and implement policy, legislation, deliver services, trade and perform functions that affect livelihoods. Processes are the 'software', which determine the way in which these structures and individuals operate and interact. Both the 'hardware' and 'software' influence livelihood strategies and outcomes.

(4) *Livelihood strategies:* comprise activities and choices people make to achieve their livelihood goals. A changing asset may influence strategies depending on policies and institutions.

(5) *Livelihood outcomes:* are the achievement or outputs of livelihood strategies. They can include more income, increased well being,

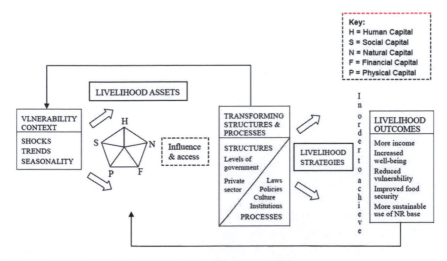

Figure 8.3 The sustainable livelihoods framework
Source: Shen *et al.* (2008), with permission.

Table 8.2 SLA livelihood assets and capital dimensions

Asset or capital dimension	Description
Physical assets/ Capital	Basic infrastructure (e.g. affordable transport, secure shelter, adequate water supplies and sanitation, affordable energy and access to information) and producer goods (e.g. tools and equipment needed to support livelihoods).
Natural assets/ Capital	Natural resource stocks from which resource flows and services useful for livelihoods are derived (e.g. land, trees and fish stocks).
Human assets/ Capital	Skills, knowledge, ability to labour and good health that collectively enable people to pursue different livelihood strategies.
Financial assets/ Capital	Available stocks that are void of attached liabilities and usually independent of third parties (e.g. cash, bank deposits, liquid assets such as livestock or jewellery), and regular inflows of money which are predominately dependent on others and require reliability (e.g. labour income, pensions, remittances).
Social assets/ Capital	The social resources from which people draw whilst seeking for their livelihood outcomes (e.g. kinship networks which increase people's trust and ability to cooperate, and membership in more formalised groups and their systems of rules, norms and transactions).

Source: Modified after Mubarak (2007: 62).

reduced vulnerability, improved food security and more sustainable use of natural resources. The outcomes directly influence assets impacting upon other strategies and outcomes.

The SLF has guided some interventions in disaster situations by the UNDP, CARE International and Oxfam, according to Mubarak (2007), because many aid agencies and donors see disaster aid intervention as part of a relief development continuum emphasising the need for livelihood strategies, which may vary depending on those who are most vulnerable and are the worst affected by a natural disaster. However, this approach could be used for developed countries that may also experience a natural disaster. Perhaps even this approach could be translated for organisational crisis recovery considering organisations as a system which will have a vulnerability context, livelihood assets, transforming structures and processes as well as livelihood strategies and outcomes. The role of livelihood assets and capital would also be important for their long-term recovery and resolution from the impact of crises and disasters.

An understanding of livelihood assets/capital is important from a tourism crisis and disaster management perspective for several reasons. First, from assistance perspective organisations and government should consider long-term recovery policies that help their stakeholders (including tourism businesses and communities) to provide long-term access to livelihood assets and support livelihood strategies, which will ultimately help to integrate recovery policies into sustainable development. Second, policies should include the full range of livelihood assets or capital outlined in Table 8.2 including physical, natural, human, financial and social. A crisis or disaster provides an opportunity to 'take stock' and plan for long-term sustainable development for both developing and developed communities and organisations. Social capital is particularly important in this context as a livelihood asset.

Social capital differs from physical and human capital as 'physical capital refers to physical objects and human capital refers to the properties of individuals, social capital refers to connections among individuals – social networks and norms of reciprocity and trustworthiness that arise from them' (Putnam, 2000: 19). Connections include interpersonal networks and relationships between families, communities and organisations and can include horizontal associations (within a family unit, organisation or destination) or vertical associations (that occur between a family, organisation or destination unit). Social capital can be increased or decreased over time, and can be used as a vehicle to acquire resources to help with community development.

A disaster may have long-term benefits for communities or businesses by providing the impetus to address social problems, improve livelihood assets, social capital and reduce vulnerability to future incidents. For example, Bolin and Stanford's study of responses to the Northbridge Earthquake in California in 1994 found that the earthquake renewed pressure to respond to long standing housing problems (such as a lack of low cost housing) as part of the reconstruction effort (in Camilleri *et al.*, 2007). Bernsdorf (2004) identified the community and tourism industry cohesion and their readiness to help shown by the extent of donations collection after the 2002 Saxony floods in Germany. The donations were the highest amount collected in Germany after the Second World War, helping to build social capital and a community spirit. Gurtner (2006) suggests that after the Bali bombings, numerous projects were undertaken to improve public health and sanitation issues and that local community and social networks were strengthened developing social capital that would benefit the future development of the tourism industry.

Strengthened social capital can be harnessed by organisations to help reduce future vulnerability to natural disasters through the mobilisation of volunteer environmental or mitigation programmes. For instance, Camilleri *et al.* (2007) found that people affected by the Canberra bushfires stated the importance of links with communities of interest and noted that volunteering could help empower residents and create a positive basis for the future. Furthermore, the bushfire disaster provided an opportunity to plan and develop new tourism precincts and products (or natural and social assets) such as the International Arboretum and Gardens, Tidbinbilla Nature Reserve, Mt Stromlo Observatory, and Stromlo Forest Park (which has been used recently to hold international mountain biking and running events).

The Singapore government's SARS Relief Tourism Training Assistance programme helped to retrain employees in approved tourism-related courses, to minimise redundancies, but to also help stimulate human capital so that if made redundant, workers may find alternative employment or even start their own businesses. Micro credit financing to help people in developing countries to establish tourism businesses after a natural disaster is another way that government and aid agencies can help provide financial assets or capital to help victims of natural disasters to recover with long-term sustainable development in mind. Long-term recovery and resolution requires good planning and foresight in order to turn a negative event into a positive event. At the very least, it focuses on the positive transformation opportunities and reduces the negative transformations through appropriate structures and processes, therefore an understanding of livelihood assets and social capital is crucial for long-term recovery and building resilient and adaptive destinations.

Conclusion

This chapter has focused on the long-term recovery and resolution phase of tourism crises and disasters. The chapter began by defining the resolution phase where a routine is restored or a new and improved state established. An improved state is possible as incidents provide opportunities as well as threats for those concerned. However, the time required between the long-term recovery and resolution stage can vary, based upon the size, complexity and nature of a crisis or disaster as well as an understanding of the dimensions of resolution (which can include human recovery elements).

Long-term positive and negative transformation can occur at an organisational, destination and human/community level, as a result of a tourism crisis or disaster. Organisations can increase their vitality and longevity, examine relationships with industry stakeholders and customers, and develop new products, markets and programmes to reduce their costs. Organisational team spirit and cohesion can also be established. At a destination level dealing with a crisis or disaster can also increase destination cohesiveness, within the tourism industry and between the tourism industry and associated groups (such as emergency workers, government and the community). Policy changes may occur as a result of disasters acerbating change and a realisation of the positive impact and value of tourism. Infrastructure may be rebuilt and improved and greater planning and mitigation measures may also be introduced. However, community tensions may exist over the allocation of recovery funding and development options, while some workers may leave the destination due to trauma.

Human and community transformation may also occur as a result of physical and mental exhaustion and post-traumatic stress for the local community, emergency workers and tourists themselves. Support services and intervention is required, especially for those people most vulnerable including children, elderly and emergency workers. The roles of family, peers, co-workers and the nature of the incident will influence the nature of recovery and the speed of resolution. Further work and research is required on the long-term recovery and resolution phase of crises and disasters. In particular, research is required on the role of social capital and livelihood assets as a way to integrate long-term recovery and resolution strategies into broader sustainable development, in order to increase human, destination and organisation resilience and reduce future vulnerability.

Chapter 9
Knowledge Management and Organisational Learning

Introduction

This chapter follows on from the previous one and suggests that one of the most positive outcomes from a crisis or disaster can be the generation and sharing of knowledge associated with a tourism crisis or disaster, which can be used in future tourism crisis and disaster planning. The chapter begins by outlining the knowledge management imperative, defines knowledge management and suggests the importance of knowledge for the survival and adaptation of tourism organisations facing a tourism crisis or disaster. This part of the chapter acknowledges the differing knowledge types and the knowledge requirements throughout the crisis or disaster lifecycle for acquisition, storage, distribution, interpretation and action of knowledge. The next section of the chapter focuses on organisational learning and feedback by focusing specifically on the review and reflection phase of the crisis or disaster lifecycle. It suggests that new knowledge enables the re-evaluation of currently understood ideas and beliefs and leads to the possibility of future change. However, limited research has been undertaken on the link between organisational learning and tourism crises and disasters. This section outlines the difference between single- and double-loop learning, and notes that double-loop learning facilitates a higher level of knowledge generation and organisational learning as it may challenge existing assumptions and mental models.

The next section suggests that managing the reflection process to encourage organisational learning is needed, including implementing evaluative enquiry and tools to encourage the generation of new explicit and tacit knowledge to challenge existing mental models. The chapter then discusses the role and importance of knowledge brokers and spanners in developing and sharing such knowledge across diverse groups and domains. Potential knowledge brokers and spanners could include DMOs, industry associations and government agencies, who have a role to play in facilitating tourism crisis and disaster knowledge management through the use of boundary objects such as repositories, forms, models and maps. The final section of the chapter brings these concepts together by proposing steps for boundary spanners and brokers to consider in developing evaluative enquiry and critical reflection at the review stage of a tourism crisis or disaster. In particular, this section outlines the need to ask tough questions designed to challenge existing values, beliefs and assumptions; the promotion of reflection and dialogue between stakeholders; the collection, analysis and interpretation of data, and importantly, the use of this data to develop and test new tourism crisis management strategies and policies as a result of this new knowledge.

The Knowledge Management Imperative

Like tourism management, the discipline of knowledge management is relatively young and involves the integration of several disciplines including computer and management science, sociology, human resource management and strategy. The definitions of knowledge management vary, depending on the perspective and approach of authors. According to Malhotra (1997: np):

> [k]nowledge management caters to the critical issues of organisational adaptation, survival and competence in the increasingly discontinuous environmental change ... essentially, it embodies organisational processes that seek synergistic combination of data and information processing capacity of information technologies, and the creative and innovative capacity of human beings.

This definition suggests that knowledge management is a complex activity, involving the integration of information, technological and human elements to produce and diffuse organisational knowledge. Jashapara (2004: 12) provides an integrated definition of knowledge management as 'the effective learning processes associated with exploration, exploitation and sharing of human knowledge (tacit and explicit) that use appropriate technology and cultural environments to enhance an organisation's intellectual capital and performance'.

However, it is important to note that knowledge management is not just required for individual organisations. As Schianetz *et al.* (2007) acknowledge, approaches are needed that promote stakeholder collaboration and learning at a destination or regional level, as well as an organisational level. The authors note that this is increasingly important due to the dynamic of the tourism system and for long-term sustainability. In particular, Schianetz *et al.* (2007: 1486) note that a learning organisation approach to destination management would help create a shared understanding of:

(1) how the tourism destination functions;
(2) how the market possibilities may be enhanced;
(3) the requirements for adaptation to changing environments;
(4) how to promote collective awareness of eventual economic, social and environmental risks and impacts; and
(5) how risks can be minimised and/or counted.

Points 3 to 5 in the list are concerned with dealing with tourism crises and disasters through developing a learning approach for their potential management, and fit with an adaptive approach to strategic management as proposed by Hofer (1973) and discussed in Chapter 3. As Mistilis and Sheldon (2006: 42) state, 'at the destination level a shared knowledge system is needed to address crisis and disasters with all tourism stakeholders involved in its creation'.

Knowledge management is increasingly recognised as an important tool that can augment the chances of adaptation and survival of organisations (Bahra, 2001; Cooper, 2006; Malhotra, 2002; Mistilis & Sheldon, 2006; Newell *et al.*, 2002), and is an important part of identifying, recording and sharing disaster lessons (Robert & Lajtha, 2002). Although in much of the literature the emphasis is upon the creation of organisations' developing competitive advantage (Davidson & Voss, 2002; Grant, 1996), knowledge management is also recognised more broadly as important for a range of tourism organisations (Bouncken & Pyo, 2002; Cooper, 2006). Knowledge can be identified as a series of stocks – what is known, and flows – how it is communicated (Cooper, 2006; Davidson & Voss, 2002), and can be crucial for the effectiveness of quick reactions to any crisis. Nevertheless, knowledge management is often focused on simply storing knowledge and innovation, rather than developing supporting processes to enable new knowledge creation, recognition and utilisation (Earl, 2001). Knowledge acquisition and storage is only one part of the process with information distribution, while interpretation and organisational memory are other important parts.

Knowledge can take two main forms: explicit and tacit knowledge. Explicit knowledge can be made explicit by being thought, written and communicated to others, whereas tacit knowledge represents knowledge that cannot be clearly articulated to others, and may include personal beliefs, thoughts and perspectives which are hard to communicate. The transfer of tacit knowledge requires commitment and involvement in a specific context (Nonaka & Takeuchi, 1995).

The first stage in any knowledge management strategy is to identify who has important knowledge and what format it takes. Here, it will be important to recognise the difference between information and knowledge (Blackman, 2006; Fahey & Prusak, 1998), since simply to move more information around the system will not be sufficient. In many cases there will be tacit knowledge held by individuals, which should be shared within, and perhaps even outside of the specific organisation. Often the argument is made that tacit knowledge needs to be made explicit (Nonaka & Takeuchi, 1995), but this is frequently not realistic to achieve, especially in short time frames. Consequently, Blackman and Ritchie (2007) argue that for successful crisis management, knowledge

Table 9.1 Knowledge base components for tourism crisis and disaster management

KB 1: Preventative planning	KB 2: Management plan for tourism disasters	KB 3: Recovery handling
• Assessment of possible disaster scenarios • Assignment of probabilities to those scenarios • Local, national and global situation monitoring • Historic studies of previous disasters • Capacity audit of human and physical resources • Inventory of outside sources and emergency relief • Prediction of forecasting models • Case base of tourism disasters in other destinations • Proven disaster prevention/mitigation strategies • Set of standard protocols of information collection and process	• Decision support system for managers • A recognised and tested process to automate the knowledge base • Identification of a tourism crisis control centre that is connected to generic centres • Situation awareness scanning • Policy manuals for different operational areas	• Data from KB 2 to capture knowledge of the disaster situation • An appropriate recovery plan • Media communication and marketing resources and strategy

Source: Mistilis and Sheldon (2006: 45), reproduced with permission from Cognizant Communications Corporation.

management approaches focused upon the creation and movement of knowledge will be more effective. In this context, the role of the DMO and industry associations (on behalf of the industry) as knowledge brokers or spanners becomes particularly important, which is discussed later in this chapter.

One way to consider how tourism crisis and disaster knowledge can be developed and managed is to use the stages of the crisis lifecycle, to indicate knowledge management actions (see Table 9.1). According to Mistilis and Sheldon (2006), knowledge base 1 includes mostly knowledge (or information) retrieval and storage, while knowledge base 2 includes information processing and knowledge base 3 includes dissemination and action based on knowledge management. As discussed in previous chapters on tourism and disaster prevention and planning, information and the use of scenarios, forecasting and establishment of protocols are all-important activities at the pre-event stage of a crisis or disaster. The development of policy manuals, crisis control centres and decision support systems are all vital for planning actions to deal with tourism crises and disasters, which are outlined in detail in Chapters 5 and 6 of this book. However, according to Barnett and Pratt (2000), after the onset of a crisis, increased centralisation leads to the overloading of information, and decision-makers tend to depend on old knowledge based on past experience and seek fewer sources of information. Furthermore, as noted in Table 9.1 and Chapters 6 and 7, it is important to not only gather data and information from key stakeholders to help shape responses and recovery activities, but to also to engage them developing new knowledge and foresight.

However, two important aspects arise from examining the work of Mistilis and Sheldon (2006). First, the need to move beyond simply collecting information to actually building new knowledge, which includes actions and activities discussed in more detail in the remainder of this chapter. Second, the need for a knowledge management stage that includes organisational learning and feedback into future tourism crisis and disaster planning, which should occur after recovery.

Organisational Learning and Feedback

Organisational learning has been defined in many ways (Blackman, 2006; Prange, 1999). A common thread amongst these various definitions is that of being a set of processes, which enable organisational behaviour to change in some way as a result of new knowledge that has been developed. The traditional goals of the learning process are the acquisition of new knowledge (know what), development of skills (know how) and a change in attitude of the learner (Jashapara, 2004: 61). New knowledge enables the re-evaluation of currently understood ideas and beliefs and leads to the possibility of change. It may be argued that, without the creation of new knowledge, no change will ever be possible (Blackman, 2006; Cook & Brown, 1999). In terms of the framework proposed in Figure 3.6 in Chapter 3, learning and adaptive management should occur at all stages of the strategic crisis or disaster management process. As Mistilis and Sheldon (2006) note, each stage needs certain knowledge from the pre-crisis stage through the disaster management stage and the recovery handling. However, for effective evaluation and feedback, long-term learning from current experience also needs to be captured and understood in order to ensure that: (1) the same mistakes/problems do not re-occur, and (2) that new strategies are increasingly better informed through adaptive management. Without such learning, the same problem can occur again even though they may have been purportedly 'managed' and 'dealt with' previously.

Previous research (Armstrong & Ritchie, 2007; Cioccio & Michael, 2007; Hystad & Keller, 2006, 2008) has illustrated that DMOs involved in crisis or disaster response and recovery activities may not use this experience to develop crisis or disaster management adaptation strategies. Ritchie *et al.* (2003) noted that despite going through the Foot and Mouth Outbreak in the UK in 2001/2002, regional and local agencies suggested that future crisis plans would not be established because of the unpredictability of planning for tourism crises. Furthermore, as de Sausmarez (2003) notes in research on tourism crises in the late 1990s, the Malaysian government and private sector were uncertain about developing a tourism crisis plan that may never be needed, due to a false sense of security and inability to fund such a plan. This in part may be because there is an assumption that large-scale incidents are unique and unlikely to reoccur (Turner & Toft, 2006).

The benefit of hindsight should allow destinations and organisations to develop even better crisis management strategies and plans, and there are some examples of this occurring. DMOs located in the Maldives, Charleston, USA, Singapore, Malaysia and South Carolina have developed crisis management plans as a result of previous crisis and disaster experiences (Carlsen, 2006; Henderson, 1999, 2002; Litvin & Alderson, 2003; Soñmez & Backman, 1992). In the airline sector, Britton (2003) acknowledges that September 11, 2001 was a unique experience for American Airlines and they have learnt how to rebuild a positive image after a major terrorist attack. In the public sector, policy structure changes can be developed as a response to incidents, and can be beneficial for reducing potential future crises and disasters. For instance, after September 11, 2001, an Office of Homeland Security was formed in the USA, and in Australia, the Tourism Working Group was established to develop strategies to deal with future crises (Hall, 2002). Further evidence of positive change and transformation as a result of tourism crises and disasters were outlined in the previous chapter (Chapter 8).

Yet as Pforr and Hosie (2007: 257) note, the PPRR model suggests that '... the preparation, response and recovery elements of this crisis management model are interrelated, and therefore, have a crucial relationship to the "learning" purpose. Learning is therefore an axiomatic and critical recurrent feature of this model'. One of the few studies to focus on organisational learning and feedback in the context of tourism crisis and disaster management was that of Faulkner and Vikulov (2001), who tested Faulkner's (2001) tourism disaster management framework using the case of the 1998 Katherine floods in Australia.

The authors encouraged stakeholders to reflect on lessons learnt through the disaster by posing three major questions in their research in order to get respondents to reflect on their actions and changes to the organisation and destination as a result of the disaster:

(1) With the benefit of hindsight, is there anything you or any other partner could have done which would have enabled you to cope with the situation more effectively?
(2) Has the experience of the floods resulted in any permanent changes to your firm/agency's approach to management planning?
(3) Have there been any permanent changes in the planning and organisation of the destination as a whole?

Resulting from the above study, Faulkner and Vikulov (2001) revised the tourism disaster framework to include a reappraisal of the marketing, planning and policy regime at the review/resolution stage. However, no discussion occurred on what constituted such a review, how it should occur with respect to knowledge acquisition and development, and what stakeholders should have been involved in the review.

Henderson (2003) is also one of the few tourism crisis management researchers to note explicitly the importance of organisational learning, including it as her final stage in airline crisis management, directly after the resolution phase. Henderson (2003: 281) suggests that '[r]esolution, even if only partial, provides an opportunity for review and reflection leading to reforms in pursuit of improvements in structures and systems and a heightened preparedness for future crises'. However, no feedback loop from learning to crisis preparation was specifically indicated in her model. Henderson (2003) also suggests, in writing about Singapore Airline's (SIA) response to the flight SQ006 crash in 2000, that there was an assumption that SIA's management conducted a review, but questioned whether it was conducted formally or informally. No discussion occurred as to how the review was carried out, despite reassurances about preventing further accidents and assertions made by the company that no effort would be spared to uncover the full circumstances of the crash. Henderson's (2003) work illustrates that in order for such a model to work, those involved with the strategy planning and preparation need to effectively review their actions, in order to make new choices. Whilst organisational learning is used explicitly within the model of some authors (Faulkner, 2001; Henderson, 2003; Ritchie, 2004), it is clear that a broader knowledge management process could assist tourism organisations to develop better crisis and disaster plans and responses, in a way that would be beneficial to the organisation and their tourism stakeholders.

Differences in the nature and extent of organisational learning, discussed above, may be due to the local cultural context, organisational culture and perhaps even the way that learning and reflection are managed by organisations. Defensive routines or a defensive organisational culture can also inhibit learning. This phenomenon can be described by what Argyris and Schon (1996) refer to as single-loop learning, where the values and norms underpinning a strategy or action are left unchallenged and unchanged, preventing organisation's learning from their errors, and potentially, leading to failure. As a result, they advocate double-loop learning which will promote inquiry and challenge current assumptions and actions, thus leading to new 'theories-in-use' and better foresight.

The example commonly given to explain the difference between single- and double-loop learning is taken from cybernetics (Argyris, 1991, 1999). A thermostat reacts to the condition 'too hot' or 'too cold' by turning heat on or off as appropriate to maintain a fixed temperature. This is single-loop learning, since the thermostat does not question why either state is unsatisfactory. The single-loop learning commences with a mismatch between expectations and experiences (the temperature is not as set), which leads to a required action based on previous patterns of action. This can be corrected in a straightforward, single-loop process, which does not add to the stock of knowledge, since it only applies what was already known. It is not even necessary for the thermostat to 'know' why or how its actions create changes in temperature. If the thermostat could ask questions, and wondered why it was set for a particular temperature, or what the significance of temperature was in the wider scheme of things, it would be commencing double-loop learning as it would be beginning to develop consciousness in its routines and thus examine the problem (Argyris, 1991, 1999).

Single- and double-loop learning has been considered in the crisis management literature by authors such as Richardson (1994), in discussions on organisational foresight (Blackman & Henderson, 2004) and could be applied to tourism crisis and disaster management. In particular, the concept could be applied to ways in which DMOs and industry associations evaluate their tourism crisis and disaster activities. As Faulkner and Vikulov (2001: 343) suggest, loop learning 'emphasises the importance of a fundamental reassessment of the destination's management and planning approaches at the post disaster stage if the positive enduring effects are to be accentuated and the negatives ameliorated'. However, the reappraisal of the destination crisis response should not simply be an internal process, but a process involving all stakeholders and should be as important as the implementation of crisis and disaster responses and should thus be provided with relevant resources.

As Pforr and Hosie (2007: 258) argue:

> [o]rganizational learning resulting from double loop learning is therefore a complex undertaking which takes time and commitment by all concerned to be achieved. Deep organizational learning is more likely to result when there is constant iterative design of learning opportunities about crisis management. Creating and maintaining a suitable organizational configuration will assist to embed the necessary culture into an organization's repartee.

In organisational terms, the difference between single- and double-loop learning is the difference between responding to a problem in a formulaic, procedures driven way, versus considering why the problem is occurring and capturing such understanding for future use (see Figure 9.1). A defensive reaction to a crisis could lead to avoidance of double-loop learning. Without a form of managed reflection, it may not be possible for an organisation to subsequently acquire the new knowledge that is needed in order to be able to develop effective strategies, contributing to adaptive systems management. It is by reflecting that new ways of conceptualising the problem can be developed which will lead to the development of new 'theories-in-use'. As Miller and Ritchie (2003: 165) note:

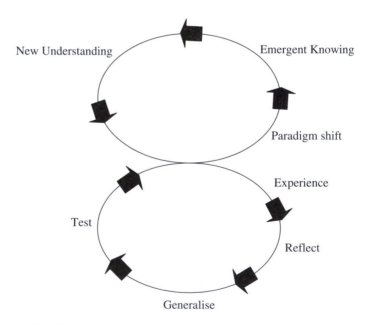

Figure 9.1 Double-loop learning
Source: Modified from Kolb (1984).

double-loop learning requires a paradigmatic shift as a result of the experience and so emergent knowledge is produced and ultimately new understanding is derived ... [c]onversely, and as evidenced by history, those who suffer the effects of a disaster react to events and are contained to single-loop actions, if not single-loop thinking, unless a larger body can enforce the necessary changes to prevent the events repeating themselves.

Larger bodies may enforce or implement external forces such as government policies or changes from other external stakeholders. For instance, government regulations as a result of mitigation measures could ensure tourism businesses in bushfire-prone locations have adequate insurance, or are built away from hazard locations (Cioccio & Michael, 2007).

Managed Reflection for Organisational Learning

Reflection helps to develop a learning cycle, and if people don't have time to think and reflect, then the level of organisational learning will be diminished (Jashapara, 2004). To be effective in the long term, organisations need to undertake systematic strategy development, which is underpinned by effective learning processes. One of these processes is ongoing reflection, enabling new knowledge to be recognised, captured and reused when needed. It is important to understand that this is an ongoing process which ensures that knowledge is constantly updated as the use of incorrect or incomplete knowledge is potentially extremely dangerous (Chapman & Ferfolja, 2001; Gibb, 2002). Preskill and Torres (1999: 92) argue that what is needed is evaluative enquiry, which requires organisational members to 'critically consider what they think, say and do in the context of the work environment'. They use this term because evaluation is used to seek answers and information about an object or outcome, which should include not only the action or object itself, but also the values, standards and assumptions that relate to it. By critically evaluating all the aspects of strategy formulation, implementation and outcomes, it should be possible to gain important knowledge for the future and change the currently held collective mental models of organisational members, leading to double-loop organisational learning. Seven processes are outlined as making up the core of evaluative enquiry and are identified in Table 9.2.

Whilst reflection is listed as a process within evaluative enquiry, it could be argued that it also equates with the process of evaluative inquiry itself. Reflection is the process whereby knowledge, beliefs, assumptions and processes are considered in order to establish how they influence behaviour and understanding, and consequently, experiences. The importance of reflection can be understood if the way that

Table 9.2 Core processes of evaluative enquiry

Asking questions	Clarifies issues; Identifies misconceptions; Determines additional information required
Identifying and challenging values, beliefs and assumptions	Makes public what is done and why; Creates opportunities for change
Reflection	Considers impacts of actions and behaviours
Dialogue	Shares ideas and experiences; Translates and interprets learning
Collecting, analysing and interpreting data	Produces information
Action planning	Using the learning to make new plans
Implementation	Testing the new knowledge

Source: Modified after Preskill and Torres (1999).

knowledge is developed and considered. It is increasingly argued that knowledge is constructed within organisations by making inquiries into situations of uncertainty (Dewey, 1986 in Elkjaer, 2004) and developing new theories about such situations. This occurs through reflection upon the relationship between how the problem or situation is defined and the chosen resolution. This indicates that learning will be contextual and needs to be related to both the organisation and the organisational community in order to develop knowledge that is relevant and useful for the crisis or disaster situation being examined. For reflection to be effective it must be a managed process, which seeks to understand why things did or did not work in a particular set of circumstances. Furthermore, in many cases reflection does not occur because people are simply too busy. As Hystad and Keller (2008) discovered from repeated research after a Canadian bushfire, only 11% more respondents had a disaster plan (up to 38%) after actually experiencing a severe bush fire. Most respondents felt that it was the responsibility of emergency organisations and tourism organisations to prepare for disasters and to respond to such incidents, emphasising the role of DMOs and local agencies.

In terms of tourism crisis and disaster strategies and actions, reflection will need to occur at every stage of the crisis or disaster management framework in order to challenge the currently accepted norms that might otherwise lead to mental models constricting the range of possibilities (Blackman & Henderson, 2004; Chapman & Ferfolja, 2001). However, the most important time for reflection, as indicated by the frameworks of Ritchie (2004), Henderson (2003) and Faulkner (2001) will be at the end of the crisis or disaster in the form of evaluating response and recovery strategies. As outlined earlier, this is posited in some of the literature but there is inadequate detail as to how this should actually occur. This is important since often evaluation, which should be a double-loop learning process leading to new knowledge, is actually a self-reflexive and adaptive process, whereby all ideas are judged purely by what is already known to an individual or entity, which merely acts to confirm the knowledge that is already understood (Blackman & Henderson, 2004). Those involved seek out ideas and information that support the actions already in place and do not challenge the current 'givens' and 'mind set' (Mellahi *et al.*, 2002). As Barnett and Pratt (2000: 81) note, 'once a policy has been formulated to cope with the crisis, a search for information to support policy choices re-intensifies. Paradoxically, throughout the ebb and flow of information gathering ... the number of new alternatives introduced to the organisation may be relatively low'.

This is illustrated in the tourism crisis publications (Frisby, 2002; Hooper, 2002) written by representatives from DMOs who present research and data on the number of press releases, media interviews, value and extent of media coverage or recovery marketing funds gained to justify their decisions. For instance, in discussing 'The Greatest Show on Earth' campaign to increase visits to London theatres after crisis events, Hooper (2002: 85) stated '... the overall marketing spend for the campaign was £720,000. The campaign generated accommodation bookings totalling 7,290 bed nights. The estimated audience reach for supporting press coverage was over 7.5 million and page views on the campaign website reached 202,000'. However, these data only seek to confirm and illustrate the success of previously implemented tourism crisis response and recovery strategies, without collecting data on possible alternative actions or even inaction. Blackman and Henderson (2004) argued for a process of 'doubting' that could actively explore the current context and the nature of the solutions that were chosen compared with other possible scenarios and the implementation of managed skepticism or double-loop doubting. The traditional approach to evaluate crisis activities is unlikely to create new knowledge and yet, if the status quo is to change and more effective policies and strategies are to be developed new knowledge and ideas will be vital. As identified in Figure 9.2, Cook and Brown (1999) argue that there are four distinctive types of knowledge based upon the social context and the locus of the knowledge (i.e. whether internal or external to those holding it), which are important to understand in the pursuit of generating new explicit and tacit knowledge.

	Individual	*Group*
	Concepts	**Stories**
Explicit	Including things an individual can know, learn and express explicitly (concepts, rules and equations).	Typically expressed explicitly as a group through stories about how work is done or about famous successes or failures. Also can include metaphors or phrases with meaning for a particular group.
Tacit	Skills that are tacit and used in making use of concepts, rules and equations.	Most difficult to define. Various social and physical artefacts such as different types of things (products) and activities (ways of doing tasks) and meanings in literary artefacts.
	Skills	**Genres**

Figure 9.2 Four forms of knowledge
Source: Adapted from Cook and Brown (1999: 391).

Cook and Brown (1999) argue that for new knowledge to be created, the existing knowledge will need to be 'moved' into a new form and therefore a new square. For example, if an individual understands a particular 'Concept', it will remain static until they try to explain and share it and move it to 'Stories' by enabling a group to understand the same concept. This 'dance' generates the process of knowing which leads, in turn, to the generation of something new. Thus, evaluation processes will need to ensure that such movement between knowledge types occurs, and DMOs along with industry associations and government agencies, have a role in acting as knowledge brokers or spanners enabling the movement of knowledge, perhaps through this 'dance' and the use of boundary objects.

The Role of Knowledge Brokers, Spanners and Objects

Boundaries are present within, and between, all aspects of organisations and between different stakeholders within a system, including the tourism system. The wide range of tourism stakeholders will need to work together to integrate their different fields of knowledge in order to develop and implement effective tourism crisis and disaster strategies and actions. As Turner and Toft (2006: 203) suggest '. . . lessons identified need to be passed on effectively to those who need to know about them, and that they be passed on in such a way that appropriate action indicate by them is encouraged'. Such a situation will require stakeholders to share knowledge and develop a system to enable sharing and re-interpretation of knowledge spanning across boundaries and diverse groups. In simple terms, a broker or spanner is an individual or organisation who acts as an intermediary between at least two other parties or communities of practice. A broker's role is to facilitate the movement of ideas and knowledge by bringing people and diverse communities of practice together and enabling them to create and share new ideas, thereby supporting the creation and flow of knowledge. In undertaking this role, knowledge brokers add value to their own organisational activities. Consequently, a knowledge broker plays an important role in matching different (and often dispersed) knowledge sources together (Aalbers *et al.*, 2004; Hargadon, 1998, 2002; Sharon *et al.*, 2000).

A knowledge boundary spanner is an individual or organisation that recognises a problem and may facilitate the transfer of knowledge from one party to another through facilitation that enables the recognition and understanding of the knowledge of others. This may mean organising meetings and bringing stakeholders together, but it may also include the need for translation across language boundaries and domains to enable common understanding and reducing political rivalries in order to facilitate the generation of knowledge. Nevertheless, boundary spanners do not have the information or knowledge themselves, but act as facilitators. Spanners can be brokers, however, the difference between the two lies in that a spanner does not possess the knowledge that is to be transferred, whereas a broker does. Boundary spanners are 'a means of cultivating the organisational ability to deal with the challenges of managing across boundaries' (Levina & Vaast, 2005: 338). Boundary spanners can be perceived as:

- agents who identify, interpret and facilitate the movement of ideas, knowledge and innovative practices between domains and diverse groups (such as tourism, emergency management and aid agencies in the context of tourism crisis and disaster management);
- able to work with stakeholders to understand their explicit and implicit knowledge, and translate this across a boundary to unite different domains and groups for the benefit of all parties; and
- having a difficult role merging a diverse range of domains and groups, each with their own sets of ideas, understanding and knowledge (both tacit and explicit).

Boundary spanners and knowledge brokers are more likely to be those organisations in the tourism system that can enable the sharing of knowledge between stakeholders. The types of agents that can act as boundary spanners or brokers include DMOs (from national, regional and local levels), industry associations and government agencies. Paraskevas and Arendell (2007) suggest that DMOs should advocate a 'no-fault learning culture' within the destination in order to facilitate learning transfer and the sharing of crisis knowledge and experience without fear of failure or blame. Other parts of this book have also advocated the role of the DMO in tourism crisis and disaster preparation and planning, not just recovery management. Brokers and spanners may identify where useful knowledge might be, who else needs to know it and how to link these parties together to enable the flow and creation of knowledge, not just information. However, importantly potential spanners and brokers should also consider how new knowledge can be created and developed. This will also be a brokerage role, but this time it will also include enabling different parties and organisations to share all forms of knowledge (including tacit and explicit), and helping them to learn through challenging and testing existing mental models for more effective adaptive management of crises and disasters.

The difficult role of boundary spanning will be determined by the nature and complexity of knowledge held at the boundary. Table 9.3 outlines three properties that can be held by the knowledge at the boundary, with an application to tourism crisis and disaster management. The table suggests that for crises or disasters that have been encountered in the past and information has been perhaps gathered on those, the focus of boundary spanning will be on difference and dependence in order to adapt an already formulated strategy or approach to tourism crisis and disaster management. This will most likely ensure access to and transfer of existing knowledge. If novelty of explicit or tacit knowledge is required, then the focus may have to be on the development of new ideas, meanings and actions. In this case, the type of boundary to be spanned becomes particularly important.

Table 9.4 outlines the types of boundary, their definitions and potential application to tourism crisis and disaster management. The pragmatic or political boundary and knowledge properties of novelty pose the greatest challenge to boundary spanners and tourism crisis knowledge management. Such situations will require stakeholders to share knowledge, possibly across locations and between organisations that may have different goals, history, expectations, budgets and knowledge levels. Identification of boundary spanners and their role in facilitating knowledge management is vital. The use of boundary objects, which is something that can be used across different contexts to share both explicit and tacit knowledge (Carlile, 2002; Miller, 2005), can include three different types according to Carlile (2002):

(1) *Repositories* which supply a common reference point that provides shared definitions and values for solving problems.
(2) *Forms* to provide a shared format for solving problems across different settings.

Table 9.3 Knowledge properties applied to tourism crisis and disaster management

Properties of knowledge at a boundary	Theoretical explanation	Application to tourism crisis and disaster management
Difference	Difference in the amount or type of knowledge held by agents within different domains at the boundary.	When a disaster occurs, the knowledge locally may differ from different agents and domains such as emergency managers, tourism organisations and DMOs. Previous experiences may highlight differences in knowledge and actions, rather than enabling integrated and coordinated crisis management responses.
Dependence	Where entities or agents must combine (or at least take into account) their knowledge in order to achieve a specific goal.	Hotels involved in hosting emergency workers and tourists after a natural disaster will rely on knowledge from emergency managers on the needs of both groups for access to shelter and resources.
Novelty	This may either be novelty in the case of new knowledge being needed and created, or that there is novelty across the boundary as different agents are unaware of each other's knowledge.	It may become apparent that the media need to be made aware of the realities of recovery efforts, so that negative images and stories can be reduced during the recovery phase. Tourism recovery marketers may be unaware of the needs of media for timely communication, relevant images and story leads due to a lack of experience in crisis communication.

Source: Adapted from Carlile (2002).

(3) *Objects, models and maps* can act as simple or complex representations that can be observed and then used between and across different settings systematically.

Boundary objects that are simply based on information processing and, not knowledge management, may not be complex enough to develop new knowledge through managed reflection and organisational

Table 9.4 Types of knowledge boundary and application to tourism crisis and disaster management

Type of boundary	Definition and Application to Tourism Crises and Disasters
Syntactic or information processing	This is where the focus is upon transferring knowledge across the boundary in order that all agents understand it. For such an approach to be successful, there will need to be a common lexicon developed which will enable the effective communication and mutual understanding of knowledge. This will usually need stable conditions, rarely found within contemporary organisations. Shared boundary objects such as repositories, forms and reports can help span boundaries to clarify facts, differences in meanings and agreed upon tasks. In the case of tourism crisis management, this could include knowledge brokers and boundary spanners facilitating the sharing of information on tourism crisis protocols, mobilisation systems, and defining who is responsible for certain responses and actions. Workshops may be required to discuss and clarify meanings, develop a common language and allocate responsibilities. Repositories of information and data, such as the National Tourism Incident Plan in Australia, can help identify responsibilities for tourism crisis management at a national level and define key concepts.
Semantic or interpretive	This boundary focuses upon translating knowledge. It will occur when novelty affects the levels of difference or dependency. Here, the new knowledge will necessitate the creation across the boundary of new meanings to explain the discrepancies and enabling shared understandings. This may occur through the translation of meanings and/or negotiation between agents in order to reach a common agreement. This will occur in tourism crisis management where there is a new incident to be addressed but where current knowledge will enable a solution, providing everyone can access and understand what is being planned and meant. The focus will be upon effectively sharing the ideas being implemented, so that one group can translate localised knowledge into forms that the other group can understand. A specific example is the 'Prepared and Protected Video' developed to communicate to the Australian accommodation industry the important role they would need to play in a potential influenza pandemic. The video was initially designed for health care professions, but was adapted for accommodation staff.
Pragmatic or political	The focus here is upon transforming knowledge. It will occur when novelty presents different knowledge outcomes or requirements which lead to different interests among agents

Table 9.4 (*Continued*)

Type of boundary	Definition and Application to Tourism Crises and Disasters
	needing to be resolved. This boundary recognises that knowledge is invested in practice and that there are potential conflicts and/or costs to do with sharing if to do so creates negative consequences for those in another domain. This is where resistance to innovation and adaptation may occur and where the most complex processes will need to be developed to overcome such potential difficulties. It is expected that some progress is made on the previous two categories to develop shared meanings and understanding.
	In tourism crisis management terms this will be where currently understood and applied strategies are ineffective and new ones must be developed either, because some parties simply are unaware of current possibilities, or because the way the problem is being addressed may be unsuitable. Boundary objects, maps and models may need to be used to transform embedded knowledge into knowledge that all stakeholders can understand and share rather than simply exchanging or transferring knowledge. An example is the use of scenario planning workshops undertaken by Visit Scotland, which brought out tacit knowledge and explicit knowledge in workshops on how to deal with tourism crises. Possible responses were then modelled showing the potential impact on the tourism economy.

Source: Adapted from Carlile (2002).

learning, but may be useful for syntactic or information processing. Knowledge needs to be diffused and used through expressions of organisational knowledge including boundary objects such as organisational models, policies, procedures, products and services, information systems and artefacts. These may be, according to Jashpara (2004) structured (financial and business data), semi-structured (policies, plans) and unstructured (videos, e-mail, presentations). Pforr and Hosie (2007) suggest that because many tourism organisations are geographically dispersed, the use of technology such as learning content management and digital storage devices may be an effective strategy.

However, how this knowledge is developed, stored and transferred to stakeholders depends upon the view of the knowledge broker or spanner. According to Jashpara (2004) two main approaches exist:

(1) *A codification-based strategy*, which is technology-led, based on explicit knowledge that is codified and is database driven. This

tends to result in a focus on the creation of knowledge objects and templates for stakeholders to access.

(2) *A personalisation-based strategy,* which is people-led, based on tacit knowledge, is developed through engagement in dialogue and where expertise is channelled. This approach emphasises knowledge sharing and mentoring amongst colleagues.

Drew (1999) outlines four types of business knowledge and the tools associated with these types:

(1) *What we know we know:* knowledge sharing, access and inventory. Tools include benchmarking and developing communities of practice.
(2) *What we know we don't know:* knowledge seeking and creation. Tools include research and development, market research and competitive intelligence.
(3) *What we don't know we know:* uncovering hidden and tacit knowledge. Tools include knowledge maps, audits, training and networks.
(4) *What we don't know we don't know:* discovering key risks, exposures and opportunities. Tools include creative tension, audits, dilemmas and complexity science.

These important points from the knowledge management literature suggest knowledge brokers and boundary spanners should carefully consider what information and knowledge their stakeholders require regarding the tourism crisis or disaster, what type of knowledge management philosophy should be followed, and finally, what business tools or boundary objects should be used to assist the knowledge management process and organisational learning for tourism crises and disasters.

The next section of this chapter brings together some of these concepts in proposing the need for evaluative enquiry and managed reflection in order to: (1) consider how to avoid reflexivity and (2) to ensure that new knowledge development is actively encouraged by focusing on the potential role of boundary spanners in producing and diffusing tourism crisis and disaster knowledge. Table 9.5 provides recommendations for applying to effective crisis and disaster strategy evaluation. Although these principals may be able to be applied throughout the tourism crisis lifecycle, the remainder of this chapter focuses on the review stage, where organisational learning and feedback hold the most importance. The following section expands upon each of the ideas in the table, developing a set of recommendations for potential boundary spanners and brokers, in order for them to embed a more reflective, critical and managed review of tourism crisis and disaster response strategies.

Table 9.5 Crises evaluation processes using core processes of evaluative enquiry

Asking questions	• Questions that ask about alternatives • Questions that ask why what was done has to be right • Questions that ask why what was done could not be wrong • Questions that frame alternatives that could have happened • Were there unexpected consequences from the actions taken • How does one action compare with another
Identifying and challenging values, beliefs and assumptions	• The key here is to identify assumptions about the solutions and the choices made. • Why was the strategy chosen accepted – what did it assume about the context
Reflection	• All stakeholders need to have the opportunity to feed in to the dialogue and challenge values, beliefs and assumptions
Dialogue	• All stakeholders need to be included in discussions about the new strategy • All need to be involved in setting the questions for the next stage. • Alternative scenarios need to be developed – even if they were ones that were rejected at the time to allow further evaluation at this stage
Collecting, analysing and interpreting data	• Too often data is collected that will show why what happened worked, thus data should be collected about alternatives – even ideas previously rejected. • Data should be collected by a variety of stakeholders, not just the project team.
Action planning and implementation	• A variety of scenarios should be developed and evaluated and incorporated into future tourism crisis communication and recovery strategies and plans. • These should be communicated to stakeholders and publics and tested through simulations, media training exercises and audits.

Source: Adapted from Preskill and Torres (1999).

Steps to Encourage Evaluative Enquiry and Managed Reflection

Asking questions

As discussed previously, when evaluating crisis response and recovery strategies it is very tempting to consider what actions worked and then to frame questions in a way that supports the current mental models. If evaluation of these strategies is to be truly effective, the questions will need to challenge the status quo and encourage a form of mild skepticism (Blackman & Henderson, 2004). Questions should ask about alternatives and rather than ask whether what was done was right, there should be questions that ask why what was done could not be wrong – a form of falsification. Questions that frame alternatives that might have happened should be used, to enable a wider range of discussion to evolve. Such questions may be asked prior to choosing and implementing crisis management strategies, but they will be dependent upon the speed and intensity of the crisis and whether adequate information is available to the organisation to assist decision-making. As Turner and Toft (2006) noted, learning about disasters is often constrained by a limited range of potential comparisons being scanned.

As noted below, and summarised in Table 9.5, all steps in an effective crisis evaluation procedure must involve external as well as internal stakeholders. Key questions in analysing the response/recovery of an organisation or destination include:

- Were crisis and disaster resources allocated effectively and efficiently?
- What were the early warning signs or triggers of the crisis and disaster, and did we pick these up quickly?
- How well were we prepared, and how well did the testing or scenario planning work? Was there a gap between tourism crisis and disaster planning and management?
- Was our leadership visible and appropriate?
- How was the decision-making undertaken? Did decision-making processes work effectively during the crisis or disaster?
- Did we re-deploy our resources effectively and efficiently during the response and recovery?
- How well did the crisis communication strategies meet stakeholders goals and needs?
- What changes could be made in the future to meet the needs of key publics based on their reaction to the strategies?
- What were our biggest mistakes? How could we have dealt with these better?

Based on previous suggestions for crisis communication and recovery marketing (Berry, 1999; Coombs, 1999) alternative framing questions could include: Was the response of the DMO and industry quick enough? Were the messages consistent for all stakeholders? Were appropriate response strategies developed for all stakeholders (government, tourists, industry, media) and were communication channels accessible? Were DMOs proactive or reactive at communicating with stakeholders? To illustrate the importance of this point, as discussed in Chapter 7, only

60% of Tourist Information Centres in the South East of England, had e-mail facilities during the Foot and Mouth Outbreak and only six out of 10 Regional Tourist Boards had websites (DCMS, 2001), yet the national DMO used e-mail as a major crisis communication channel for stakeholders. Alternative framing may have led to a wider range of crisis communication strategies being adopted.

Questions can be used to move tacit or explicit individual knowledge to a group-owned set of understandings, considering the DMO as an organisation but also the 'tourism industry' as a group. By developing questions that would elicit what each individual or stakeholder currently believed happened and why, new stories can be generated that can then be discussed. One technique might be to get each stakeholder to do a self-interview and answer the framing questions individually in a relatively formal manner (i.e. written format). These ideas can then be shared through the use of boundary objects such as written reports, models or maps. By doing this, pre-judging will not occur during the discussions, as can otherwise happen. For instance, comments from the British Hospitality Association in 2001, before the Foot and Mouth Outbreak and recovery marketing had ended, stated that the response was too little too late (Cotton, 2001). Perhaps these public statements were premature and unproductive prior to any reappraisal at the resolution and review stage of the crisis.

These questions can also be seen to be looking at comparisons and consequences. Such discussions are argued by Davenport and Prusak (1998 in Teodorescu, 2006) to be two ways of developing new knowledge. The idea is not to rank one idea as better than another but to look at each (even if one was initially rejected) as serious alternatives and evaluate the differences emerging as a series of potential outcomes. The comparisons may also help to identify and challenge some of the assumptions and beliefs being made as a basis for decision-making.

Identifying and challenging values, beliefs and assumptions

One of the hardest things to do is to open the shared mental models and surface the beliefs and assumptions that have been used as the basis for the decision-making by organisations during the crisis or disaster. Those involved in crisis response and recovery need to look at each decision point and explore why they chose that particular action – what was the conversation that occurred and what does it indicate about what they believed at that time. What is hard is to keep the conversation open, is tempting to keep remaking the decisions and re-judging the events to justify the decision. This is not the point of this exercise, the validity of the decision is not in question, what matters is why it was taken. As Anderson (2006: 192) argues, 'the extent to which organisational members are open to learning and the duration of this phase ['openness'] are largely dependent on the behaviour of the top management'.

In all likelihood, a third party facilitator or broker is needed to talk to as many internal and external stakeholders as possible and develop an understanding of the knowledge assumptions in place. Certain assumptions may have been made about the likely impact of a crisis on the image or reputation of a destination because of a lack of information, preparedness or organisational beliefs of the organisation. Therefore, organisations should consider what assumptions were in place at the time of the crisis or disaster and challenge these for developing more effective strategies in the future. On what grounds were these values, beliefs and assumptions based? They should reflect on assumptions and involve stakeholders where possible to provide critical reflection.

Reflection

This is where all the stakeholders need to compare the espoused 'theories-in-action' with the actual 'theories-in-use' (Argyris & Schon, 1996). Espoused theory is the theory that is put forward to explain what is done and to justify a particular pattern of activity, whereas 'theory-in-use' is that which is implicit in the performance of the given activity. The latter is much harder to achieve and must be constructed from evidence gained by observing and analysing what was actually done. It is easy to assume that an action emerges from espoused theory but this is often not the case, especially at a time of crisis when reaction may take over from consideration.

Thus, reflection on the 'theory-in-use' will matter as, if it is different from espoused theory and this is not what is desired, this may be a serious area for reconsideration. It may be that policy and culture do not match, for example, or that different stakeholders do not actually espouse the same theory. Differences that emerge will be a part of the dialogues that ensue. In order to consider these two areas, it may require someone who was less involved to track the actual actions and determine what the 'theory-in-use' really was. As Blackman et al. (2004: 24) state, 'controlling knowledge, keeping it from critical scrutiny, can lead to various forms of the closed society incapable of change and intelligent response and politically totalitarian'.

Dialogue

Mistilis and Sheldon (2006) suggest that all public and private stakeholders are involved in creating knowledge for tourism disasters, while collaboration is considered vital in triggering knowledge creation and organisational learning (Clegg et al., 2006). Dialogue has been identified as an important part of knowledge management (Groff &

Jones, 2003) and an important part of looking outside of an industry sector to improve learning about disasters (Turner & Toft, 2006). During the crisis it is likely that a very wide range of stakeholders will have been involved in trying to overcome the problems, although it has been noted that the DMO or industry associations usually take a coordinating role (Henderson, 1999b, 2002; Stafford *et al.*, 2002). It is important, therefore, that all these parties are involved in the conversations that occur as a co-sequence of the reflective process (Davenport & Prusak, 1998 in Teodorescu, 2006).

Dialogue or conversation is not about sending reports from one place to another, but is about situating the current knowledge. Nonaka and Konno (1998) describe socially based knowledge generation and note that participation in a social situation defines what is knowledge and what is information. Knowledge is described as useful only at a specific time and place if it is to be of value. Knowledge that is separated from its situation reverts to information to be communicated between situations. This processual perspective of knowledge (Newell *et al.*, 2002) indicates that it is the interaction between the different stakeholders that will enable the new knowledge to be developed within and around the context of the crisis or disaster. This interchange of knowledge between a wider range of people will again enable the movement of knowledge between knowledge types (as indicated in the squares in Figure 9.2): stories can be compared so that new scenarios and concepts can be developed. People with differing skills and current knowledge will analyse the ideas and develop their own 'theories-in-use' (Argyris & Schon, 1996) as to how such ideas would develop if there were another crisis or disaster. Dialogue is important part of developing trust and respect and valuing diverse view points of stakeholders, which are important in reducing homogeneity and blind support for policies or actions.

DMOs and industry associations have been recognised as having an important role to play in developing dialogue and coordinating messages in tourism crisis recovery (Henderson, 1999b, 2002; Stafford *et al.*, 2002), as well as their potential to facilitate dialogue through their roles as knowledge spanners or brokers. However, few studies have been conducted on the role and mechanisms for creating dialogue or the degree of trust needed to help develop organisational learning from tourism crises. For instance, Hooper (2002) notes that continuous dialogue with the industry was vital to monitor the impact of the Foot and Mouth Outbreak and also used to discuss recovery marketing options and opportunities. Furthermore, Stafford *et al.* (2002) suggested that dialogue was vital with government officials to help raise funds for crisis recovery activities with respect to 9/11 in Washington, DC.

However, the evaluation and reflection of such activities in tourism crisis response and recovery appears to be limited. The British national DMO, for instance, did realise that their previous dialogue with the media, and in particular London-based foreign correspondents, was reactive and that 'successful targeting of these individuals was crucial to the success of the [marketing and communication] programme' (Frisby, 2002). Frisby (2002) suggested that good communication and relations with foreign media should have been developed before the crisis hit, to enable a speedy and more positive response from foreign media outlets based in London. Schianetz *et al.* (2007) suggest that systems thinking tools can be used in workshops, in networks and partnerships to analyse complex problems and hopefully enhance systemic awareness. The use of scenario workshops by Visit Scotland (discussed in Chapter 5), which included interaction and dialogue, are another example of developing knowledge, not just information sharing.

Collecting, analysing and interpreting data

It would be very tempting to start by considering existing data and then seeking more confirmatory data early in the reflection process, as noted earlier in the chapter. This needs to be avoided. The order of the processes of evaluative enquiry is very important as it is designed to ensure that those involved have taken the time to develop alternative scenarios and will, therefore, gather data about those, as well as the actual choices made. What will be made possible is the opportunity for novel connections (Davenport & Prusak, 1998 in Teodorescu, 2006). Organisations should consider gathering data and information from internal and external stakeholders and critically evaluate the implications of the findings to develop new espoused theory for future crisis and disaster planning and management.

Gathering information is critical, not only in the implementation of crisis response strategies, but also at the end in facilitating a formal review. This may also include stakeholders such as emergency managers, aid agencies, government consulate officials in foreign countries as well as foreign journalists and news agencies. Data and information from a range of sources is required, perhaps including:

- crisis action plans;
- log of actions undertaken;
- copies of press releases and media monitoring;
- data on visitor numbers, occupancy and room rates;
- minutes of crisis management team meetings; and
- damage assessments and costs.

Action planning and implementation

Information and new knowledge from the managed reflection and critical enquiry should be then used to develop more effective plans and strategies as illustrated by the crisis and disaster framework outlined by Ritchie (2004). As discussed in Chapter 8, tourism crises and disasters can lead to transformations and positive outcomes through the generation of new knowledge, relationships and policy. Some destinations have reduced their reliance on key markets, increased government support and funding for tourism, developed new products and tourism-related policies to help reduce their vulnerability to incidents or increased their resilience.

Changes to resort location and design including safer rooms and escape routes were found in newly designed resort proposals after the 2004 tsunami in southern Thailand (Garcia *et al.*, 2006). Other examples include Australia after the Asian Economic Crisis (Prideaux, 1999) and the Foot and Mouth Outbreak in the UK (Miller & Ritchie, 2003; Sharpley & Craven, 2001). However, such knowledge is likely to be stronger if it has been created through a reflective and critical way at the review stage and used to produce organisational learning. Organisational learning should lead to the development of better crisis response and recovery plans which then need to be communicated to stakeholders, tested through simulations and audits, modified and ultimately implemented when the next crisis or disaster occurs.

Conclusion

This chapter began by outlining the knowledge management imperative, defined knowledge management and argued the importance of knowledge for the survival and adaptation of tourism organisations facing a tourism crisis or disaster. This part of the chapter acknowledged the differing knowledge types and the knowledge requirements throughout the crisis or disaster lifecycle for acquisition, storage, distribution, interpretation and action of knowledge. Following on from this, the chapter focused on organisational learning and feedback by focusing specifically on the review and reflection phase of the crisis or disaster lifecycle. It suggests that new knowledge enables the re-evaluation of currently understood ideas and beliefs and leads to the possibility of future change. Discussion took place over the difference between single- and double-loop learning, where it was noted that double-loop learning facilitates a higher level of knowledge generation as it may challenge existing assumptions and mental models and assist the future adaptive management of tourism crises and disasters.

The next section of the chapter suggested that managing the reflection process to encourage organisational learning is needed, including implementing evaluative enquiry and tools to encourage the generation of new explicit and tacit knowledge to challenge existing mental models. The chapter then discussed the role and importance of knowledge brokers and spanners in developing and sharing such knowledge across diverse groups and domains. The final section of the chapter brought these concepts together by proposing steps for boundary spanners and brokers to consider in developing evaluative enquiry and critical reflection at the review stage of a tourism crisis or disaster. In particular, this section outlined the need to ask tough questions designed to challenge existing values, beliefs and assumptions; the promotion of reflection and dialogue between stakeholders; the collection, analysis and interpretation of data, and importantly, the use of this data to develop and test new tourism crisis management strategies and policies as a result of this new knowledge.

Acknowledgements

I would like to acknowledge Associate Professor Deborah Blackman and Dr Monica Kennedy at the University of Canberra for their valuable input and feedback, which helped immensely in the production of this chapter.

Chapter 10

Conclusion and Reflections on Tourism Crisis and Disaster Management

Introduction

This chapter concludes the book by summarising the main contents of the book and looking forward to future challenges and research opportunities. The chapter begins with a summary of each part of the book (from Parts 1 to 4) before outlining future challenges and research issues, questions and topics, which have been identified from the theory and research identified in the book. This chapter acknowledges that effective tourism crisis and disaster planning and management is only possible if it is underpinned by sound research. The final section of this chapter outlines a 'post-disciplinary' approach to research that would ensure better understanding by undertaking research projects in an interdisciplinary way. This would mean tourism researchers need to work with a wide range of researchers from disciplines including education, sociology, management, allied health, geography in order to address the complex problems associated with tourism crisis and disaster management.

Book Summary

Setting the context

Part 1 provided an introduction and context to crisis and disaster planning and management for the tourism industry. Chapter 1 first, defined tourism and the tourism industry and acknowledged tourism from a systems perspective. It noted the main characteristics that make tourism unique but also susceptible to change as a result of shocks, crises and disasters. It suggested that decision-making of consumers could be vastly impacted by crises or disasters impacting upon business and society and noted a growing number of issues associated with global environmental change that affect the tourism industry and are affected by it through reductions in biodiversity, climate change, land alteration, loss of non-renewable resources and unsustainable use of renewable resources. Second, the chapter proposed a move from crisis and disaster management to prevention and planning, suggesting a growing aware-ness of the impact of natural hazards, extreme weather events, disasters, and crises on society. It advocated that far from ignoring crises, disasters and global environmental change and viewing them simply as a threat, tourism managers and destinations should embrace them as a part of the tourism system and should strategically plan for such change by identifying and understanding crises and disasters, developing and implementing management plans, and evaluating the success of those plans for more effective future planning. The chapter concluded with an overview of the two main fields of theory and literature included in the book: organisational crisis management, and disaster and emergency management.

Chapter 2 focused on the need to both define and understand crises and disasters in order to develop more effective responses with respect to their planning and management. It explained the difference between crisis and disaster definitions, the interrelationship between the two and how the 'ripple effect' can turn a crisis into a disaster or vice versa. It then outlined the type of crises and disasters that exist and can impact upon the tourism industry through the use of examples demonstrating their impacts on the tourism industry, with particular focus on large-scale natural/technical disasters (often as a result of global environmental change), and political and economic crises. The chapter noted that an increase in biosecuirty, health scares and global environmental change could pose serious challenges to the tourism industry, with their spread exacerbated by the tourism industry and greater levels of mobility.

An anatomy of a crisis or disaster was presented and the lifecycle of such incidents were identified and discussed in this chapter. Under-standing when an 'issue' becomes a crisis or disaster was discussed with the use of appropriate models. It outlined the difficulty in predicting or responding to crises and disasters as each one has different character-istics and are often seen as impossible to control. Discussion was undertaken concerning chaos and complexity theory and various ways of viewing crisis and disaster management. However, this chapter concluded by suggesting that a strategic and integrated approach to crisis and disaster management can help limit the potential impact of crises and disasters and is particularly relevant for the tourism industry, despite the complexity of such incidents.

The final chapter in the context setting Part 1 of the book (Chapter 3) suggested that an understanding of planning, management and strategic planning/management are crucial for the effective adaptive manage-ment of tourism crises and disasters. The concept of strategic planning and management were outlined, while debates were also presented on strategic planning and management perspectives. The elements of a strategic planning and management approach were outlined and discussed, including strategic analysis, choice, implementation and control, and the link between planning and management functions. Key concepts in strategic management were introduced including understanding the internal and external operating environment, organisational culture and the allocation of resources. These aspects were integrated in Parts 3 and 4 of the book. The final half of Chapter 3 outlined a rationale for a strategic approach to both planning for, and managing, tourism crises and disasters. An overview of crisis and disaster planning and management models were provided before a proposed strategic framework was presented, linked to the structure of the book. The framework noted that the crisis and disaster lifecycle has a clear similarity to the strategic management framework stages, and thus was integrated in the model and book chapters.

Tourism crisis and disaster prevention and planning

The first chapter in Part 2 of the book (Chapter 4) outlined the role of organisational strategic planning to prevent or reduce the chance of crisis and the role of disaster reduction and mitigation. Although forecasting techniques can signify the likelihood of emerging crises and disasters, they are limited with respect to their forecasting of immediate shocks including economic and political crises. As this chapter argued, despite the growing threat of natural disasters to tourism businesses and destinations, few tourism businesses are prepared to handle the impacts of such threats, yet crisis planning should be a core competency of tourism managers. The chapter also outlined key literature from the hazards, natural disasters and emergency management field to consider ways that natural disasters may be reduced or mitigated. Understanding risk and vulnerability and their broader links to sustainable development and sustainable tourism are vital and suggest the need for long-term reduction of global environmental change and natural disasters. The concept of 'invulnerable development' should be considered in combination with structural and non-structural mitigation measures.

If prevention or mitigation of crises and disasters is not possible, then contingency plans have to be developed and tested for dealing with these incidents at an organisational and destination level. Chapter 5 commenced by discussing preparedness measures for dealing with tourism disasters if prevention is not possible, including an understanding of emergency planning, the nature of precursors and warning systems, and finally, the development of training and simulations for emergency and tourism managers. Limited academic attention by tourism researchers and tourism managers has explored tourism disaster preparation. Due to the nature of the tourism industry comprising a large number of small businesses, this chapter argued that NTOs, DMOs or industry associations have an important role to play in assisting their stakeholders to change their reactive mindset and develop readiness strategies and initiatives. Recent efforts by such organisations, such as Visit Scotland are promising, but more effort is required.

Tourism organisations and destinations should set up a system to identify emerging issues and potential crises consisting of a core number of staff from various functional areas and even from related organisations (such as tourist associations and law enforcement officials).

This group should undertake scenario brainstorming to improve their understanding of the types of risks and possible response strategies and their impacts. Contingency plans should be developed which include the development of manuals and procedures, staff training and simulation exercises. The role of human resource development in effective crisis and disaster preparation should not be underestimated. All of these activities can help ensure an organisation is prepared and able to respond more effectively to both emerging incidents and unpredictable shocks. To date, the evidence suggests that the tourism industry has had less formal planning than other industries, possibly because of its nature (many small enterprises and interconnected with many sectors).

Tourism crisis and disaster response, implementation and management

The first chapter of this part of the book (Chapter 6) outlined the implementation of strategies to source, administer and control resources and systems for effective crisis and disaster management. It emphasised the importance of coordination between stakeholders, both within the tourism industry and between the tourism industry and external stakeholders such as emergency services personnel in order to effectively and efficiently use resources. Furthermore, leadership is required at a local, regional, national, and perhaps even international level depending on the size and scale of the tourism crisis or disaster. An understanding of the influence of cultural backgrounds in tourism crisis or disaster management decision-making and resource allocation was deemed important. The debate about the characteristics that make effective leaders in crisis and disaster situations, effective decision-making, and the degree to which leadership should be (de)centralised were all outlined in this chapter as significant issues in the strategic implementation phase.

Government may have to provide substantial resources not only towards reassurance and recovery marketing activities to assist the recovery of the tourism industry, but provide measures such as tax relief or tax credits to help businesses to continue operations. At an organisational level, resources may have to be (re)deployed to communication and information strategies and undertake activities to stimulate tourism demand. In conjunction with these activities, organisations may need to diversify their businesses away from tourism to reduce the impact and vulnerability. Other organisations will need to implement cost control measures such as reducing costs, postponing payments to creditors, reducing operations and reallocating human resources. In some aspects, staff will be asked to undertake unpaid leave or may lose their jobs completely due to a tourism crisis or disaster.

The second chapter in Part 3 of the book (Chapter 7) outlined the importance of image and perceptions for the tourism industry and the effect crises and disasters can have on consumer destination choice. In particular, it suggests that the media have an important role to play in crisis communication, perceptions management and recovery marketing. The media can encourage the flow and the intensity of a crisis or disaster or even help turn an incident or issue into a crisis due to negative media coverage. Subsequently, organisations need to work with the media to ensure that a consistent and accurate message is transmitted to the various public and stakeholders. A crisis or disaster communication plan should be part of the pre-event strategy but also needs to be flexible depending on the nature of the crisis and the response of stakeholders. Key target audiences should be identified and a communication and public relations plan developed and implemented paying particular attention to concepts such as the issue–attention cycle and understanding the information needs of key publics. Symmetrical two-way communication may be the best way to communicate to public during the emergency and intermediate stage of a crisis or disaster. Quick communication is required while destinations and organisations should develop a consistent set of messages through a nominated spokesperson, provide access to information for stakeholders and should be open, honest and express sympathy to victims at all times.

In the long-term recovery phase, recovery marketing initiatives are often undertaken using integrated marketing communication programmes that include persuasive consumer advertising as well as partnership marketing between government and industry stakeholders. Timing of marketing campaigns is crucial in order to limit wasting resources and misjudging consumer sentiment. The use of credible and unbiased third parties, such as celebrities, politicians and the like may be used to provide more credibility to marketing efforts, while the travel trade and media can be invited to take part in trade shows, events and familiarisations in order to increase positive exposure to the destination seeking to reverse negative images. Recovery marketing activities can be costly and fundraising and collaboration between the public and private sectors are often required, with good monitoring systems developed for providing feedback and information on the return on investment of long-term recovery marketing initiatives.

Tourism crisis and disaster recovery, resolution and feedback

The first chapter of Part 4 (Chapter 8) focused on the long-term recovery and resolution phase of tourism crises and disasters. The chapter began by defining the resolution phase as where a routine is restored or a new and improved state established. An improved state is possible as incidents provide opportunities as well as threats for those concerned. However, the time required between the long-term recovery and resolution stage can vary, based upon the size, complexity and nature of a crisis or disaster as well as an understanding of the dimensions of resolution (which can include human recovery elements).

Long-term positive and negative transformation can occur at an organisational, destination and human/community level, as a result of a tourism crisis or disaster. Organisations can increase their vitality and longevity, examine relationships with industry stakeholders and customers, and develop new products, markets and programmes to reduce their costs. Organisational team spirit and cohesion can also be established, and the role of destinations as social networks was identified. At a destination level, dealing with a crisis or disaster can also increase destination cohesiveness, within the tourism industry and between the tourism industry and associated groups (such as emergency workers, government and the community). Policy changes may occur as a result of disasters acerbating change and a realisation of the positive impact and value of tourism. Infrastructure may be rebuilt and improved, and greater planning and mitigation measures may also be introduced. However, community tensions may exist over the allocation of recovery funding and development options, while some workers may leave the destination due to trauma. Human and community transformation may also occur as a result of physical and mental exhaustion and post-traumatic stress for the local community, emergency workers and tourists themselves. Support services and intervention may be required, especially for the most vulnerable groups including children, elderly and emergency workers. The roles of family, peers, co-workers and the nature of the incident will influence the nature of recovery and the speed of resolution.

The final chapter of Part 4 (Chapter 9) focused on knowledge management and organisational learning from tourism crises and disasters. This chapter began by outlining the knowledge management imperative, defined knowledge management and argued the importance of knowledge for the survival and adaptation of tourism organisations facing a tourism crisis or disaster. This part of the chapter acknowledged the differing knowledge types and the knowledge requirements throughout the crisis or disaster lifecycle for acquisition, storage, distribution, interpretation and action of knowledge. Following on from this, the chapter focused on organisational learning and feedback by focusing specifically on the review and reflection phase of the crisis or disaster lifecycle. It suggests that new knowledge enables the re-evaluation of currently understood ideas and beliefs and leads to the possibility of deep learning and future change. Discussion took place over the difference between single- and double-loop learning, where it was proposed that double-loop learning facilitates a higher level of knowledge generation as it may challenge existing assumptions and mental models.

The chapter also suggested that managing the reflection process to encourage organisational learning is needed, including implementing evaluative enquiry and tools to encourage the generation of new explicit and tacit knowledge to challenge existing mental models. It discussed the role and importance of knowledge brokers and spanners in developing and sharing such knowledge across diverse groups and domains. The final section of the chapter brought these concepts together by proposing steps for boundary spanners and brokers to consider in developing evaluative enquiry and critical reflection at the review stage of a tourism crisis or disaster. In particular, this section outlined the need to ask tough questions designed to challenge existing values, beliefs and assumptions; the promotion of reflection and dialogue between stakeholders; the collection, analysis and interpretation of data, and importantly, the use of this data to develop and test new tourism crisis management strategies and policies as a result of this new knowledge.

Future Crisis/Disaster Challenges

Although it is difficult to predict the future, this section of the conclusion outlines some current issues and challenges which may pose an even bigger threat to the tourism system in the future. In particular, security issues provide a significant number of interrelated challenges to the tourism system which are likely to increase over the coming decades, and are outlined below. Finally, as noted earlier, the potential opportunities and the ability of the tourism system to self-regulate itself through adaptive management is noted at the end of this section.

As Hall *et al.* (2003) note, security is central to tourism and the concept has moved beyond national security issues to broader security issues including global environmental change, environment and resource security, health, biosecurity, and economic security. Resource shortages are placing increased pressures on society which are likely to grow in the future, creating the potential for linked disasters and crises to occur which could affect the tourism system. For instance, food shortages in developing countries may cause political unrest disrupting tourism flows and economic development as a result of tourism, affecting already vulnerable populations. As the IPCC (2007: 19) note, '[v]ulnerable regions face multiple stresses that affect their exposure and sensitivity as well as their capacity to adapt. These stresses arise from, for example, current climate hazards, poverty and unequal access to resources, food insecurity, trends in economic globalisation, conflict, and incidence of diseases such as HIV/AIDS'.

The potential of future biological threats to animals as well as humans is a very real threat to the tourism industry that has largely been ignored. As Hall (2006: 174) states, 'there is very little to suggest that the tourism industry is concerned or even aware of many [pandemics] such global health and disease issues'. Moreira (2007) notes, in a study of both tourists and residents, that an epidemic disease outbreak was the highest rated perceived risk for both groups. The potential for bioterrorists to contaminate the food chain through the use of biological agents or spread diseases such as smallpox or even foot and mouth could have a catastrophic impact upon industry and society including the tourism system, and are only recently being highlighted by industry and tourism researchers (Hall, 2006). Such crises and disasters will maintain the interest of health and food officials and have the potential to dramatically influence the tourism industry. The process of globalisation and the tourism industry itself has facilitated the spread of such disease impacting upon global security. More recently, the potential outbreak of bird flu and/or a global influenza pandemic have caused some concern amongst the tourism industry (Page *et al.*, 2006).

The increase of temperatures in particular locations as a result of climate change are set to exacerbate health-related disease and illness. Climate change impacts are complex and spread to other industries due to their linkages (IPCC, 2007), while the loss of biodiversity as a result of climate change will affect tourism resources in coastal areas, while population growth in these areas will further exacerbate risks from increases in storms and coastal flooding by 2050. Mountainous areas will face glacier retreat, reduced snow cover and winter tourism, and extensive species losses, according to the IPCC (2007). Tourism demand is often climate related and will obviously change, plunging some destinations into major crises and a need for rejuvenation strategies (both product and market related) in order to develop a sustainable competitive advantage into the future.

Economic security is increasingly becoming an issue at the present time of writing. The global 'credit crunch' of 2007 and possible world-wide recession could have a major impact upon consumer consumption and may dramatically affect tourism demand patterns. Furthermore, fuel price rises and concern over levels of oil production could dramatically increase the economic cost of travel and may affect demand and tourism services. As Becken (2008: 695) notes, 'the awareness of energy security and peak production of oil has traditionally been low in the tourism industry', yet concerns are mounting over the potential impacts a global decline in oil could produce. The dependency of tourism, and in particular, aviation to oil, is a major challenge to the tourism system and substantial risks are present for tourist transportation. The recent push for biofuels by Richard Branson (owner of Virgin airlines group) could be viewed with some caution as some media reports that biofuel production could affect agricultural crops and contribute to greater levels of food shortages.

Despite these challenges from future security issues, opportunities also exist for tourism destinations. The ability of the tourism system to self-regulate and adapt has been described in Chapter 2 in discussions over complexity, chaos and tourism crises. For instance, revenues will be created from the creation of new attractions as a result of climate change (IPCC, 2007), while increased fuel prices may lead to a modal shift towards more locally based or sustainable holidays (such as walking and cycling). As Becken (2008) notes, destinations that are reliant on international air travel might (re)invest in domestic tourism including developing fossil-free transport systems. The tourism system will adapt to these challenges, but as Gössling and Hall (2006) suggest, it is more likely that individual tourists will be flexible enough to adapt the easiest, both spatially and temporally, to global environmental change, whilst hotels and resorts might be the least flexible. Becken and Hay (2007) suggest that although some parts of the tourism industry may benefit from climate change, these benefits are likely to be small compared to negative impacts.

The Stern Review Report (Stern, 2006) suggests higher latitude countries, such as Canada, Russia and Scandinavia may benefit from tourism as a result of climate change but that the same regions will have rapid rates of warming affecting infrastructure, health and economic livelihoods. Mitigation measures could include involving tourists in conservation efforts to contribute to destination resilience activities as well as sustainable economic development for local livelihood strategies. The reduction of tourism businesses' carbon footprint could also improve their bottom line as well as contributing to carbon emissions and reducing the impacts of global environmental change.

Future Research Issues and Topics

This book attempts to provide a research base for understanding tourism crisis and disaster planning and management. Therefore, this part of the conclusion chapter outlines some key research issues, questions and topics that require future research to better understand, prepare and manage tourism crises and disasters (see Table 10.1). Although not an exhaustive list, the following research issues, questions

Table 10.1 Future research themes, questions and issues

Research theme	Questions and issues
Understanding tourism crises and disasters	• Chaos and complexity perspectives in tourism crises and disasters to better understand the triggers, planning and management associated with these incidents. • How can complexity and chaos perspectives be applied to tourism crises and disasters? • In what way does the 'ripple effect' or escalation of linked crises and disasters occur in the tourism system? • In what way can natural disaster planning actually exacerbate disaster by increasing vulnerability and risk? • What can be done to avoid crises and disasters in tourism in light of the interconnectiveness of the industry? • What methods and methodologies can be used to unpick the complexity of these incidents?
Planning, preparation and preparedness	• What are the current level of tourism industry preparedness and planning for crises and disasters? How does this compare to other sectors? A planning and preparedness scale could be developed to examine levels of preparedness, or qualitative research undertaken to examine reasons for planning or preparedness decisions? • Are forecasting techniques used by industry in crisis and disaster planning? Which ones should or could be used? • What planning tools are used in businesses and destinations (such as scenario planning, forecasting, environmental scanning, etc.)? Can scenario planning help with planning and systems thinking? Literature and theory on scenario planning, long-range planning and strategic management could be used in research. • What structural and non-structural mitigation techniques are used at a destination and organisation level for reducing vulnerability to natural hazards? To what extent are they working? • What preparation tools are used in tourism crisis and disaster planning (such as simulations, drills, development of response teams)? • What barriers or impediments exist in the adoption of tourism crisis and disaster planning/management? What are the perceptions of industry towards planning and prevention? Are barriers concerned with a 'locus of responsibility'; a reactive mindset; experience levels; social norms, values or organisational culture; or a lack of awareness of plans? • How can crisis and disaster planning and preparedness be linked to broader sustainable development? • What training needs are required for the tourism industry? A training needs analysis could be created based on the results of research on levels of planning/preparation and industry attitudes.

Table 10.1 (*Continued*)

Research theme	Questions and issues
Response, implementation and management	• Do plans actually work in reality? What works or does not work and for what reasons? Are plans too specific or not updated or lack commitment or knowledge from organisational members? • How are decisions made effectively in an organisation or destination facing a crisis or disaster? Should decision-making be centralised or de-centralised? What are the roles of various stakeholders with respect to response? What conflicts have occurred and how could they be resolved? How coordinated are stakeholders and what role do tourism agencies or organisations have with respect to the implementation of responses? Stakeholder collaboration theory or network analysis could be used to understand the actions of stakeholders and their involvement in the management of a tourism crisis or disaster. • What decision-making models are used or work most effectively in tourism crises and disaster management? What models have the best flow of information and communication, vital to effective management? • Do cultural differences exist with respect to decision-making processes, and how do these effect crisis or disaster management? • How are organisational decisions made in stable environments compared to complex environments, and how effective are they? • What policy measures should government implement to deal with large-scale tourism crises and disasters? Should tourism receive offset measures, and what types of measures would be best for tourism and the economy as a whole? Modelling is required on the best return on investment. • What lobbying has the tourism industry undertaken for government funding and resource allocation? How effective has this been compared to other sectors, and why is this the case? • Are measures easy to access by the tourism industry and what are the uptake levels? • Is aid and relief given as a result of natural disasters going to those who need it? • What organisational resource deployment is the best for dealing with tourism crises and disasters? What measures are best for reducing costs and increasing demand from tourists? What creative ways are there to (re)deploy workers or reduce costs? • Developing an understanding of risk perceptions, types of information and response to recovery marketing from consumer segments? How does a crisis or disaster affect perceptions of risk or image from key source markets? In

Table 10.1 (*Continued*)

Research theme	Questions and issues
	what way does a crisis or disaster affect the destination choice model of consumers?
	• Which type of image development techniques work best in recovery marketing (induced, organic, autonomous) and what is the role of unbiased third parties such as media in endorsing a destination during the recovery phase?
	• Does an issue–attention cycle exist with respect to tourism crises and disasters? In what way is this useful for crisis communication research and media management?
	• In what way can the media be used in the recovery marketing process? What forms of crisis communication work best (one way, two way, symmetrical) for different publics?
	• What role does and should the public relations departments have and does autonomy of this department improve recovery efforts?
	• What crisis communication techniques and distribution channels are most effective for key publics (government, industry, consumers)?
	• Can situational theory be used and applied in tourism crisis and disaster communication?
	• Timing on recovery marketing campaigns and the possible exploitation of 'pent up demand' for travel after crises and disasters.
	• Conversion studies and evaluation of recovery marketing campaigns. How effective are recovery marketing campaigns? Why do some campaigns fail, and what constitutes poor practice?
Long-term recovery, resolution and feedback	• When the resolution phase is complete? Does this depend on business recovery or human recovery dimensions? A holistic model of recovery and resolution is required.
	• What long-term positive and negative transformations occur as a result of a crisis of disaster at an organisational, destination and human/community level? Here, longitudinal research may be required.
	• What is the long-term recovery needs of tourists, the tourism industry and community? What support services and interventions are required and when should recovery resources be halted? What roles do peers, family or interventions such as debriefing play in the human recovery process?
	• What role does social capital play in recovery and resolution? How can vulnerability be reduced through recovery and resolution initiatives and strategies? What role should policy-makers have in building long-term resilience and reducing vulnerability into recovery initiatives?

Table 10.1 (*Continued*)

Research theme	Questions and issues
	• Can the Sustainable Livelihoods Framework (SLF) be used in a destination tourism disaster context and be modified to be used in an organisational crisis context? How could it be operationalised and tested at an organisational level? • Developing a knowledge management model for tourism crises and disasters at a destination and organisation level. How should the tourism industry gather explicit and tacit knowledge related to tourism crises and disasters? • How is information used and knowledge developed and transmitted during a tourism crisis or disaster? How should knowledge be stored, retrieved, processed and disseminated? • How can organisational learning be used to feedback into more effective crisis and disaster strategies? Can double- and single-loop learning be applied and in what instances does it apply? Is managed reflection applied by organisations or destinations in reviewing crisis or disaster management? • What role can knowledge brokers and spanners play in transmitting and developing knowledge? Who are the knowledge brokers and spanners? What are effective boundary objectives that can be used to help organisational learning and knowledge management? • What steps for evaluative enquiry and managed reflection actually work? How can managed skepticism be applied in tourism organisations and stakeholders involved in the review stage of a crisis or disaster? • Do reviews actually lead to changes in tourism crisis or disaster planning or prevention? Why or why not?

and potential topics are considered important priorities for future research linked to issues or theory outlined earlier in the book. In particular, it should be noted that a lack of research exists concerned with the planning/prevention and resolution/feedback stage of tourism crises and disasters. Most research to date has focused on the response of organisations and destinations and has limited theoretical or conceptual focus. For a comprehensive research agenda for crisis and disaster management for tourism see Carlsen and Liburd (2007) who identified research priorities based on six categories:

(1) clarification of definitions, concepts and typologies;
(2) risk identification and assessment;
(3) managing recovery and restoration;
(4) marketing and promotion during and after a crisis;

(5)   rebuilding the destination; and
(6)   sustainable tourism development from a risk management perspec-
      tive.

This section of the chapter ends with a call for a 'post-disciplinary approach' to researching tourism crises and disasters, which will encourage more interdisciplinary research and better understanding of these phenomena.

Understanding tourism crises and disasters

One of the biggest issues in understanding tourism crises and disasters is the chaotic and complex nature of these phenomena. In particular, due to the complexity in the tourism system it is often difficult to understand the key triggers of a tourism crisis or disaster and ways to limit or reduce vulnerability to incidents as the world is interconnected. Research issues, questions and future research in this area are identified in Table 10.1 and relate to understanding the interdependence of tourism to the broader human and natural system, as well as the application of chaos and complexity perspective and methods to tourism crisis and disaster planning and management.

Models for assessing and understanding tourism crises and disasters (based on their lifecycles) have largely been prescriptive. More work is required to develop and test models in the tourism field. However, the balance between developing a generic or broad model that can capture enough detail for both the macrolevel generality and microlevel comprehensiveness has eluded researchers to date. The development, testing and refinement of models are required by tourism researchers, particularly models that are less linear and capture the continuous and dynamic nature of tourism crisis and disaster management. To date, few have even tested Faulkner's (2001) tourism disaster framework, while detailed models for each phase of the crisis or disaster lifecycle may be required (reduction, readiness, response, recovery). Researchers are encouraged to further develop, expand and/or test the model or components of the model presented in Figure 3.6, which this book is based on.

Understanding also needs to be improved with respect to the blurring of human and natural systems, which can create security threats and risks as well as creating natural disasters and crises for the tourism industry. These pose the greatest challenge to the tourism industry as the tourism industry itself can facilitate the spread of security threats and risks through facilitating global mobility.

Planning, preparation and preparedness

Further research on a number of topics associated with crisis and disaster planning and readiness are urgently required. Tourism crisis and disaster literature appears to be dominated by response and recovery at the expense of planning and prevention. Such research can assist tourism managers and policy-makers to develop effective policies and strategies. In particular, researchers should attempt to understand the current level of industry reduction and readiness efforts as well as potential barriers or impediments in tourism crisis and disaster planning. Research from the hazards, emergency planning and tourism disaster planning field suggest that the tourism industry can play an important role in planning for natural disasters. However, as Figure 5.3 illustrates, a lack of awareness, understanding and capacity of tourism managers may be restricting tourism crisis and disaster planning. This may be in part due to a lack of experience in dealing with such incidents, certain values and beliefs, personal attributes or social/cultural norms. Therefore research issues, questions and future topics related to this theme should explore these issues and questions.

Furthermore, as noted in Chapter 5, tourists are often considered more vulnerable in a natural disaster as they are not aware of the local conditions or resources and rely on tourism operators to provide necessary information, which may not be available. Research is urgently required on the hazard and disaster information strategies for different tourist groups and target markets, and how differences between local perceptions and knowledge may assist the development of relevant information for tourists. Each tourist market may require separate messages and information located in different sources to ensure that they are read and understood by these groups.

Response, implementation and management

It is widely held that crisis and disaster planning may not translate into effective management for several reasons outlined in Chapter 5 including a lack of planning, limited testing of plans and decision-making structures. Therefore, future research issues, questions and topic concerning the link between tourism crisis and disaster planning and management are required and could examine the role of organisational culture, decision-making and leadership on the effective development and implementation of tourism crisis and disaster responses.

Furthermore, there are questions that arise as to the allocation of resources by government and organisations, including relevant policy measures for responses, as well as the scope and nature of resource (re)allocation at a destination level as well as an organisational level. Finally, research is required to understand the information needs of key publics, help establish when recovery marketing campaigns should start and should be used to evaluate their effectiveness. Such information is vital for the future support of recovery marketing campaigns by government and industry.

Long-term recovery, resolution and feedback

As noted in Chapter 8, further work and research is required on the long-term recovery and resolution phase of crises and disasters. In particular, research issues, questions and topics should explore when the recovery phase is actually completed and what long-term impacts and transformations occur as part of a tourism crisis or disaster, and what support do local communities and tourists need to assist their full recovery. The role of capital and sustainable livelihoods are particularly important and should be considered in the development of recovery strategies and actions.

Furthermore, research is required into the capture, storage and use of knowledge, as well as organisational learning, outlined in Chapter 9. In particular, key research issues, questions and topics should focus on the development and communication of both tacit as well as explicit knowledge, and the role of knowledge brokers and spanners in the transformation of information into knowledge and the process of managed reflection, which is an important part of adaptive management.

Finally, this book has advocated a greater role in tourism crisis and disaster planning, response and organisational learning by DMOs, NTAs and industry associations, due to the size of tourism businesses. These organisations have an important role to play in educating the industry and facilitating readiness, response and recovery actions. Therefore, research is also required into their activities before, during and after a tourism crisis or disaster, particularly in regard to leadership and collaboration (both within the industry and with emergency departments).

A post-disciplinary approach to research

Future research and the development of theoretical or conceptual frameworks are required on crisis and disaster management generally, but particularly focusing on the tourism industry. In particular, there is a need for researchers to move beyond simplistic prescriptive models which may provide check lists or information on *what* managers should do before, during or after crises toward descriptive models which develop and/or test models, concepts or theories related to crisis management to examine *why* crises were managed (in)effectively in the tourism industry. Future research should consider a 'post-disciplinary' (Coles *et al.*, 2006) approach to the problem of tourism crisis and disaster planning and management.

As Coles *et al.* (2006) suggest a more problem-focused approach beyond disciplines, based on more flexible modes of knowledge production, plurality, synthesis and synergy, may be important for advancing tourism knowledge especially in complex areas. Synthesis of different discipline areas is important, as Coles *et al.* (2006: 301) suggest there is a 'tendency for scholars to restrict themselves to the boundaries of their own disciplines ... reflective is a common ignorance of what lies beyond the disciplinary divide'. This may be achieved by involving researchers from education, communication, emergency planning, environmental science, security, sociology, geography (physical and applied) and tourism to better understand the reasons behind tourism disaster and crisis planning and preparation levels. As Larsson and Enander (1997) observed, social values and norms may have an influence on disaster planning, and cross-cultural studies are suggested to examine these issues. In complex areas, such as tourism crisis and disaster planning/management, a single disciplinary approach is perhaps not significant to advance knowledge and understanding.

Furthermore, as noted in this book, tourists are often considered more vulnerable in a natural disaster as they are not aware of the local conditions or resources and rely on tourism operators to provide necessary information, which may not be available. Research is urgently required on the hazard and disaster information strategies for different tourist groups and target markets. Researchers in the communication, education, media and sociology field could work with tourism researchers to explore these issues. Awareness campaigns, training needs analysis and other educational programmes can be developed once a better understanding of industry and tourist attitudes are held by policy-makers.

Media and communications specialists may need to work with tourism researchers to understand the media effect during the crisis communication and recovery marketing phase of a crisis or disaster. Theory such as framing analysis, representation analysis, and communication and public relations theory could also be used to further understanding of crisis and disaster communication techniques. Content analysis could be used to examine how the messages are framed by different audiences. Economists may be involved in modelling the economic benefits and costs of government assistance measures or tax policies to help the industry recover from shocks, such as that undertaken by Blake and Sinclair (2003). This would provide useful information and models to assist government policy making. Psychologists may be required to help better understand perceptions of risk and marketers to assist how risk perceptions affect image and decision-making of consumers. Management researchers, especially in the field of leadership, organisational behaviour and strategic management, could work with tourism researchers to better understand leadership, human resource development and decision-making in tourism crises.

Finally, with respect to the long-term recovery and resolution phase, psychologists and allied health researchers could work with tourism researchers on the important issue of the human dimension of recovery (for workers in the tourism industry, tourists themselves and the broader community). Community development specialists, human geographers and anthropologists may be able to assist in integrating recovery initiatives with sustainable livelihoods and understanding the role of social capital in resolving crises and disasters. Knowledge management specialists, and educators, could assist in research to better understand the nature and process of organisational learning from crises and disasters.

There is also a need for research following different paradigmatic positions to improve our understanding of crisis and disaster management in the tourism industry, including:

- chaos and complexity theory applied to crises and disasters;
- positivistic approaches to quantify levels of preparedness and reactions of the industry to crises and disasters and help predict incidents through computer stimulation modelling;
- phenomenological approaches to explore attitudes and opinions of managers in the public and private sector towards crisis and disaster management; and
- case study approaches are needed to test models and concepts surrounding crisis management in the tourism industry.

A 'post-disciplinary' approach to researching this complex field would help research to go beyond discipline boundaries for more detailed research insights, more interesting and valuable methodological approaches. This is particularly important bearing in mind the complexity of future security challenges and crises/disasters. A 'post-disciplinary' approach would provide benefits to researchers, enhancing our understanding of tourism crises and disasters and hopefully develop better planning and management techniques for managers and policy-makers. However, such an approach is not without its challenges and potential costs to tourism researchers. I hope that students and researchers consider taking up this challenge.

Conclusion

This chapter has summarised the main contents of the book, acknowledged possible future risks, crises and disasters resulting from security issues, and outlined future research opportunities. It has suggested a number of research issues, questions and potential topics exist in this field, and proposed that models need to be developed and tested using a range of different research approaches, methods and disciplinary perspectives. In particular, this chapter has proposed a 'post-disciplinary' approach to research that would hopefully move researchers 'beyond disciplines' to examine the complexity surrounding tourism crisis and disaster management. This would provide opportunities for a deeper understanding of these phenomena, which would hopefully lead to more effective planning and management. It is hoped that this research book has made some small contribution to knowledge in this field, and helps provide some assistance to future researchers (whether they are students, academics or practioners).

References

Aalbers, R., Dolfsma, W. and Koppius, O. (2004) On and off the beaten path: How individuals broker knowledge through informal and formal networks. *ERIM Research Series*. On WWW at http://www.erim.eur.nl. Accessed 24.6.2007.

Alexander, D. (2000) *Confronting Catastrophe*. Harpenden: Terra Publishing.

Allen, K. (2003) Vulnerability reduction and the community based approach: A Philippines study. In M. Pelling (ed.) *Vulnerability Reduction and the Community Based Approach: A Philippines Study* (pp. 170–184). London: Routledge.

Allinson, R.E. (1994) *Global Disasters: Inquiries into Management Ethics*. New York: Prentice-Hall.

Anderson, B.A. (2006) Crisis management in the Australian tourism industry: Preparedness, personnel and postscript. *Tourism Management* 27, 1290–1297.

Andrai, D. (2007) *Crisis Management: A Case Study of the Indonesian Government Tourism Public Policy after the First and Second Bali Bombs*. Canberra: MA. Tourism Discipline. University of Canberra.

Anon. (2003) *Crisis Management Plan to be in Place to Bolster Tourism Trade*. Business Times, Singapore.

Ansoff, I. and McDonnell, E. (1990) *Implanting Strategic Management*. Hemel Hampstead: Prentice Hall.

Arbel, A. and Bargur, J. (1980) A planning model for crisis management in the tourism sector. *European Journal of Operational Research* 5 (2), 77–85.

Argyris, C. (1991) Teaching smart people how to learn. *Harvard Business Review* May/June, 98–105.

Argyris, C. (1999) *On Organizational Learning*. Oxford: Blackwell Business.

Argyris, C. and Schon, D.A. (1996) *Organizational Learning II: Theory, Method and Practice*. Massachusetts: Addison-Wesley.

Armstrong, E.K. (2008) Destination recovery after natural disasters – A case study of the recovery of the ACT tourism industry after the 2003 bushfires. PhD thesis, Tourism Discipline. University of Canberra. Canberra.

Armstrong, E.K. and Ritchie, B.W. (2007) The heart recovery marketing campaign: Destination recovery after a major bushfire in Australia's national capital. *Journal of Travel & Tourism Marketing* 23 (2/3/4), 175–190.

Ashcroft, L.S. (1997) Crisis management – public relations. *Journal of Managerial Psychology* 12 (5), 325–332.

Au, A.K.M., Ramasamy, B. and Yeung, M.C.H. (2005) The effects of SARS on the Hong Kong tourism industry: An empirical evaluation. *Asia Pacific Journal of Tourism Research* 10 (1), 85–95.

Augustine, N. (1995) Managing the crisis you tried to prevent. *Harvard Business Review* (November–December), 148.

Australian Capital Tourism (2004) *Market Research – Autumn/Post-Bushfire Campaign Evaluation*. Canberra: ACTC. On WWW at http://www.tourism.act.gov.au. Acccessed 5.12.2004.

Aziz, H. (1995) Understanding attacks on tourists in Egypt. *Tourism Management* 16 (2), 91–95.

Bahra, N. (2001) *Competitive Knowledge Management*. Basingstoke: Palgrave.

Baral, A., Baral, S. and Nigel, M. (2004) Marketing Nepal in an uncertain climate: Confronting perceptions of risk and insecurity. *Journal of Vacation Marketing* 10 (2), 186–192.

Barnett, C.K. and Pratt, M.G. (2000) From threat-rigidity to flexibility: Toward a learning model of autogenic crisis in organizations. *Journal of Organizational Change Management* 13 (1), 74–88.

Barton, L. (1994a) Preparing the marketing manager for crisis: The use and application of new strategic tools. *Marketing Intelligence & Planning* 12 (11), 41–46.

Barton, L. (1994b) Crisis management: Preparing for and managing disasters. *Cornell Hotel and Restaurant Administration Quarterly* April, 59–65.

Barton, L. and Hardigree, D. (1995) Risk and crisis management in facilities: Emerging paradigms in assessing critical incidents. *Facilities* 13 (9/10), 11–14.

Baxter, E. and Bowen, D. (2004) Anatomy of tourism crisis: Explaining the effects on tourism of the UK Foot and Mouth disease epidemics of 1967–68 and 2001 with special reference to media portrayal. *International Journal of Tourism Research* 6, 263–273.

Becken, S. (2008) Developing indicators for managing tourism in the face of peak oil. *Tourism Management* 29, 695–705.

Becken, S. and Hay, J. (2007) *Tourism and Climate Change: Risks and Opportunities.* Clevedon: Channel View Publications.

Beeton, S. (2001) Horseback tourism in Victoria, Australia: Cooperative, proactive crisis management. *Current Issues in Tourism* 4 (5), 422–439.

Beeton, S. (2002) The cost of complacency: Horseback tourism and crisis management revisited. *Current Issues in Tourism* 5 (5), 467–470.

Beirman, D. (2002) Marketing of tourism destinations during a prolonged crisis: Israel and the Middle East. *Journal of Vacation Marketing* 8 (2), 167–176.

Beirman, D. (2003) *Restoring Tourism Destinations in Crisis: A Strategic Marketing Approach.* Wallingford: CABI Publishing.

Beirman, D. (2006) Best education network think tank V keynote address: "Marketing tourism destinations from crisis to recovery." *Tourism Review International* 10, 7–16.

BERI (2003) BERI – Business Environment Risk Index. On WWW at http://www.beri.com/. Accessed 22.4.2003.

Beritelli, P. and Gotsch, H. (1999) Crisis-PR for tourist enterprises: Chosen examples and practical recommendations. *Tourismus Journal* 3 (3), 325–355.

Berke, P. (1998) Reducing natural hazard risks through state growth management. *Journal of American Planning Association* 64 (1), 76–87.

Berman, R. and Roel, G. (1993) Encounter with death and destruction: The 1985 Mexico City earthquake. *Group Analysis* 26, 81–89.

Berno, T. and King, B. (2001) Tourism in Fiji after the coups. *Travel & Tourism Analyst* 2, 75–92.

Bernsdorf, S. (2004) *The Impact of the Floods on Tourism: A Case Study of the August 2002 Floods in Saxony, Germany.* Diploma in Tourism. Department of Tourism. University of Otago. Dunedin.

Berry, S. (1999) We have a problem ... call the press! (crisis management plan). *Public Management* 81 (4), 4–15.

Billings, R.S., Milburn, T.W. and Schaalman, M.L. (1980) A model of crisis perception: A theoretical and empirical analysis. *Administrative Science Quarterly* 25, 303–316.

Blackman, D.A. (2006) Knowledge creation and the learning organization. In P. Murray, D. Poole and G. Jones (eds) *Contemporary Management Issues in Management and Organisational Behaviour* (pp. 246–273). Melbourne: Thomson.

Blackman, D., Connelly, J. and Henderson, S. (2004) Does double loop learning create reliable knowledge? *The Learning Organization* 11 (1), 11–27.

Blackman, D. and Henderson, S. (2004) Double loop doubting: Challenging past experience to frame the future. *Futures* 36 (2), 253–266.

Blackman, D. and Ritchie, B.W. (2007) Tourism crisis management and organizational learning: The role of reflection in developing effective DMO crisis strategies. *Journal of Travel and Tourism Marketing* 23 (2/3/4), 45–58.

Blaikie, P., Cannon, T., Davis, I. and Wisner, B. (1994) *At Risk: Natural Hazards, People's Vulnerability and Disasters*. London: Routledge.

Blake, A., Sinclair, T. and Sugiyarto, G. (2001) The economy-wide effects of foot and mouth disease in the UK economy. Unpublished paper. Travel and Tourism Reasearch Institute, Nottingham University, UK.

Blake, A. and Sinclair, M.T. (2003) Tourism crisis management: US response to September 11. *Annals of Tourism Research* 30 (4), 813–832.

Bland, M. (1995) Training managers to handle a crisis. *Industrial and Commercial Training* 27 (2), 28–31.

Bonham, C., Edmonds, C. and Mak, J. (2006) The impact of 9/11 and other terrible global events on tourism in the United States and Hawaii. *Journal of Travel Research* 45, 99–110.

Bonn, I. and Rundle-Thiele, S. (2007) Do or die – Strategic decision-making following a shock event. *Tourism Management* 28, 615–620.

Bouncken, R. and Pyo, S. (2002) *Knowledge Management in Hospitality and Tourism*. New York: Haworth.

Bowman, C. (1992) Charting competitive strategy. In D. Faulkner and G. Johnson (eds) *The Challenge of Strategic Management*. London: Kogan Page.

Brammer, H. (1990) Floods in Bangladesh: A geographic background to the 1987 and 1988 floods. *Geographical Journal* 156 (1), 12–22.

Brewton, C. (1987) Managing a crisis: Model for the lodging industry. *Cornell Hotel and Restaurant Administration Quarterly* 28 (3), 10–15.

BBC News. (2003a) *SARS: Global Hotspots*. London: BBC News. On WWW at http://www.news.bbc.co.uk/1/hi/health/2969247.stm. Accessed 19.8.2003.

BBC News. (2003b) *Killer Bug Traced to HK Hotel*. London: BBC News. On WWW at http://www.news.bbc.co.uk/1/hi/health/2867055.stm. Accessed 19.8.2003.

British Tourist Authority (BTA) (2001) *Foot and Mouth Disease Briefing*. London: BTA.

British Tourist Authority (BTA) (2002) *Media Releases*. London: BTA. 28 April. http://www.tourismtrade.org.uk/pdf/PPR_MVC_OnlyBritain.pdf.

Britton, R. (2003) *Rebuilding Credibility after a Crisis*. Tourism and Travel Research Association (TTRA) Conference, St. Louis, Missouri, USA, 15 June.

Buchanan, D.A. and Huczynski, A.A. (1985) *Organizational Behaviour: An Introductory Text*. Hemel Hempstead: Prentice Hall.

Buckle, P., Marsh, G. and Smale, S. (2001) *Assessing Resilience & Vulnerability: Principles, Strategies & Actions*. Canberra: Emergency Management Australia.

Burnett, J.J. (1998) A strategic approach to managing crises. *Public Relations Review* 24 (4), 475–488.

Burton, I., Kates, R. and White, G. (1978) *The Environment as Hazard*. New York: Oxford University Press.

Calantone, R.J., Di Benedetto, A. and Bojanic, D. (1987) A comprehensive review of the tourism forecasting literature. *Journal of Travel Research* 25, 28–39.

Calder, S. (2003) Never mind terrorism – the real risks are on your hotel balcony. *The Independent.* London. 1.

Camilleri, P., Healy, C., MacDonald, E., Nicholls, S., Sykes, J., Winkworth, G. and Woodward, M. (2007) *Recovering from the 2003 Canberra Bushfire: A Work in Progress.* Canberra: Emergency Management Australia.

Campiranon, K. and Arcodia, C. (2007) Market segmentation in time of crisis: A case study of the MICE Sector in Thailand. *Journal of Travel & Tourism Marketing* 23 (2/3/4), 151–161.

Carlile, P.R. (2002) A pragmatic view of knowledge and boundaries. *Organization Science* 13 (4), 442–455.

Carlsen, J. (2006) Post-tsunami tourism strategies for the Maldives. *Tourism Review International* 10, 66–79.

Carlsen, J. and Liburd, J. (2007) Developing a Research Agenda for Tourism Crisis Management, Market Recovery and Communications. *Journal of Travel &Tourism Marketing* 23 (2/3/4), 265–276.

Cassedy, K. (1991) *Crisis Management Planning in the Travel and Tourism Industry: A Study of Three Destinations and a Crisis Management Planning Manual.* San Francisco: PATA.

Cavlek, N. (2002) Tour operators and destination safety. *Annals of Tourism Research* 29 (2), 478–496.

CDC (Centres for Disease Control and Prevention) (2003a) Severe Acute Respiratory Syndrome – frequently asked questions about SARS. CDC, 19.8.2003. On WWW at http://www.cdc.gov/ncidod/sars/sars-faq.pdf.

CDC (Centres for Disease Control and Prevention) (2003b) Severe Acute Respiratory Syndrome – SARS information for travelers. CDC, 19.8.2003. On WWW at http://www.cdc.gov/ncidod/sars/travel.htm.

Chacko, H.E. and Marcell, M.H. (2007) Repositioning a tourism destination: The case of New Orleans after hurricane Katrina. *Journal of Travel & Tourism Marketing* 23 (2/3/4), 223–235.

Chaffee, E. (1985) Three models of strategy. *Academy of Management Review* 10 (1), 89–98.

Chandler, A. (1962) *Strategy and Structure.* Cambridge, MA: MIT Press.

Chandler, J.A. (2004) An analysis of the economic impact of Hurricanes Dennis, Floyd, and Irene on North Carolina's lodging industry. *Journal of Hospitality & Tourism Research* 28 (3), 313–326.

Chapman, J. and Ferfolja, T. (2001) Fatal flaws: The acquisition of imperfect mental models and their use in hazardous situations. *Journal of Intellectual Capital* 2 (4), 398–409.

Chen, R.J.C. and Noriega, P. (2003) The impacts of terrorism: Perceptions of faculty and students on safety and security in tourism. *Journal of Travel & Tourism Marketing* 15 (2/3), 81–97.

Cheung, C. and Law, R. (2006) How can hotel guests be protected during the occurrence of a Tsunami? *Asia Pacific Journal of Tourism Research* 11 (3), 289–295.

Chien, G.C.L. and Law, R. (2003) The impact of the severe acute respiratory syndrome on hotels: A case study of Hong Kong. *Hospitality Management* 22, 327–332.

Christoplos, I. (2003) Actors in risk. In M. Pelling (ed.) *Actors in Risk* (pp. 95–109). London: Routledge.

Chong, J.K.S. and Nyaw, M.K. (2002) Are Hong Kong companies prepared for crisis? *Disaster Prevention and Management* 11 (1), 12–17.

Cigler, B. (1988) Emergency management and public administration. In M.T. Charles and J.C.K. Kim (eds) *Emergency Management and Public Administration* (pp. 5–19). Springfield: Charles C. Thomas.

Cioccio, L. and Michael, E.J. (2007) Hazard or disaster: Tourism management for the inevitable in Northeast Victoria. *Tourism Management* 28, 1–11.

Clegg, S., Kornberger, M. and Pitsis, T. (2006) *Managing and Organisations: An Introduction to Theory and Practice*. London: Sage.

Cole, G. (1994) *Strategic Management*. London: DP Publishers.

Cole, G. (1996) *Strategic Management*. London: DP Publishers.

Coles, T. (2003) A local reading of a global disaster: Some lessons on tourism management from an *Annus Horribilis* in South West England. *Journal of Travel & Tourism Marketing* 15 (2/3), 173–197.

Coles, T., Hall, C.M. and Duval, D.T. (2006) Tourism and post-disciplinary enquiry. *Current Issues in Tourism* 9 (4/5), 293–319.

Comfort, L.K. (1999) *Shared Risk: Complex Systems in Seismic Response*. Oxford: Pergamon Press.

Cook, S.D.N. and Brown, J.S. (1999) Bridging epistemologies: The generative dance between organizational knowledge and organizational knowing. *Organization Science* 10 (4), 381–400.

Coombs, T. (1999) *Ongoing Crisis Communication: Planning, Managing and Responding*. Thousand Oakes, CA: Sage.

Cooper, C. (2006) Knowledge management and tourism. *Annals of Tourism Research* 33 (1), 47–64.

Cooper, M. (2005) Japanese tourism and the SARS epidemic of 2003. *Journal of Travel & Tourism Marketing* 19 (2/3), 117–131.

Cosgrave, J. (1996) Decision-making in emergencies. *Disaster Prevention and Management* 5 (4), 28–35.

Cotton, B. (2001) Foot and Mouth: The lessons we must learn. *Tourism: Journal of the Tourism Society* Autumn, 5.

Crompton, J. (1979) An assessment of the image of Mexico as a vacation destination and the influence of geographical location upon that image. *Journal of Travel Research* 17 (4), 18–24.

Crondstedt, M. (n.d.) Prevention, preparedness, response, recovery – an outdated concept? *Australian Journal of Emergency Management* 1–4.

Cushnahan, G. (2003) Crisis management in small-scale tourism. *Journal of Travel & Tourism Marketing* 15 (4), 323–338.

Darling, J., Hannu, O. and Raimo, N.T. (1996) Crisis management in international business: A case situation in decision-making concerning trade with Russia. *The Finnish Journal of Business Economics* 4, 12–25.

Darling, J.R. (1994) Crisis management in international business: Keys to effective decision-making. *Leadership & Organization Development Journal* 15 (8), 3–8.

Davidson, C. and Voss, P. (2002) *Knowledge Management*. Auckland: Tandem.

Davies, H. and Walters, M. (1998) Do all crises have to become disasters? Risk and risk mitigation. *Disaster Prevention and Management* 7 (5), 396–400.

De Freitas, C.R. (2006) Extreme weather events. In S. Gössling and C.M. Hall (eds) *Tourism and Global Environmental Change: Ecological, Social, Economic and Political Interrelationships* (pp. 195–210). London: Routledge.

De Jong, P. (2004) *Tourism Recovery Strategies for the Region*. CAUTHE 2004: Creating Tourism Knowledge. Brisbane, 11 February.

De Sausmarez, N. (2003) Malaysia's response to the Asian financial crisis: Implications for tourism and sectoral crisis management. *Journal of Travel & Tourism Marketing* 15 (4), 217–231.

De Sausmarez, N. (2004) Crisis management for the tourism sector: Preliminary considerations in policy development. *Tourism & Hospitality: Planning & Development* 1 (2), 157–172.

De Sausmarez, N. (2005) The Indian Ocean Tsunami. *Tourism & Hospitality: Planning & Development* 2 (1), 55–59.

Department of Culture, Media and Sport (DCMS) (2001) *Press Releases*. London: On WWW at http://www.culture.gov.uk/tourism/search.asp?Name = press releases/tourism/2001/dcms.

Ditto, W. and Manukata, T. (1995) Principles and applications of chaotic systems. *Communications of the ACM* 38 (11), 96–102.

Downs, A. (1972) Up and down with ecology – the issue attention cycle. *Public Interest* 28, 38–50.

Dozier, D., Grunig, L. and Grunig, J. (1995) *Managers Guide to Excellence in Public Relations and Communication Management*. New Jersey: Lawrence Erlbaum Associates Inc.

Drabek, T.E. (1995) Disaster responses within the tourism industry. *International Journal of Mass Emergencies and Disasters* 13 (1), 7–23.

Drabek, T.E. (1996) *Disaster Evacuation Behavior: Tourists and other Transients*. Boulder, CO: Institute of Behavioral Science, University of Colorado.

Drabek, T.E. (1999) *Disaster-Induced Employee Evacuation*. Boulder, CO: Institute of Behavioral Science, University of Colorado.

Drabek, T.E. (2000) Disaster evacuations: Tourist-business managers rarely act as customers expect. *Cornell Hotel and Restaurant Administration Quarterly* August, 48–57.

Drew, S. (1999) Building knowledge management into strategy: Making sense of a new perspective. *Long Range Planning* 32 (1), 130–136.

Dwyer, L., Forsyth, P., Spurr, R. and VanHo, T. (2006) Economic effects of the world tourism crisis on Australia. *Tourism Economics* 12 (2), 171–186.

Earl, M.J. (2001) Knowledge management strategies: Toward a taxonomy. *Journal of Management Information Systems* 18 (1), 215–233.

Elkjaer, B. (2004) The learning organization: An undelivered promise. In C. Grey and E. Antonacopoulou (eds) *The Learning Organization: An undelivered promise* (pp. 71–88). London: Sage.

Elliot, D. (2006) Crisis management into practice. In D. Smith and D. Elliot (eds) *Crisis Management into Practice* (pp. 393–414). London: Routledge.

Emergency Management Australia (EMA) (1995) *National Emergency Management Competency Standards*. Canberra: Emergency Management Australia.

English Tourism Council (ETC) (2001) *Press Briefing*. London: ETC.

Enz, C.A. and Canina, L. (2002) The best of times, the worst of times: Differences in hotel performance following 9/11. *Cornell Hotel and Restaurant Administration Quarterly* October, 41–52.

Evans, N., Campbell, D. and Stonehouse, G. (2003) *Strategic Management for Travel and Tourism*. Wallingford: CABI Publishing.

Evans, N. and Elphick, S. (2005) Models of crisis management: An evaluation of their value for strategic planning in the international travel industry. *International Journal of Tourism Research* 7, 135–150.

Fahey, L. and Prusak, L. (1998) The eleven deadliest sins of knowledge management. *California Management Review* 40, 265–275.

Fall, L.T. (2004) The increasing role of public relations as a crisis management function: An empirical examination of communication restrategising efforts among destination organisation managers in the wake of 11th September, 2001. *Journal of Vacation Marketing* 10 (3), 238–252.

Faulkner, B. (2001) Towards a framework for tourism disaster management. *Tourism Management* 22, 135–147.

Faulkner, B. and Russell, R. (2000) Turbulence, chaos and complexity in tourism systems: A research direction for the new millennium. In B. Faulkner, G. Moscardo and E. Laws (eds) *Turbulence, Chaos and Complexity in Tourism Systems: A Research Direction for the New Millennium* (pp. 328–349). London: Continuum.

Faulkner, B. and Vikulov, S. (2001) Katherine, washed out one day, back on track the next: A post-mortem of a tourism disaster. *Tourism Management* 22, 331–344.

Federal Department of Industry Tourism and Resources (2007) *National Tourism Incident Response Plan: An Action Plan for Governments across Australia*. ACT: Commonwealth of Australia.

Field, S. (2003) *Tourism: Recovery in the aftermath of Disaster*. BA (Hons). School of Service Management. University of Brighton. Eastbourne.

Fink, S. (1986) *Crisis Management: Planning for the Inevitable*. New York: American Association of Management.

Fink, S. (2000) *Crisis Management: Planning for the Inevitable*. Lincoln: iUniverse. com Inc.

Floyd, M.F., Gibson, H., Pennington-Gray, L. and Thapa, B. (2003) The effect of risk perceptions on intentions to travel in the aftermath of September 11, 2001. *Journal of Travel & Tourism Marketing* 15 (2/3), 19–38.

Frechtling, D. (1996) *Practical Tourism Forecasting*. Oxford: Butterworth Heinemann.

Freeman, R.E. (1984) *Strategic Management: A Stakeholder Approach*. Boston: Pitman.

French, T. (1991) European airline profitability – Part 1. *Travel & Tourism Analyst* 5, 5–23.

Frisby, E. (2002) Communicating in a crisis: The British Tourist Authority's responses to the Foot-and-Mouth outbreak and 11th September, 2001. *Journal of Vacation Marketing* 9 (1), 89–100.

Garcia, R., Lau, S.S.Y., Chau, K.W., Kanitpun, R., Shimatsu, Y., Grunder, P., Koo, R. and Baharuddin (2006) Sustainable resorts: Learning from the 2004 Tsunami. *Disaster Prevention and Management* 15 (3), 429–447.

Gartner, W.C. (1993) Image formation process. In M. Uysal and D. Fesenmaier (eds) *Image Formation Process* (pp. 191–216). New York: Harworth.

Gartner, W.C. (1996) *Tourism Development: Principles, Processes and Policies*. New York: Van Nostrand Reinhold.

Gartner, W.C. and Shen, J. (1992) The impact of Tiananmen Square on China's tourism image. *Journal of Travel Research* 30 (4), 47–52.

Gee, C., Makens, J. and Choy, D. (1994) The travel industry. In *The Travel Industry*. New York: Van Nostrand Rheinhold.

Geipel, R. (1982) *Disaster and Reconstruction*. London: Allen and Unwin.

Getz, D. (1987) *Tourism planning and research: Traditions, models and futures*. The Australian Travel Research Workshop. Bunbury, Western Australia, 5–6th November.

Gibb, S. (2002) *Learning and Development: Processes, Practices and Perspectives at Work*. Basingstoke: Palgrave Macmillan.

Glaesser, D. (2003) *Crisis Management in the Tourism Industry*. London: Butterworth-Heinemann.

Glaesser, D. (2006) *Crisis Management in the Tourism Industry*. Oxford: Butterworth-Heinemann.

Gleick, J. (1987) *Chaos: Making a New Science*. London: Abacus Books.

Gonzalez Herrero, A. (1997) Preventive marketing: Crisis reporting in the tourism sector. *Estudios Turisticos* 133, 5–28.

Gonzalez Herrero, A. (1999) Product commercialization and crisis planning in the tourist sector: Corporative image and consumer-centred marketing. *Papers de Turisme* 24, 6.

Gonzalez-Herrero, A. and Pratt, C.B. (1995) How to manage a crisis before – or whenever – it hits. *Public Relations Quarterly* Spring, 25–29.

Gonzalez-Herrero, A. and Pratt, C.B. (1996) An Integrated Symmetrical Model for Crisis-Communications Management. *Journal of Public Relations Research* 8, 79–105.

Gonzalez-Herrero, A. and Pratt, C.B. (1998) Marketing crises in tourism: Communication strategies in the United States and Spain. *Public Relations Review* 24 (1), 83–98.

Goodrich, J.N. (2005) The big American blackout of 2003: A record of the events and impacts on USA travel and tourism. *Journal of Travel & Tourism Marketing* 18 (2), 31–37.

Gössling, S. and Hall, C.M. (eds) (2006) *Tourism and Global Environmental Change: Ecological, Social, Economic and Political Interrelationships*. London: Routledge.

Granot, H. (1995) Proposed scaling of communal consequences of disaster. *Disaster Prevention and Management* 4 (3), 5–13.

Grant, H.D., Murray, R.H. and Bergeron, J.D. (1989) *Emergency Care*. Englewood Cliffs, NJ: Prentice-Hall.

Grant, R.M. (1996) Toward a knowledge-based theory of the firm. *Strategic Management Journal* 17, 109–122.

Grewe, T., Marhsall, J. and O'Toole, D. (1989) Participative planning for a public service. *Long Range Planning* 22, 110–117.

Groff, T. and Jones, T. (2003) *Introduction to Knowledge Management*. London: Butterworth-Heinemann.

Gunn, C. (1972) *Vacationscape: Designing Tourist Environments*. Austin: University of Texas.

Gunn, C. (1977) Industry pragmatism vs tourism planning. *Leisure Sciences* 1 (1), 85–94.

Gunn, C. (1988) *Tourism Planning*. New York: Taylor & Francis.

Gurtner, Y. (2006) Understanding tourism crisis: Case studies of Bali and Phuket. *Tourism Review International* 10, 57–68.

Gurtner, Y. (2007) Crisis in Bali: Lessons in tourism recovery. In E. Laws, B. Prideaux and K. Chon (eds) *Crisis in Bali: Lessons in Tourism Recovery* (pp. 81–97). Wallingford: CABI Publishing.

Hall, C.M. (1994) *Tourism and Politics: Policy, Power and Place*. Chichester: John Wiley and Sons.

Hall, C.M. (1995) *Introduction to Tourism in Australia: Impacts, Planning and Development*. Melbourne: Longman.

Hall, C.M. (1998) *Introduction to Tourism: Development, Dimensions and Issues*. Melbourne: Addison Wesley Longman.

Hall, C.M. (2000) *Tourism Planning: Policies, Processes and Relationships*. Melbourne: Addison Wesley Longman.

Hall, C.M. (2002) Travel safety, terrorism and the media: The significance of the issue-attention cycle. *Current Issues in Tourism* 5 (5), 458–466.

Hall, C.M. (2005) Biosecurity and wine tourism. *Tourism Management* 26 (6), 931–938.

Hall, C.M. (2006) Tourism, biodiversity and global environmental change. In S. Gössling and C.M. Hall (eds) *Tourism and Global Environmental Change: Ecological, Social, Economic and Political Interrelationships* (pp. 211–226). London: Routledge.

Hall, C.M., Jenkins, J.M. and Kearsley, G. (1997) *Tourism Planning and Policy in Australia and New Zealand: Cases, Issues and Practice*. Sydney: Irwin.

Hall, C.M. and O'Sullivan, V. (1996) Tourism, political instability and violence. In A. Pizam and Y. Mansfeld (eds) *Tourism, Political Instability and Violence* (pp. 105–122). Chichester: John Wiley and Sons.

Hall, C.M., Timothy, D.J. and Duval, D.T. (2003) *Safety and Security in Tourism: Relationships, Management, and Marketing*. New York: The Haworth Hospitality Press.

Harder, J. (2003) Epidemic From China is Encircling Globe (Morbid Mystery Tour), 29 March. *Science News* 163, 198.

Hargadon, A.B. (1998) Firms as knowledge brokers: Lessons in pursuing continuous innovation. *California Management Review* 40 (3), 209–227.

Hargadon, A.B. (2002) Brokering knowledge: Linking learning and innovation. *Research in Organizational Behavior* 24, 41–85.

Heath, R. (1995) The Kobe earthquake: Some realities of strategic management of crises and disasters. *Disaster Prevention and Management* 4 (5), 11–24.

Heath, R. (1997) *Strategic Issues Management*. London: Sage Publications.

Heath, R. (1998) *Crisis Management for Managers and Executives*. London: Financial Times Management.

Henderson, J.C. (1999a) Tourism management and the Southeast Asian economic and environmental crisis: A Singapore perspective. *Managing Leisure* 4, 107–120.

Henderson, J.C. (1999b) Managing the Asian financial crisis: Tourist attractions in Singapore. *Journal of Travel Research* 38, 177–181.

Henderson, J.C. (2002) Managing a tourism crisis in Southeast Asia: The role of national tourism organizations. *International Journal of Hospitality & Tourism Administration* 3 (1), 85–105.

Henderson, J.C. (2003) Communicating in a crisis: Flight SQ 006. *Tourism Management* 24, 279–287.

Henderson, J.C. (2003) Terrorism and tourism: Managing the consequences of the Bali bombings. *Journal of Travel & Tourism Marketing* 15 (1), 41–58.

Henderson, J.C. (2005) Responding to natural disasters: Managing a hotel in the aftermath of the Indian Ocean Tsunami. *Tourism and Hospitality Research* 6 (1), 89–96.

Henderson, J.C. (2007) Corporate social responsibility and tourism: Hotel companies in Phuket, Thailand, after the Indian Ocean Tsunami. *Hospitality Management* 26, 228–239.

Henderson, J.C. and Ng, A. (2004) Responding to crisis: Severe Acute Respiratory Syndrome (SARS) and hotels in Singapore. *International Journal of Tourism Research* 6, 411–419.

Herman, C. (1972) *International Crises: Insights from Behaviour Research*. New York: The Free Press.

Higgins, B.A. (2005) The storms of summer: Lessons learned in the aftermath of the hurricanes of '04. *Cornell Hotel and Restaurant Administration Quarterly* 46 (1), 40–46.

Hills, A. (1998) Seduced by recovery: The consequences of misunderstanding disaster. *Journal of Contingencies and Crisis Management* 6 (3), 162–170.

Hitchcock, M. and Putra, I.N.D. (2005) The Bali bombings: Tourism crisis management and conflict avoidance. *Current Issues in Tourism* 8 (1), 62–76.

Hofer, C. (1973) *Some Preliminary Research on Patterns of Strategic Behaviour.* Academy of Management Proceeding.

Hofstede, G. (1984) *Culture's Consequences: International Differences in Work-Related Values.* Beverly Hills, CA: Sage.

Hofstede, G. (2001) *Culture's Consequences: Comparing Values, Behaviors, Institutions, and Organizations across Nations.* Thousand Oaks, California: Sage.

Hoogenraad, W., Eden, R.V. and King, D. (2004) Cyclone awareness amongst Backpackers in Northern Australia. *The Australian Journal of Emergency Management* 19 (2), 25–29.

Hooper, P. (2002) Marketing London in a difficult climate. *Journal of Vacation Marketing* 9 (1), 81–88.

Horsley, S.I. and Barker, R.T. (2002) Toward a synthesis model for crisis communication in the public sector. *Journal of Business and Technical Communication* 16(4), 406–40.

Hoyois, P., Scheuren, J.M., Below, R. and Guha-Sapir, D. (2007) *Annual Disaster Statistical Review: Numbers and Trends 2006.* Brussels: Centre for Research on the Epidemiology of Disasters (CRED).

Huang, J.H. and Min, J.C.H. (2002) Earthquake devastation and recovery in tourism: The Taiwan case. *Tourism Management* 23, 145–154.

Huimin, G. and Wall, G. (2006) SARS in China: Tourism impacts and market rejuvenation. *Tourism Analysis* 11 (6), 367–379.

Hystad, P. and Keller, P. (2006) Disaster management: Kelowna tourism industry's preparedness, impact and response to a 2003 major forest fire. *Journal of Tourism and Hospitality Management* 13 (1), 44–58.

Hystad, P. and Keller, P. (2008) Towards a destination tourism disaster management framework: Long-term lessons from a forest fire disaster. *Tourism Management* 39 (1), 151–162.

Ichinosawa, J. (2006) Reputational disaster in Phuket: The secondary impact of the tsunami on inbound tourism. *Disaster Prevention and Management* 15 (1), 111–123.

Intergovernmental Panel on Climate Change (IPCC) (2001) *IPCC Third Assessment. Climate Change 2001.* Report of the Intergovernmental Panel on Climate Change. Cambridge: Cambridge University Press.

Intergovernmental Panel on Climate Change (IPCC) (2007) Summary for policymakers. In M.L. Parry, O.F. Canziani, J.P. Palutikof, P.J. van der Linden and C.E. Hanson (eds) *Climate Change 2007: Impacts, Adaptation and Vulnerability* (pp. 7–22). Contribution of Working Group II to the Fourth Assessment Report of the Intergovernmental Panel on Climate Change. Cambridge: Cambridge University Press.

Irvine, W. and Anderson, A.R. (2005) The Impacts of Foot and Mouth Disease on a peripheral tourism area: The role and effect of crisis management. *Journal of Travel & Tourism Marketing* 19 (2/3), 47–60.

ISDR (2004) *Living with Risk: A Global Review of Disaster Reduction.* Geneva: United Nations.

Israeli, A.A. and Reichel, A. (2003) Hospitality crisis management practices: The Israeli case. *Hospitality Management* 22, 353–372.

Jashapara, A. (2004) *Knowledge Management: An Integral Approach.* Harlow: Prentice Hall.

Jessop, B. (1999) Reflections on globalisation and its (il)logic(s). In K. Olds, P. Dicken, P.F. Kelly, L. Kong and H.W. Yeung (eds) *Reflections on Globalisation and Its (il)logic(s)* (pp. 19–38). London: Routledge.

Johnson, G. (1988) Rethining incrementalism. *Strategic Management Journal* 9 (1), 75–91.

Johnson, G. and Scholes, K. (1993) *Exploring Corporate Strategy.* Oxford: Butterworth-Heinemann.

Johnston, D., Becker, J., Gregg, C., Houghton, B., Paton, D., Leonard, G. and Garside, R. (2007) Developing warning and disaster response capacity in the tourism sector in coastal Washington, USA. *Disaster Prevention and Management* 16 (2), 210–216.

Joyce, P. (1999) *Strategic Management for the Public Services.* Maidenhead: Open University Press.

Kash, T.J. and Darling, J.R. (1998) Crisis management: Prevention, diagnosis and intervention. *Leadership & Organization Development Journal* 19 (4), 179–186.

Kates, R. and Kasperson, J. (1983) Comparative risk analysis of technological hazards (a review). *National Academy of Science* 80, 7027–7038.

Keown-McMullan, C. (1997) Crisis: When does a molehill become a mountain? *Disaster Prevention and Management* 6 (1), 4–10.

Kim, P.S. and Lee, J.E. (1998) Emergency management in Korea and its future directions. *Journal of Contingencies and Crisis Management* 6 (4), 189–201.

Kim, S.S., Chun, H. and Lee, H. (2005) The effects of SARS on the Korean hotel industry and measures to overcome the crisis: A case study of six Korean five-star hotels. *Asia Pacific Journal of Tourism Research* 10 (4), 369–377.

Knable, C.R.J. (2002) September 11, 2001 recovering hospitality at ground zero. *Cornell Hotel and Restaurant Administration Quarterly* October, 11–26.

Kolb, D. (1984) *Experiential Learning.* New Jersey: Prentice-Hall.

Kondro, W. (2003) SARS back in Canada. *The Lancet* 361, 1876.

Konecnik, M. (2004) Evaluating Slovenia's image as a tourism destination: A self-analysis process towards building a destination brand. *Brand Management* 11 (4), 307–316.

Kotler, P. (1988) *Marketing Management.* Hemel Hempstead: Prentice Hall.

Kouzmin, A., Jarman, A.M.G. and Rosenthal, U. (1995) Inter-organizational policy processes in disaster management. *Disaster Prevention and Management* 4 (2), 20–37.

Kozak, M., Crotts, J.C. and Law, R. (2007) The impact of the perception of risk on international travellers. *International Journal of Tourism Research* 9, 233–242.

Kwortnik, R.J. (2006) Shining examples of service when the lights went out: Hotel employees and service recovery during the blackout of 2003. *Journal of Hospitality & Leisure Marketing* 14 (2), 23–45.

Larsson, G. and Enander, A. (1997) Preparing for disaster: Public attitudes and actions. *Disaster Prevention and Management* 6 (1), 11–21.

Laws, E. and Prideaux, B. (2005) Crisis management: A suggested typology. *Journal of Travel & Tourism Marketing* 19 (2/3), 1–8.

Layfield, L. (2003) *Europe Promises £6.2m for SARS Research.* The Guardian. 19th August. On WWW at http://www.guardian.co.uk/sars/story/0,13036,990668,00.html.

Lee, G., O'Leary, J.T. and Hong, G.S. (2002) Visiting propensity predicted by destination image: German long-haul pleasure travellers to the US. *International Journal of Hospitality and Tourism Administration* 3 (2), 63–92.

Lee, Y.J. and Harrald, J.R. (1999) Critical issue for business area impact analysis in business crisis management: Analytical capability. *Disaster Prevention and Management* 8 (3), 184–189.

Leiper, N. (1989) *Tourism and Tourism Systems*. Occasional Paper No. 1. Palmerston North: Massey University.

Leiper, N. (2000) Are destinations 'the heart of tourism'? The advantages of an alternative description. *Current Issues in Tourism* 3 (4), 364–368.

Leiper, N. and Hing, N. (1998) Trends in Asia-Pacific tourism in 1997–98: From optimism to uncertainty. *International Journal of Contemporary Hospitality Management* 10 (7), 245–251.

Lenthan, G. (1995) *Qantas Flies in as Philippines Pulls Out*. Sydney: The Sydney Morning Herald.

Lenthan, G. (1998) *Qantas Flies in as Philippines Pulls Out*. The Sydney Morning Herald 18 June.

Levina, N. and Vaast, E. (2005) The emergence of boundary spanning competence in practice: Implications for implementation and use of information systems. *MIS Quarterly* 29 (2), 335–363.

Litvin, S. and Alderson, L. (2003) How Charleston got her groove back: A convention and visitors bureau response to 9/11. *Journal of Vacation Marketing* 9 (2), 188–197.

Lloyd, J., La Lopa, J. and Braunlich, C. (2000) Predicting Changes in Hong Kong's Hotel Industry Given the Change in Sovereignty from Britain to China in 1997. *Journal of Travel Research* 38 (4), 405–410.

Lo, A., Cheung, C. and Law, R. (2006) The survival of hotels during disaster: A case study of Hong Kong in 2003. *Asia Pacific Journal of Tourism Research* 11 (1), 65–79.

Malhotra, Y. (1997) Knowledge management, knowledge organizations and knowledge workers: A view from the front lines. BRINT. 2.7.2007. On WWW at http://www.brint.com/interview/maeil.htm.

Malhotra, Y. (2002) Why knowledge management systems fail? Enabler and constraints of knowledge management in human enterprises. In C. Holsapple (ed.) *Why Knowledge Management Systems Fail? Enabler and Constraints of Knowledge Management in Human Enterprises* (pp. 577–599). Heidelberg: Spriner Velag.

Marra, F.J. (1998) Crisis communication plans: Poor predictors of excellent crisis public relations. *Public Relations Review* 24 (4), 461–474.

Martín-Consuegra, D., Esteban, Á. and Molina, A. (2007) The role of market orientation in managing crises during the post-crisis phase. *Journal of Travel & Tourism Marketing* 23 (2/3/4), 59–71.

Massey, J.E. (Forthcoming) Public relations in the airline industry: The crisis response to the September 11th attacks. *Journal of Hospitality & Leisure Marketing*.

Mathieson, A. and Wall, G. (1985) *Tourism: Economic, Physical and Social Impacts*. London: Harlow.

McEntire, D.A. (1999) Sustainability or invulnerable development? Proposals for the current shift in paradigms. *Australian Journal of Emergency Management* 15 (1), 58–61.

McEntire, D.A. (2001) Triggering agents, vulnerabilities and disaster reduction: Towards a holistic paradigm. *Disaster Prevention and Management* 10 (3), 189–196.

McIntosh, R., Goeldner, C. and Ritchie, J.R.B. (1995) *Tourism: Principles, Practice, Philosophies*. New York: John Wiley and Sons.

McKercher, B. (1999) A chaos approach to tourism. *Tourism Management* 20, 425–434.

McKercher, B. and Chon, K. (2004) The over-reaction to SARS and the collapse of Asian tourism. *Annals of Tourism Research* 31 (3), 716–719.

McKercher, B. and Pine, R. (2005) Privation as a stimulus to travel demand? In E. Laws and B. Prideaux (eds) *Privation as a Stimulus to Travel Demand?* (pp. 107–116). New York: Haworth.

Méheux, K. and Parker, E. (2006) Tourist sector perceptions of natural hazards in Vanuatu and the implications for a small island developing state. *Tourism Management* 27 (1), 69–85.

Mellahi, K., Jackson, P. and Sparks, L. (2002) An exploratory study into failure in successful organizations: The case of marks and spencer. *British Journal of Management* 13 (1), 15–30.

Michael-Leiba, M., Granger, K. and Scott, G. (2000) Lanslide risk in cairns. *Australian Journal of Emergency Management* Winter, 32–34.

Mileti, D. (1999) *Disasters by Design: A Reassessment of Natural Hazards in the United States.* Washington, DC: Joseph Henry Press.

Mill, R. and Morrison, A. (1985) *The Tourism System: An Introductory Text.* Englewood Cliffs: Prentice-Hall International.

Miller, G.A. and Ritchie, B.W. (2003) A farming crisis or a tourism disaster? An analysis of the Foot and Mouth Disease in the UK. *Current Issues in Tourism* 6 (2), 150–171.

Miller, G.A. and Ritchie, B.W. (2004) Sport tourism in crisis: Exploring the impact of the Foot and Mouth Crisis on sport tourism in the United Kingdom. In B.W. Ritchie and D. Adair (eds) *Sport Tourism in Crisis: Exploring the Impact of the Foot and Mouth Crisis on Sport Tourism in the United Kingdom* (pp. 206–225). Clevedon: Channel View Publications.

Miller, K. and Waller, G. (2003) Scenarios, real options and integrated risk management. *Long Range Planning* 36 (1), 93–107.

Miller, R. (2005) Creating boundary objects to aid knowledge transfer. *KM Review* 8 (2), 12–15.

Mills, R. and Snow, C. (1978) *Organisational Strategy, Structure and Process.* Maidenhead: McGraw-Hill.

Mintzberg, H. (1987) The strategy concept I: Five Ps for strategy. *California Management Review* 30, 11–24.

Mistilis, N. and Sheldon, P. (2006) Knowledge management for tourism crises and disasters. *Tourism Review International* 10, 39–46.

Moreira, P. (2007) Stealth risks and catastrophic risks: On risk perception and crisis recovery strategies. *Journal of Travel & Tourism Marketing* 23 (2/3/4), 15–27.

Mubarak, K. (2007) *Analyzing Post-Tsunami Livelihoods Recovery: The Case of Masons in Polhena Village, Sri Lanka.* Melbourne: The University of Melbourne.

Murphy, P. (1996) Chaos theory as a model for managing issues and crises. *Public Relations Review* 22 (2), 95–113.

Murphy, P.E. (1985) *Tourism: A Community Approach.* New York: Methuen.

Murphy, P.E. and Bayley, R. (1989) Tourism and disaster planning. *Geographical Review* 79 (1), 36–46.

Newell, S., Robertson, M., Scarborough, H. and Swan, J. (2002) *Managing Knowledge Work.* Basingstoke: Palgrave.

Nicholls, S. and Glenny, L. (2005) Communicating for recovery: A case study in communication between the Australian Capital Territory Government and the ACT community after the ACT bushfires, January 2003. In C. Galloway and

K. Kwansah-Aidoo (eds) *Communicating for Recovery: A Case Study in Communication between the Australian Capital Territory Government and the ACT Community after the ACT Bushfires, January 2003* (pp. 41–58). Australia: Thomson.

Nielsen, C. (ed) (2001) *Tourism and the Media.* Sydney: Hospitality Press Pty Ltd.

Nonaka, I. and Konno, N. (1998) The concept of "ba": Building a foundation for knowledge creation. *California Management Review* 40 (3), 40–54.

Nonaka, I. and Takeuchi, H. (1995) *The Knowledge Creating Company.* Oxford: Oxford University Press.

Nothiger, C., Burki, R. and Elsasser, H. (2006) The example of the avalanche winter 1999 and the storm Lothar in the Swiss Alps. In S. Gössling and C.M. Hall (eds) *Tourism and Global Environmental Change: Ecological, Social, Economic and Political Interrelationships* (pp. 286–292). London: Routledge.

Office Fédéral de l'Environnement, des Forêts, et du Paysage (OFEFP) (1999) *La Fôret.* Suisse: Un bilan.

O'Mahony, B., Whitelaw, P. and Ritchie, B.W. (2006) The effect of fuel price rises on tourism behaviour: An exploratory Australian study. Paper for *ATLAS Asia-Pacific Conference*, December, Unpublished manuscript. Dunedin, New Zealand.

O'Neil, M. and Fitz, F. (1996) Northern Ireland tourism: What chance now? *Tourism Management* 17, 161–163.

Okumus, F. and Karamustafa, K. (2005) Impact of an economic crisis: Evidence from Turkey. *Annals of Tourism Research* 32 (4), 942–961.

Oloruntoba, R. (2005) A wave of destruction and the waves of relief: Issues, challenges and strategies. *Disaster Prevention and Management* 14 (4), 506–521.

Oxford Economic Forecasting (2001) *The Economic Impacts of the Terrorist Attacks in the US.* Oxford, UK: World Travel and Tourism Council.

Page, S., Yeoman, I., Munro, C., Connell, J. and Walker, L. (2006) A case study of best practice—Visit Scotland's prepared response to an influenza pandemic. *Tourism Management* 27, 361–393.

Paraskevas, A. (2006) Crisis management or crisis response system? A complexity science approach to organizational crises. *Management Decision* 44 (7), 892–907.

Paraskevas, A. and Arendell, B. (2007) A strategic framework for terrorism prevention and mitigation in tourism destinations. *Tourism Management* 28 (6), 1560–1573.

Parsons, W. (1996) Crisis management. *Career Development International* 1 (5), 26–28.

Paton, D. (1997) Post-event support for disaster workers: Integrating recovery resources and the recovery environment. *Disaster Prevention and Management* 6 (1), 43–49.

Pauchant, T. and Mitroff, I.I. (1992) *Transforming the Crisis-Prone Organization: Preventing Individual, Organizational, and Environmental Tragedies.* San Francisco: Jossey-Bass Publishers.

Payne, W. (1994) How do we handle emergency information in our borough? *Disaster Prevention and Management* 3 (1), 42–46.

Pearce, D. (1989) *Tourist Development.* Harlow: Longman Scientific and Technical.

Pearson, C.M. and Mitroff, I.I. (1993) From crisis prone to crisis prepared: A framework for crisis management. *Academy of Management Executive* 7 (1), 48–59.

Peattie, K. and Moutinho, L. (2000) The marketing environment for travel and tourism. In L. Moutinho (ed.) *Strategic Management in Tourism* (pp. 17–38). Wallingford: CABI Publishing.

Pelling, M. (2003) Paradigms of risk. In M. Pelling (ed.) *Paradigms of Risk* (pp. 1–16). London: Routledge.

Pender, L. (1999) *Marketing Management for Travel and Tourism*. Cheltenham: Stanley Thornes Publishers Ltd.

Perez-Lugo, M. (2001) The mass media and disaster awareness in Puerto Rico: A case study of the floods in Barrio Tortugo. *Organization & Environment* 14 (1), 55–73.

Peters, M. and Pikkemaat, B. (2005) Crisis management in Alpine Winter Sports Resorts – The 1999 Avalanche disaster in Tyrol. *Journal of Travel & Tourism Marketing* 19 (2/3), 9–20.

Pforr, C. and Hosie, P.J. (2007) Crisis management in tourism: Preparing for recovery. *Journal of Travel &Tourism Marketing* 23 (2/3/4), 249–264.

Phillips, P. and Moutinho, L. (1998) *Strategic Planning Systems in Hospitality and Tourism*. Wallingford: CABI Publishing.

Pine, R. and McKercher, B. (2004) The impact of SARS on Hong Kong's tourism industry. *International Journal of Contemporary Hospitality Management* 16 (2), 139–143.

Pizam, A. and Mansfeld, Y. (1996) *Tourism, Crime and International Security Issues*. Chichester: John Wiley and Sons.

Poirier, R. (1997) Political risk analysis and tourism. *Annals of Tourism Research* 24 (3), 675–686.

Porter, M. (1980) *Competitive Strategy: Techniques for Analysing Industries and Competitors*. New York: Free Press.

Porter, M. (1990) *The Competitive Advantage of Nations*. New York: Basic Books.

Pottorff, S.M. and Neal, D.M. (1994) Marketing implications for post-disaster tourism destinations. *Journal of Travel & Tourism Marketing* 3 (1), 115–122.

Prange, C. (1999) Organizational learning – Desperately seeking theory. In M. Easterby-Smith, J. Burgoyne and L. Araujo (eds) *Organizational Learning – Desperately Seeking Theory* (pp. 23–43). London: Sage.

Preskill, H. and Torres, R.T. (1999) The role of evaluative enquiry in creating learning organizations. In M. Easterby-Smith, J. Burgoyne and L. Araujo (eds) *The Role of Evaluative Enquiry in Creating Learning Organizations* (pp. 92–114). London: Sage.

Prideaux, B. (1999) The Asian financial crisis: Causes and implications for Australia's tourism industry. *Australian Journal of Hospitality Management* 6 (2), 35–44.

Prideaux, B. (2003) The need to use disaster planning frameworks to respond to major tourism disasters: Analysis of Australia's response to tourism disasters in 2001. *Journal of Travel & Tourism Marketing* 15 (4), 281–298.

Prideaux, B., Coghlan, A. and Falco-Mammone, F. (2007) Post crisis recovery: The case of after cyclone Larry. *Journal of Travel and Tourism Marketing* 23 (2/3/4), 163–174.

Prideaux, B., Laws, E. and Faulkner, B. (2003) Events in Indonesia: Exploring the limits to formal tourism trends forecasting methods in complex crisis situations. *Tourism Management* 24, 475–487.

Putnam, R. (2000) *Bowling Alone: The Collapse and Revival of American Community*. New York: Simon and Schuster.

Quarantelli, E.L. (1984) Organisational behaviour in disasters and implications for disaster planning. *Monographs of the National Emergency Training Center* 1 (2), 1–31.

Quarantelli, E.L. (1988) Disaster crisis management: A summary of research findings. *Journal of Management Studies* 25 (4), 377–385.

Quarantelli, E.L. (1998) *What is Disaster? Perspectives on the Question*. London: Routledge.

Quinn, J. (1978) Strategic change: Logical incrementalism. *Sloan Management Review* 20 (1), 7–19.

Ready, K.J. and Dobbie, K. (2003) Real and perceived terrorist threats: Effects of September 11, 2001 events on the U.S. motorcoach-based tourism industry. *Journal of Travel & Tourism Marketing* 15 (1), 59–76.

Reddy, M.V. (2005) Tourism in the aftermath of the Tsunami: The case of the Andaman and Nicobar Islands. *Current Issues in Tourism* 8 (4), 350–362.

Reilly, A.H. (1987) Are organizations ready for crisis? A managerial scorecard. *Columbia Journal of World Business* 22 (1), 79–88.

Ren, C.H. (2000) Understanding and managing the dynamics of linked crisis events. *Disaster Prevention and Management* 9 (1), 12–17.

Richardson, B. (1994) Crisis management and management strategy – Time to "Loop the Loop"? *Disaster Prevention and Management* 3 (3), 59–80.

Richardson, B. (1995) Paradox management for crisis avoidance. *Management Decision* 33 (1), 5–18.

Richardson, B. and Richardson, R. (1992) *Business Planning: An Approach to Strategic Management*. London: Pitman.

Ritchie, B.W. (2004) Chaos, crises and disasters: A strategic approach to crisis management in the tourism industry. *Tourism Management* 25, 669–683.

Ritchie, B.W., Dorrell, H., Miller, D. and Miller, G.A. (2003) Crisis communication and recovery for the tourism industry: Lessons from the 2001 Foot and Mouth disease outbreak in the United Kingdom. *Journal of Travel & Tourism Marketing* 15 (2/3), 199–216.

Ritchie, J.R.B. and Crouch, G. (2003) *Tourism Management: The Competitive Destination*. Wallingford: CABI Publishing.

Rittichainuwat, B.N., Beck, J.A. and Qu, H.L. (2002) Promotional strategies and travelers' satisfaction during the Asian financial crisis: A best practice case study of Thailand. *Journal of Quality Assurance in Hospitality & Tourism* 3 (1/2), 109–124.

Robert, B. and Lajtha, C. (2002) A new approach to crisis management. *Journal of Contingencies and Crisis Management* 10 (4), 181–191.

Roberts, V. (1994) Flood management: Bradford paper. *Disaster Prevention and Management* 3 (2), 44–60.

Rodway-Dyer, S. and Shaw, G. (2005) The effects of the Foot-and-Mouth outbreak on visitor behaviour: The case of Dartmoor National Park, South–West England. *Journal of Sustainable Tourism* 13 (1), 63–81.

Rousaki, B. and Alcott, P. (2007) Exploring the crisis readiness perceptions of hotel managers in the UK. *Tourism and Hospitality Research* 7 (1), 27–38.

Russell, R. and Faulkner, B. (1999) Movers and shakers: Chaos makers in tourism development. *Tourism Management* 20, 411–423.

Sadi, M.A. and Henderson, J.C. (2000) The Asian economic crisis and the aviation industry: Impacts and response strategies. *Transport Reviews* 20 (3), 347–367.

Salt, J.E. (2003) The insurance industry: Can it cope with Catastrophe? In M. Pelling (ed.) *The Insurance Industry: Can it Cope with Catastrophe?* (pp. 124–138). London: Routledge.

Salter, J. (1997) Risk management in a disaster management context. *Journal of Contingencies and Crisis Management* 5 (1), 60–65.

Santana, G. (2003) Crisis management and tourism: Beyond the rhetoric. *Journal of Travel & Tourism Marketing* 15 (4), 299–321.

Sautter, E. and Leisen, B. (1999) Managing stakeholders a tourism planning model. *Annals of Tourism Research* 26 (2), 312–328.

Schianetz, K., Kavanagh, L. and Lockington, D. (2007) The learning tourism destination: The potential of a learning organisation approach for improving the sustainability of tourism destinations. *Tourism Management* 28 (6), 1485–1496.

Schmidt, D.A. (1986) Analyzing political risks. *Business Horizons* 29 (4), 43–50.

Schneider, S.K. (1995) *Flirting With Disaster: Public Management in Crisis Situations*. New York: M. E. Sharpe Inc.

Scott, N., Laws, E. and Prideaux, B. (2007) Tourism crises and marketing recovery strategies. *Journal of Travel & Tourism Marketing* 23 (2/3/4), 1–13.

Seaton, A.V. and Bennett, M.M. (1996) *Marketing Tourism Products: Concepts, Issues, Cases*. London: International Thomson Business Press.

Seymour, M. and Moore, S. (2000) *Effective Crisis Management: Worldwide Principles and Practice*. London: Cassel Publishing.

Sharon, J., Sasson, L., Parker, A., Horvath, J. and Mosbrooker, E. (2000) Identifying the key people in your KM effort: The role of human knowledge intermediaries. *Knowledge Management Review* 3 (5), 26–29.

Sharpley, R. (2005) The tsunami and tourism: A comment. *Current Issues in Tourism* 8 (4), 344–350.

Sharpley, R. and Craven, B. (2001) The 2001 Foot and Mouth crisis – Rural economy and tourism policy implications: A comment. *Current Issues in Tourism* 4 (6), 527–537.

Shen, F., Hughey, K.F.D. and Simmons, D.G. (2008) Connecting the sustainable livelihoods approach and tourism: A review of the literature. *Journal of Hospitality and Tourism Management* 15, 19–31.

Shrivastava, P. and Mitroff, I.I. (1987) Strategic management of corporate crises. *Columbia Journal of World Business* Spring, 5–11.

Simmons, D. and Leiper, N. (1998) Tourism systems in New Zealand and Australia. In H. Perkins and G. Cushman (eds) *Tourism Systems in New Zealand and Australia* (pp. 86–108). Auckland: Addison Wesley Longman.

Simpson, P. and Siguaw, J. (2008) Perceived travel risks: The traveller perspective and manageability. *International Journal of Tourism Research* 10, 315–327.

Skertchly, A. and Skertchly, K. (2001) Catastrophe management: Coping with totally unexpected extreme disasters. *Australian Journal of Emergency Management* Autumn, 23–33.

Smallman, C. (1997) Read all about it – Risk trends in the media: A research note. *Disaster Prevention and Management* 6 (3), 160–164.

Smallman, C. and Weir, D. (1999) Communication and cultural distortion during crises. *Disaster Prevention and Management* 8 (1), 33–41.

Smith, K. (1995) *Environmental Hazards: Assessing Risk and Reducing Disaster*. London: Routledge.

Smith, S.L.J. (1988) Defining tourism: A supply-side view. *Annals of Tourism Research* 15 (2), 179–190.

Soñmez, S.F. and Backman, S.J. (1992) Crisis management in tourist destinations. *Visions in Leisure and Business* 11, 25–33.

Soñmez, S., Backman, S. and Allen, L. (1994) *Managing Tourism Crises: A Guidebook*. Department of Parks, Recreation and Tourism Management: Clemson University.

Soñmez, S. and Graefe, A. (1998) Influence of terrorism risk on foreign tourism decisions. *Annals of Tourism Research* 25 (1), 112–144.

Soñmez, S.F. (1998) Tourism, terrorism, and political instability. *Annals of Tourism Research* 25 (2), 416–456.

Soñmez, S.F., Apostolopoulos, Y. and Tarlow, P. (1999) Tourism in crisis: Managing the effects of terrorism. *Journal of Travel Research* 38 (1), 3–9.

Stafford, G., Yu, L. and Armoo, A.K. (2002) Crisis management and recovery how Washington, DC. Hotels responded to terrorism. *Cornell Hotel and Restaurant Administration Quarterly*, 27–40.

Stanbury, J., Pryer, M. and Roberts, A. (2005) Heroes and villains – Tour operator and media response to crisis: An exploration of press handling strategies by UK adventure tour operators. *Current Issues in Tourism* 8 (5), 394–423.

Stern, N. (2006) *Stern Review on the Economics of Climate Change.* HM Treasury. On WWW at http://www.hm-treasury.gov.uk/independent_reviews/stern_review_economics_climate_change/sternreview_index.cfmS. Accessed 18.4.08.

Tarlow, P. (2006) Best education network think tank V keynote address: Disaster management: Exploring ways to mitigate disasters before they occur. *Tourism Review International* 10, 17–25.

Taylor, M.S. and Enz, C.A. (2002) Voices from the field GMs': Responses to the events of September 11, 2001. *Cornell Hotel and Restaurant Administration Quarterly* February, 7–20.

Taylor, P.A. (2006) Getting them to forgive and forget: Cognitive based marketing responses to terrorist acts. *International Journal of Tourism Research* 8, 171–183.

Templeton, T. (2003) *Escape: News: Terror Threat Now Priority.* The Observer: London.

Teodorescu, D. (2006) Institutional researchers as knowledge managers in universities: Envisioning new roles for the IR profession. *Tertiary Education and Management* 12, 75–88.

Then, S.K. and Loosemore, M. (2006) Terrorism prevention, preparedness, and response in built facilities. *Facilities* 24 (5/6), 157–176.

Thompson, J.L. (1998) Strategic crisis aversion: The value of a "style audit". *The Learning Organization* 5 (1), 36–46.

Tiernan, S., Igoe, J., Carroll, C. and O'Keefe, S. (2007) Crisis communication response strategies: A case study of the Irish Tourist Board's response to the 2001 European Foot and Mouth scare. In E. Laws, B. Prideaux and K. Chon (eds) *Crisis Management in Tourism* (pp. 310–326). Wallingford: CABI Publishing.

Toh, R.S., Khan, H. and Erawan, S.D. (2004) Bomb blasts in Bali: Impact on tourism. *Tourism Analysis* 9, 219–224.

Tribe, J. (1997) *Corporate Strategy for Tourism.* Suffolk: International Thomson Business Press.

Tse, A.C.B., So, S. and Sin, L. (2006) Crisis management and recovery: How restaurants in Hong Kong responded to SARS. *Hospitality Management* 25, 3–11.

Turner, B. and Toft, B. (2006) Organizational learning from disasters. In D. Smith and D. Elliot (eds) *Organizational Learning from Disasters* (pp. 191–204). London: Routledge.

Turner, D. (1994) Resources for disaster recovery. *Security Management* 28, 57–61.

Turner, L. and Witt, S.F. (2001) Forecasting tourism using univariate and multivariate structural time series models. *Tourism Economics* 7 (2), 135–148.

Van Biema, D. (1995) When Kobe died. *Time*, 30 January, 14–23.

Viljoen, J. (1994) *Strategic Management: Planning and Implementing Successful Corporate Strategies.* Melbourne: Longman.

Wahab, S. (1996) Tourism and terrorism: Synthesis of the problem with emphasis on Egypt. In A. Pizam and Y. Mansfeld (eds) *Tourism and Terrorism: Synthesis of the Problem with Emphasis on Egypt* (pp. 175–186). Chichester: John Wiley and Sons.

Wall, G. (1996) Terrorism and tourism: An overview and an Irish example. In A. Pizam and Y. Mansfeld (eds) *Terrorism and Tourism: An Overview and an Irish Example* (pp. 143–158). Chichester: John Wiley and Sons.

Weaver, D. and Oppermann, M. (2000) *Tourism Management*. Brisbane: John Wiley and Sons.

Wen, Z., Huimin, G. and Kavanaugh, R.R. (2005) The impacts of SARS on the consumer behaviour of Chinese domestic tourists. *Current Issues in Tourism* 8 (1), 22–39.

Wiik, S. (2003) *Crisis Management Strategies amongst Tour Operators in the UK*. BA (Hons). School of Service Management. University of Brighton, Eastbourne.

Wilks, J. and Moore, S. (2004) *Tourism Risk Management for the Asia-Pacific Region: An Authoritative Guide for Managing Crises and Disasters*. Gold Coast: CRC for Sustainable Tourism.

Williams, C. and Ferguson, M. (2005) Biting the hand that feeds: The marginalisation of tourism and leisure industry providers in times of agricultural crisis. *Current Issues in Tourism* 8 (2/3), 155–164.

Williams, C. and Ferguson, M. (2006) Recovering from crisis strategic alternatives for leisure and tourism providers based within a rural economy. *International Journal of Public Sector Management* 18 (4), 350–366.

Witt, S.F. and Moutinho, L. (2000). Demand modelling and forecasting. In L. Moutinho (ed.) *Demand Modelling and Forecasting* (pp. 293–314). Wallingford: CABI Publishing.

Witt, S.F. and Song, H. (2001) Forecasting future tourism flows. In A. Lockwood and S. Medlik (eds) *Forecasting Future Tourism Flows* (pp. 29–38). Oxford: Butterworth-Heinemann.

Woodside, A. and Sherrell, D. (1977) Traveler evoked, inept, and inert sets of vacation destinations. *Journal of Travel Research* 16, 14–18.

World Market Research Centre. (2003) WMRC – Research reports. 26.8.2003. On WWW at http://www.wmrc.com/.

World Tourism Organization (WTO) (1998) *Handbook on Natural Disaster Reduction in Tourist Areas*. Madrid: World Tourism Organization and World Meteorological Organization.

World Tourism Organization (WTO) (2003) Facts and figures. Madrid: World Tourism Organization. 29.9.2003. On WWW at http://unwto.org/facts/menu.html.

World Tourism Organization (WTO) (2005) Facts and figures. Madrid: World Tourism Organization. 12.4.2005. On WWW at http://unwto.org/facts/menu.html.

World Tourism Organization (WTO) (2007) Facts and figures. Madrid: World Tourism Organization. 18.12.2007. On WWW at http://unwto.org/facts/menu.html.

World Travel and Tourism Council (WTTC) (2003) SARS has a massive impact on travel and tourism in affected destinations. WTTC. 22.8.2003. On WWW at http://www.wttc.org/News11.htm.

World Travel and Tourism Council (WTTC) (2007) World travel and tourism council – Research. WTTC. 21.12.2007. On WWW at http://www.wttc.travel/eng/Research/.

Wright, R. (2003) *Crisis What Crisis? The Management of Tourism in Eastbourne during the 2001 Foot and Mouth Outbreak.* BA (Hons). School of Service Management. University of Brighton. Eastbourne.

Xinghua News Agency (2003) Asian-Pacific countries unite for tourism promotion. Xinghua News Agency, 22.8.2003. On WWW at http://www.china. org.cn/english/2003/Jul/70055.htm.

Yeoman, I., Galt, M. and Mcmahon-Beattie, U. (2005a) A case study of how visit Scotland prepared for war. *Journal of Travel Research* 44 (1), 6–20.

Yeoman, I., Lennon, J. and Black, L. (2005b) Foot-and-Mouth disease: A scenario of reoccurrence for Scotland's tourism industry. *Journal of Vacation Marketing* 11 (2), 179–190.

Yeoman, I., Lennon, J.J., Blake, A., Galt, M., Greenwood, C. and McMahon-Beattie, U. (2007) Oil depletion: What does this mean for Scottish tourism? *Tourism Management* 28 (5), 1354–1365.

Yew, L. (2003) A biological attack: SARS. *Forbes* 172 (2), 31.

Young, W.B. and Montgomery, R.J. (1998) Crisis management and its impact on destination marketing: A guide for convention and visitors bureaus. *Journal of Convention & Exhibition Management* 1 (1), 3–18.

Zeng, B., Carter, R.W. and Lacy, T.D. (2005) Short-term perturbations and tourism effects: The case of SARS in China. *Current Issues in Tourism* 8 (4), 306–317.

Zerman, D. (1995) Crisis communication: Managing the mass media. *Information Management & Computer Security* 3 (5), 25–28.

Index

accidents 6, 18, 27, 29, 140, 192, 232
actions, organisational 18, 30
adaptive management ix, 6, 23-4, 62, 230-1, 251, 259, 268
advertisement 196-8, 204
advertising vii, 119, 121, 194, 199, 205, 257
advisories 92-5, 169, 171
airlines 36, 38, 40, 61, 159, 164-5, 170, 191-2
Alexander 43, 97, 113-14, 152-3, 155-6, 272
American Airlines 29, 180-1, 192-3, 231
analysis, strategic 57, 62-4, 79, 254
Annals of Tourism 276, 288-9
Annals of Tourism Research 274-5, 284-6, 288
Ansoff 68, 85-7, 97, 272
Argyris 233, 272
Armstrong 196, 198, 203, 213, 272
Asia Pacific Journal of Tourism Research 272, 275, 282-3
Asia-Pacific region 13, 31, 39-40, 134
Asian financial crisis 41, 44, 276, 280, 286-7
attention cycle 180, 205, 257, 264
Australia x, 19, 28-9, 31-2, 34, 40, 46, 53, 119-20, 135, 150, 166, 198, 231, 272-3, 277-8

Bali 38, 158, 203, 217, 279, 289
Bali bombings x, 38, 93, 134, 139, 141, 170, 189, 201-2, 223, 280-1
barriers 66, 126, 262
Barton 19, 22, 138-40, 179, 184, 190, 273
Becken 260-1, 273
Beirman 18, 36-7, 39, 51, 94, 167-9, 171, 177, 179-80, 188-9, 193-4, 199-201, 210, 218, 273
BERI (Business Environment Risk Index) 90-3, 273
biosecurity 20-1, 33-4, 55, 259, 279
Blackman 228, 230, 237, 248, 274
Blake 34, 38, 163-6, 174, 269, 274, 291
Blake & Sinclair 38, 164, 166
Bonn 159-60, 274
British Tourist Authority *see* BTA
BTA (British Tourist Authority) 134, 163, 168, 179-80, 188, 190, 200, 202, 204, 274
Burnett 41-2, 45, 48, 51, 77-8, 87, 274
bushfires 21, 32, 120, 169, 196, 198, 203, 211-12, 272
Business Environment Risk Index *see* BERI

Canberra 32, 196-8, 203-4, 272, 274-5, 277

Canberra bushfires x, 203-4, 210-11, 213, 224
capacity 7, 84, 101-3, 105, 150, 170-2, 260, 267
Carlsen 21, 32, 162, 166, 169, 171, 202, 231, 265, 275
Cassedy 114-15, 129, 158, 275
Cavlek 180-1, 202, 275
Chaffee 60, 275
chaos v, 17, 26, 50, 53-6, 68-70, 76, 95, 213, 254, 261-2, 266, 270, 278-9, 287
chaos theory 52-4, 284
chaotic 14, 22, 49-50, 52, 54, 69-70, 77-8, 266
China 20, 35, 89, 94, 171, 280-1, 283, 291
Chong 131-2, 275
climate change 8, 13-14, 17, 20-1, 28, 31-2, 52-3, 71, 104, 253, 260-1, 273, 281, 289
CMT (Crisis Management Team) 84, 113, 115, 129, 132, 140-1, 217, 250
Coles 21, 171, 173, 212, 216, 268-9, 276
collaboration vi, 50, 76, 146-8, 151-3, 155, 205, 209, 248, 257, 268
communication vii, ix, 16-17, 67, 96, 115, 140, 155-6, 174-5, 181-2, 184, 205, 250, 256-7, 268-9, 284-5
complexity v, 11, 17, 23, 26, 50, 52-4, 56, 69-70, 79, 88, 95, 211-12, 261-2, 270-1, 278
consumers vii, 3, 8, 12, 16, 21, 25, 64, 93-4, 146, 167-8, 180, 194, 253, 264, 269
contingency plans 23, 48, 84, 112-16, 118, 128-9, 131, 136, 142, 158, 255-6
control vi-vii, 5-7, 11, 26, 30, 50, 56-7, 62-3, 75-6, 78-9, 139, 145-6, 153, 155-7, 178, 254
Control and Resource Allocation vi, 145, 147, 149, 151, 153, 155, 157, 159, 161, 163, 165, 167, 169, 171, 173
Cook 237-8, 276
Coombs 26, 29, 45, 179, 181, 183, 185, 188, 190, 192, 246, 276
Cooper 35, 228, 276
coordination vi, 23, 50, 59, 78, 105, 115, 122, 126, 140, 145-53, 155, 157, 159, 161, 173-4
coups 28, 37, 44, 91, 133, 187, 273
Craven 163-5, 216, 288
Crisis and Disaster Communication and Recovery Marketing 175, 177, 179, 181, 183, 185, 187, 189, 191, 193, 195, 197, 199, 201, 203, 205
crisis communication vii, 18, 24, 55, 76, 78, 130-1, 145, 148, 174-5, 178-81, 184-8,

192-3, 204, 241, 246
crisis events, linked 51, 54, 287
crisis management, organisational 3, 18-19, 21, 25, 45-6, 70, 254
crisis management plans 95, 131-3, 139, 182, 231, 272-3
crisis management policy 50, 129
crisis management team 84, 113, 115
Crisis Management Team *see* CMT
crisis planning 4, 18, 23, 69, 72, 84, 114, 132, 214, 255, 269, 279
Current Issues in Tourism 273, 276, 279, 281, 283-4, 287-91
customers 40, 60-1, 64, 123-5, 136, 169-70, 189, 191, 199, 214, 216, 258, 277
cyclones 19, 106, 117

damage 4, 23, 27, 32-3, 42-3, 48-9, 70, 77, 104, 108-9, 114, 133, 154, 176, 179, 210
Darling 5, 17, 69-70, 77, 83, 276, 282
DCMS *see* Department of Culture, Media and Sport
Delphi technique 89
Department of Culture, Media and Sport (DCMS) 191, 247, 277
Destination Marketing Organisations *see* DMOs
destinations, tourist 6, 8, 37, 48, 51, 53, 109, 133, 288
Disaster Communication vii, 175, 177, 179, 181, 183, 185, 187, 189, 191, 193, 195, 197, 199, 201, 203
disaster lifecycle v, ix, 24, 44-7, 48, 52, 58, 74, 79, 116, 118, 209, 226, 251, 255, 258-9
disaster management plans 52, 84, 116, 120-1, 126
Disaster Management Team (DMT) 116, 119, 152
disaster planning v, ix, 57, 59, 61, 65, 67, 69-71, 73, 79, 112-13, 122, 126, 253, 261-2, 265-9
disaster preparedness vi, 113-14, 116, 118, 122, 127
Disaster Recovery vii-viii, 17, 49, 207, 210, 212, 214, 216, 218, 220, 222, 224, 228, 230, 232, 234
disaster reduction 20, 22, 70-1, 98, 105, 111, 255, 281, 283
diseases 21, 34, 36, 188-9, 191, 193, 199, 212, 260
DMOs (Destination Marketing Organisations) 127, 141, 148-9, 151, 200, 203, 226, 229, 231, 233, 236-41, 246-7, 249, 255, 268
DMT (Disaster Management Team) 116, 119, 152
double-loop learning 226, 233-5, 251, 259
Dozier 182, 185, 277

Drabek 16, 114-15, 119-22, 124-5, 152, 212, 277

earthquakes 19, 21, 26, 28, 32, 43, 44, 97, 110, 118, 150, 154, 156, 158, 202, 223
economic crises 16, 19, 27-8, 31, 39, 55, 95, 97, 172, 214-15, 254, 285
EMA *see* Emergency Management Australia
emergency 5, 48, 51-2, 113-14, 141, 149-50, 159, 175, 181, 185, 188, 193, 196, 204-5, 209, 212
emergency management 3, 18, 25, 54, 71, 113-14, 122, 239, 254, 276, 281, 283
Emergency Management Australia (EMA) 97, 150, 274-5, 277
emergency organisations 48, 151, 156, 158
emergency planning vi, 19, 76, 113-14, 141, 149, 155, 255, 267, 269
employees 4-5, 29, 60, 76, 115, 118, 126, 132, 157, 161, 173, 175, 179
England x, 34, 170, 172-3, 218
evaluation 18, 50, 58-9, 62-3, 67-8, 72, 74, 76-8, 101, 117, 165, 214, 235, 237, 245-6, 250
Evans 61, 63-5, 67, 169, 171-2, 277

Faulkner ix, 4, 6, 16-17, 41, 46-8, 53, 74-5, 114-16, 118, 158, 179-80, 218, 232, 278, 286-7
Faulkner and Vikulov 32, 46, 119-20, 122, 126, 211-13, 218-19, 231-3
Federal Department of Industry 135, 138
Federation of Tour Operators (FTO) 140-1
feedback vii-viii, 23-4, 49, 62-3, 68, 72, 74, 76-7, 207, 216, 221, 226, 230-1, 251-2, 257-9, 264-5
Fink 5, 17, 46-8, 52, 54, 278
floods 19, 22, 26, 28, 32-3, 43, 49, 107-8, 110, 122, 126, 141, 169, 212-13, 218-19, 273-4
forecasting vi, 44, 84, 88-90, 95, 112, 129, 230, 255, 262, 290
forecasts 84, 88-90, 92, 95-7, 116-18, 128, 134
framework 22, 44, 48, 53, 58, 74-5, 79, 95, 98, 100, 130, 220, 230, 237, 255, 278
Frisby 134, 163, 168, 188, 190, 193, 200, 202-4, 237, 250, 278
funding 162-6, 185, 200, 251

Gartner 177-9, 278
Glaesser 88, 91-3, 278
Global Disasters 272, 276
global environmental change 8, 14, 17, 21, 23, 25-6, 55, 109, 112, 253-5, 259, 261, 276, 279-80, 285
Gonzalez-Herrero 16, 18-19, 45, 48, 73, 135, 140, 182-3, 279
Gurtner 149, 166, 189, 201-2, 217, 223, 279

Hall 10-12, 14, 20-1, 29, 33-7, 58-9, 148, 176, 179-80, 231, 259-61, 276, 279-80, 285
hazards 7, 19, 42-3, 49, 97-102, 106-10, 112, 114-15, 117-20, 122, 255, 267, 269, 274, 276
Heath 42, 45, 49, 51-2, 71-3, 77, 83, 85, 139, 150, 153, 155-9, 162, 167, 280
Henderson 16-19, 21, 31-2, 133, 138-9, 165, 181-2, 189-92, 199, 202-3, 210, 231-2, 237, 249, 274, 280
Henderson & Ng 21, 35, 170, 173
Hills 6-7, 42, 44, 50-2, 216, 280
Hofstede 156, 281
Hong Kong 35, 89, 94, 131, 163, 168, 170-1, 173, 191, 199, 212, 272, 275, 283, 289
hotels 11, 19, 35-6, 108, 110, 123, 139, 154, 165, 170, 172-3, 189, 191-2, 197, 212, 280
Hystad and Keller 49, 73, 120, 126, 147-8, 151, 169, 236

image vii, 24, 36, 39, 49, 175-8, 181, 185, 188, 191, 193, 202-4, 241, 248, 257, 276
Indonesia 40-1, 203, 286
industry associations 127, 141, 148-9, 151, 226, 229, 233, 238-9, 249, 255, 268
industry sectors 9, 11, 18, 22, 50-1, 71, 76, 158, 181, 188, 249
information processing 182-3, 194, 229, 241-3
infrastructure 15-16, 32, 49, 64, 104, 108, 193, 218, 225, 258, 261
International Journal of Tourism Research 273, 277, 280, 282, 288-9
interventions 220, 222, 225, 258, 264, 282
IPCC (Intergovernmental Panel on Climate Change) 20, 33, 71, 104-5, 260-1, 281
Irish Tourist Board 163, 191, 196
ISDR 7, 19-20, 22, 57, 70-1, 98-101, 103-4, 107, 281
Israeli 39, 160, 162, 281
Israeli hotel managers 161, 163, 173

Johnson 60, 67-8, 274, 282
Journal of Travel Research 274-6, 278, 280, 283, 289-91
Journal of Vacation Marketing 273, 277-8, 283, 291

knowledge management 24, 76-7, 226-8, 230, 240-1, 248, 251, 258, 265, 276-7, 279, 281, 283-4
Knowledge Management and Organisational Learning vii, 226-7, 229, 231, 233, 235, 237, 239, 241, 243, 245, 247, 249, 251

Laws 4, 6, 41, 275, 278-9, 282-4, 286, 288-9
leadership vi, 24, 59, 62-3, 67, 137, 140, 145-6, 152, 156, 158-9, 174, 188, 246, 256, 267-9

learning 52, 71-2, 74, 76, 79, 98, 130, 227, 230-3, 236, 243, 246, 248-9, 259, 278
Lee 6, 17, 113, 131, 150, 177, 282-3
Leiper 11-12, 19, 31, 39-40, 90, 177, 283, 288
lifecycle 16-17, 23, 26, 44-6, 48, 50, 56, 71, 74, 78, 183, 254, 266
likelihood 23, 33, 42-3, 46, 69-70, 83, 106, 108-9, 120, 127, 176-7, 189, 214, 248
London 34, 155, 250, 272, 274-80, 282-3, 285-9
long-term recovery vii-viii, x, 24, 49, 77, 147, 149, 170, 209, 213, 218, 223-5, 258, 264, 268, 270
Loosemore 96, 138-9, 289

Madrid 290
Maldives 32, 169-71, 202, 231, 275
Malhotra 227-8, 283
manuals 23, 113, 130-1, 140-2, 256
marketing vii, 37, 59, 65, 94, 145, 148, 160-3, 165, 171, 194, 196, 200, 203, 214-15, 280-1
markets 60, 65-6, 101, 131, 136, 159, 169-71, 173, 188, 195-6, 213, 225, 258, 260
Marra 18, 179, 184, 283
Massey 191-3, 283
McDonnell 85-7, 97, 272
McKercher 53-5, 148, 173, 176, 194, 203, 284, 286
media coverage 180-1, 204, 237
Melbourne 274, 279, 284, 289
Miller 46, 98, 212, 234, 240, 284, 287
Mistilis 228-30, 248, 284
mitigation vi, 15, 83, 97-8, 101, 104-5, 107, 109, 112-13, 120, 150, 190, 255, 285
Mitroff 4-5, 30, 146-7, 285, 288
monitor 67, 84, 86, 204, 249
Moutinho 12-14, 60, 64, 68, 87, 285-6, 290
Mubarak 220-2, 284

National Tourism Administrations (NTAs) 140, 149, 151, 268
National Tourist Organisations *see* NTOs
natural hazards ix, 7-8, 20-2, 43, 48, 53, 70, 79, 97-9, 102, 105-10, 117-18, 120-1, 128, 155, 284
Nepal Tourism Board (NTB) 200, 202
New Orleans 33, 190, 195-6, 203, 275
New Zealand 40, 93, 103, 285, 288
NGOs *see* Non-Governmental Organisations
Non-Governmental Organisations (NGOs) 109, 148, 200, 220
normality 46-7, 76, 78, 95, 209
NTAs (National Tourism Administrations) 140, 149, 151, 268
NTOs (National Tourist Organisations) 127, 133-4, 141, 181, 255

OMT (operational management triage) 153-4

organisational behaviour 157, 230, 269, 274, 286
organisational culture 65-6, 79, 159, 184-5, 233, 255, 262, 267
organisational learning vii-x, 6, 24, 76, 79, 146, 210, 226-7, 229-33, 235, 243-5, 247-9, 251, 258-9, 265, 268
organisational structures 59, 62-3, 65, 85, 118, 129, 158, 216
Oxford 272, 276, 278, 282, 285, 290

Pelling 7, 52-4, 272, 275, 286-7
Phillips 60, 64, 68, 286
physical vulnerability 15, 101, 103
Poirier 90-2, 286
political crises 18, 28, 36, 112, 168, 255
political instability 14, 16-18, 27, 31, 37, 39, 51, 90, 133, 139, 169, 177, 180, 195, 200, 213
Political Risk Index (PRI) 91
Porter 62-4, 68, 286
power 4, 37, 41, 61, 126, 156, 171, 179-80, 184, 188, 279
Pratt 45, 48, 73, 140, 159, 182-3, 213, 230, 237, 273, 279
preparedness viii, 19, 46, 71-2, 84-5, 99, 105-6, 112, 120, 123, 125, 127, 137, 248, 262, 266
prevention 3, 6, 23, 25, 34, 42, 45, 46, 73-4, 77, 79, 83, 105, 112-14, 255, 275-6
Prideaux 3-4, 6, 40-1, 44-5, 48, 52, 95-7, 106, 135, 166, 251, 279, 282, 284, 286, 288-9
probability 8, 42-4, 87, 101-4, 115, 229
products 11-12, 28-9, 31, 65-6, 131, 169, 175, 216-17, 224, 238, 243, 260
public relations ix, 18, 175, 178-9, 181, 184-5, 187, 199, 203, 272, 277, 283

Quarantelli 7, 113-15, 118, 126, 152-3, 159, 286-7

readiness 22-3, 66, 72, 84, 120, 158, 183, 223, 266, 268
recover 7, 76, 78, 162, 166, 181-2, 210, 212, 220, 224
recovery campaigns 193, 197, 199, 204
recovery marketing vii, 17-18, 24, 49, 78, 145, 148, 163-4, 169, 175, 181, 193, 197, 199-205, 246-7, 263-4
recovery marketing activities 133, 145, 174, 204-5, 256-7
recovery marketing campaigns 163, 165-6, 189, 193, 201-2, 204-5, 264, 267-8
recovery plans 72, 137, 229, 251
recovery strategies 180, 237, 245, 268
reduction vi, 13-14, 19-20, 23, 32, 34-5, 40, 50, 52, 66, 69-70, 72, 83, 94, 97, 107-8
Ren 50-2, 210, 287
resolution vii-viii, 20, 24, 47-9, 52, 74, 76, 174, 207, 209-13, 215, 219-21, 223-5, 258, 264
resolution stage 4, 49-52, 74, 79, 149, 209-10, 213, 216-17, 219, 224, 258
resource allocation vi, 60, 78-9, 145, 147, 149, 151-5, 157, 159, 161-3, 165-9, 171, 173-4, 181, 255-6, 263
Richardson 19, 22, 45, 58, 68-70, 233, 287
risk analysis 76-7, 95, 97, 101-4, 113, 116, 118, 127-9, 134
risk assessment 72, 92, 96-7, 101-4, 114-15
risk perceptions vii, 39, 104, 108, 120, 133, 167, 175-7, 263, 269, 273, 278, 282, 284
Ritchie 18, 21, 46, 76, 127, 134, 138, 148, 168, 187, 191, 193, 196, 231-2, 283-5, 287
Roberts 46-9, 287, 289
Rundle-Thiele 159-60, 274

safety 18, 36, 104-5, 141, 176-7, 190, 194, 217, 275, 279-80
Santana 4, 14, 16-17, 22, 74, 287
SARS (Severe Acute Respiratory Syndrome) 21, 34-6, 93, 148, 163, 168-70, 172-3, 176-7, 200-1, 212, 272, 274-5, 280-2, 284, 289-91
SARS virus 34-5, 53
Sausmarez 21, 50-1, 74, 129, 133, 148, 165, 199, 201, 231, 276-7
scenario planning 76, 89, 97-8, 120, 130, 134, 262
scenarios 69, 84, 89, 95-8, 103-4, 126, 128, 130, 134, 140, 229-30, 237, 245, 249-50, 284, 291
Scotland 136-7, 291
security 176, 186-7, 193, 217, 231, 259, 269, 275, 280
severity 42-3, 50, 75, 78, 104, 139, 149, 179
Sharpley 163-5, 216, 288
Sheldon 228-30, 248, 284
shocks 3, 5, 8, 26, 40, 44, 50, 52, 58, 84, 90, 95-7, 112, 127, 163, 221
signals 42, 71, 78, 84, 96-7
Sinclair 38, 163-6, 174, 269, 274
Singapore 18, 31, 34-5, 40, 94, 170, 199, 231, 272, 280
SLF (Sustainable Livelihoods Framework) 220-2, 265
Smith 7-8, 10, 42-3, 45, 97, 101-4, 106-7, 109-10, 116-17, 128, 166-7, 277, 288-9
Soñmez 5, 18, 37-9, 133, 172, 177, 179, 181-2, 195, 203, 213, 288-9
Stafford 33, 38, 173, 196, 249, 289
Stanbury 177, 185, 188-90, 289
strategic management 16, 27, 45, 57, 61, 65, 68-9, 72, 74, 77, 79, 228, 254, 262, 269, 276-8
sustainable development 23, 99-100, 105, 112, 220, 223, 225, 255, 262

Sustainable Livelihoods Approach (SLA) 220, 288

Taylor 170, 185, 194-5, 289
Templeton 93-4, 289
terrorism 16, 18, 28, 31, 36-7, 39, 92-4, 135, 177, 201, 203, 275, 279-80, 289-90
terrorist attacks 17, 19, 29, 38, 44, 92, 97, 139, 158, 176, 189, 194-5, 203, 213, 231, 285
threats 3, 16, 23-5, 41, 46, 48, 57, 63-4, 79, 87, 93, 104, 112, 117, 152, 209, 254-5
tools vi, 77, 87-8, 91, 95-6, 99, 129, 159, 168, 188, 222, 226, 228, 244, 252, 259
Tourism Action Group (TAG) 133, 187
Tourism Management 41, 75-6, 128, 137, 151, 160, 218, 227, 272-4, 276, 278-81, 284-8, 290-1
tourism managers 3, 14, 18, 25, 55, 57, 70, 84, 121-2, 132, 139, 141, 175, 254-5, 267
Tourism Marketing 17, 198, 272, 274-6, 278-84, 286-8
tourism organisations 14, 16, 22-3, 31, 49, 69, 84, 90, 92, 112, 121, 127, 141, 146, 151, 164
tourism planning 58-9, 217, 278-9
tourism system 3, 8, 25, 31, 36, 51, 53-4, 59, 65, 69, 84-5, 147, 238-9, 259-62, 278, 283-4

Tourist Information Centres 191, 247
training 63, 66, 72-3, 115, 117, 122, 126-7, 129-30, 132, 140-1, 173, 188, 244, 255, 262, 269
Tribe 61, 63-6, 289
turbulence 53-5, 278
Turner 114-15, 158, 238, 246, 289

UK 9-10, 19, 21, 27, 34, 46, 49, 51, 92-3, 107, 134, 153, 172, 188, 202, 216, 284-5
USA 19, 40, 46, 94, 122, 139, 150, 189, 198, 200, 202, 231, 274, 279, 282

Vietnam 35, 94
violence 29, 36, 39, 179, 280
Visit Scotland 127, 134, 136-7, 141, 243, 250, 256, 285
vulnerability, reducing 105, 109, 262, 264
vulnerability reduction 105, 272

war 14, 16, 18, 36, 92, 134-5, 210-11, 291
warnings 27, 30, 34, 39, 46, 84, 93-4, 115-17, 121
World Tourism Organization *see* WTO
WTO (World Tourism Organization) 13, 20, 101-2, 106, 108, 117-18, 140, 290
WTTC (World Travel and Tourism Council's) 13, 35, 290

Yeoman 90, 134, 137, 285, 291